INTERNET BUSINESS GUIDE

THE INTERNET BUSINESS GUIDE: RIDING THE INFORMATION SUPERHIGHWAY TO PROFIT

Rosalind Resnick and Dave Taylor

SAMS
PUBLISHING

DEDICATIONS

For my grandmother, Jean Resnick, who loved math and would have loved computers
Rosalind Resnick

To the jewels in my life—Linda, Jasmine, and Karma
Dave Taylor

International Standard Book Number: 0-672-30530-5

Library of Congress Catalog Card Number: 94-66276

97   96   95   94   4   3   2

Interpretation of the printing code: the rightmost double-digit number is the year of the book's printing; the rightmost single-digit, the number of the book's printing. For example, a printing code of 94-1 shows that the first printing of the book occurred in 1994.

Composed in Palatino and MCPdigital by Macmillan Computer Publishing

Printed in the United States of America

Publisher
Richard K. Swadley

Associate Publisher
Jordan Gold

Acquisitions Manager
Stacy Hiquet

Managing Editor
Cindy Morrow

Acquisitions Editor
Grace Buechlein

Development Editor
Mark Taber

Editor
Katherine Stuart Ewing

Editorial Coordinator
Bill Whitmer

Editorial Assistants
Carol Ackerman
Sharon Cox
Lynette Quinn

Technical Reviewer
Kevin Savetz

Marketing Manager
Gregg Bushyeager

Cover Designer
Jay Corpus

Book Designer
Alyssa Yesh

Director of Production and Manufacturing
Jeff Valler

Imprint Manager
Juli Cook

Manufacturing Coordinator
Paul Gilchrist

Production Analysts
Dennis Clay Hager
Mary Beth Wakefield

Graphics Image Specialists
Tim Montgomery
Dennis Sheehan
Susan VandeWalle

Production
Nick Anderson
Carol Bowers
Mona Brown
Elaine Brush
Ayrika Bryant
Amanda Byus
Elaine Crabtree
Mike Dietsch
Rob Falco
Kimberly K. Hannel
Debbie Kincaid
Ayanna Lacey
Stephanie J. McComb
Jamie Milazzo
Shelly Palma
Nanci Sears Perry
Chad Poore
Casey Price
Kim Scott
Marc Shecter
Scott Tullis
Dennis Wesner
Michelle Worthington

Indexer
Rebecca Mayfield

OVERVIEW

	Introduction	xxi
1	Putting the Internet to Work for You	1
2	Getting Connected: Your Ticket to Ride	45
3	Risks and Realities	63
4	Doing Business on the Internet	83
5	Marketing Do's and Don'ts	111
6	The Electronic Schmooze	147
7	Dialing for Data	175
8	Connecting the World with Internet E-Mail	209
9	Customer Support	231
10	The Virtual Corporation	253
11	Internet Cybermalls	271
12	The Commercial Online Services	299
13	The Future of Internet Business	321
A	Internet On-Ramps	335
B	How to Start Your Own Usenet Newsgroup	365
C	The World According to the Internet	371
D	Working with the World Wide Web: Tips and Tools	377
E	The Full Scoop on Gopher	383
	Index	389

CONTENTS

1   Putting the Internet to Work for You   1

A Virtual Storefront 2

Around the World with E-Mail 4

   Using the Internet Post Office 5

Joining the Crowd with Mailing Lists 9

   Types of Mailing Lists 12

   Business Benefits of Mailing Lists 12

   Getting on the List 14

Spreading the News with Newsgroups 16

   A Sample Session 19

   Usenet's Hierarchies 21

   The Benefits of Usenet 21

Dialing into the World with Telnet 22

   Accessing Business Services with Telnet 23

Moving Files with FTP 26

Accessing Archives with Archie 30

Searching for Data with Gopher 33

   A Sample Gopher Session 34

   Gopher and Internet Shopping Malls 35

Searching Gopherspace with Veronica 37

Winging Your Way with World Wide Web 39

   The Multimedia Interface: Mosaic 41

Conclusion 43

2   Getting Connected: Your Ticket to Ride   45

Internet Economics 101: How the Internet Works 47

   Analyzing Your Internet Needs 48

Choosing an Internet Access Provider 50

   Network Reliability 50

   Network Performance 51

   Network Security 52

   Network Restrictions 52

   Local Phone Access 53

   User Services and Support 53

The Three Types of Internet Connections 54

   Online Accounts 54

   SLIP/PPP Connections 57

   Leased-Line Connections 60

The Future of Internet Pricing and Connections 61

3 Risks and Realities   63

The Internet and Security: A Troubled Past 64
Internet Risks and Realities 66
   Real-Life Experience 67
   What the Experts Say 70
Creating a Secure Environment 71
   Staying Off the Net 72
   Passwords 73
   Firewalls 75
   Data Encryption 75
   Putting it All Together 77
Emergency Measures: What to Do if a Break-In Occurs 78
   CERT 79
Additional Resources 80
   Mailing Lists and Usenet Newsgroups 80
   Books 81
Conclusion 81

4 Doing Business on the Internet   83

A Brief History of Internet Commerce 85
Hot Opportunities in Cyberspace 86
   Communications 87
   Business Services 89
   Sales and Marketing 93
   Customer Support 96
   Research and Development 99
   Publishing 100
   Internet Services 104
The Future of Internet Commerce 105
How Your Company Can Do Business on the Internet 106
Internet Business Resources 107
   Mailing Lists (Discussion Groups) 108
   Newsgroups 108
   Newsletters and Magazines 109

5 Marketing Do's and Don'ts   111

Internet Marketing: Not Ready for Prime Time? 113
Rules and Regulations 117
A Direct Marketer's Dream Come True 118
Caveat Vendor—Let the Seller Beware 119
   Internet Marketing: The Consumer's View 122
   Internet Advertising: The Marketer's View 122

Marketing Strategies That Work 123
    Direct Mail 125
    Press Release Postings 126
    Billboards on the Net 131
    Relationship Marketing 133
    Display Advertising (World Wide Web) 136
The Downside of Internet Marketing—Flame Wars and Worse 140
    Tips on Avoiding Flame Wars 143
    The Contrarian View: In-Your-Face Marketing 143
Future of Internet Marketing 144

6   The Electronic Schmooze   147
Choosing a Discussion Group to Join 149
Joining and Participating in a Discussion Group 150
    The Fine Points of Netiquette 152
    The Rules of Netiquette 154
Tapping into Internet Discussion Groups for Fun and Profit 156
    Sales and Marketing 156
    Trend-Surfing on the Net 158
    Customer Support 160
    Employee Recruitment 161
Creating Your Own Discussion Group 163
    How to Start Your Own Mailing List 166
Conclusion 167
Business-Related Discussion Groups 167
    Business-Professional Interest 167
    Geographic 170
    Company, Product, User Groups 172

7   Dialing for Data   175
Infomania on the Internet 176
Bargain-Hunting on the Internet 177
    EDGAR 178
    State Department Travel Advisories 179
Exploring the Internet with a Map 180
    Stock-Picking with EDGAR 181
    Globe-Trotting with Telnet 185
    Finding Your Way with Wide-Area Information Servers 187
Who's on First? (Tracking Down Internet Names and Addresses) .. 189
Is Company X on the Internet? 190
So Many Databases, So Little Time 191
Business Databases on the Internet 196
    General Reference 197
    Demographics and Market Research 198

Technology 199
Economics and Business 200
Government Regulation 203
International Trade 205
Law 206

8   Connecting the World with Internet E-Mail   209

Around the World with Internet E-Mail 210
Internet E-Mail Versus the Rest of the Pack 212
How Internet E-Mail Works 214
Internet E-Mail Software 216
Internet Addressing 220
Internet Directory Assistance 221
The Pitfalls of Using Internet Mail 222
Reliability 222
Versatility 222
Integration 224
E-Mail Solutions 225
The Future of Internet E-Mail 227
Graphical Interfaces 227
Interoperability 228
Multimedia 228
Mobility 229

9   Customer Support   231

Evaluating Customer Support Options 232
Net Results: Why Internet Support Is Good Business 234
Getting Feedback with E-Mail 235
Spreading the News with Usenet Newsgroups 237
Anticipating Questions with FAQs 240
Do-It-Yourself Support with FTP Sites 241
Publishing Information with Gopher and WAIS 243
Point-and-Click with Mosaic and World Wide Web 245
The Bottom Line: the Cost of Providing Customer Support
on the Internet 249
The Keys to Good Customer Support 251

10   The Virtual Corporation   253

The Rise of the Virtual Corporation 255
R&D on the Internet: From Medical Imaging to Oil and Gas 256
Brigham and Women's Hospital 256
Global Basins Research Network 257
Monterey Bay Aquarium Research Institute 257

Big Business on the Net 258
    Motorola 258
    Sun Microsystems 259
Linking Small Businesses Worldwide 259
    KnowledgeNet: a Corporation in Cyberspace 260
    The Pros and Cons of Being a Virtual Worker 261
Virtual Transactions: Where Do I Sign and How Do I Pay? 262
    Digital Signatures 263
    Digital Currency 265
Virtual Liabilities 266
    Libel on the Internet 267
Internet Legal Tips 268
Additional Reading 269
    Books 269
    Magazine Articles 269

11   Internet Cybermalls   271
Internet Shopping Malls 272
    The Company Mailbox: Information Researchers 273
    The Storefront: Harmony Games 276
    The Store: The Electronic Newsstand 278
    The Cybermall: Internet Distribution Services 282
Surfing the Web with Mosaic 287
Mosaic: The Internet's "Killer App"? 290
    Special Uses of Mosaic 290
Drawbacks to Using Mosaic 294
Owning Versus Leasing: Setting up Your Own Web Server 295
The Future of Internet Retailing 296

12   The Commercial Online Services   299
Commercial Online Services Versus the Internet 300
Making Money on the Commercial Networks 302
The World of Commercial Online Services 304
CompuServe 304
    Business Opportunities 306
    Demographics 307
Prodigy Services Co. 307
    Business Opportunities 310
    Demographics 310
America Online 310
    Business Opportunities 312
    Demographics 313

GEnie 313
    Business Opportunities 315
    Demographics 315
Delphi Internet Services 315
    Business Opportunities 317
    Demographics 317
The Future of Commercial Online Services 317
Striking a Balance: Integrating Commercial Networks and the
    Internet 318
Further Reference: Pricing and Contact Information 319

13 The Future of Internet Business   321

Continued Internet Population Growth 322
Lower Network Access Costs with Wider Availability
    of Internet Tools 323
Easier On-Ramps 323
An Explosion of E-Mail 324
More Sophisticated Multimedia Technologies 324
Tighter Security 326
More Outlets for Flame-Proof Advertising 328
    MecklerWeb 328
    Internet Shopping Network 330
Persistence of In-Your-Face Advertising 331
Geographic Specialization 332
Internet Is Everywhere 333
Before You Go...So What Does All This Mean for
    Your Company? 334

A Internet On-Ramps   335

Geographical and Area Code Summary—US
    and Canadian Providers 336
    Alabama 336
    Alberta 336
    Arizona 336
    British Columbia 336
    California 337
    Colorado 338
    District of Columbia 339
    Florida 339
    Georgia 339
    Illinois 339
    Louisiana 340
    Manitoba 340
    Maryland 340

Massachusetts 341
Michigan 341
Missouri 341
Nevada 341
New Hampshire 342
New Jersey 342
New York 342
North Carolina 343
Ohio 343
Ontario 343
Oregon 344
Pennsylvania 344
Rhode Island 344
Quebec 344
Texas 344
Utah 345
Virginia 345
Washington 345
    Packet Network/Toll-Free Access 346
Providers in United States and Canada 347
Agora 347
Alberta SuperNet Inc. 347
CAPCON Library Network 347
CCI Networks 348
CCnet Communications 348
CERFnet 348
CICNet 348
ClarkNet (Clark Internet Services, Inc.) 349
CNS 349
Colorado SuperNet 349
Communications Accessibles Montreal, Inc. 349
CRL 350
CTS Network Services (CTSNet) 350
CyberGate 350
Cyberstore Systems Inc. 350
DataFlux Systems Limited 351
Data Basix 351
Data Tech Canada 351
Delphi 351
Digital Express Group (Digex) 352
Echo 352
Eskimo North 352
Evergreen Internet 352

Freelance Systems Programming 353
Gateway to the World 353
Global Enterprise Services, Inc. 353
HoloNet 353
Hookup Communication Corporation 353
IDS World Network 354
Institute for Global Communications (IGC) 354
InterAccess Co. 354
Internet Online Inc. 354
Interpath 355
Maestro Information Service 355
MBnet 355
Meta Network 355
Mindvox 356
Msen 356
MV Communications, Inc. 356
Neosoft 356
Netcom Online Communications Services 357
North Shore Access 357
Northcoast Internet 357
Nuance Network Services 357
OARNet 358
Olympus 358
Panix Public Access UNIX and Internet 358
Pipeline 358
Portal Communications Company 359
PSI 359
Teleport 359
Telerama 359
Texas Metronet 360
UUNorth Incorporated 360
VNet Internet Access, Inc. 360
The WELL 360
Wimsey Information Services 361
The World 361
XNet Information Systems 361
Australia 361
Aarnet 361
Connect.com.au P/L 362
Germany 362
Contributed Software 362
Individual Network e.V. 362
Inter Networking System (INS) 362

Netherlands 363
Knoware 363
NetLand 363
Simplex 363
New Zealand 363
Actrix 363
Switzerland 363
SWITCH—Swiss Academic and Research Network 363
United Kingdom 364
Almac 364
Cix 364
Demon Internet Limited 364
The Direct Connection (UK) 364

B   How to Start Your Own Usenet Newsgroup   365

Requirements for Group Creation 366
The Discussion 366
The Vote 367
The Result 368

C   The World According to the Internet   371

D   Working with the World Wide Web: Tips and Tools   377

More Information on the Web and Mosaic 378
The World Wide Web FAQ 378
World Wide Web Guide 378
World Wide Web Discussion Groups 379
The Wide World of Webs 379
Viewing the Web: World Wide Web Browsers 380
Creating Web Documents (HTML Editors) 382

E   The Full Scoop on Gopher   383

Gopher Client Software 384
Publicly Available Gopher Logins 384
Gopher Server Software 385
Discussion Lists 386
gopher 386
comp.infosystems.gopher 386
gopher-news 386
VMSgopher 386
MVSGOPHER 386
Hooking Your Gopher Server into Gopherspace 387

Index 389

ACKNOWLEDGEMENTS

I'd like to offer my special thanks to all the people who generously contributed their time and expertise to help me write this book, including Michael Tague of Computer Witchcraft, Tom Benham and Jason Kurtz of CyberGate, Marc Fleischmann of Internet Distribution Services, Andrew Currie of Cyberspace Development, Debra Young of CompuServe, Margaret Ryan of America Online, Debra Borchert of Prodigy, Barbara Byro of GEnie, and Nancy Morrisroe of Delphi.

—Rosalind Resnick

I'd like to profusely thank Linda for putting up with this writing project—and just when we thought the previous book was my last! I'd also like to acknowledge the help I received from technical-editor-and-self-taught Internet Wizard Kevin Savetz and my ever-reliable mates James Armstrong, Marvin Raab, and Tai Jin.

This book has been great fun to work on, and the team at Sams has been a delight to work with. Special thanks to Grace, Mark, and Kathy for even making the editing process an amusing task, though even now it seems hard to believe.

Finally I'd like to thank Apple for being so responsive in fixing my haunted PowerDuo, upon which much of my portion of the book was written. In a true testimony to the Internet and how it's changing how we do business, I've never seen a single page of this book on paper: All discussion, development, composition and editing has been done through e-mail and file transfer, with the pipeline between CompuServe and Netcom getting quite a bit of traffic.

Thanks also to Joel, Mike (the new guy), Tom, Crow, and the rest of the Mystery Science Theater crew for helping me keep some semblance of sanity, and Sting and Thomas Dolby for ensuring that it was never too quiet around the office.

—Dave Taylor

ABOUT THE AUTHORS

Rosalind Resnick

Rosalind Resnick (`rosalind@harrison.win.net`) is a former *Miami Herald* business reporter and now a freelance writer and author specializing in business and technology. Her articles have appeared in *The New York Times, Forbes, Nation's Business, Internet World, Compute, Home Office Computing, PC Today,* and other major newspapers and magazines. She is the author of *Exploring the World of Online Services* (Sybex, 1993), a beginner's guide for small businesses; editor and publisher of *Interactive Publishing Alert*, a monthly newsletter about electronic newspaper and magazine publishing, and a consultant to publications seeking to go online. She recently launched a syndicated newspaper column called "CyberBiz" to advise companies seeking to do business in cyberspace.

Dave Taylor

Dave Taylor (`taylor@netcom.com`) has been involved with the Internet since early in 1980 when he logged on for the first time and learned about Usenet and e-mail. Since then he's been a research scientist with Hewlett-Packard Labs, reviews editor for *SunWorld* magazine, and now president of Intuitive Systems. He has published over 500 articles, is a columnist for *Internet World* and *Open Computing*, and has two prior books: *Global Software* and *Teach Yourself UNIX In A Week*. In his spare time he's finishing up a graduate degree in Educational Computing at Purdue University, trying to train his dogs to sit, cooking gourmet vegetarian foods, and watching innumerable old movies.

INTRODUCTION

These days, everyone from the vice president on down seems to be jumping onto the information superhighway bandwagon. In fact, if you haven't been bombarded by the breathless hyperbole surrounding the information highway, you must have lived in a cave.

Despite all this hype surrounding what is more formally known as the *National Information Infrastructure*—an all-encompassing network allowing businesses to connect with customers, suppliers, and researchers worldwide—the system itself is still a long way from reality. Even big corporations are starting to realize the scope of the challenge, and recent months have seen a variety of deals and mergers fail as the glossy veneer begins to dull. Although some corporate dealmakers continue to lay down their billion-dollar bets on the future, the goal of universal videoconferencing, document sharing, and multimedia electronic mail (e-mail) remains out of reach.

What's perhaps most ironic is that there *is* a network up and running already that offers much of the information highway's promise. That network is the Internet. Although the routes aren't well marked, the signs are often incomprehensible, some lanes are closed to commercial traffic, and on-ramps are in short supply, for a tiny investment, the Internet offers enormous commercial potential for your business today.

What Is the Internet?

Put simply, the Internet is a "network of networks," a global web of 25,000 computer networks of all shapes and sizes, ranging from huge research institution mainframes to modest personal computers tucked into the corners of home offices.

Information on the Internet flows across all sorts of wires—from copper-wire telephone lines and satellite dishes to fiber-optic cable and cable TV. Once a government-funded research network that linked teams of bureaucrats and academics, the Internet now connects more than 20,000,000 people worldwide, a community that encompasses high school students, college professors, writers, programmers, and even florists and real estate brokers. And the Internet's growing at over 150,000 new users each month.

Although the Internet's academic flavor remains, many new users represent businesses and other commercial ventures. These days, corporate giants such as IBM, General Electric, J.P. Morgan, Xerox, Merrill Lynch, Motorola, and Schlumberger are tapping into the Internet for everything from electronic mail to international research and development. Most excitingly to us, so are thousands of electronic entrepreneurs selling everything from cheap and easy Internet access to software, books, music, computer chips, toys and flowers.

Marketing experts are also starting to recognize that the Internet promises a veritable bonanza—20,000,000 people who have conveniently sorted themselves into interest groups that focus on topics ranging from medieval literature to drag racing, C programming to dating. On the Internet, no one has to buy a mailing list and pay for printing and postage. Post a product announcement or press release on the appropriate Internet discussion list, and without any further effort or cost, your message is zapped automatically to every subscriber.

But don't run out and log onto the Internet yet! Although the Internet represents a huge, easily accessible market that doubles as the world's largest post office and library, doing business on the Internet can be perilous for the uninformed.

Internet-connected companies point to increased productivity, better collaboration with strategic partners, and access to a seemingly infinite array of information, but businesses also are quick to agree that the Internet is virgin territory when it comes to marketing and advertising. As a result, savvy entrepreneurs are moving cautiously to avoid alienating Internet users—their potential customer base—by being sensitive to the network's not-for-profit heritage, which emphasizes free information and egalitarian access to markets.

Realize before you set out that the Internet isn't just another magazine in which to advertise. On the Internet, you can't distribute empty puffery, breathless hype, or innuendo about your competitors—and expect to get away with it. Instead, proceed cautiously and view the Internet as a sort of supertown square, where different corners have different values and expectations but all have a basic set of expectations of how newcomers will behave.

Tip: The best advice we have is to start out in any new Internet arena as a *cybertourist*, exploring and experimenting but not becoming a full-fledged participant until you've had a chance to learn about the culture and interaction style of the Internet community in which you plan to do business. Some communities, you'll find, are quite hostile to newcomers, whether corporate or otherwise; others eagerly extend a virtual welcome mat, delighted at your interest, attention, and participation.

Who Runs This Show Anyway?

The world of business has always been a pretty rough and tumble place, with competitors using innuendo, unfair trade practices, monopolies, bribes, and other unsavory techniques to ensure their individual success in the marketplace. More recently, consumers have become a little savvier. These days, companies that thrive are those that work with the community, becoming "good corporate citizens," and trying to make a positive addition to their communities.

The Internet is no different from any other community, and those companies that "go native" by brushing up on the network's culture and mores will gain a competitive advantage in the electronic marketplace .

Taking time to learn about the Internet now can pay big dividends in the future. If the current growth rate is sustained, more than 50,000,000 people will be accessible through the Internet by the turn of the century. Companies that jump in early and learn how to work with the Internet community will become productive, valued members of cyberspace; those that don't may end up as roadkill on tomorrow's Infobahn.

The quickest way to hitch a ride on the information highway is by hopping aboard the Internet. Created in 1969 as a way to link the U.S. Defense Department with high-level university researchers working on sensitive government projects, the Internet has no central computer that stores its millions of gigabytes of information. That's because the government feared that, in the event of a nuclear attack, all its valuable military data could be destroyed. As a result, the Internet became a decentralized network with data stored on each of thousands of computers.

That's good news for our country's defense but not for today's business users. Unlike traditional online services such as CompuServe, Prodigy, and America Online, the Internet has no central mainframe to dial into, no 800 number to call for a starter kit, precious little easy-to-use navigational software, and no technical support staff to call with problems or questions. Check with some of your colleagues, and you'll find that the Internet interface they see is probably very different from your own, with Mac and PC systems vying with UNIX systems for greatest popularity and dialup access offering a primitive text-based view of the information highway.

The Internet is not a corporation; it's a computer cooperative. Nobody owns the Internet and there's no one you can hold accountable if the system breaks down, which it occasionally does.

Even so, the Internet's quirky infrastructure is remarkably efficient at transmitting information from point A to point B. One way to understand the Internet is to compare it with the phone company. Due to public access laws, phone companies are required by law to offer a connection to anyone who wants one; no analogous requirements are yet in place for Internet connections (an important consideration for many businesses that we examine later in the book).

If you imagine how a phone system that connected only subscribers would work, you have a rough idea of how e-mail and other messages are transmitted through the network. You compose and address a message with the Internet equivalent of an area code and phone number: an e-mail address. Your local system then consults various databases to identify the unique computer address for the remote system, then directly feeds the message to that system.

The main backbone of the Internet is the National Science Foundation-funded *NSF Network* (NSFNet). The primary artery for research and academic Internet information flow, NSFNet prohibits all commercial traffic. Its acceptable-use policy excludes any advertising except for announcements of new products and services that would be of interest to the research and education community.

However, a second, parallel backbone run by the *Commercial Internet Exchange* (CIX), a private cooperative venture, has no such restrictions. Because most Internet access providers and online services offer underlying CIX connectivity in addition to or instead of NSFNet, the remaining barriers to doing business on the Internet today are more cultural than regulatory. The government, meanwhile, is getting out of the Internet business; it's planning to start reducing its $11,500,000 subsidy beginning in 1994.

As federal restrictions on Internet use drop away, the main barrier to advertising on the Internet is the Internet purists who believe that advertising is out of place there. Many users, especially those affiliated with government research institutions and universities, can be downright hostile to any sales pitches or junk mail that litter their electronic frontier. With that in mind, we advise you to adopt more passive strategies for making your corporate presence known on the information highway.

The National Information Infrastructure

Though the Internet has been around in various forms since Richard Nixon was president, Bill Clinton and, in particular, Vice President Al Gore, have been the first high-ranking government officials to promote the information highway actively. Whether the Internet will retain its status as the de facto information superhighway or simply ride along with whatever data highway eventually emerges from the ongoing mergers of telephone, cable, and communications companies is too soon to predict. Either way, the commercialization and privatization of the Internet fits neatly into the Clinton Administration's vision of a *national information infrastructure.*

The Administration's publicly stated goals are

> To encourage private investment in the national information infrastructure

> To promote and protect competition

> To provide open access by consumers and service providers to the national information infrastructure

> To preserve and advance universal service

> To ensure flexibility so that the newly adopted regulatory framework can keep pace with the rapid technological and market changes that pervade the telecommunications and information industries.

Vice President Gore told the National Press Club in Washington, late in 1993,

> The impact on America's businesses will not be limited just to those who are in the information business, either. Virtually every business will find it possible to use these new tools to become more competitive. And by taking the lead in quickly employing these new information technologies, America's businesses will gain enormous advantages in the worldwide marketplace.

Key Business Benefits of the Internet

The Internet offers businesses an impressive number of competitive advantages, including these six key benefits: electronic mail, access to research, tracking competitors, inexpensive remote collaboration, enhanced customer service, and low-cost marketing and advertising.

Let's look at them one by one.

Electronic Mail

Much of the traffic on the Internet today is electronic mail. Indeed, it's been estimated that well over 4,000 messages are sent each second of the day on the Internet.

Being able to send messages in seconds to a user anywhere in the world is probably the single most important reason so many companies find the Internet so appealing.

The Internet is also cheaper and more cost-efficient than comparable commercial online networks such as CompuServe, GEnie, or MCI Mail. Once you're connected to the information highway, there are no additional per-minute or per-message charges. In the world of commercial online services, by contrast, flat-fee plans by which users send unlimited messages are quickly giving way to pay-as-you-go schemes as the services learn to compete in this new market.

There's another important aspect to this, too: In addition to enabling your employees to communicate in an effective and inexpensive manner, the Internet links your company with the Internet's more than 20,000,000 users.

To be fair, we're not talking 20,000,000 potential customers, but even if only 1 percent are vaguely interested…well, you get the picture.

Research

Imagine that every book in your local library were actually a gateway to another library and that each of those libraries had another two to fifty times as many volumes as the first one. That's what makes the Internet such a treasure trove of information for your business. For starters, the Internet provides

- Access to the Library of Congress and just about every major university library in the United States
- Business-oriented databases such as Commerce Business Daily, the Federal Register, and the U.S. Chamber of Commerce's Economic Bulletin Board
- U.S. and Canadian Census data
- Supreme Court decisions
- World health statistics
- Security and Exchange Commission corporate financial reports
- International weather forecasts (including up-to-the-hour satellite pictures)
- United Nations information
- And even transcripts of daily White House press briefings

The Internet has more than statistical data, however. The network's lifeblood is its widely varying and often freewheeling discussion forums, split between public bulletin boards (called *Usenet*) and private electronic mailing lists. Both offer forums packed with experts discussing new developments in their fields. There are Internet discussion groups about almost anything you can think of—chemical engineering, entrepreneurship, computer programming, franchise opportunities, Eastern European trade and politics, semiconductor manufacturing, continuing employee education, and over 10,000 other forums.

Competitive Tracking

One of the most important ingredients of business success is being aware of what your competitors are doing. Frequently-asked questions include

Are my competitors working on a new product?

What areas of research are they contributing expertise to on the network?

What do customers say about their products, both good and bad?

All this information and more is on the Internet, awaiting your careful analysis.

Note: By the same token, it's important to recognize that information about your company will also appear on the network once you become involved. If you start an electronic mailing list for customers, for example, your competitors may join to find out what you're doing. At the same time, joining the Internet gives your company a chance to offer valuable information to the user community and enhance your reputation with your customers, too.

Collaboration

The Internet can also help your company work with colleagues throughout the world to develop new products and services. By using the Internet to exchange and search for information, many businesses are facilitating collaboration and lowering the costs of research and development.

When IBM does development work with other companies, for example, its engineers use the Internet to communicate with counterparts rather than set up an expensive private data connection.

Marketing and Advertising

With more than 20,000,000 users worldwide— many of whom are affluent and highly educated professionals, the Internet is a fertile field for companies advertising everything from silicon chips to luxury cars.

Businesses that explicitly target the Internet's technocratic culture can gain a competitive edge and boost sales. Some companies also have found that supplying a free sample of what they're offering can whet Internet users' appetites for a product or service they're willing to buy. It's the same idea as giving away a free taste of an ice cream flavor at a soda fountain; bait the hook right and the customers will reel themselves in.

Advertising on the Internet can be perilous, however, especially for those who don't know or don't respect the Internet culture. Witness the Arizona law firm that blitzed the Internet with direct-mail—and became Internet pariahs.

Remember that business success on the Internet comes from treading lightly and learning the culture before launching any commercial ventures. There are many opportunities for profit, but there is just as much potential for failure, too—failure that can ultimately prove quite damaging to a company.

Profile: One company that learned the importance of treading lightly in the Internet culture is Magma, a small San Diego-based computer board manufacturer. Late in the summer of 1993, the company used the Internet to send a blatantly promotional new-product announcement to over 3,000 e-mail addresses concerning its newest products.

The direct mail blitz brought in more than $30,000 in new business, but the company also was pummeled with hate mail from almost 100 Internet users, all of whom were outraged that the network was being used for such a blatantly commercial purpose. These sorts of experiences leave a permanent record in the collective memory of the online community. As Michael Seidel, vice president of sales and marketing, notes, "It was as if we had molested their daughters."

E-mail address: `seidel@magma.com`

Even marketers that do everything right must recognize that the Internet isn't a mass market. In cyberspace, software still sells better than soap pads. Though there is more diversity in the cyberspace market than there was five years ago, there's certainly less than in the mainstream markets reached by newspaper and television marketing campaigns.

One problem is that blue-collar workers are still unlikely to be connected to the Internet. What's more, people who aren't so-called early adopters are only now beginning to consider the possibility of going online.

Most top executives are also unlikely to be directly on the network; the CEOs of many computer companies have e-mail addresses, but almost always someone else reads and screens their mail for items of value and import. When John Young was CEO of Hewlett-Packard in the early 1990s, he would "read" his e-mail by having his administrative assistant print it and leave it on his desk. John Scully, former head of Apple Computer, put two assistants on the job.

Customer Service

Increasingly, companies are turning to the Internet to set up customer support bulletin boards offering technical advice, monitoring customer satisfaction, providing new product information, and making software upgrades available electronically.

For many companies, it's a cost-effective way to do business. By supporting customers electronically, they save the expense of 800 numbers and corporate newsletters announcing upgrades. Customers, meanwhile, save on long-distance phone calls. What's more, simple upgrades can be quickly distributed to your customer base at no expense—a technique used extensively by Apple with its Macintosh software suite.

Profile: An interesting example of how the Internet can improve customer service with minimal financial outlay is EDI Strategic Services in Medford, Oregon. EDI uses the Internet to provide technical support to clients throughout the West Coast—services provided by a technician who works from home. Karen Loban, the technician, uses her personal computer to dial in to the UNIX-based computer at the consulting firm's offices a few miles away and then uses the Internet to log in remotely to the remote client's computer system. This way, EDI can diagnose, support, and configure its software without interfering with the client's day-to-day computing operations and without incurring hefty long-distance telephone or air fare charges.

E-mail address: `info@edihost.ediss.com`

On the Internet, small businesses can tap into a global community of more than 20,000,000 users to swap mail, make contacts, market products, search databases and other reference sources, and even engage in real-time discussions for less than $20 a month. Larger companies can buy their own direct Internet hookups starting at about $160, and high-speed, leased-line connections to the network—connections capable of supporting hundreds of employees using the Internet simultaneously—can be maintained for under $1,500 per month.

Risks and Rewards

Although there are unquestionably many advantages of doing business on the Internet, there are also many risks and problems. In addition to the business-averse Internet culture, there are also security breaches, traffic jams, and reliability problems that crop up from time to time.

Another problem is that much of the underlying Internet technology is based on the somewhat arcane UNIX operating system; low-cost, dialup connections are likely to plop you right in the middle of a UNIX session, leaving novice users hopelessly lost.

> **Note:** The good news is that there are several excellent UNIX tutorial books on the market, including one from Sams Publishing that can get you up to speed on UNIX in no time—Dave Taylor's *Teach Yourself UNIX In A Week*.

Right now, security is probably the most pressing concern that most businesses have about connecting to the Internet. Late in 1993, for instance, electronic "crackers" broke into the Internet and began stealing account passwords for a variety of different machines. By the time anybody noticed, the bandits had already learned thousands of passwords, the keys to public and private computer accounts throughout the world. No one knows exactly how many passwords were stolen, but according to *The New York Times,* officials at the government-funded Computer Emergency Response Team (CERT) estimate that tens of thousands of computers around the world have been put at risk—computers not just on the Internet but on any computer network attached to it.

Michael DeFazio, executive vice president and general manager of the UNIX Systems Group subsidiary of Novell, Inc., told *The Times,*

> A network of computers, especially one as extensive as the
> Internet, is not as secure as a stand-alone computer. With a stand-
> alone computer, you can limit access in physical ways, locking it
> in a room policed by gun-toting security guards if you want. You
> can't do that on a global network.

Then there are the traffic jams. On the Internet, as on any real-world roadway, traffic tie-ups occur when thousands of people try to tap into a particular computer at once. One example is the Illinois National Center for Supercomputer Applications computer, which offers free copies of the popular Internet browsing software, Mosaic. So many users try to download the software from the machine that it often slows to a veritable crawl trying to meet the demand. Other times, due to its traffic load, it simply refuses entry to users trying to connect. Internet computers and data providers are working to add capacity, although it seems a safe bet that however fast networks are expanded, there will always be places where user demand will exceed computer capacity. Call it rush hour on the information highway!

Another occasional problem is network reliability. Unlike centralized for-profit services like CompuServe and Prodigy, there's no guarantee that your message or data will get to where you send it in a timely manner, and there are precious few reliable ways of checking or confirming receipt. Our experience shows that the system is nonetheless quite reliable, with hundreds of messages transmitted without incident to Eastern Europe, India and the People's Republic of China for every message that vanishes or bounces back.

Can I Really Profit From the Internet?

At the beginning of this introduction, we noted that the media hasn't really noticed the Internet in its zeal to talk about the NII, with its sexy combination of interactive cable TV, telephone, video conferencing, and just about anything else reporters can fantasize about. That's a simplification, because some savvy businesses are already taking advantage of the Internet for their own commercial uses, albeit cautiously. Here's a sampling of how some companies are using the Internet to improve their business and turn a profit.

Profile: Recognizing that many companies which want to utilize the Internet for marketing purposes lack technical expertise, The Internet Company (info@internet.com) of Cambridge, Massachusetts, offers a commercial presence for client companies through its own computer systems. The Internet Company also offers consulting on the culture and community of the Internet to help its clients market their products and services in a manner that's appropriate and compatible with the prevailing culture.

One of the firm's most ambitious projects is the *Electronic Newsstand*, a joint venture between The Internet Company and *The New Republic* magazine of Washington, D.C. The Newsstand is a collection of popular and scholarly journals and magazines from which the table of contents and one or more articles or editorials per issue are available to Internet users electronically, with no fee. Currently almost thirty magazines are involved with this experimental project, including *The National Review, The New Yorker, The Economist, ComputerWorld, Foreign Affairs, Outside,* and *Eating Well.* Internet Company President Robert Raisch indicates that The Newsstand fields almost 10,000 requests for information each day.

E-mail address: `info@enews.com`

Mail order retailers are jumping on the network, too, cracking new markets while saving on postage, phone calls, and advertising. On the Internet, even a startup operation can wield the direct-marketing clout of a well-funded giant like L.L. Bean.

Profile: Two mail-order retailers—The Corner Store (`ADD paolop@pipeline.com`) of Litchfield, Conn., and Indelible Blue, Inc. (`bbohac@mercury.interpath.net`) of Raleigh, North Carolina—are racking up millions of dollars by selling software via the Internet, and revolutionizing the way software is sold. Paolo Pignatelli, owner of The Corner Store, and Buck Bohac and Katherine Ansardi, co-owners of Indelible Blue, say their ventures sprang out of their familiarity with the needs of the inhabitants of cyberspace. Both companies specialize in selling the OS/2 operating systems and associated software and applications.

Bohac and Ansardi didn't plan initially on doing business. Rather, they had planned to launch an advertising campaign for their software catalog in the spring of 1993 and began letting users know ahead of time through discussion groups on Prodigy and the Internet. The couple, who hoped they might make a small profit from the catalog, have been shocked by the huge demand.

"By the time our first print ads appeared in April, 1993, we were already out of our first 3,000 catalogs and had to reprint," Ansardi told *The Wall Street Journal* in January. "Everybody already knew about us" from the Internet and services.

Their formula appears to work well; since last March, Indelible Blue's average monthly sales have been about $250,000. Ansardi says that the company hopes to exceed $5,000,000 in revenues for 1994.

The Corner Store's Pignatelli opened for business with an actual storefront on a local corner but soon closed it when he realized that 95 percent of his sales were through online services. Last year, Pignatelli says the company generated sales of about $1,000,000, up from about $100,000 in 1989. Even more attractively, his profit margin improved, once he stopped paying for print advertising.

Bookstores have rapidly become one of the most popular businesses on the Internet. Booksales are a type of business uniquely suited to the information-rich environment that the Internet offers. With shared ordering capabilities and references like *Books in Print*, the challenge of differentiation for an electronic bookstore also offers an advantage to the small chain: unlike a walk-in mall, the investment required to have an attractive and interesting Internet shop is minimal.

Profile: Internet readers order and receive books electronically from The Online Bookstore (obs@marketplace.com) of Rockport, Massachusetts. Once they type their credit card number, an electronic copy of the requested book is instantly transmitted to their computer through the Internet, saving them a trip to the bookstore. Laura Fillmore, formerly an editor at Little, Brown, who launched the venture early in 1993, points out that distributing books on the Internet is a faster and cheaper way to reach readers than traditional publishing methods. Because there are no paper, printing, binding, or warehousing costs to worry about, books can also be produced at half the normal price. Only a limited number of titles are available through the Online Bookstore, though they're not all technical titles as you might expect. Two popular electronic texts offered range from a comprehensive guide to bed-and-breakfast lodging to an oral history of sexuality.

Cost and speed are not the only advantages to online publishing. The Internet also enables publishers to do things they can't in print or even on CD-ROM, such as linking electronic books to far-flung databases containing related material on music, video, photos, and other texts on the worldwide network. An art history book, for example, might include a link to a library of images from the Vatican's collection of sculpture.

Meanwhile, the Online Bookstore is branching out into another novel venture—turning readers into authors. In January, Fillmore started posting notes on the Internet seeking electronic manuscripts from Internet subscribers and offering to split the profits 50-50.

The Internet Business Guide: Your Personal Passport to Doing Business Online

Now that you've gotten a taste of what the Internet can offer, let's take a look at what this book can offer you. In a nutshell, our purpose in writing this book is to offer you a guide through the maze of commercial, cultural, and technical issues surrounding the use of the Internet.

Together, we'll explore the tremendous number of valuable resources now available on the Internet, including many that you won't find anywhere else at any price. We don't shy away from nuts-and-bolts technical information; you'll learn everything you need to know about working with Internet mailing lists and Usenet newsgroups. You can even watch over our shoulders as we use the FTP file transfer program to download press releases from companies on the Net and then sign up for, and participate in, a mailing list that discusses the Internet's commercialization.

Who Should Read This Book?

This book is for anyone who wants to make his or her business more efficient and profitable. Whether you're a home-based startup or a Fortune 500 company, a computer-savvy network administrator, or a marketing VP who has never gone online before, there's something in this book that can either make you money or help you save it.

You don't need to be a computer expert, you don't need to have ever even logged in to the Internet or connected to a specific information service — though we're willing to bet that you've encountered the Net at some point and just didn't realize it. Our goal here is to present a vision of the Internet and how businesses can work within the community and technologies thereon in a positive manner.

On the other hand if you are already an expert on all these topics, there's a lot in this book that you'll find valuable and thought-provoking too. From novel ways to build your client base with e-mail to how Usenet can help you identify what your competitors are up to, this book will prove helpful for all.

How Is This Book Organized?

We've organized this book to help you learn about the business face of the Internet with minimal fuss. Our hope is that you read it straight through, but if there are particular sections that sound exciting, feel free to flip directly to them! Also make sure you browse through the various appendixes for a list of Internet access providers; guides to Web and Gopher setup, configuration, and use; a map of what countries are hooked into the Internet; and an explanation of how you can create a Usenet newsgroup for your own uses.

Chapter 1, "Putting the Internet to Work for You," will show you how to use the Internet to make your company more efficient and profitable. You'll learn how to use the Internet to market your products and services, make contacts with colleagues and prospective customers, cut your company's mailing costs, improve customer service, develop new products, and search for business leads. The chapter will also explore the hottest business-related Internet tools, including e-mail, mailing lists, Usenet newsgroups, telnet, Gopher, file-transfer protocol (FTP), Wide Area Information Services (WAIS), and the World Wide Web (WWW).

Chapter 2, "Getting Connected: Your Ticket to Ride," offers practical information on how to get onto the Internet and how to choose an Internet access provider, pricing plan and front-end software. This chapter will help you evaluate the pros and cons of the three major access alternatives.

> Dial-up service to an Internet access provider

> Serial Line Interface Protocol (SLIP) or Point-to-Point Protocol (PPP) connection through a regular dialup line to the Internet

> A leased telephone line, which provides very high speed Internet access. Such a line also turns your company's computer or local area network into a full member of the Internet.

Chapter 3, "Risks and Realities," provides an in-depth look at the reality and technological hazards of doing business on the Internet. This chapter offers detailed information on network security issues (viruses, crackers and network crashes) and privacy risks, including criminals monitoring your corporate electronic mail and unauthorized users gaining access to customers' credit card numbers and company financial information. The chapter will also suggest ways to minimize these risks and offer an overview of encryption software and other security tools now available.

Chapter 4, "Doing Business on the Internet," will explore the Internet culture. Just like doing business in any other new market, entrepreneurs must understand the Internet's traditions and culture before they can succeed in doing business there. Despite Internet users' traditional aversion to any kind of commercialization of the network, businesses that master the rules of the game can do brisk sales there—as many are already.

Chapter 5, "Marketing Do's and Don'ts," shows you what to do and what not to do to win customers on the Internet. Not only does junk mail tend to fall on deaf ears, for example, but it often drives away the very customers it was meant to attract. You'll also see some actual examples of how companies work with the Internet community and how other firms have alienated potential customers with inappropriate activities. This chapter will also provide an overview of the basic rules of network etiquette.

Chapter 6, "The Electronic Schmooze," shows you how to tap into Internet discussion groups to meet colleagues and find customers worldwide. You'll find out where the business-oriented action is—for example, the com-priv discussion group, which focuses on the commercialization and privatization of the Internet. You'll also get an annotated list of Internet discussion groups specific to businesses and professions and see the steps involved as we sign up for a mailing list and receive a few messages to read.

Chapter 7, "Dialing for Data," will show you how to use the Internet to search for business leads and information. The chapter will show you how to find and use business-oriented databases such as Commerce Business Daily, the Federal Register, the Library of Congress catalog and the U.S. Chamber of Commerce's Economic Bulletin Board.

Chapter 8, "Connecting the World with Internet E-Mail," will demonstrate how to set up a low-cost e-mail network for your company's employees, customers and vendors, saving your company money over postal mail, long-distance telephone service and videoconferencing. This chapter will include case studies and price comparisons to help you design the best e-mail system for your business. You'll also learn how to integrate Internet access with your existing local area and wide area networks and find out how small, medium and large companies can set up Internet mail gateways.

Chapter 9, "Customer Support," will show you how to set up a customer support service on the Internet to provide technical support, monitor customer satisfaction, provide new product information and make software upgrades available electronically. You'll also learn about Internet information servers that allow companies to provide detailed product information, announcement of new offerings, and other public relations information for Internet-connected customers.

Chapter 10, "The Virtual Corporation," will show you how to use the Internet to work with colleagues worldwide to develop new products and services. This chapter will look at how companies such as IBM, General Electric, Intel and Motorola use Internet tools such as e-mail, FTP, telnet, and Usenet newsgroups to facilitate and lower the costs of research and development.

Chapter 11, "Internet Cybermalls," will show you how to set up your own retail sales centers to distribute information and peddle products and services along the information superhighway. You'll read about companies that have used the Internet to sell and deliver products electronically and to perform credit-card transactions. You'll also get the low-down on "renting" a storefront from an information mall provider and spend some time strolling through the Internet Mall.

Chapter 12, "The Commercial Online Services," shows you ways in which you can integrate your use of commercial services such as CompuServe, Prodigy and America with the Internet to enhance your company's ability to do business. Commercial services are typically less strict than Internet newsgroups and mailing lists as to what constitutes an ad. However, they also cost more than the Internet, both for users and for advertisers. You'll get detailed information about networking areas on CompuServe, Prodigy, and America Online, plus detailed information about advertising, marketing, and other aspects of doing business there.

Chapter 13, "The Future of Internet Business," examines the future of the Internet and the information superhighway. You'll find out how you can position your business to profit from these impending changes. You'll also find out more about the Clinton Administration's plans to use the Internet as the basis for the National Information Infrastructure and what the private-sector information businesses have on their drawing boards.

What Conventions Are Used?

To ensure that you can quickly find information within each chapter and throughout the book, we use a variety of typographical conventions and small margin illustrations. Throughout the book when you see lines of output in monospace

```
this is a typical line of computer output
```

it means that it's the output of a specific Internet program or application. If you see it in monospace boldface

```
Here's what you would type
```

it's exactly what you would type in to the indicated program.

The graphics conventions are

Note: These boxes will highlight interesting information to make your work with the Internet and business communities more enjoyable.

Tip: These focus on ways to streamline your interaction with the Internet or other valuable information.

Profile: An abstract business book is of little value, so we include extensive profiles of real businesses that are really using the Internet today, all tucked into these profile boxes.

It's an Art, Not a Science

As you read this book, keep in mind that doing business on the Internet means developing the right mix of marketing, research, sales, and staff. It's really more of an art than a science.

Right now, most of the companies tapping into the Internet are still experimenting, and there are no hard and fast rules to Internet business success. Some firms will succeed; others will fail. We can't tell you who the winners will be, but we can help you learn how to properly evaluate the various business opportunities there.

The most important difference between success and failure on the Internet, after all, is the same as for any other business venture—meeting the demands of the customer in an innovative and cost-effective manner. Of course, it also helps to have a little bit of luck.

Our advice is to approach the Internet with an open mind, just as you would an overseas business trip. Wander around a little. Take in the sights. Join a discussion group and post a few notes there. Tap into a database that looks intriguing. Start an e-mail exchange with a colleague in Japan or Hungary. Most of all, don't be afraid to step off the beaten track, because on the Internet, the old adage is especially true, "If you don't know where you're going, it's impossible to get lost." As we've learned time and again, when you travel on the Internet, you're guaranteed to be surprised at where you end up. For a growing number of businesses, that destination is proving to be an extremely profitable place to be.

PUTTING THE INTERNET TO WORK FOR YOU

There are a thousand different ways to use the Internet for business purposes and just as many companies trying each one. Unlike a real highway, composed of relatively few parts, the information highway is littered with more tools, services, and elements than a jet engine. Different tools offer dramatically differing capabilities, and how each company opts to use the network is as much a function of the needs, interests, and technological savvy of the business as are the capabilities of the tools.

For some companies, doing business on the Internet means using the network's international electronic mail system to send memos and documents from corporate headquarters to satellite offices and sales sites throughout the world.

For other companies, doing business means searching Internet-accessible databases for market data, competitive intelligence, and university research reports—without paying a dime.

For still others, doing business on the Internet means exchanging ideas with colleagues around the world in specialized public and private discussion groups and "networking" online to get new clients.

For some aggressive entrepreneurs, it means sending low-cost targeted mailings or otherwise making commercial product information and order forms available electronically to small groups of potential buyers who hang out on Internet newsgroups discussing subjects as varied as Star Trek and auto racing.

And that's not counting all the Net-repreneurs who are selling Internet-related products and services to newcomers in need of help. These days, thousands of companies large and small are offering everything from Internet access, training, and consulting to books, magazines, computers, software, and flowers that can be ordered online.

A Virtual Storefront

The logistics of setting up a storefront in the local strip mall or office building are fairly straightforward, but doing business on the information highway is nowhere near as easy. Indeed, few companies fully understand the various tools and services they could offer, the tradeoffs involved, and the best way to ensure profitable results from their investment. Part of the reason this is more difficult is because unlike in the real world, in cyberspace, you can't see where you're going.

If you're driving down Interstate 95 to attend a meeting in downtown Fort Lauderdale, for example, you can look for—and hope to find—the sign that indicates the desired exit ramp. Even if you get hopelessly lost, you can always pull off the highway, pull in at a gas station, and ask for directions.

Cruise the Internet in search of a program stored on a university computer system, by contrast, and you can spend hours poking about, vainly attempting to summon the exact commands needed without so much as a virtual gas station in sight. Unlike centralized commercial online services such as CompuServe and Prodigy, there's no toll-free technical support department you can call for help when you get lost on the Internet.

What if you want to put your business on the Internet and access millions of potential customers? If it's a struggle for you to find information on the Internet, imagine the trouble your customers will have trying to locate your Internet "store." How will your customers know that you're even online? Complicating the picture further, the Internet provides a dizzying array of information services that you can offer customers and potential customers, ranging from a simple file and information archives to electronic catalogs to elaborate multimedia documents. Remember that your customers will need to know in advance not only what

Internet services you offer but how you offer them. If they send e-mail to an information archive, for example, they may hit a dead end—and go looking for another company that offers more accessible information. These are only a few of the problems involved in doing business on the Internet. Despite the Internet's massive human and informational resources and its enormous potential as a worldwide marketplace, the Internet is still, to a large extent, an uncharted frontier. Imagine New York City without street signs, the Kalahari Desert without a map, and hieroglyphics without the Rosetta stone, and you're starting to get an idea of what navigating the Internet can be like if you don't know what you're doing.

Don't despair! There are a growing number of Internet tools and navigational software programs now becoming available that will make it much easier to find the information you're seeking and where you're going. If you pack the right tools and learn how to use them, you'll be cruising the information highway in no time. At the same time, it's hard to know which Internet services to offer until you know the lay of the land, so climb aboard and let us be your travel guides for this introduction to the Internet and its capabilities.

The rest of this chapter will focus on the tools and services available through the Internet. When possible, we'll show you the "nuts and bolts" of what we're doing; however, the key is not so much to master all the tools but to try to understand how you can use them to enhance your business and offer information to your customers.

Note: Odds are good that you have some sort of personal computer that you'll use as the basis of your connection to the Internet, whether through expensive leased lines or an economical dialup line.

It used to be that regardless of what system you used, you would be working with a text-based interface that ran on top of the UNIX operating system. Today, you can obtain many graphical interfaces for free or little expense, programs that allow you to accomplish the same tasks without mastering cryptic commands.

Despite the increasing availability of graphical interfaces, however, we believe that the best approach to explaining Internet tools is to demonstrate the standard UNIX way of doing things, because that's still how most dialup accounts work. However, we'll also show you snippets of the more attractive Macintosh and PC Windows interfaces that are available for the many services.

Around the World with E-Mail

Twenty-five years ago, English teachers were decrying the death of the art of letter writing and its replacement by the telephone call. The good news is that the dire predictions appear to have been premature and that the art of interpersonal communications is enjoying a virtual renaissance thanks to electronic mail, perhaps the single most popular facet of the Internet. Based on statistics released by the National Science Foundation, over 4,000 e-mail messages are sent *each second* on the Internet. The oft-quoted 20,000,000 users number is based on their e-mail connectivity to the network; these days, it's getting to the point where just about everyone is hooked up to the network in some fashion or other. Today, more than 145 countries are connected, and it's a sure bet that once we meet up with extraterrestrial residents, they'll be hooked in, too. Through Internet gateways, users from CompuServe, MCI Mail, GEnie, and other commercial networks are also "on the Net."

For businesses, being able to connect with lots of people is a boon, but for many companies the greatest advantage to Internet e-mail is its low cost. Not only do you save on postage and printing compared to postal mailings, but by paying a monthly fee to an Internet access provider, you can send and receive all the e-mail you want without paying extra for messages or the time you spend online composing them. That's a refreshing change from commercial networks where you pay by the hour or the byte. In fact, if you send a message to a colleague on CompuServe, the recipient must pay to receive your e-mail if it's sent from the Internet.

The third advantage is universality. Through the Internet, you can send e-mail to people who use CompuServe, America Online, MCI Mail, AppleLink, eWorld, AT&T EasyLink, and other commercial networks even if you don't have an account on that system. You can also swap mail with colleagues and friends connected to government, military, and university e-mail systems and even local computer bulletin boards. This means that you don't have to pay fees to a dozen individual computer networks just to reach their subscribers or to log on and off each one every time you wanted to send a message to one of its users. Thanks to the Internet, sending mail electronically is faster and easier than carting a batch of company fliers to the post office.

Profile: As an example, Dave makes his living as a free-lance writer and editor, and every morning he starts his day by logging into Netcom (a commercial Internet access provider) to check for e-mail. A typical day sees messages from Macmillan, sent from CompuServe, messages from colleagues at universities and online services, clients on MCI Mail and commercial Internet systems, a message or two from overseas, and even family members accessible through the Internet gateway to MILNET, the United States Military Network. There's no charge for the messages—even when they're huge—and just about all of them are delivered in his mailbox within seconds of being sent.

A variety of messages from colleagues on various Internet mailing lists are also shuffled into his mailbox, providing information comparable to high-priced newsletters but without any fee. Without the Internet to link everyone together, the only people with whom Dave would be able to swap mail and documents would be the several thousand or so users on Netcom.

Using the Internet Post Office

Although there's a wide variety of individual programs you can use to send electronic mail, they all have some features in common. Each program works by requesting one or more e-mail addresses for the recipients and offers you the ability to specify a brief (5–10 word) subject heading. Then you can use the program to compose or upload a message from your personal computer. Think of the message *body* as the text of the letter; think of the addressing information as the envelope.

We go into great detail on e-mail's various aspects and capabilities in Chapter 8, "Connecting the World with Internet E-Mail." For now, we'll spend some time considering the components of an electronic mail address and briefly examine several of the most common electronic mail composition programs.

The E-Mail Address

To send mail to someone, you must have their Internet e-mail address. All addresses are composed of the following three portions:

> The individual's name or *account name*
> The name of the *computer* the person uses
> And what's called the *domain* that describes the type of network that hooks the computer to the Internet

Here's an example: `taylor@netcom5.netcom.com` is a typical Internet e-mail address. Here, `taylor` is the account name, `netcom5` is the name of the computer Dave uses to receive electronic mail, and `netcom.com` is the domain name. The at-sign (@) serves as a separator, and the overall notation is then *user@host.domain*.

The domain is read from right to left (`com` and then `netcom` in the preceding example) with the most important, highest level information farthest to your right.

The rightmost item of information (`com` in the example) is known as the *top-level domain*. These are the seven most common domains used in the United States:

> `com` is for commercial sites and service providers.
> `edu` is for educational sites, including all K-12 schools and colleges.
> `mil` is for military sites or other computers on MILNET.
> `gov` denotes a government system.
> `net` indicates that it's a completely different network (remember that the Internet is a network of networks).
> `org` is for non-profit and other private organizations.

Most international electronic mail follows a similar domain naming strategy, but the top-level domain is the two-letter International Standards Organization (ISO) country abbreviation. In this internationally recognized scheme, `mx` stands for Mexico, `au` is Australia, `uk` is the United Kingdom, `no` is Norway, `fr` is France, and so on.

Here are some examples of Internet addresses:

```
mtaranto@noc.sura.net
plieb@umd5.umd.edu
jstraw@navy.mil
tai@nsa.hp.com
cat@kodak.com
jackson@dftnic.gsfc.nasa.gov
```

These examples refer, respectively, to a user on the SURA network, the University of Maryland at Delaware educational facility, the United States Navy, and the Network Software groups of Hewlett-Packard, Kodak, and the GSFC division of the National Aeronautics and Space Administration.

Making the Message

That's what an address looks like. How does an e-mail message look? Glance over our shoulders as we send a brief message back and forth on our computers. Dave used the Elm Mail System on a UNIX computer through his dialup account, and Rosalind used WinNET Mail on her PC in the Windows environment. Text shown in boldface shows what's typed on the UNIX system.

```
% elm rosalind@harrison.win.net

Subject of message: Quick question about chapter five
Cc:

Please enter your message, using '.' to end it.

Rosalind, I'm revising some of our earlier text in Chapter 5 and wanted to
know how strongly you felt about the holographic illustration you've included
in the current draft? I also wanted to remind you that our next deadline is in
four days...
Dave
.

message sent.

%
```

That's all it takes for a quick note to be sent the thousands of miles between us,
and a scant few minutes later Rosalind sees the message shown in Figure 1.1.

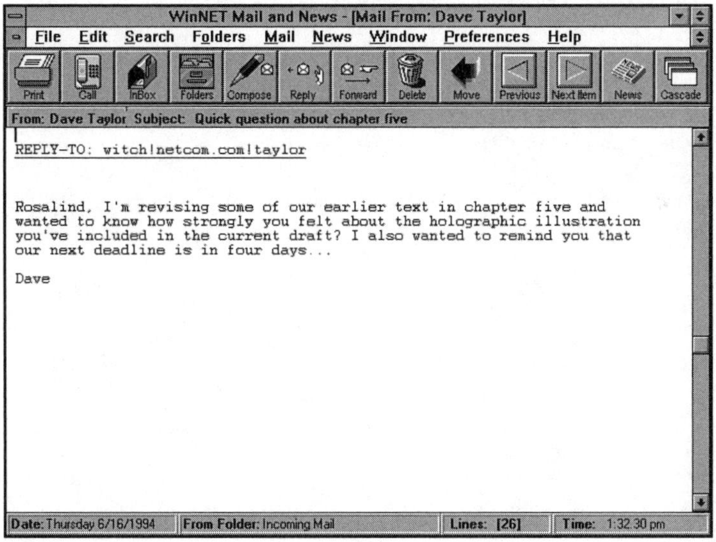

Figure 1.1. Message received.

To respond, Rosalind uses the compose feature of WinNET Mail to bring up a
blank message template and then types the message shown in Figure 1.2.

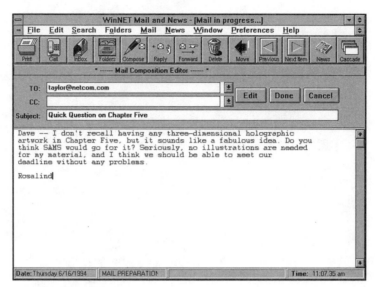

Figure 1.2. The WinNET Mail message composition blank.

Once sent, the response is quickly and automatically routed back to Dave, who sees

```
>> Rosalind Resnick — Re: Quick question on chapter five
```

informing him that a new message has arrived. Typing elm and pressing Return reveals

```
Message from Rosalind Resnick              25 May, 1994 at 4:15pm
            Re: Quick question on chapter five

Dave,
I don't recall having any three dimensional holographic art work in
Chapter 5, but it sounds like a fabulous idea. Do you think SAMS
would go for it? Seriously, no illustrations are needed for my material
and I think we should be able to meet the deadline without any problems.

Rosalind


End of message. Press <space> to continue:
```

Elapsed time of this transaction: four minutes, including typing and transmission across the United States.

Another important capability of electronic mail is automated mail servers that are available on the Internet—both for retrieving documents and information and for companies wanting to distribute information through that means. An automated mail server works similar to a fax-back service; simply place an electronic copy of your company's brochure or price list on an Internet-connected computer and customers can retrieve it automatically any time of day or night. For example, the Internet Shopping Network offers an electronic software shop on the Internet through electronic mail. Here's what you get when you send a message to `info@internet.net`.

```
Message 1/6  From info@news.internet.net          May 27 '94 at 5:44 am -480
                    re: Internet Shopping Network


HERE IS THE INFO YOU REQUESTED FROM:

THE INTERNET SHOPPING NETWORK

GENERAL INFORMATION

The Internet Shopping Network is an electronic shopping system available on the
worldwide internet.  It is set up like a virtual mall with a variety of stores
selling various products.

Today, the network offers twenty thousand computer software and hardware
products available from nearly one thousand different companies.  More than
95% of these products, representing more than $500 million dollars worth of
inventory, are in stock and can be shipped to you the next business day.
Anyone can browse the stores and catalogs of the shopping network from anywhere
on the internet.  All you need is an internet connection and a copy of a Web
browser like Mosaic -  and you can connect.  The connection address is
http://shop.internet.net
 65 lines more (35%). Press <space> for more, 'i' to return.
```

From there, you can see how to request specific documents and information from the server. A message with the subject send prices, for example, might result in a price list automatically being sent back within seconds of the request, without any human intervention. Chapter 6, " The Electronic Schmooze," looks at how to set up these automated mail servers—what we like to think of as e-mail robots.

If there's a lingua franca of the Internet and of computer networks overall, it's surely electronic mail. Whether you use a Mac or PC product that sends messages through gateways or whether you're using a product directly connected to an Internet line, the basics of Internet electronic mail are going to be the same: you specify the user and their location and then type in the message to send.

Joining the Crowd with Mailing Lists

Once you become familiar with the idea of sending a message to an individual through the Internet, it isn't much of a leap to imagine that with a slight change or two, you could actually send the same message to a group of dozens, hundreds, or even thousands of users, all without incurring any charge.

Imagine that you're sending a letter to a post office with a really fast copying machine and a big list of addresses. If you send a letter to, for example, all homeowners in your neighborhood, you'd need to send only one copy of the letter, and the post office would duplicate it and send copies to every registered homeowner—for free.

That's exactly how mailing lists work on the Internet. A central computer somewhere on the network maintains a list, and then anyone on the list can send e-mail easily to everyone else on that discussion list by addressing it to the so-called list server machine.

If you've ever thought about what it must be like to maintain current names and addresses for a magazine like TV Guide, you wouldn't be surprised to find that it's quite a lot of work. Electronic mailing lists on the Internet are quite involved also, but the good news is that computers can make the process considerably easier.

The most common software package used to maintain lists on central computers is called *Listserv* (without the trailing *e* for mundane historical reasons). To sign up for a list that uses the Listserv software, send an e-mail message directly to the Listserv program, requesting that you be added (or removed) from the specified list.

With 20,000,000 users, there are also a *lot* of mailing lists, enough that a list of them with one-line descriptions come to almost 400,000 bytes. At last count, there are almost 8,000 mailing lists, ranging from medieval literature and issues surrounding consulting to a list that offers tips on working with Microsoft Word on the Macintosh and a popular list that discusses the commercialization of the Internet itself.

You can obtain your own list of these mailing lists by sending a request to the Listserv program that resides on the BITNET network information center computer. Send the message to LISTSERV@BITNIC.BITNET with the message body (not the subject—an important distinction) containing the words list global. It should look like this:

```
% elm listserv@bitnic.bitnet
    Subject: none
    Cc:
    Please enter your message, press '.' to end
    list global
    .
    %
```

It will take about fifteen minutes to an hour to process your request, and the result will be enormous. Here's a sampling of the first page or two:

```
Network-wide ID  Full address      List title
--------------   ------------      ----------
'I-AMIGA-UIUC...  I-AMIGA@UIUCVMD   Archive of I-AMIGA list elsewhere on net (Do+
'NEW-SUPERCOM...  S-COMPUT@UGA      (Peered) SuperComputers List (UGA)
'UPDATE-ELECT...  UPNEWS@MARIST     Update Electronic Music Newsletter renamed t+
A-GROUP           A-GROUP@UMSLVMA   The A-Group (Kind of like the A-Team)
AAAE              AAAE@PURCCVM      American Assoc. for Agricultural Education (+
AAAE-C            AAAE-C@PURCCVM    American Assoc. for Agricultural Education (+
AAAE-E            AAAE-E@PURCCVM    American Assoc. for Agricultural Education (+
AAAE-S            AAAE-S@PURCCVM    American Assoc. for Agricultural Education (+
AAAE-W            AAAE-W@PURCCVM    American Assoc. for Agricultural Education (+
AAASHRAN          AAASHRAN@GWUVM    AAAS Human Rights Action Network
AAASMSP           AAASMSP@GWUVM     AAAS Minority Perspectives on Ethics in Scie+
AACRL             AACRL@UABDPO      Alabama Association of College and Research +
AACUNY-L          AACUNY-L@CUNYVM   AACUNY-L: Asian Americans Culture mailing li+
AAHESGIT          AAHESGIT@GWUVM    AAHE Info. Tech. Activities & Projects Steve+
AARPUB-L          AARPUB-L@JPNIMRTU AAR Electronic Publication list
AASCU-L           AASCU-L@UBVM      American Association of State Colleges and U+
AASIG-L           AASIG-L@GSUVM1    GSU Academic Administrators
AATG              AATG@INDYCMS      American Association of Teachers of German
AAUA-L            AAUA-L@UBVM       American Association of University Administr+
AAVLD-L           AAVLD-L@UCDCVDLS  American Assoc of Vet Lab Diagnosticians
ABE-L             ABE-L@BRLNCC      Forum da Associacao Brasileira de Estatistica
ABEP-L            ABEP-L@BRUFSC     Associacao de Brasileiros Estudantes e Pesqu+
ABILITY           ABILITY@ASUACAD   Journal for the study and advancement of the+
ABLE-JOB          ABLE-JOB@SJUVM    St. John's University Job Opportunity List
ABLE-L            ABLE-L@ASUACAD    ABILITY Journal - Discussion & submission
ABOG-L            ABOG-L@UCSBVM     UCSB Academic Business Officers Group (ABOG)
                  ABOG-L@UCSFVM     UCSF Academic Business Officers Group
ABSAME-L          ABSAME-L@MSU      ABSAME-L
ABSJRN-L          ABSJRN-L@CMUVM    ABS Journal Committee
ABSLST-L          ABSLST-L@CMUVM    Association of Black Sociologists
ABUSE-L           ABUSE-L@UBVM      Professional Forum for Child Abuse Issues
ACADDR-L          ACADDR-L@MCGILL1  Academic Computing Centre Directors Forum
ACADEMIA          ACADEMIA@TECHNION Academia  -  Forum on Higher Education in Is+
ACADEMIC          ACADEMIC@BRUFMG   Forum de Ciencia Computacional
ACADLIST          ACADLIST@CESPIVM2 Lista Secretarios Academicos UNLP
ACADNEWS          ACADNEWS@TECHNION Acadnews  -  Bulletin on Higher Education in+
ACADV             ACADV@NDSUVM1     ACADV Academic Advising Forum
ACC-L             ACC-L@GITVM1      ACC-L: "Advanced Computer Controls Discussio+
ACCES-L           ACCES-L@UNBVM1    Associated Competitions for Can. Eng. Studen+
ACCESS-L          ACCESS-L@BRUFPB   List for MS ACCESS
                  ACCESS-L@INDYCMS  Microsoft Access Database Discussion List
ACCI-CHI          ACCI-CHI@URIACC   Consumer Economics and Chinese Scholars
ACDGIS-L          ACDGIS-L@AWIIMC12 Geographische  Informationssysteme
ACE-COM           ACE-COM@WSUVM1    ACE Communication Management SIG
ACES-L            ACES-L@UNBVM1     Atlantic Congress of Engineering Students (F+
ACEWEST           ACEWEST@WSUVM1    Ag Communicators in Education
ACH-EC-L          ACH-EC-L@BROWNVM  ACH Executive Council Discussion List
ACHNEWS           ACHNEWS@UCSBVM    Newsletter of the Association for Computers +
ACLA-L            ACLA-L@WSUVM1     Association of Collegiate Licensing Administ+
ACM-L             ACM-L@KENTVM      ACM-L List for discussing ACM; gatewayed to +
```

```
                 ACM-L@PACEVM       Association for Computing Machinery
ACMET-L          ACMET-L@TEMPLEVM   Academic Metal Crafts discussion
ACMMEX-L         ACMMEX-L@ITESMVF1  ACM MEXICO
ACMR-L           ACMR-L@UHCCVM      Association for Chinese Music Research Netwo+
ACMSTCHP         ACMSTCHP@SUVM      ACM Student Chapters
ACORN-L          ACORN-L@TREARN     ACORN computers Discussion List
```

Types of Mailing Lists

There are three major types of mailing lists: unmoderated, moderated, and in digest format.

Unmoderated lists are the most common. Any message sent to an unmoderated list is automatically distributed to everyone on the list without any human intervention.

Moderated lists offer a valuable alternative with an editor, or moderator, screening all messages to ensure that they're appropriate for the list. If the messages are appropriate, they're distributed to the list. If they're not appropriate, they're returned to the sender with an explanation. The difference between the unmoderated and moderated lists is akin to the difference between graffiti on a wall and the letters published in a magazine.

There's a cost to this sort of mailing list, however. Messages aren't immediately distributed to everyone and might sit for hours or days before being checked and forwarded by the moderator.

The third type of list, *digest format*, is a variant on the second type; instead of sending each submission as a separate e-mail message, they're compiled into a single, quite large message. Our experience suggests that moderated lists that distribute submissions in a digest format are becoming less common, though for lists with lots of shorter messages, having them show up as a single multi-message digest can be quite helpful.

Business Benefits of Mailing Lists

There are two main business benefits to Internet mailing lists—access to experts and access to potential customers. Almost all mailing lists seem to be populated with a surprising and often eclectic variety of users, ranging from the top experts in the area to neophytes monitoring the discussion, hoping to learn about the subject.

When compared to the time and expense involved in attending a professional conference or workshop, joining an Internet mailing list can be an amazingly efficient alternative. Because all these experts are accessible electronically, you can bounce ideas off them any time without incurring exorbitant fees. But beware that your competitors might be quite interested in your fledgling ideas, too!

The other advantage to mailing lists is that you can use them to disseminate product- and service-related information to your target community without any associated expenses. Beware of violations of the spirit of mailing lists and other netiquette *faux pas* (see Chapter 5, " Marketing Do's and Don'ts," for an in-depth exploration of this topic). Also remember that you can create your own mailing lists that might focus exclusively on new product announcements from your company—a list to which you can add customers when they first purchase a product from your firm.

Profile: Here's an example of how this can work: Last fall, Rosalind began a consulting business to help newspapers and magazines expand into online services and interactive media. Later, she launched an electronic newsletter, *Interactive Publishing Alert,* that tracks trends and developments in the electronic newspaper and magazine field. In addition to the word-of-mouth networking she did among her contacts in the publishing world, she also joined four Internet mailing lists—two discussing Internet trends and developments (with an eye toward commercialization of the network), one about computer-assisted journalism, and another about online newspapers and magazines.

Every day since then, she's devoted about an hour to reading the messages distributed on the lists, adding comments of her own, and where appropriate, including information about her consulting services (though in a low-key way). It has proven a most efficient way for her to find out what key members of the media community are thinking about, to learn how the Internet is evolving, and to network with colleagues and potential clients throughout the world. All without paying anything more than her basic monthly connection fee—and all without leaving her home in Florida.

Internet discussion and mailing lists can be a direct marketer's dream—if used judiciously. Unlike the bulletin boards on CompuServe and other commercial services, you don't have to wait until your prospective customers drop by and happen to glance at your company's information; they get your message automatically as subscribers to the list.

Of course, this can be a double-edged sword. If you misjudge your market or word your press release in too promotional a way, you run the risk of alienating your entire target market in one fell swoop, and, on the Internet, apologies often aren't accepted.

Getting on the List

Joining an Internet mailing list is as easy as sending a single piece of electronic mail. There are no cards to fill out, no authorizations, qualifications, and, best of all, no checks to include. Instead, you need only identify the name of the mailing list and the name of the computer that hosts the list.

Most mailing lists are run through Listserv software, so your request to subscribe to the list is sent directly to the Listserv program rather than to the list itself. That's an important distinction: Mail sent to the mailing list itself *is sent to everyone on the list*—the last thing you want to do before you join up!

As an example, Dave earlier requested the list of mailing lists from BITNIC (a message sent to LISTSERV@BITNIC.BITNET with the message body containing the words list global) and noticed that buried deep in the file was a mailing list AAVLD-L that described itself as "American Assoc of Vet Lab Diagnosticians". It sounded interesting, so Dave checked the list of mailing lists, saw that it was listed as AAVLD-L@UCDCVDLS, and knew that address meant he could join by sending a subscription request, as in the following, to the Listserv program at that computer:

```
To: listserv@ucdcvdls.bitnet
Subject: none
Message : SUBSCRIBE AAVLD-L Dave Taylor
```

The message you'll send to sign up for a mailing list is almost identical to this message; the only changes you'll need to make are the e-mail address, the name of the list, and your own name. If Dave wanted to sign up for the valuable "net-happenings" list, a clearinghouse for new products, services, and activities of interest to the Internet community, here's what he would send instead:

```
To: majordomo@is.internic.com
Subject: none
Message : SUBSCRIBE NET-HAPPENINGS Dave Taylor
```

The net-happenings mailing list recently switched to a new mailing list manager program—majordomo—so you'll notice that the destination address for this message is majordomo rather than listserv. The commands you need to subscribe to a list managed by either program are quite similar.

Most of the time, subscription requests are processed within seconds of receipt. Don't be surprised if less than a minute after you send your subscription request, you receive an acknowledgment similar to this:

```
You have been added to list net-happenings@is.internic.net.
The system has recorded your address as taylor@netcom.com
and in order for your messages to get posted, you will
have to send them from this address.

If a message is ever rejected, please contact the list's owner:

sackman@plains.nodak.edu

All requests should be addressed to listserv@is.internic.net.

The net-happenings list is a service of InterNIC Information Services. The
purpose of the list is to distribute to the community announcements of
interest to network staffers and end users. This includes conference
announcements, call for papers, publications, newsletters, network tools
updates, and network resources. Net-happenings is a moderated,
announcements-only mailing list which gathers announcements from many
Internet sources and concentrates them onto one list. Traffic is
around 5-10 messages per day.
```

If after a few days or weeks, you decide that you want to drop the list; the conversation isn't of value, there are just too many messages to read each day, or any other reason, you can easily "unsubscribe" by sending another message to the Listserv program, substituting UNSUBSCRIBE for SUBSCRIBE in the message body. If Dave was tired of net- happenings and wanted to remove himself from the list, he could send the following message:

```
To: majordomo@is.internic.com
Subject: none
Message : UNSUBSCRIBE NET-HAPPENINGS Dave Taylor
.
%
```

One helpful hint here is that if you find a number of mailing lists that sound interesting, sign up gradually: without actually being involved, it's impossible to tell whether a particular mailing list will have a few messages each week or a hundred messages per day. Sign up for too many too quickly and you might quickly find yourself innundated with mail!

Note: Because you can now send electronic mail to and from Internet addresses (even if you're hooked into one of the commercial services like CompuServe), you can subscribe to any Internet mailing list, too. Be careful, however, because many of these lists can result in a considerable amount of electronic mail being received each day, and on commercial services you pay per-message for e-mail that travels through the system gateway from the Internet.

In summary, think of Internet mailing lists as your own private broadcasting network—without the expense of buying a TV or radio station. Or think of them as "virtual" conferences with top experts available day and night to inform you about the latest industry trends and debate the hottest issues. For more information about mailing lists and how you can use them to benefit your company, check out Chapter 5, "Marketing Do's and Don'ts," and Chapter 6, "The Electronic Schmooze."

Spreading the News with Newsgroups

The next step up in Internet information dissemination is Usenet newsgroups. If mailing lists are like a post office that can automatically make copies of your message and distribute it worldwide, Usenet is the public library, where each book covers a discussion on a specific topic.

Currently, there are over 7,000 Usenet newsgroups with far-ranging discussions on a dizzying array of topics ranging from HyperCard programming on the Macintosh to magazine writing, the best places to eat in the San Francisco area to the moral implications and ramifications of abortion in U.S. society.

As with mailing lists, the two primary types of Usenet newsgroups are *moderated* and *unmoderated*. Most groups are unmoderated, and anything anyone submits, or "posts," in Internet lingo, to the group is quickly distributed to all sites on the network and available to everyone who participates in that particular discussion group.

Moderated groups have all submissions automatically sent to an individual or committee that screens the articles for appropriateness, and if acceptable, posts them to the group. Delays of many days are common with moderated newsgroups, but when a small Usenet group can have 5,000 participants, you might find yourself quickly seeking shelter from the barrage of information.

Note: The technological underpinnings of Usenet offer an intriguing model for distributed information systems. In an unmoderated Usenet group, you post an article on your local machine, which

> keeps a copy and sends another copy to its virtual electronic neigh-
> bors. Upon receipt of the copy, each machine then makes another
> copy of your article, adding it into the disk directory set aside for
> that particular discussion group and sending another copy to its
> virtual neighbors. In a matter of a few hours, an article you wrote
> on your machine can be duplicated thousands of times, with your
> comments and insight occupying disk space on each machine.

As with mailing lists, you also have to subscribe to Usenet newsgroups, but the
good news is that the entire process takes place on your local Internet service
provider computer rather than through electronic mail on a remote computer.

Now for the catch: A wide variety of programs are available for reading Usenet
news, and they are dramatically different from each other. With the proliferation
of Mac and PC computers on the Internet, graphically-based readers are also
becoming available, further complicating things. Worse yet, different Internet
access providers offer a different subset of the Usenet readers. For example, Dave
prefers a program called *tin* for reading Usenet news, and although it's available
on Netcom, it isn't available on the computer he uses at Purdue University, so he
uses another program called *rn* for Purdue-related newsgroups. Rosalind, by
contrast, relies on WinNET Mail, a Windows-based news reader.

> **Tip:** The best recommendation we can give you is that if you have
> access to any sort of graphical interface to Usenet, use it. If you don't,
> we recommend that you look for tin, a friendly screen-based Usenet
> reader that works quickly and understandably on inexpensive
> dialup lines. If you're interested in the possibility of customizing
> your reader—and you have some programming experience or a
> good consultant available—the rn or trn programs could be a good
> choice.

As a result of the plethora of Usenet interfaces, we debated (through electronic
mail!) which would be the best reader to use for the examples in this book. Our
conclusion was that tin offered the best balance between common accessibility
and sophisticated interface.

Don't be surprised, however, if things aren't immediately obvious. Like all Usenet
software, tin takes a while to master. Worse, it's difficult to figure out what Usenet
groups are available, and few of the programs offer any capabilities to help. Your
best bet is to ask your Internet access provider for a listing of the groups available including descriptions (if that puzzles them, ask whether they have a file on

the system called /usr/lib/news/newsgroups). It's a huge file, and we used a simple utility to show just the groups that have the phrase biz within their names. Here's what we found:

```
biz.americast            AmeriCast announcements.
biz.americast.samples         Samples of AmeriCast. (Moderated)
biz.books.technical           A place to contact book sellers & buyers.
biz.clarinet             Announcements about ClariNet.
biz.clarinet.sample           Samples of ClariNet newsgroups for the outside w
orld.
biz.comp.hardware             Generic commercial hardware postings.
biz.comp.services             Generic commercial service postings.
biz.comp.software             Generic commercial software postings.
biz.comp.telebit              Support of the Telebit modem.
biz.comp.telebit.netblazer    The Telebit Netblazer.
biz.config               Biz Usenet configuration and administration.
biz.control              Control information and messages.
biz.dec          DEC equipment & software.
biz.dec.ip               IP networking on DEC machines.
biz.dec.workstations          DEC workstation discussions & info.
biz.digex.announce       Announcements from Digex. (Moderated)
biz.jobs.offered              Position announcements.
biz.misc                 Miscellaneous postings of a commercial nature.
biz.next.newprod              New product announcements for the NeXT.
biz.sco.announce              SCO and related product announcements. (Moderate
d)
biz.sco.binaries              Binary packages for SCO Xenix, UNIX, or ODT.
biz.sco.general          Q&A, discussions and comments on SCO products.
biz.sco.magazine              To discuss the magazine and its contents.
biz.sco.opendesktop           ODT environment and applications tech info, q&a.
biz.sco.sources          Source code ported to an SCO operating environment.
biz.stolen               Postings about stolen merchandise.
biz.tadpole.sparcbook         Discussions on the Sparcbook portable computer.
biz.test                 Biz newsgroup test messages.
biz.zeos                 Information about Zeos International and its products.
biz.zeos.announce             Zeos product announcements. (Moderated)
biz.zeos.general              Zeos technical support and general information.
clari.biz.commodity      Commodity news and price reports (Moderated)
clari.biz.courts         Lawsuits and business related legal matters (Moderated)
clari.biz.economy        Economic news and indicators (Moderated)
clari.biz.economy.world  Economy stories for non-US countries (Moderated)
clari.biz.features            Business feature stories (Moderated)
clari.biz.finance        Finance, currency, Corporate finance (Moderated)
clari.biz.finance.earnings    Earnings & dividend reports (Moderated)
clari.biz.finance.personal    Personal investing & finance (Moderated)
clari.biz.finance.services    Banks and financial industries (Moderated)
clari.biz.invest         News for investors (Moderated)
clari.biz.labor          Strikes, unions and labor relations (Moderated)
clari.biz.market         General stock market news (Moderated)
clari.biz.market.amex    American Stock Exchange reports & news (Moderated)
clari.biz.market.dow     Dow Jones NYSE reports (Moderated)
clari.biz.market.ny      NYSE reports (Moderated)
clari.biz.market.otc     NASDAQ reports (Moderated)
clari.biz.market.report  General market reports, S&P, etc. (Moderated)
clari.biz.mergers        Mergers and acquisitions (Moderated)
```

```
clari.biz.misc          Other business news (Moderated)
clari.biz.products      Important new products & services (Moderated)
clari.biz.top           Top business news (Moderated)
clari.biz.urgent        Breaking business news (Moderated)
clari.canada.biz        Canadian Business Summaries (Moderated)
```

A Sample Session

Follow along as we step through a brief sample session with tin, starting at the first screen, which indicates what groups we subscribe to and how many articles have arrived in each group since the last time we read Usenet.

```
Group Selection (15)                        h=help

    1          netcom.announce              Announcements from Netcom Staf
    2     2    netcom.general               General discussions about Netc
    3     1    netcom.internet              Internet access at Netcom: ftp
    4          ed.vr
    5    606   misc.entrepreneurs           Discussion on operating a busi
    6          netcom.programmers           Discussions about software dev
    7          ucb.extension.class.telewriting
    8     1    biz.comp.services            Generic commercial service pos
    9          school.subjects.languages    English, Deutsch, Francais etc
   10     3    clari.feature.miss_manners   Judith Martin's Humourous Etiq
   11    22    clari.biz.briefs
   12    19    clari.biz.industry.print_media
   13    16    clari.biz.industry.services
   14    22    clari.news.education.higher
   15    11    clari.news.education

   <n>=set current to n, TAB=next unread, /=search pattern, c)atchup,
g)oto, j=line down, k=line up, h)elp, m)ove, q)uit, r=toggle all/unread,
s)ubscribe, S)ub pattern, u)nsubscribe, U)nsub pattern, y)ank in/out

                    *** End of Groups ***
```

If you look carefully, you'll see that we subscribe to 15 newsgroups and that the group misc.entrepeneurs, for example, has 606 articles that have arrived since the last time we read the group. To see what's there, press Return (the group is already highlighted in bold, though on your screen it might be an inverse video bar), which results in the following screen:

```
misc.entrepreneurs (321T 606A 0K 0H R)              h=help

    1  +   Can you teach entrepeneur             Ben M. Schorr
    2  +   On commercial use of the 'net         Randal L. Schwartz
    3  +   COMPLETE BUSINESS ON DISK             Christopher D. Col
```

```
   4   +      Free Report! How to m                  Scott Tengen
   5   + 9    A straw-man: Use "Distribution: ad"     Thomas F Lee
   6   + 3    Vending Business Opp                     epsinc@delphi.com
   7   + 2    Earn Free Travel & Cash                  epsinc@delphi.com
   8   + 2    CASH Generator                           epsinc@delphi.com
   9   +      FREE Closing Costs & Appraisals          epsinc@delphi.com
  10   + 5    ALMOST FREE MLM Newspaper Sample         epsinc@delphi.com
  11   + 2    PROTECTING YOUR DESIGN                   Michael Sellers
  12   + 4    Has anyone heard of Incomnet?            acanton@delphi.com
  13   +      Data Detectives Wanted                   Daniel Hunsinger
  14   + 3    The IDEA Association, Free Newsletter.   Donald Miller
  15   +      Help: Bottle Mfr. and Bottling Company   Charleen Bunjiovia
  16   +      where can I get a list of govt auctions, date  Michael Grommet
  17   +      Apologies for reposting due to technical prob   Brookfield Economi

    <n>=set current to n, TAB=next unread, /=search pattern, ^K)ill/select,
  a)uthor search, c)atchup, j=line down, k=line up, K=mark read, l)ist thread,
   ¦=pipe, m)ail, o)print, q)uit, r=toggle all/unread, s)ave, t)ag, w=post
```

Here we've zoomed into the virtual magazine that is misc.entrepreneurs and are viewing the table of contents of new articles. At the bottom of the screen is a brief reminder of the most commonly used commands at this level of tin. To read a particular article, we could either enter the number to the left of the article or because we're already at an article of interest, just press Return. Here's what we see:

```
Thu, 26 May 1994 11:37:00      misc.entrepreneurs        Thread  1 of  321
Lines 24                  Can you teach entrepeneur        No responses
ben.schorr@bcsbbs.com  Ben Schorr at The BCS BBS - Los Angeles, CA - 213-962-29

CJ> Can it be taught in business schools or is it something an individual
CJ> is born with?

Now THAT'S an interesting question. I think it can be taught, but there
is a certain attitude that can be very difficult for people that don't
have it inherent as part of their personality.

I think that there needs to be a little bit of swashbuckler in an
entrepreneur that the meek may never be able to get ahold of.

Just a thought.

-Ben-
Ben M. Schorr                              21000 Osborne, #6
Director of Operations                     Canoga Park, CA. 91304

    <n>=set current to n, TAB=next unread, /=search pattern, ^K)ill/select,
       a)uthor search, B)ody search, c)atchup, f)ollowup, K=mark read,
        ¦=pipe, m)ail, o)print, q)uit, r)eply mail, s)ave, t)ag, w=post

                                               —More—(79%) [933/1175]
```

Usenet's Hierarchies

Usenet is divided into nine primary hierarchies, or categories, focusing on

> computers (`comp`)
> science (`sci`)
> recreation (`rec`)
> miscellaneous topics (`misc`)
> alternative topics (`alt`)
> Usenet software and organizational discussion (`news`)
> social topics (`soc`)
> hotly debated topics (`talk`)
> business (`biz`)

The alternative newsgroups (`alt`) merit special mention; these groups have even fewer constraints than the rest of Usenet. Some alternative groups are sophomoric, such as `alt.sex.bestiality`, but others are actually valuable and interesting to business users, such as `alt.education.distance` and `alt.internet.services`.

For businesses with computers, some of the most valuable newsgroups are the ones dealing with computer-related topics. For example, there are newsgroups for users of Sun, NeXT, DEC, and Macintosh computers; newsgroups for Windows, spreadsheet, and database users, and newsgroups for people who want to share information and exchange ideas about everything from virtual reality to artificial intelligence.

The Benefits of Usenet

The great thing about newsgroups is that there's no charge to access them—unlike CompuServe's technical support bulletin boards, for example, where you pay by the minute. In fact, a small number of companies are creating their own newsgroups as a way of offering low-cost customer support, though we favor other alternatives, particularly mailing lists and Web pages, as we'll discuss throughout this book.

Newsgroups can also be a valuable marketing tool to announce new products and boost your company's visibility—but as with mailing lists, overly promotional or off-topic messages will assuredly result in hostile reactions from your potential customers on the Internet. In April, for example, an Arizona immigration lawyer was pummeled with hate mail and lost his Internet account after plastering thousands of Usenet newsgroups with online advertisements.

As commercial online services such as America Online and GEnie incorporate more Internet features and information in a quest to compete, they will undoubtably add access to a subset of the many Usenet newsgroups. If they meet your needs and include the groups you want, such a subset can be an alternative, but we recommend that you investigate full Internet access providers and ensure that they include the majority of Usenet.

From invaluable business information to keeping up with the latest trends in your market niche to just plain gossip and recreational chit-chat, Usenet can't be beat. With over 7,000 different discussion areas, many of which can contain a hundred or more new messages each day, there's a group of people talking about subjects of interest to you, too! As a marketing and research tool for businesses, Usenet can be particularly valuable, and we explore its facets extensively in Chapter 7, "Dialing for Data," and Chapter 6, "The Electronic Schmooze."

Dialing into the World with Telnet

Electronic mail and Usenet are both focused on offering discussion forums through various means, but there's a world of additional information available through the Internet, too.

There are a number of ways to access the far-flung databases in cyberspace, but the most popular, and easiest, is probably something called *telnet*, for *telephone network*.

The program works by connecting you to a remote computer and then sending to that computer everything you type on your screen; once you're logged on, everything from the remote machine appears on your local display. With telnet, you can dial into thousands of computers connected to the Internet—even those overseas—without ever worrying about remembering phone numbers or racking up long-distance phone bills. Electronic mail addresses require you to know names of users and the full names and domains of their computers, but for telnet, you only need to know the computer name.

Sitting in California, for example, you can use telnet to connect directly to the United States Library of Congress Information System (LOCIS) and search its card catalog. You can also try connecting to the Wharton School of Business at the University of Pennsylvania to search for business information or the holdings catalog at the University of Melbourne in Australia. Once you have an Internet account, you can also telnet directly to a variety of commercial networks such as CompuServe and Dialog. You'll still need to open an account on these services before you can access the information stored there, however.

Accessing Business Services with Telnet

Telnet offers a wide variety of services of interest to business users.

For example, you're meeting with your CEO, and she mentions that she saw a book on managing interpersonal conflict and thought you'd find it of value. You could ask for a full citation, or you could use the Internet to find it yourself. Let's see what you could find with a quick check of the Duke University Library. To connect, we'll type `telnet ducatalog.lib.duke.edu` and wade through the first few screens of startup information to get to the following main screen:

```
                  MAIN SEARCH MENU    (1 of 2)           DUKE_CATALOG


AUTHOR      a=faulkner william      (enter last name first)
            a=american chemical soc (you may truncate search statements)


TITLE       t=scarlet letter        (omit initial articles a, an, the)


SUBJECT     s=substance abuse
            s=king, martin luther   (searching for works about a person)


KEYWORD     To start the keyword search program, type K at the >> prompt.

DATABASES   To search other databases, including the catalogs of NCSU and UNC-CH
            type d at the >> prompt.

QUIT        To leave the Library Catalog, type quit at the >> prompt.

Enter your search below. Press (RETURN) to continue or type ?? to see Help Menu.
>>
```

We'll want to do a keyword search, so entering K results in this display on the screen:

```
WELCOME
        ENTER           TO SEARCH           EXAMPLE

        fi              KEYWORD             fi games

        fi ti           TITLE               fi ti america

        fi au           AUTHOR              fi au asimov

        fi su           SUBJECT             fi su united states
```

```
**************************************************
* Enter   DISPLAY  to display a record        *
*         START    to start over              *
*         STOP     to finish                   *
*         HELP     for more information        *
**************************************************

1>>
```

Based on these examples, we should be able to find the book by searching for the keywords interpersonal and conflict, so at the prompt, we enter find interpersonal conflict and see what happens. Astoundingly, only one book is matched, and the display command shows that this information is available:

```
1>> fi nd managing interpersonal
        1> MANAGING INTERPERSONAL occurs 1 time in 1 record.


2>> display
Record #1
        Title: Managing interpersonal conflict / William A. Donohue
               ; with Robert Kolt.
       Author: Donohue, William A., 1947-
    Published: Newbury Park : Sage Publications, c1992.
      Subject: Interpersonal conflict.
               Negotiation.
               Conflict management.
               Interpersonal relationships


LOCATION: Fuqua   — CALL NUMBER: BF637.I48 D66 1992
     c.1                                                  NotCheckedOut

2>>


he - for help   fi - to find a term  di - to display results  sto - to stop
```

Here we can type stop to quit the library catalog and return to our regular session. Don't be too intimidated if it seems difficult to work with these library catalogs; as you'll see, there are different, and easier, ways to work with this type of database.

These days, many electronic merchants are using telnet as a way to let potential customers throughout the world access their computer systems and software directly for the price of a local phone call. Thanks to telnet, shoppers can browse books, CDs, software, flowers, and hundreds of other items online and order them direct from the vendor.

For example, let's say you've found the book you were looking for by logging in to the New York Public Library's computer system and now want to buy a copy for yourself. There's no need to leave the telnet program; just connect to books.com, the computer run by Book Stacks Unlimited of Cleveland, Ohio. Once connected, you'll be asked to type your name, address, phone number, and other information to uniquely identify yourself for future transactions. The next display is the following main menu, the central spot for user interaction:

```
*****************************************
*      Book Stacks Unlimited, Inc.    *
*              MAIN MENU              *
*****************************************


        <B>ook Store

        <M>essages

        <N>ews/Notes

        <F>iles/Magazines

        <U>tilities

        <H>elp

        <G>oodBye

Command:
```

We choose B to search for a book and learn that there are quite a variety of ways to accomplish this:

```
************************************************************
*                 The Book Store                          *
*                 200,000+  Titles                        *
************************************************************

 <A>uthor Search              <R>eview Your Selections

 <T>itle Search               <O>rder (when done)

 <K>eyWord Title Search       <C>heck Order Status

 <I>SBN Search

 <S>ubject Search \ Just Published


 ----------------------------------------------------
       <P>revious Menu     <H>elp     <G>oodbye

Command:
```

We select T to search by title and enter interpersonal conflict and find that the book we want is available online:

```
YOU HAVE SELECTED THE FOLLOWING TITLE:

Author   : Donohue, William A./Kolt, Robert

Title    : Managing Interpersonal Conflict (Interpersonal Commtexts, Vol 4)


ISBN     : 0803933126
Volume   :
Subject  :
Dewey #  : 303.69
Publisher: Sage Pubns
Date Pub : 07/92
Binding  : Paperback
Edition  :
Bookmarks:    0
Price    : $ 16.50
Reviews  : 0

How many copies would you like? <R>eviews <ENTER> To Exit :
```

We choose the book, enter our credit card number, and log off. Three days later, the book arrives via United Parcel Service. We never even had to leave our computers.

The real value of telnet is that you can let your fingers do the walking through the Internet without ever making a long-distance phone call. For businesses, it's a wonderful way for customers all over the world to browse your merchandise electronically at absolutely no cost. For consumers, it's like being able to travel to any building, library, or organization anywhere in the world—instantly—for free. We talk about this facet of the Internet in both Chapter 7, "Dialing for Data," and Chapter 11, "Internet Cybermalls."

Moving Files with FTP

Telnet is a great way to access remote computers—or let Internet users access yours, but it doesn't help disseminate files, documents, press releases, or software. That's where file transfer protocol (FTP) comes in.

There are two basic ways of working with FTP. For confidential information distribution, files can be deposited in a specific account with a secret password. If the information is intended for the general public, you can make it available through a service known as *anonymous FTP*, in which users don't need an account to connect, search available files, or download them to their computers.

Many computer companies, including Digital, Apple, Sun Microsystems, and Silicon Graphics, use FTP to enable their customers to download software fixes, press releases, and other informational files.

Unfortunately, the FTP program that is available through most dialup Internet access providers is very primitive and remains one of the most difficult Internet tools to use. Thankfully, a number of attractive graphical interfaces are now available for DOS, Windows, and Macintosh systems, and many are available for free or little cost. In this section, we'll demonstrate how to work with the UNIX-based FTP program because that's what your dialup account will probably require you to use. We'll also show how the same collection of files would appear within the Mac Fetch and a Windows-based FTP program.

To transfer a file using UNIX FTP, you need to connect to the remote computer, enter the word anonymous or FTP as an account and, by tradition, your e-mail address as password. Then you need to change to the directory where the desired file is stored and use the get command to download that file to your local account. By default, all files are transmitted as if they are text, which usually works.

If the file you want to download is a program file or another type of file that mustn't be altered in transmission, you can switch into *binary mode* by using the binary command. By contrast, if you're sure what you seek is text—a document, for example— you might use the ascii command. ASCII is the set of characters used by most Internet computers; it stands for American Standard for Computer Information Interchange.

Suppose that while reading a recent article in a technology-oriented business magazine, you notice a note at the end of the story that says, "The text of the intellectual property portion of the North American Free Trade Agreement is available via FTP from wiretap.spies.com as file NAFTA/17.intellect." Based on that description, it's a pretty safe bet that NAFTA/17.intellect is a text file.

Here's what a UNIX session to retrieve that file would look like. (In FTP, cd changes directory and dir lists the files in a specific directory.)

```
% ftp wiretap.spies.com
Connected to wiretap.spies.com.
220 wiretap.spies.com FTP server (Version wu-2.3(2) Wed May 4 14:08:55 PDT 1994)
 ready.
Name (wiretap.spies.com:taylor): anonymous
331 Guest login ok, send your complete e-mail address as password.
Password:
230-
230-wiretap.spies.com
230-
230-Welcome to the Internet Wiretap FTP server.
230-Tar and compressed tar archive output is enabled.
230-
```

```
230-Gopher access to this material is available on port 70.
230-
230-Logging has also been enabled on file transfers.
230-Anyone uploading pictures to this machine will have
230-their kneecaps broken.
230-
230-Look at ".files" in each directory for a better
230-description of contents. Please note that ".cap" files
230-are intended for use by Gopher, and are generally
230-meaningless to FTP users.
230-
230-Read the files in About/ if you desire more detailed
230-information regarding the Internet Wiretap.
230-
230-Comments to: archive@wiretap.spies.com
230-
230 Guest login ok, access restrictions apply.
ftp> cd NAFTA
250 CWD command successful.
ftp> dir 17.intellect
200 PORT command successful.
150 Opening ASCII mode data connection for /bin/ls.
-r—r—r—  1 9013      42           63957 Mar  5  1993 17.intellect
226 Transfer complete.
remote: 17.intellect
68 bytes received in 0.01 seconds (6.6 Kbytes/s)
ftp> ascii
200 Type set to A.
ftp> get 17.intellect
200 PORT command successful.
150 Opening ASCII mode data connection for 17.intellect (63957 bytes).
226 Transfer complete.
local: 17.intellect remote: 17.intellect
65434 bytes received in 2.3 seconds (28 Kbytes/s)
ftp> quit
221 Goodbye.
```

As you can see, the text-based FTP program is helpful but tricky to use. How might graphical interfaces help with the problem? Figures 1.3 and 1.4 show how the same directory of files would look on a PC running Windows or a Macintosh directly connected to the network. We're sure you'll agree that it's considerably easier to use FTP with a graphical program.

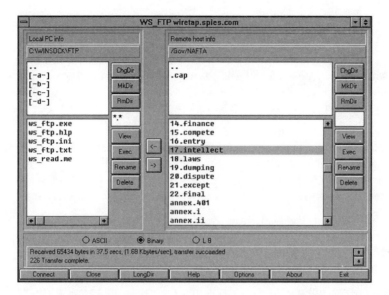

Figure 1.3. Downloading the file, NAFTA/17.intellect, using WS_FTP, a Windows-based FTP program graphical program.

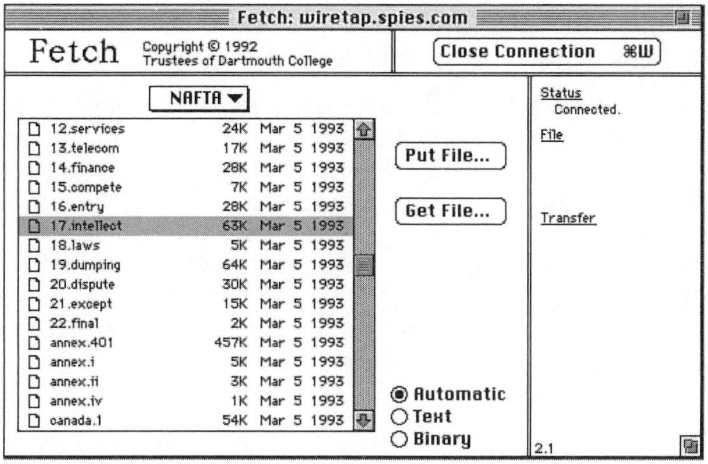

Figure 1.4. Macintosh version.

Accessing Archives with Archie

For all the advantages of the FTP system, there's also a basic problem: how do you know what files are available where? Indeed, this is part of a more fundamental problem on the Internet that has to do with the missing road maps and still-unfinished highways that we've been talking about through this book.

A group of students at the McGill University school of computer science recognized the problem and, with some ingenuity and skillful programming, solved it by creating an FTP database system called *Archie*. The Archie system automatically gathers and indexes the hundreds of FTP archives available and then distributes the comprehensive index to a variety of Archie sites through the Internet.

With Archie, you can locate any file available through FTP. The downside is that there really isn't much information contained in the Archie database. Archie filenames don't tell you much about the contents of the file, and, unfortunately, that's all you have to work with.

Nevertheless, you can often infer some information about a file by its location, which may offer some assistance. Let's take a look at directory naming that can help you find what you're looking for. A directory such as `pub/archives/mac/business/stocks`, for example, is a likely place to find stock-market-related files and applications. You can use this to help your searches. In this case, if we search for `mac` and `stocks`, we could match the files in this directory.

Archie's Internet archives database contains an entry including the name, location, host system, size, and file type of more than 2,250,000 files at more than 1,000 anonymous FTP archive sites. To give you some sense of how popular Archie has become, public Archie servers currently receive more than 50,000 queries each day. With more than 2,000,000 files available, you won't be surprised to find that the Archie database is massive, far too massive to be found on lots of different sites on the Internet. Fortunately, that's not a problem because a number of computer systems offer public access to Archie for anyone who can use telnet (see preceding section on telnet) to connect to their machines. Here are some of the public access Archie sites:

Hostname	Site Location
archie.au	Australia
archie.edvz.uni-linz.ac.at	Austria
archie.univie.ac.at	Austria
archie.uqam.ca	Canada
archie.funet.fi	Finland
archie.univ-rennes1.fr	France
archie.th-darmstadt.de	Germany
archie.ac.il	Israel

`archie.unipi.it`	Italy
`archie.wide.ad.jp`	Japan
`archie.hana.nm.kr`	Korea
`archie.sogang.ac.kr`	Korea
`archie.uninett.no`	Norway
`archie.rediris.es`	Spain
`archie.luth.se`	Sweden
`archie.switch.ch`	Switzerland
`archie.nctuccca.edu.tw`	Taiwan
`archie.ncu.edu.tw`	Taiwan
`archie.doc.ic.ac.uk`	United Kingdom
`archie.hensa.ac.uk`	United Kingdom
`archie.unl.edu`	USA (NE)
`archie.internic.net`	USA (NJ)
`archie.rutgers.edu`	USA (NJ)
`archie.ans.net`	USA (NY)
`archie.sura.net`	USA (MD)

Let's connect to the closest Archie site and look to see whether there are any files that can help Macintosh users track their stocks and other securities. To connect to the Archie database, we'll use the telnet program, connecting to the hostname specified in the preceding table. As with FTP, using the Archie program directly through telnet can be quite confusing:

```
% telnet archie.internic.net
Trying...
Connected to ds.internic.net.
Escape character is '^]'.
              InterNIC Directory and Database Services

Welcome to InterNIC Directory and Database Services provided by AT&T.
These services are partially supported through a cooperative agreement
with the National Science Foundation.

First time users may login as guest with no password to receive help.

Your comments and suggestions for improvement are welcome, and can be
mailed to admin@ds.internic.net.

AT&T MAKES NO WARRANTY OR GUARANTEE, OR PROMISE, EXPRESS OR IMPLIED,
CONCERNING THE  CONTENT OR  ACCURACY OF THE  DIRECTORY  ENTRIES AND
DATABASE FILES  STORED  AND  MAINTAINED BY  AT&T.  AT&T EXPRESSLY
DISCLAIMS AND EXCLUDES ALL EXPRESS WARANTIES AND IMPLIED WARRANTIES
OF MERCHANTABILITY AND FITNESS FOR A PARTICULAR PURPOSE.

SunOS UNIX (ds2)

login:
```

As with all Archie servers, logging in here as `archie` will drop us into the Archie client program:

```
**************************************************************************

              Welcome to the InterNIC Directory and Database Server.

**************************************************************************

# Bunyip Information Systems, 1993

# Terminal type set to 'vt100 24 80'.
# 'erase' character is '^?'.
# 'search' (type string) has the value 'sub'.
archie> find stocks
# Search type: sub.
# Your queue position: 1
# Estimated time for completion: 00:50
working... /


Host sunsite.unc.edu    (152.2.22.81)
Last updated 11:07 22 Dec 1993

    Location: /pub/packages/TeX/fonts/postscript/adobe/Updates
       FILE    -r—r—r—    1315 bytes  22:42 14 Jul 1993  930709.StockSplit.press
```

Dozens of matches are shown on-screen, all in the format demonstrated here. This particular match is available at the FTP archive site `sunsite.unc.edu` in the specified directory, and it's 1,315 bytes in size. Looking through all the matches reveals the following:

```
Host wuarchive.wustl.edu    (128.252.135.4)
Last updated 11:27 22 Dec 1993

    Location: /systems/mac/umich.edu/misc/demo
       FILE    -r--r--r--  266426 bytes  15:15  5 Sep 1993  stockstack2.1g.cpt.hqx
```

Looks promising. We could use FTP to connect to `wuarchive.wustl.edu`, change to the directory `systems/mac/umich.edu/misc/demo`, and retrieve the file `stockstack2.1g.cpt.hqx` to see whether it has what we're looking for.

> **Note:** Archie can be a bit confusing to work with, as can many of the other Internet services we introduce in this initial chapter. Rather than writing yet another book on how to use the tools themselves, however, we'd like to suggest that an excellent companion to this book for those of you seeking more information on these tools is *Navigating the Internet* by Richard Smith and Mark Gibbs, and *The Internet Unleashed,* both from Sams Publishing.

As a card catalog is an essential part of any library, so Archie is the key to finding files and documents through the many FTP archives available on the Internet. It's a bit awkward to use at first, and unfortunately its only knowledge of the items in its archive are the actual file names used (a significant limitation, in our view), but it's definitely a tool to learn.

Searching for Data with Gopher

Telnet is a terrific tool, but it requires a fair amount of knowledge about the Internet. In particular, you'd need to know a lot of computer names to be able to exploit fully the many services available. This is doubly true for FTP, and even with the Archie service, it's still quite difficult to find information on the Internet.

The computer services group at the University of Minnesota found the same problem when they began to make online documentation available to their students. As a result, they invented Gopher, a menu-based front-end to documents, information, and services available on the Internet.

Gopher is a one-stop shopping source for Internet information. A menu-driven document-delivery service, you can use Gopher to browse the Internet's resources, read text files, and access information of all kinds. With Gopher, you "burrow" through a series of nested menus to find the information you need on any computer system connected to the network and running Gopher software.

As does FTP, a variety of Gopher programs offer access to the data through Mac, PC, or dialup systems. All the software is free, and we will show the dialup service again, so you can see how to step through menus and then show the same information on TurboGopher (the Mac Gopher client) and Winsock Gopher, a shareware Windows client.

The most powerful aspect of the Gopher service is that any system can include a variety of links to other Gopher servers. The result is a network-wide information source called *Gopherspace*.

Gophers also provide gateways to other Internet information systems such as World Wide Web, WAIS, Archie, and Whois and to network services such as telnet and FTP. When you access a Gopher site, the files you see listed on the menu in front of you could be housed anywhere on the network—on your local server or on a computer system thousands of miles away. By simply choosing an item from the menu on your screen, you can access that information within minutes.

A Sample Gopher Session

Here's the main menu of the Gopher site put up by the U.S. Census Bureau. We connect by typing gopher gopher.census.gov at the command line, and the screen shows

```
               Internet Gopher Information Client v1.12S

               Root gopher server: gopher.census.gov

  ->  1.  About This Gopher Server ( Help and Information )/
      2.  About The U.S. Census Bureau/
      3.  Directory of Services and Information/
      4.  Our Organizations and Divisions/
      5.  Other Servers on the Web That Offer Census Data/
      6.  U.S. Government Gopher Servers/
      7.  University Gopher Servers/
      8.  Other Gopher Servers on the Web/
      9.  Internet Documents/
      10. Online Internet/UNIX User Reference/


Press ? for Help, q to Quit, u to go up a menu              Page: 1/1
```

Pressing 3 followed by Return chooses the Directory of Services and Information menu item, which immediately burrows in to that level, changing the center information on the screen to

```
      1.   What you will find in this menu.
  ->  2.   News Releases Hot Off the Press/
      3.   News and analysis from the Center for Economic Studies
      4.   International programs that collect global information/
      5.   Census Bulletin Board System <TEL>
      6.   Statistical Briefs like never before!!! (Postscript)/
      7.   Who's Who at the Census Bureau/
      8.   "We The People" Series!!! (Postscript)/
      9.   Financial data from state and local governments and schools
      10.  The Census Bureau Anonymous Ftp/
      11.  Census Bureau BBS Bulletins/
      12.  Sipp On Call/
```

Choosing 2 brings up a list of news releases organized into thirteen categories: Construction, Population, 2000 Census, Economic Census and Surveys, Education, Foreign Trade Monthly, Governments, Health and Health Care, Income, Wealth and Poverty, International, Housing, Agriculture, and Publications. If your business is involved in international trade, for example, you might choose 6 to see what's in *Foreign Trade Monthly*.

```
—>  1.  About the January Press Releases (Jan '92 to '94).
    2.  U.S. International Trade in Goods and Services.
    3.  U.S. International Trade in Goods and Services 3 month avgs.
    4.  U.S. Services by Major Category — Exports.
    5.  U.S. Services by Major Category — Imports.
    6.  U.S. Trade in Goods.
    7.  Exports and Imports of Goods by Principal End-Use Category.
    8.  Exports of Goods by End-Use Category and Commodity.
    9.  Imports of Goods by End-Use Category and Commodity.
   10.  Exp/Imp/Bal of Goods, Petroleum, & Non-Petroleum End-Use Cat. Tot..
   11.  Exports/Imports of Goods by Principal End-Use Cat.(Const. $ Basis).
   12.  U.S. Trade in Goods.
   13.  Exports and Imports of Goods by Principal End-Use Category.
   14.  Exp./Imp./Bal. of Goods by Selected Countries & Geo. Areas '94.
   15.  Exp./Imp./Bal. of Goods by Selected Countries & Geo. Areas '93.
   16.  Exp/Imp of Goods by Principal SITC Commodity Groupings- '94 & '93.
   17.  Exports, Imports & Balance of Advanced Technology Products.
   18.  Imp. of Energy-Related Petroleum Products, Inc. Crude Petroleum.
```

Without ever leaving your computer, you can get up-to-the-minute foreign trade data directly from the U.S. Census Bureau.

Gopher and Internet Shopping Malls

Gopher can be also valuable for companies seeking to market their products and services online. Many Internet "shopping malls" being set up these days are actually Gopher sites. If you're an Internet shopper, you simply connect to your Internet access provider, type gopher at the prompt followed by the Internet address of the Gopher site, and you're connected to the remote system.

If you've got products to sell or information to distribute, you can set up your own Gopher site or rent space on someone else's.(For more information, see Chapter 11, " Internet Cybermalls.") *The News & Observer*, a daily newspaper in Raleigh, North Carolina, recently created a Gopher site so that its print subscribers (and anybody else on the Internet) can access an online edition of the newspaper. To check it out, type gopher gopher.nando.net at the system prompt. Here's a recent sampling:

```
                    Internet Gopher Information Client v1.12S

                    Root gopher server: gopher.nando.net

—>  1.  READ ME!.
    2.  About this Gopher service.
    3.  About The News & Observer Publishing Co./
    4.  Today's edition of The News & Observer (a sampler)/
    5.  The Insider: North Carolina Government/
```

```
 6.  Other sources of news, sports and weather/
 7.  Education resources/
 8.  Exploring the Internet/
 9.  Government information/
10.  Just for fun/
11.  Kidslink/
12.  Libraries/
13.  MetroMUD: You're not in Raleigh anymore ... <TEL>
14.  Misc. Triangle-area resources/
15.  News and Observer Searchable Classified Advertisements/
16.  Test Section/
17.  The Armchair Traveler/
18.  The Bookshelf/

Press ? for Help, q to Quit, u to go up a menu              Page: 1/2
```

Figure 1.5 shows how this same screen of information would appear if we were using TurboGopher, a Gopher interface that works on the Macintosh. Using this version, you use your mouse to click any items of interest, making the process easier and faster.

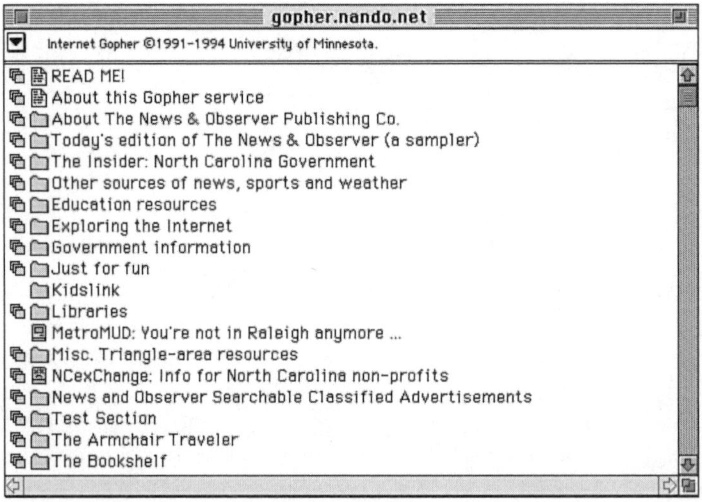

```
                          gopher.nando.net
  ▼   Internet Gopher ©1991–1994 University of Minnesota.
  🖹 READ ME!
  🖹 About this Gopher service
  📁 About The News & Observer Publishing Co.
  📁 Today's edition of The News & Observer (a sampler)
  📁 The Insider: North Carolina Government
  📁 Other sources of news, sports and weather
  📁 Education resources
  📁 Exploring the Internet
  📁 Government information
  📁 Just for fun
  📁 Kidslink
  📁 Libraries
  🖥 MetroMUD: You're not in Raleigh anymore ...
  📁 Misc. Triangle-area resources
  📁 NCexChange: Info for North Carolina non-profits
  📁 News and Observer Searchable Classified Advertisements
  📁 Test Section
  📁 The Armchair Traveler
  📁 The Bookshelf
```

Figure 1.5. TurboGopher.

Internet storefronts, or "cybermalls," are popping up, too, to accommodate those businesses that would rather "rent space" online than put up a mall of their own. Here is the main menu of the Gopher site operated by Cyberspace Development in Boulder, Colorado:

```
              Internet Gopher Information Client v1.12S

                 Root gopher server: marketplace.com

  —>  1.  About MarketPlace.com - The Internet Information Mall.
      2.  Online Bookstore/
      3.  The Maloff Company (Internet Reseller Market Report)/
      4.  Information Law Alert/
      5.  Interactive Publishing Alert/
      6.  *Alternative-X*/
      7.  INFOMARK - International Telecom Information/
      8.  Harmony Games/
      9.  How to open a storefront in Marketplace.com.
     10.  Commercial Internet Directory/
     11.  Cyberspace Development: Builders of Internet Storefronts.
     12.  Frequently Asked Questions about Internet Commerce.
```

Companies listed here include the Online Book Store, Maloff Company, Information Law Alert, Interactive Publishing Alert, Harmony Games, and several other online information vendors. By accessing this Gopher site, potential customers interested in buying any of these products can browse samples, view descriptive information, and if they like what they see, type their name, address, and credit card information and can place an order directly. There are some security risks and limitations, however, as we explore in both Chapter 3, "Risks and Realities," and Chapter 11, "Internet Cybermalls." Gopher is one of the best tools available for those searching for specific information on the network and that'll be demonstrated in Chapter 7, "Dialing for Data."

Searching Gopherspace with Veronica

Unlike FTP and telnet data, and even mailing lists, the documents and information available in Gopher is uniquely suited for a comprehensive database and search capability. This is available in Gopherspace through a tool called *Veronica*.

The basic concept is simple: Certain sites accessible through Gopher have a huge database containing an entry for each menu item on each of thousands of Gopher servers throughout the Internet. Type a keyword or two and you get a list of all the Gopher menu entries that match.

The problem is that the searching and matching capabilities can vary, and in an attempt to help manage the overwhelming traffic, certain keywords are presearched or otherwise recognized for special behavior. If the keyword by itself would generate too many matches, Veronica won't go any further with your query but instead will say, too many matches or something similar. This can be frustrating when you're searching for, say, Internet stock reports and use internet stock as keywords. Most of the Veronica servers will see `internet` and immediately return a `too many hits` error. With some judicious choice of keywords, however, this shouldn't be too much of a problem, even given our explanation here.

Veronica is a simple search tool. As a result, all lists of keywords are implicitly considered as *or* choices. Therefore, `internet stock` will return all entries that contain either `Internet` or `stock` in their descriptions, hence the error. There is currently no way to have searches that build on each other.

Here's an example of what you might see on your screen if you used Veronica to search the NYSERNet system, one of several Veronica servers available to the public. Your first stop would be a menu item, probably at the first set of choices, called `Search Gopherspace using Veronica`. Choose that and here's what you'll see:

```
          Search Gopherspace using Veronica

 ->   1.  Search gopherspace by veronica at NYSERNet <?>
      2.  Search gopherspace by veronica at SCS Nevada  <?>
      3.  Search Gopher+ ABSTRACTs (50 sites) via SCS Nevada  <?>
      4.  Search gopherspace by veronica at PSINet <?>
      5.  Search gopherspace by veronica at University of Pisa <?>
      6.  Search gopherspace by veronica at U. of Manitoba <?>
      7.  Search gopherspace by veronica at University of Koeln <?>
      8.  Search gopherspace by veronica at UNINETT/U. of Bergen <?>   .
      9.  Search gopherspace by veronica at U.Texas, Dallas <?>
     10.  Search Gopher Directory Titles using NYSERNet <?>
     11.  Search Gopher Directory Titles using SCS Nevada  <?>
     12.  Search Gopher Directory Titles using PSINet <?>
     13.  Search Gopher Directory Titles using University of Pisa <?>
     14.  Search Gopher Directory Titles using U. of Manitoba <?>
     15.  Search Gopher Directory Titles using University of Koeln <?>
     16.  Search Gopher Directory Titles using UNINETT/U. of Bergen <?>
     17.  Search Gopher Directory Titles using U.Texas, Dallas <?>
     18.                                 .

Press ? for Help, q to Quit, u to go up a menu            Page:1/2
```

We choose #1 and then are prompted for keywords. Entering `finance stocks` produces quite a few matches. The first 18 are summarized on the screen of our dialup account, as follows:

```
          Search gopherspace by veronica at NYSERNet: finance or stocks

 ->   1.  Top Technology Stocks by Volume and Change, 3-15.
      2.  Most active OTC stocks 7-20.
      3.  Finance Division (organizationalUnit)/
      4.  FIN  FINANCE/
      5.  Most active OTC stocks 3-17.
      6.  Finance Office (organizationalUnit)/
```

```
 7.  Search Finance <?>
 8.  Top Technology Stocks by Volume and Change, 7-2.
 9.  Stocks rise to record heights in London.
10.  1993 Volume 17 Issue 1 Journal of Banking and Finance.
11.  Top Technology Stocks by Change at Midday, 7-22.
12.  15 most active NYSE stocks 4-8.
13.  Read Bnking and Finance Assist. Center .. for EastWest Studies entry.
14.  15 most active NYSE stocks 7-15.
15.  Stocks edge up in Japan.
16.  Stocks recover a little.
17.  Search ACCOUNTING AND FINANCE <?>
18.  Most active AMEX stocks 8-7.

Press ? for Help, q to Quit, u to go up a menu          Page: 1/12
```

Veronica is a valuable tool, particularly if you take the time to try your queries with different keywords (think synonyms) and occasionally try the same query at multiple Veronica sites. Because the sites aren't all identical, the results can vary depending on where you query.

It's difficult to find files in FTP archives without using the Archie service, and it's similarly difficult, if not impossible, to find specific information in Gopher without using the Veronica search tool therein. Veronica is a bit quirky, particularly in its very limited understanding of Boolean searches (for example, a and b a or b). You'll see how we use it to best advantage in Chapter 7, "Dialing for Data."

Winging Your Way with World Wide Web

Gopher is a valuable service for people using the Internet as a place to find information and make information available to others. The biggest problem with Gopher, however, is that the entry for each item of information is confined to a single line of text. If a paragraph of explanation is required for users to fully understand a particular file or software package, Gopher's not much help.

That's where the *World Wide Web* comes in. The newest of the Internet information tools, the Web, as it's known, is the first truly universal multimedia environment for publishing information on the network. It's a harbinger of what the information superhighway will look like 10 years from now.

In a nutshell, the Web is built of thousands of *pages* of information distributed throughout the network, with each page containing audio and video clips, graphics, and/or text-based information. On the Web, words can be presented in bold, italics, and a variety of fonts, and any word or phrase can serve as a hypertext button moving the user from place to place with the click of a mouse.

Let's take a look at the World Wide Web in action. Figure 1.6 shows a Web home page, or "welcome screen," for *Internet Distribution Service*—a cybermall on the information highway. Notice the inclusion of attractive graphics and particularly notice the phrase `click here for more information`. Clicking any of the words in that phrase automatically displays another document.

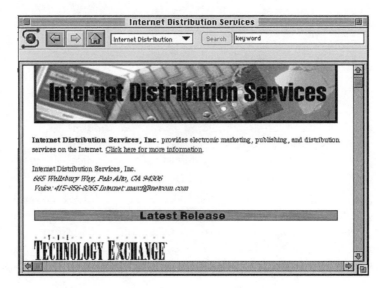

Figure 1.6. The Internet Distribution Service on the World Wide Web.

Once you're connected to a Web server, you can click on a "hyperlinked" word, phrase, picture, or multimedia icon to access related documents elsewhere on that computer or on other computer systems throughout the network. The Web enables information to be shared internationally and disseminated to a large number of people at different sites. Because World Wide Web is so easy to use, it's also fast becoming the method of choice for accessing a wide range of other Internet tools.

Originally designed for the high-energy physics community, the World Wide Web has spread to other fields and attracted a lot of interest among newspapers, magazines, advertisers, and electronic merchants as they seek ways to publish their information on the Internet in an eye-catching, accessible format. Internet-watchers predict that, by the end of the decade, even McDonald's customers may be clicking their Web servers to order a hamburger and fries (though we're not sure we agree.)

Although the World Wide Web is attractive and interesting, we need to mention that it's not accessible through electronic mail, and users with basic dialup accounts are limited to accessing it with a primitive text-based-based Web interface called *Lynx* that has no graphics, audio, or font capabilities. The attractive page of information shown in Figure 1.6 looks quite different when only the following words can be displayed:

```
Internet Distribution Services (p1 of 6)

   [IMAGE] [IMAGE]

   Internet Distribution Services, Inc. provides electronic marketing,
   publishing, and distribution services on the Internet. Click here for
   more information.

   Internet Distribution Services, Inc.
    665 Wellsbury Way, Palo Alto, CA 94306
    Voice: 415-856-8265 Internet: marcf@netcom.com


   [IMAGE] Latest Release


   Technology Board of Trade

   Technology Board of Trade serves as a trading floor for companies
   seeking and/or providing reusable software technology. It assists
   businesses in defining, valuing and exchanging intellectual property
 — press space for next page —
   Arrow keys: Up and Down to move. Right to follow a link; Left to go back.
 H)elp O)ptions P)rint G)o M)ain screen Q)uit /=search [delete]=history list
```

High-speed dialup connections with certain additional capabilities (SLIP or PPP connections) can work with Mosaic and other graphical interfaces to the Internet, albeit slowly. See Chapter 2, "Getting Connected: Your Ticket to Ride," to learn about the specifics of what you can do with different types of Internet connections.

The Multimedia Interface: Mosaic

After you see how plain the Web's text-based interface looks, you won't be surprised to learn that the graphical interface, known as *Mosaic,* is by far the preferred way to explore. Developed by the National Center for Supercomputer Applications at the University of Illinois, Champaign-Urbana, this free program is available for Macintosh, PCs running Microsoft Windows, and UNIX hosts running the X Window System. With Mosaic, you can point and click your way to the information you want on the World Wide Web. Another Mosaic page is shown in Figure 1.7.

Figure 1.7. Mosaic running on a Macintosh.

In this starting point for what's called *a virtual computer exposition,* for example, you might click a familiar smiling Macintosh icon and be connected to the Apple Computer central Web server in Cupertino, California. Clicking Olivetti might move you to a computer system in Italy, and the phrase, `click here to see the latest products from Toshiba`, could zap you across the Pacific to Japan. You can use Mosaic also to access other Internet tools such as Gopher, World Wide Web, FTP, Usenet newsgroups, Archie, WAIS, and Veronica.

Mosaic works on both PCs and UNIX machines. Figure 1.8 shows yet another interesting Web site, this time with the Windows version of Mosaic.

There's a downside to Mosaic, a problem that is more pervasive than the requirement for a fast connection to the Internet. The problem is that it's difficult, if not downright impossible, to *find* things in the Web. There are precious few widely available search tools or databases analogous to Archie, Veronica, or even the centralized list of mailing lists. Instead, users must find a collection of good starting places and then wander through the Web hoping to find the information they seek. Another problem is that relatively few Internet users currently have access to Mosaic—some experts put the figure as low as 2 percent. This has some profound ramifications for commercial use of the Web, issues that we explore in depth in Chapter 11, "Internet Cybermalls."

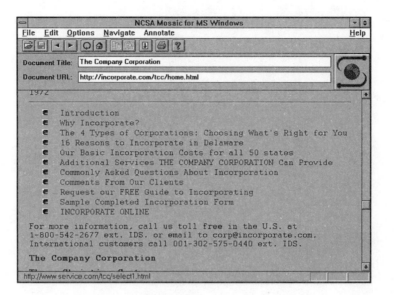

Figure 1.8. Mosaic on Microsoft Windows.

In summary, the World Wide Web and Mosaic are the Internet's colorful "storefronts," enticing gateways to a universe of hyper-linked information. Although relatively few Internet users can currently access the Web in all its multimedia splendor, that number is growing rapidly, and savvy businesses would be wise to follow their customers' lead. For more information about the Web and Mosaic and its role in online retailing and publishing, see Chapter 11, "Internet Cybermalls."

Conclusion

The Internet is clearly much, much more than just a conduit for information between computers, the function suggested—unfortunately—by the popular information highway metaphor. It's an exciting combination of people, places, and things, ranging far across culture, society, and commerce to encompass hobbies, professions, and interests. It's a personalized newspaper, a 24-hour cafe, and the biggest library in the world. It's also one heck of a great place to do business.

GETTING CONNECTED: YOUR TICKET TO RIDE

How much would you pay for the key to the world's largest library?

What would it be worth to you to be able send all the mail you wanted anywhere in the world without paying postage?

What price would you put on the opportunity to announce a new product or tell your company's story to an audience of several thousand of the top movers and shakers in your field?

$1,000? $10,000? $1,000,000?

Try $20 a month.

That's the going rate for basic individual Internet access these days; despite the fact that some Internet sharpies are trying to sell costly, all-encompassing systems to unsuspecting business owners who wouldn't know the Internet if they tripped over it.

For about $20 a month, most Internet access providers will let you send and receive as much e-mail as you want, download as much free software and information as you like, and stay online as long as you want. You'll never pay a penny more so long as it's a local phone call away.

Sound like a great deal? You bet it is! In fact, it's such a great deal that hundreds of thousands of people a month are signing up for Internet access—causing lots of anxiety at CompuServe, Prodigy, and the other commercial online services, services that make their money by billing customers for connect time. (Not to be left out, the commercial services are scurrying to offer Internet access, too, but we'll talk more about that later.)

Note: Although $20-a-month Internet access may give technologically savvy individuals and small businesses everything they need, it's a less-than-ideal solution for larger companies and less-computer-adept users. These simple dialup accounts are the "worst" for businesses wanting to ship large amounts of data over the Internet, perform multiple tasks in parallel (that is, have more than one program running at the same time), or allow more than one employee at a time to log onto the network, and access the Internet's many features through the standard DOS, Windows, or Mac interface. If that sounds like your business, then you'll probably find that it's worth investing in a more powerful—and expensive—Internet connection.

In this chapter, we take a look at the three basic types of Internet connections and identify which offers the most for your business. The three basic options are

> Dialup accounts
> Dialup network extensions—particularly Serial Line Interface Protocol (SLIP) and Point to Point Protocol (PPP)
> High-speed leased lines connecting your network to the Internet directly

In this chapter, we explore what each type of connection has to offer and how much you're likely to pay for the service, and we offer a list of vendors that can help you connect to the Internet. An extensive listing of commercial Internet access providers offering a variety of connectivity options is provided in Appendix A, "Internet On-Ramps."

Internet Economics 101: How the Internet Works

Because the Internet is a network of networks, it's not surprising that many organizations are already hooking into the information highway, sometimes without even realizing it.

For these people—oscilloscope designers at Hewlett-Packard, assembly line workers at Xerox, undergraduate students at Harvard, Ph.D. candidates at Stanford and MIT, and many branches of the government—the connection to the Internet is free; they don't have to pay a monthly fee or any connect charges to access the wealth of resources and information on the network.

"Free" is really a misnomer, however; the Internet certainly doesn't operate at no cost. Just like the interstate highway system and any other aspect of the national infrastructure, somebody—in this case, the government, universities, telecommunications companies, and other businesses—had to ante up the money to build the Internet's network of roadways and somebody—namely, the users—has to pay for its upkeep.

Who pays for the Internet? The answer is threefold:

The government. The federal government started it all when the Defense Department Advanced Research Projects Agency created the original ARPAnet. The National Science Foundation backbone (NSFnet) followed in the early 1970s, linking the ARPAnet with academic researchers. Today the NSF continues to subsidize the Internet to the tune of $11,500,000 a year. In the cards, however, is a gradual phase-out of this support from the government, leaving private sector communications companies to take over maintenance of the information superhighway.

Commercial providers. The second important source of funding for Internet maintenance and development are the various commercial Internet access providers. Because the government originally banned commercial traffic on NSFnet, a group of companies seeking to use the growing network for commercial purposes formed a loose co-operative venture called the *Commercial Internet Exchange* (CIX). The goal of the CIX is to build and maintain its own parallel backbone network wherein commercial traffic could appear without violation of the NSF network usage policies. Today, in return for paying CIX a flat fee of $10,000 a year, Internet connectivity "resellers" can buy unlimited Internet access, which they can then resell by the hour or on a flat-fee basis to individuals and businesses.

Individuals. In the early days, the list would have stopped here, but today the Internet encompasses more than 25,000 different networks, connecting over 20,000,000 users, and individual-user connectivity fees are becoming an important source of Internet revenue. Most individuals, businesses, and other users pay monthly fees or per-hour charges for Internet service. Prices vary depending on the speed and capacity of the Internet link: People who access the Internet through a simple dialup connection pay as little as $20 a month—or less. Internet service providers and larger corporations might pay $1,000 a month or more for a complete network-to-network bridge, a personal on-ramp as it were.

Most of the well-known commercial networks—CompuServe, GEnie, AppleLink—charge users a base monthly fee plus connect time charges and, often, additional charges for those users that access specialized databases, discussion forums, and other features.

If you're used to that environment, you'll be delighted to know that the standard policy for Internet service providers is a monthly access fee with no hidden or supplemental charges. No additional payment is required if you happen to receive more than, say, 20 e-mail messages in a month. Instead, Internet pricing is based on the speed, power, and capability of your connection. Generally speaking, the higher the speed of the connection, the more you have to pay.

Note: As you must with most things in this world, expect to pay a premium for convenience on the Internet. In non-virtual space, Rosalind lives in South Florida, for example, and when she wants to drive from Miami to West Palm Beach, she can take the optimal route, saving time by traveling on the Florida Turnpike. On the other hand, on those days when saving a few dollars is more important than speed, there's an alternative route that goes up S. 1, adding about thirty minutes to the trip but circumventing the toll booths. In this case, the tradeoff is clear: fast and expensive or slower but no additional fee. In cyberspace, Internet connectivity works the same way.

Analyzing Your Internet Needs

Sexy car advertisements aside, it's always a good strategy to analyze your needs before you decide exactly what you need. If you're buying a new automobile, basic questions include budget, fuel efficiency, size, utility, reliability, and so on.

For an Internet connection, the best strategy is to spend some time identifying your information needs and budget before you choose a connection.

You need to consider whether

> You want to hook up one person, a small group, or a larger department or company
> You want your business to provide information to others on the Internet
> Simple connectivity, allowing you to be a user, is acceptable
> You want to use programs like Mosaic and Gopher, with their full power and capabilities
> E-mail and Usenet groups are sufficient

Here's a checklist to get you started in assessing your Internet connectivity requirements. Your answers to these questions will determine the type of Internet connection your company needs.

> How big is your company? How big might it become in the foreseeable future?
> Is your business located all in one office, with your computers connected on a single local area network, or do you have multiple sites scattered throughout the state, country, or even the world?
> How many people at your company are going to need Internet access? everybody? the corporate library staff? the owner?
> What Internet features are you planning to use most often? electronic mail? discussion groups? information-gathering? marketing? remote-site collaboration? file-transfer? real-time conferencing?
> Will your employees need to perform multiple tasks on the Internet simultaneously? Will more than one employee need to log on at the same time?
> How much money can you afford to spend on Internet access every month? How much are you spending on phone, fax, overnight delivery, and other communications tools now?

Keep in mind that whether you're a small business operating out of the spare room of your house or a multinational corporation sprawled across the globe, you will realize some savings in your business overhead once you're connected to the Internet.

> **Note:** Three years ago, Dave had a Federal Express account for mailing data-filled floppy disks to clients around the United States. Today, Dave's account is closed, and he uses the Internet instead, saving hundreds of dollars each year and making the process of delivering completed projects much easier.

Regardless of your business, the more you learn about the capabilities of the Internet, the more you can restructure your company's communications system to take advantage of the international infrastructure that's already up and running.

Choosing an Internet Access Provider

As in buying a car or working with a real estate broker, choosing an Internet access provider requires you to consider a number of factors. The key factor, of course, is whether the provider offers the type of connection that you seek, but that's not the only element to consider.

Before we discuss the different types of Internet access, let's talk a little about the things that you should look for when selecting an Internet access provider.

The six key factors we recommend you consider are

- Network reliability
- Network performance
- Network security
- Network restrictions
- Local phone access
- User services and support

Each of these is covered in the following sections.

Network Reliability

If you run a business, you know what it's like when your computer system crashes or a lightning storm causes your power or phone line to go down: The business grinds to a halt. The same thing can happen to your Internet connection if the network that's providing your access goes on the blink. If you rely on Internet e-mail for your communications needs, a network failure can leave you out of touch with your employees, your colleagues, and most importantly, your clients and customers.

There are a variety of reasons that portions of the Internet can break down or otherwise go off-line. In the last few years, portions of the network have failed due to power outages, downed telephone connections, and poor weather conditions.

Note: The University of California at Berkeley had a problem for years with its on-campus network. Some of the network cabling wasn't buried deeply enough, and bad weather caused intermittent failures; UCB old-timers used to joke that they could forecast the weather based on the state of the network connection. Network-related causes such as system emergencies that need immediate fixing, scheduled maintenance, and glitches involving the network's hardware and software can also take the system off-line for minutes, hours, or even longer.

Tip: Reliability is an important question to consider when you're evaluating Internet access providers because different companies have different online records. Talk with the provider and several of his customers to find out how reliable the system is. Persistent problems indicate that the system is growing so fast that there aren't enough phone lines to handle all the calls or that the system is too small.

Network Performance

Network performance is the speed at which your Internet access provider can carry the e-mail and other data you want to send. There are two aspects involved—the speed with which you can connect to the provider and the speed of the connection the provider has to the Internet. For obvious reasons, it's important that your service provider has a very high speed connection to the Internet, lest your data sit idly on the system waiting to be dispatched to your customers or colleagues.

The speed of a network connection is measured in *bits per second* (bps). Because a single character of data is composed of eight bits of information, a slow 2,400 bps connection, for example, would transmit 2,400 / 8 or 300 characters per second (in reality, it's often less than that due to system overhead). This chapter is about 36,000 characters, for example, so with a 2,400 bps connection, it would take about 140 seconds, or just over two minutes, to transmit it to your machine. Contrast this with a 19,200 bps connection, which would require a transmission time of only 14 seconds. Internet service providers should have considerably faster connections to the Internet; a 56,000 bps connection between your service provider and its Internet connection is the minimum you should accept (at that speed this chapter could be transmitted in under 5 seconds).

Network Security

We'll be honest here; there are some security risks associated with connecting to a global network. The more sophisticated your connection, the higher the risk. Nonetheless, despite what you may have read about crackers and pirates swooping down on unsuspecting Internet users and pilfering passwords or reading private e-mail, chances are quite slim that it'll happen to your company.

If you plan on becoming an Internet user, you'll want to learn more about minimizing these risks. At the same time, there's no need for undue panic. Remember that your cellular phone carries major security risks—just ask anyone with a handheld scanner—and even voice mail has been the target of break-ins.

If you're planning to sell your product or service on the Internet, however, there are other problems to consider. If you're planning to sell your goods or services online, you need to consider strategies for transmitting credit card information in a secure manner. As a result, it's vital to find an Internet access provider who will work with you to set up "firewalls," passwords, and other network security measures. Security is also a reason that a provider that's been on the Internet a while may prove a safer choice than a brand-new access provider.

> **Note:** For more information about Internet security, both for users and businesses, read Chapter 3, "Risks and Realities."

Network Restrictions

Earlier, we talked about acceptable use provisions of various networks, particularly how they apply to the government-funded NSFnet Internet backbone. The Acceptable Use Policy (known informally as AUP) is a critical issue for any Internet access provider; before you begin to work with a provider, ensure that the company has access to a network that permits commercial traffic.

Major access providers have their own AUP policies, too, and we strongly recommend that you carefully read these policies before signing up for a particular service, regardless of how you anticipate using the Internet.

Local Phone Access

One advantage of using the Internet for information gathering and dissemination is its low cost and flat monthly fee.

Your cost savings can vanish instantly, however, if you choose an access provider that's a long-distance phone call away. Although the various telecommunications companies might appreciate your use, it's a sure bet that your first phone bill will be enough to make you rethink your Internet connection strategy!

This isn't a problem if you sign up with an Internet access provider in your city, but it's something to think about when considering whether to hook up with a national or international Internet network.

For example, Computer Witchcraft, one of the Internet providers that Rosalind uses, charges $8 an hour to log on if you dial direct to the company's computer in Louisville, Kentucky, but $15.20 an hour or more if you dial in through the company's toll-free number. With Delphi you pay an extra $9 an hour to log in through the local SprintNet gateway if you log on during business hours.

The good news is that many of the biggest Internet providers are beginning to offer local dialup access in a variety of locations throughout the United States. For example, Netcom Communications Service, with computers in the San Francisco area, has local dialup numbers in Los Angeles, San Diego, Seattle, Portland, New York City, Las Vegas, Chicago, and Austin, Texas. This can be a double boon if you travel and want to remain connected without paying for long-distance phone calls.

User Services and Support

Although Internet access is fast becoming a commodity, Internet providers vary widely in terms of the services they offer. For example, some networks offer the full range of Internet tools and features, including Archie, FTP, Gopher, telnet, Usenet, and the World Wide Web; others offer only Internet e-mail and a small selection of newsgroups. Some access providers offer subscriber newsletters and information update news as well as Internet training courses and technical support by telephone and online.

Before you choose a network access provider, it's important to check references. You wouldn't purchase a car based only on the information you learn from the salesperson, so don't sign up for an access provider without doing your homework.

One good way to learn about the service is to request the names of a few customers from the Internet access provider and ask them how well the access provider has met their needs. It can also be useful to check out the network's reputation by posting messages on online bulletin boards or by attending meetings of local Internet user groups. Finally, ask the Internet access provider for a service guarantee and find out—in advance of any possible problems—what kind of procedures the firm has for resolving problems quickly.

In summary, make sure you ask all the Internet access providers you interview how they're connected to the Internet, how easy it is to connect with them (both in terms of local or long-distance access numbers and number of modems versus number of dialup users), and how reliable their systems are. Then check the answers by asking their customers for the same information.

Doing your homework up front can save you considerable frustration—and money—down the road.

The Three Types of Internet Connections

Now, it's time to get down to the nitty-gritty—choosing the type of Internet connection that's right for you and your business. There are three basic kinds of Internet connections:

- An online, or dialup, account with an Internet access provider

- A SLIP or PPP connection, enabling your company's computer or local area network to connect to the Internet directly for full Internet connectivity, albeit relatively slowly.

- Leased-line service, offering Internet network access at speeds as fast as 1.544 megabits per second. At this speed, by the way, it would take just over 1/10th of a second to transmit this chapter from one computer to another over the Internet.

Online Accounts

Online accounts, sometimes known as "shell" accounts, are far and away the best value for individuals and small business owners who don't plan to log onto the Internet for more than a few hours each day.

With an online account, you use your computer and modem to dial your Internet access provider's computer system, which is linked directly to the Internet. Your computer never actually connects to the Internet directly.

These days, there are many providers offering accounts for business users. CTS Network Services (San Diego, California) and The Meta Network (Arlington, Virginia) charge $20 a month for a basic commercial dialup account. InterAccess (Chicago, Illinois) charges $23 each month and Internet Direct (Phoenix, Arizona) charges $29 a month for a similar service. Check out Appendix A, "Internet On-Ramps," for the Internet access provider nearest you.

The main advantages of this type of dialup connection are low cost, unlimited access to e-mail and other Internet services, and protection from network-wide system crashes and security problems.

Many access providers also let you make your products available throughout the Internet using this type of account. The downside is that it's slower than a more powerful Internet connection and lacks the capability of running multiple Internet sessions simultaneously. If you need a dozen Internet accounts for your employees, however, an online account for each user may actually end up costing you more than a SLIP or PPP connection, you'll see later.

Online accounts are available from three different sources—an Internet access provider, a commercial online service, and a university, government, or nonprofit organization. Here are the pros and cons of each:

Internet Access Providers

Pros: You get full Internet access, not just the e-mail that the commercial online services provide. You usually pay a flat monthly fee as opposed to per-minute charges based on usage. You can often dial in at higher speeds—14,400 bps, for example—than you can on America Online and Prodigy. You're likely to find an AUP that's consistent with your requirements.

Cons: Most Internet access providers don't offer easy-to-use Windows, DOS, or Macintosh front-ends for online accounts or navigational programs in which you can point and click on icons and pull down menus to explore the various services available. This means you'll probably have to struggle with an ungainly text-based system by typing UNIX commands at a system prompt. It also means that you might have to compose and reply to your mail online, a nuisance when you're accustomed to commercial services like CompuServe and their handy off-line text editors and filing cabinets. Because many local Internet access providers are small companies with few modems and phone connections, you may get frequent busy signals if you try to dial in during peak hours.

Commercial Online Services

Pros: You don't have to pay an additional monthly fee to set up a dedicated Internet account somewhere else. You also get a nice-looking, easy-to-use DOS, Mac, or Windows interface.

Cons: Although you have access to the Internet, it's likely to be fairly limited. Most commercial services only offer e-mail, though some, notably America Online, have begun offering access to Internet newsgroups and mailing lists and some Gopher and WAIS servers. Delphi is the only one of the five largest commercial online services that offers full Internet access; subscribers pay an extra $3 a month on top of their regular Delphi account fees. Be careful if you choose the commercial route, however. If you're not, you may find that the surcharges you pay are higher than the price of a dialup account. For example, CompuServe charges 15 cents for every Internet message you receive, whether you want that piece of mail delivered or not. Join a few mailing lists and start getting e-mail from customers. Soon you'll find yourself paying $50 a month or more just for e-mail.

University, Government, Non-Profit Groups, or Freenets

Pros: It's free.

Cons: It's hard to get an account on a government or university system unless you work or study there or know someone who does. There are also limits on the amount of time you're allowed to spend on the system at any one "sitting," and you may have a hard time getting past the busy signals during peak usage times. Most importantly, the acceptable use policies of these organizations usually prohibit any business or commercial use.

Profile: Pam Kane and her husband run Panda Systems, a home-based business in Wilmington, Delaware, that produces and sells anti-virus software. They pay $25 a month for an account through SSNET, their local Internet access provider. Their monthly fee includes complete Internet access with no limits on online time, volume of mail, or data storage. They use this account to send e-mail to friends and colleagues on the Internet, CompuServe, America Online, and Prodigy.

Kane notes that her Internet access came in handy recently for a book she's writing with a number of co-authors in different cities, each of whom has an account on a different network. "Every single contribution to the book has come to me over Internet," she says. "I save

> the file to disk, run a little program that removes formatting codes, and import it into my word processing program." Like many freelance writers, Kane notes that when she writes magazine articles, she not only submits the articles to the publisher through the Internet, but even sends electronic invoices to ensure prompt payment.

To have your own dialup account, you'll require an account on an Internet access provider, a high-speed modem, and some terminal emulation software (typically around $100, though less expensive and even free packages are available. We recommend VersaTerm for Macintosh and Procomm Plus for PC and Windows). In the latter category are a bewildering variety of options from dozens of firms. Your best bet is to ask your future service provider for a recommendation, and, indeed, many of the biggest Internet service providers can sell modems at a special discount rate. Dave has VersaTerm Pro on his Macintosh and connects with a Telebit Worldblazer at home and Telebit QBlazer on the road. Rosalind uses WinNET Mail front-end software, Crosstalk for Windows, and the 14.4 Kbps Telepath modem that came bundled with her Gateway 2000 486 computer.

SLIP/PPP Connections

However powerful the computer on your desk may be, it's really no more than a "dumb terminal" when all the files, processing, and applications are running on a remote computer connected to the Internet.

If you have a high-speed dialup connection to the Internet, however, you can use the power and capabilities of your desktop machine to run Internet programs. Instead of sending individual characters through the modem, dialup IP actually extends the Transmission Control Protocol/Internet Protocol (TCP/IP, the nervous system and underlying foundation of the Internet itself) to work with dialup connections.

What does this mean? It means that instead of being constrained to just having the actual characters to display sent to your computer, you can have graphics, audio, and various other information transmitted automatically. Further, TCP/IP allows you to have multiple services open at once, so you might be composing an email message while checking out the latest news on Usenet, and in a third window waiting for an Archie document search to complete.

There are two types of dialup Internet Protocol (IP) connections: SLIP and PPP. Both provide a full Internet connection capable of sending and receiving data from the tens of thousands of other computers on the network. Using this more powerful form of dialup connection, your computer can "talk" directly with other computers on the network in the Internet's universal "language"—the TCP/IP protocol. What's more, other computers connected to the Internet can dial your computer directly.

SLIP and PPP connections offer many advantages. One is that you can perform many network-related tasks at once. For example, you can download a program file from one computer on the network while accessing data from a Gopher site housed on another. You can also set up your system so that e-mail is delivered directly to your company's computer, enhancing security. You can also choose your own domain name—for example, Dave chose `intuitive.com` for his firm—which may be useful for marketing.

Another advantage is the ability to use sophisticated graphics software interfaces, such as Mosaic, to access a wide spectrum of information with a click of your mouse. These days, a number of commercial software programs can serve as front ends for Macs and PCs. With Netmanage's Chameleon, for example, you can access the Internet through an easy-to-use Windows interface.

Unlike the flat monthly rates of dialup accounts, dialup IP connections are based on connect time and can cost upward of $125 to $250 a month depending on how often you want to connect. The entry level prices are exemplified by ClarkNet (Washington, D.C.), with a 4-hour-per-day SLIP or PPP account for $33 a month, and Evergreen Communications (Phoenix, Arizona), charging $40 per month for 10 hours a week commercial SLIP or PPP access.

Upgrading to a 24-hour connection adds a bit to the bill: ClarkNet allows business customers 24-hour connections for a monthly fee of $120 and Netcom Communications Service (San Jose, California) offers 24-hour SLIP connectivity for $160 a month.

SLIP and PPP software for DOS, Windows, Macintosh, and UNIX computers—known as *client* software—can range in cost from nothing to upwards of $700, depending on the features, ease of use, and complexity of the program. TCP/IP software is included in almost every version of UNIX, though not all UNIX packages include the specific SLIP or PPP client software. In all cases, your best bet is to work with your Internet access provider to obtain the latest version of the connectivity software you need for your particular platform.

There are several disadvantages to a dialup IP connection, however. The main problem is that, during the time that you're connected to the Internet, your computer system and the data that's on it are exposed to crackers, viruses, and network-wide crashes. That's why we recommend your setting up a firewall to protect your system from the Internet and follow the other guidelines we explain in Chapter 3, "Risks and Realities."

Both SLIP and PPP connections can also be difficult to set up and install; sometimes it may be necessary to get an experienced computer user or technician to help. Although you can use a SLIP/PPP connection to access the Internet at speeds as high as 28,800 bits per second, you'll need a high-speed modem to achieve those speeds, which may mean spending money to outfit your computers with new modems that start at $100 each.

Profile: One company that uses a SLIP connection is Cyberspace Development, based in Boulder, Colorado. Headed by Andrew Currie (currie@marketplace.com), the company sets up and operates Internet "shopping malls," providing consulting and software development services to businesses that are interested in selling products or services via the Internet. By working with Internet tools such as Gopher, WAIS, the World Wide Web, and e-mail, Cyberspace Development helps customers set up online ordering and delivery of electronic publications and other products. Other services include support for online product catalogs and custom online services such automated help desks for companies such as Apple Computer, U.S. West, InfoNow, and Raynet.

Currie says he uses a SLIP connection to access Internet tools and features such as telnet, Mosaic, and e-mail but employs a more powerful T1 line (described in the following text) to run the computer that hosts his electronic shopping mall. To check it out, type gopher marketplace.com at the system prompt.

"When businesses create storefronts on the major online services like CompuServe and America Online, they are only accessible by customers on those services," Currie says. "When businesses create storefronts on the Internet, they are accessible by customers on the Internet and customers of the major online services that offer Internet access. Businesses can gain a strategic advantage by establishing a commercial presence on the Internet before major cable companies offer high-bandwidth Internet connections to business and residential customers. You can create a market niche via the Internet before your competitors realize there is a market."

Leased-Line Connections

Although connections through a regular phone line are inexpensive, they aren't particularly fast. Dialup connections, either a simple online account or a high-powered SLIP or PPP connection, are adequate for many purposes but insufficient for companies planning to offer lots of electronic information on the network or connecting a large number of employees to the Internet.

Fortunately, there's an alternative—leased lines. Leased lines are the connection of choice for Internet power users—large companies with lots of users spread out over multiple sites or sites with a lot of data to transmit.

With a leased line, companies can hook up their local area network to the Internet, enabling any or all of their employees to access the Internet whenever and for whatever task they need. As with a dialup IP connection, a leased line exposes your computer system to all the Internet's risks and problems, which means that you'll need to take security precautions.

The main advantage of a leased line is speed, enabling you to move large amounts of data in a short period of time.

In a typical phone-company way, the names of the different-speed leased lines are a bit cryptic. A T1 line can transmit data at speeds as high as 10 megabits per second. A T3 line can go even faster, zapping data from one end of the wire to the other at speeds as high as 357.5 megabits per second.

To put this in perspective, this 36,000 character chapter which takes over two minutes to transmit on a 2,400 bps dialup connection would move so fast over a T1 or T3 line that its journey would be over before you could start your stopwatch.

There's a price for this performance, however, and much of the cost comes from the local telephone company. For example, Netcom charges $1,000 a month for a T1 connection, and the phone company charges an additional $400 each month to provide the wire itself. Performance Systems International (Herndon, Virginia) offers similar connectivity for $2,850 a month plus local phone charges.

A less expensive alternative is a 56 Kbyte line, which offers four times the speed of a dedicated dialup link. Netcom charges $400 a month; the local phone company tacks on another $100 a month. The same connection costs $795 a month plus telephone company charges from UUNet Technologies (Falls Church, Virginia) and $850 a month plus telecom charges from PSI.

To set up a leased-line connection, you need a computer running TCP/IP software on a local area network. The networked computer—the "server" in this case—is hooked up to a router that also connects to the telephone link, a phone line with a digital conversion device on each end. The telephone link is hooked into a router or gateway at the network provider's end of the circuit. Installing a leased line is a complex, time-consuming job, and we strongly recommend you work with a skilled network administrator. Many Internet service providers can offer recommendations of groups and individuals in your local area that can help.

Profile: Many companies currently using leased lines are Internet resellers, companies that buy Internet access wholesale and retail it to small- to medium-size businesses and individuals. MCSNet (info@mcs.com) of Chicago, for example, pays $1,000 a month to lease a T1 circuit from Ameritech, the regional Bell company that provides local phone service in that area. The T1 connects MCSNet's Chicago offices to the Chicago offices of Sprint, a nationwide long-distance carrier. MCSNet also pays $2,200 a month to Sprint to buy a high-speed circuit, or routing service, that connects it to network providers throughout the country, according to company president Karl Denninger.

With a fixed overhead of $3,200 a month, MCSNet resells its Internet access to Chicago-area businesses and individuals for fees ranging from $1 an hour to a $30-a-month flat rate. The company provides both dialup and SLIP/PPP access. Denninger says the company currently has over 1,000 customers and that its user base is growing at a rate of 25 percent a month; he expects to have 2,000 customers on the system by summer.

The Future of Internet Pricing and Connections

With its flat-fee pricing, connectivity options, and unlimited access to e-mail, files, databases, and computers throughout the world, the Internet is clearly the biggest communications bargain on the market today.

But that may not always be true. As more and more individuals and businesses log onto the Internet, bogging down the information highway with an ever increasing quantity of data traffic, observers are beginning to question whether the "free lunch" that exists today can continue—or if, ultimately, users will have to buy their Internet access by the minute or by the byte just as subscribers to commercial online services do today.

We believe that connect-time-based access providers will become more prevalent than they are today but that there will still be flat-rate Internet access providers willing to offer competitive rates for those companies ready to hook their businesses onto the information highway.

RISKS AND REALITIES

Would you send cash through the mail to pay a bill?

Would you give your credit card number to a telemarketer who called you with a tip on a hot stock?

Would you leave the door to your company's R & D lab unlocked over the weekend?

Would you expose your valuable business and financial data to the Internet—and would you invite your customers to do the same?

If you're a prudent business person, you'd probably answer "No" to the first three questions; after all, you'd be foolish to take that kind of risk. But companies that conduct business on the Internet are saying "Yes" every day to the fourth question, often unaware of the enormous risk they're taking.

Any business that links its computer system to the Internet exposes itself to crackers and electronic joy-riders willing and able to vandalize data, pilfer passwords, and steal systems for fun and for profit any time of day or night. Worse, the faster your connection, the more likely you are to encounter trouble.

What makes the Internet so vulnerable to electronic mischief? Unlike centralized networks operated by commercial online services, such as CompuServe and Prodigy, the Internet is a decentralized system spread out across hundreds of thousands of computers worldwide. Each of these machines has its own passwords and security procedures—or lack thereof.

In some cases, therefore, the Internet is only as strong as its weakest link; intruders who break into one part of the system can rapidly gain access to much of the rest of it.

There are some steps in the right direction: Internet security issues are now being addressed by the government-funded Computer Emergency Response Team (CERT), an Internet security investigation squad, and the Internet Engineering Task Force, a volunteer group that is working on developing standards for message encryption and authentication. Don't be fooled, however; the Internet remains far from secure.

Given the problems, is the Internet a safe place to do business? Yes and no—though the security risks haven't stopped an estimated 11,000 companies nationwide from hooking up their internal networks to the Internet.

Do the potential rewards of doing business on the information highway outweigh the risks? They do indeed, particularly if you take proper and appropriate precautions.

Our goal in this chapter is to point out the risks and realities of doing business on the Internet. You'll get hard facts about "crackers," viruses, and other Internet security risks and find out about how unauthorized users can gain access to your company's financial information and your customers' credit card numbers.

Once you understand the risk you're taking, we show you how to ward off network intruders and point you in the direction of other security resources to help you build the Internet security plan that's best for your business.

The Internet and Security: A Troubled Past

Despite its origins at the Defense Department, the Internet was never designed to be a completely secure system, certainly not as secure as most of the popular commercial online services. Because it was created to help academic researchers and government officials interact with one another, the Internet was designed for maximum openness and interoperability—the ability of people with computers on different networks to communicate easily and seamlessly.

One of the reasons we believe that the Internet has become the harbinger of the global information highway is because of its emphasis on openness and accessibility. The Internet would have never been as successful if it had been Balkanized, or broken up into smaller subgroups. Keep in mind also that when the Internet was launched in 1969, network security wasn't a big issue, and there were far fewer people "on the Net" than there are today. Back then, the Internet resembled a small town where people didn't have to lock their doors when they went out for the evening. In fact, some computers on the network purposely left their "doors" open to allow anonymous visitors to pick up or leave files. This still happens to some extent (that's what anonymous FTP is all about), but now it's difficult to know who else is on the network interacting with your company's computer system.

With 20,000,000 users throughout the world, the Internet definitely is not a small town anymore and the small-town ethos that network users once enjoyed has given way to big-city problems, problems in need of big-city solutions.

As a result, Internet security breaches have become more and more common in recent years. In November, 1988, Cornell University graduate student Robert T. Morris, Jr. created the first major Internet security crisis by launching a computer "worm" that ended up crashing over 6,000 machines on the network and shutting down the network for days as the interloper was eradicated. Morris, who became the first person ever charged with violating the Federal Computer Fraud and Abuse Act, stated at the time that he didn't realize his rogue program would be destructive. (He was fined $10,000 and ordered to perform 400 hours of community service.)

More recent security breaches have had a more sinister overtone. In November, 1991, the United States General Accounting Office revealed that, between April, 1990, and May, 1991, computer crackers in the Netherlands broke into some military computers on the Internet and accessed sensitive U.S. military data during the Gulf War. Some of that data involved information about Gulf War personnel, the type and number of military equipment being moved, troop deployment data, and the development of new weapons systems.

Although there's little evidence that the crackers destroyed any data, there is evidence suggesting that they modified and copied some of it.

Jack L. Brock Jr., director of government information and financial management in GAO's Information Management and Technology Division, also told the Senate Governmental Affairs Subcommittee on Government Information and Regulation that the crackers were able to break into the Internet-connected systems because of three problems:

- Vendor-supplied accounts with well-known default passwords
- Easily guessed individual account passwords
- Vulnerable operating systems

(Later on in the chapter, we'll show you how to solve these problems.)

Commercial Internet networks have been vandalized, too. In October, 1993, Public Access Network Corp.—panix.com—was infiltrated by an unauthorized system cracker who then obtained access to the internals of the system, forcing it to shut down for three days. As an Internet access provider, Panix sells access to the Internet. The intruder stole account names and secret password combinations of Panix users who were connecting through telnet and other services to other machines on the Internet.

Officials said afterwards that the magnitude and consequences of the breach are still unknown, because the cracker's programs were hidden within the Panix operating system and had collected the secret information for many weeks—perhaps longer.

In February, 1994, CERT spotted what may be the largest computer security breach on the Internet so far and urged tens of thousands of Internet users to change their passwords. CERT, set up in the aftermath of the Morris virus in 1988, said it wasn't clear whether the crackers who broke into the network had vandalized computer systems or unleashed damaging viruses.

Meanwhile, security experts have speculated that the recent break-ins might have been connected to a group of students known as The Posse, a group that had been taunting Internet systems operators and taking down systems just for the thrill of it.

Whoever the crackers really were, they apparently broke into the network on the first of January and installed a sniffer program, a program that watches the network wires and logs passwords on computers at the University of California at Berkeley. The program collected more than 3,000 account and password combinations between 7 a.m. and 9 p.m. Once noticed, the security violation forced system administrators to immediately send notices to all logged users, telling them to change their passwords immediately.

Internet Risks and Realities

As the preceding examples show, the Internet continues to be a perilous place to do business—and is likely to become more dangerous as the Internet grows and the volume of commercial traffic rises.

Dain Gary, manager of CERT, says that his group logs three to four security breaches on the Internet each day. This year, he's expecting a 50 percent increase over the previous year's 773 reported intrusions. The real numbers are probably even higher: Fearing embarrassment and loss of public confidence, businesses rarely report break-ins. Experts estimate that only 15 percent of breaches are reported to law-enforcement authorities.

Crunch the numbers, and you can expect between 40 and 50 Internet security breaches a day by the time you read this chapter.

Internet vandals are also becoming more sophisticated, experts say. The typical Internet intruder is less and less likely to be a teenager out for an electronic joyride; many are now industrial spies motivated by financial gain.

Using special software, these crackers probe for weaknesses in a network's operating system, the underlying program that manages all other software programs. Once a loophole is detected, criminals spread the news through underground publications, at cracker conventions and on computer bulletin boards.

Cracker-designed programs that exploit these defects and search for crucial information are distributed in much the same way. In the Panix break-in November, 1993, for example, system administrators eventually found the "sniffer" program that the cracker had installed to watch and take notes as Panix users logged onto other computer networks. By monitoring those activities, the cracker stole the passwords to those other networks as well.

Businesses that connect their computer systems to the Internet put themselves at risk in these three ways:

- The e-mail they send and receive through the Internet may be intercepted and read.

- The business and financial records that they store on their computer system may be viewed, tampered with, or destroyed.

- If they sell products or services through the Internet, their customers' credit card numbers may be stolen and used illegally to ring up unauthorized charges.

(Later on in the chapter, we'll show you how to minimize these risks.)

Real-Life Experience

Both authors deal with security issues on a daily basis: Rosalind sometimes receives orders for her electronic newsletter via e-mail, including credit card and other information, and Dave offers information on a wide variety of commercial Internet ventures to Internet users through FTP, e-mail, and other sources. Both aspects of the Internet represent security threats, with the potential for disastrous consequences.

Profile: Cyberspace Development, which operates one of the Internet storefronts that carries Rosalind's electronic newsletter, has had to address the issue of how to handle credit card orders sent via electronic mail. When a potential subscriber asked Rosalind if it was safe to transmit his credit card number by Internet e-mail, Andrew Currie, the company's president (`currie@marketplace.com`) sent back the following response:

> The Internet is not a "secure" system as the term is used in defense and financial circles. However, many people believe that using credit card numbers on the Internet is an acceptable risk. Other acceptable risks include sending your credit card number through the U.S. mail, giving it to various mail order shops via the telephone, and having receipts at restaurants with your credit card number clearly visible. It is also an acceptable risk to carry your credit cards around with you everywhere in the world—even though your wallet may be stolen any time.

However, Currie noted,

> Credit cards are not the solution to currency on the Internet. Credit card numbers do work for now and are an acceptable risk. For those that want guaranteed protection, we will set up encryption schemes using DES or RSA technology in which the credit card numbers and associated information are encrypted during transit over the Internet.

Dave agrees with Currie's sentiment and routinely orders products through the Internet, sending his credit card directly to the vendor through electronic mail. There are thousands of e-mail in-transit messages sent each minute, so any particular e-mail message is likely to be lost in the shuffle.

Or is it? One problem that retail businesses on the Internet face is that, as their services become popular, the e-mail messages they receive are more likely to contain credit card numbers.

Profile: O'Reilly and Associates is a successful commercial technical book publisher that sells books and other information through the Internet. Customers can browse its booklist through the World Wide Web and order books online. Rather than ask customers to enter their credit card numbers into the Internet directly, however, O'Reilly displays an online form that customers are asked to fill out prior to placing their first order. The customer then faxes the form to the company's office in Sebastapol, California. O'Reilly assigns a unique identification number to the new customer, which the customer can use to make future purchases online.

It's also important to keep in mind what Cyberspace Development's Currie says: Although it is comforting to think that telephones and local shops are completely safe, there is a possibility that criminals will root through garbage, monitor cordless or cellular phone conversations, or even swoop into your mailbox one afternoon and intercept your credit card bills (Do you rip up the remainder of your bill before you throw it away? You should!). Although the world of electronic money is inherently unsafe, the consensus of the Internet community is that, with some forethought and precautions, the risks are manageable.

Tip: There are many ways to maintain security on the Internet. Perhaps the most obvious is to make sure that your machine and online account are secure. If you have a dialup account with an Internet access provider, choose a secure password for your account and keep it secret! Later in the chapter, we'll give you some helpful guidelines for choosing passwords, but, for now, it's enough to say that you must ensure that your account has a safe password. If your computer system is linked to the Internet via a SLIP connection or leased line, it's important to make certain that every known account on the system has a secure password, even diagnostic accounts and accounts set by the factory.

If you have a high-speed connection that actually places a computer in your network on the Internet itself, enabling intruders to connect and possibly break in, it's essential to enforce a strict user or site policy. It's also important to be aware of all known security problems, bugs, or patches. An upgrade today could save anguish tomorrow.

What the Experts Say

In researching this chapter, we polled experts who participate in various security-related discussion groups and Usenet bulletin boards to find out their views on Internet security. Would any of them, for example, be willing to send their credit card numbers over the Internet when purchasing a product?

The answers we got surprised us. Although every one of the more than a dozen security experts agreed the Internet was unsafe, several said they would nevertheless be willing to order a product from an Internet vendor by entering online their credit card information. *None of them knew of any instances in which a credit card number had been intercepted or otherwise stolen through the network.*

One popular viewpoint is that there's too much electronic mail being bandied about on the Internet for any individual e-mail message containing a credit card number to be an attractive target. Charles Wangersky, manager of technical services at Golfware Technologies, sums up this perspective by commenting, "The only thing that protects most communications is sheer volume. It's simply that there is too much data streaming past the routers for any human to track it all."

We find this difficult to accept completely, however, because the Internet is all too well suited for "smart" digging through the electronic dumpsters of the network traffic. As a particular commercial site becomes popular, chances increase that a message addressed to it will contain a credit card number. Therefore, a smart electronic criminal could intercept mail to that firm and then automatically extract the card numbers contained there. That's especially true if the messages are produced by a standard electronic form that would tag the information—for example, Credit Card No: as the beginning of a particular line.

Nonetheless, some security experts acknowledge the possibility but find that the convenience of using Internet-based businesses outweighs the possible dangers. Peter Karlson of Harrison & Troxell, Inc. is one of these die-hard users, asserting, "I have and will continue to send my credit card number via e-mail and also a Gopher site, given that it was a reputable site. I don't know of anyone that has experienced any Net-crime so far."

Profile: Computer journalist Kevin Savetz has also considered the problems of sending credit card information and other sensitive data through electronic mail, and he comments: "I've sent credit card information through the networks without any encryption, but for more sensitive data I use PGP. PGP, or pretty-good-privacy," he continues, "is a simple encryption tool that allows me to scramble my message sufficiently that only the intended recipient will be able to unscramble it and read it. The technology underneath is what's called public key encryption, allowing me to use one 'key' (typically a password) to scramble the message, and the recipient another key to unscramble it."

Tip: You can learn more about the PGP mail security system (it's available for Mac, PC, and UNIX systems) by using the FTP file transfer program to connect to `ftp.netcom.com` anonymously and then look in the directory `/pub/gbe`. Within you'll find five files named `pgpfaq-1.asc`, `pgpfaq-2.asc`, and so on.

There's more to Internet security than merely credit card transactions, of course. One of the most important areas involves the security of individual accounts and computer systems.

Working from an inexpensive dialup UNIX shell account on Netcom, Dave frequently checks to ensure that the access permissions on his home directory and files remain unaltered and secure. On one occasion, he found that his incoming electronic mail box—typically kept in a shared directory of the file system on UNIX—had its file permissions incorrectly set, allowing anyone on the machine to peruse any of his pending and incoming mail messages. A quick note to the system administration team fixed the problem.

There's another security issue here, too, particularly for company sites that are connecting computers or networks directly to the Internet through high-speed dedicated connections. Whether through SLIP, a 56 KB leased line, or even a faster T1 or T3 connection, any machine that's permanently plugged into the Internet is a box potentially waiting for someone sufficiently interested and devious to try and crack open. To address this issue, most experts are beginning to recommend that companies set up a single system that serves as an electronic gateway between internal and external services. Such a system is known as a *firewall*. We'll talk about firewalls and other security devices and techniques in the next section.

Creating a Secure Environment

As you've seen, there are undeniable dangers involved in hooking your company up to the Internet and even greater risks associated with doing business there. While some companies may find those risks unacceptable and simply stay away from the Internet, many others are making these risks manageable by

- Making sure that all user accounts have complex passwords
- Building firewalls
- Using public key encryption software
- Other security precautions—all designed to keep intruders at bay

Staying Off the Net

Without a doubt, the safest way to avoid Internet security problems is to stay off the Internet completely—to send e-mail and other vital data either through a wide area network routed through a major telecom carrier or to rely on a commercial online service such as CompuServe, America Online, or MCI Mail.

You can also send and receive Internet mail through commercial online services. These networks are considered fairly safe because they only offer gateways to the Internet—doors that periodically open and close for e-mail only.

Another important difference between a centralized online service and an Internet access provider is that, on a centralized system such as CompuServe, you can send e-mail to another user—without ever leaving the CompuServe system. On the Internet, unless the other user is on the same system as you are, the message or data travels through a variety of machines, forcing you to rely on the security of the systems through which it passes.

Because the Internet isn't a single network but really a network of networks, some portions of the route are safer than others. Jeffrey Shapard of University of California Berkeley says the academic networks are notoriously full of security holes, encompass open access subnetworks (once you're connected to one machine you automatically have access to all), poorly administered systems, and, as he phrases it, "lots of eyes and ears that can tap into your bitstream without a great deal of cleverness." But, he adds, " commercial Internet providers such as Performance Systems International (PSI) have tight central network management, careful routing, extensive training available for customers on security mechanisms, and even enhanced services with encryption built-in."

As we explained earlier, security considerations and administrative control are important criteria in selecting an Internet access provider. Most of the larger access providers provide continual monitoring, frequent spot checks, and explicit usage guidelines. All services should be able to help you ensure maximum security for your business, too.

Another approach is to keep your company's computer system "off the Net" by signing up for an inexpensive dialup account. This way, your company transmits and accesses Internet data through a UNIX line-oriented interface, or "shell," rather than connecting to the Internet directly through a SLIP connection or a leased line. Still another approach is to limit your use of the Internet to e-mail. Because e-mail is not interactive due to its store-and-forward nature, it's hard for "crackers" to use it to transmit viruses or worms.

The drawback to these strategies, of course, is that you greatly reduce your access to the Internet and its many tools and features. Dialup accounts also have their limitations, as we explored in Chapter 2, "Getting Connected: Your Ticket to Ride."

Passwords

The nature of banking transactions has changed dramatically since the advent of the automated teller machine and the *personal identification number* (PIN). A PIN, a secret four- or more digit number, is used in combination with an ATM card to verify that the person withdrawing cash from the automated teller is authorized to do so. Without the PIN, the card is useless. Simple but effective.

Computer systems offer a similar security strategy through account passwords, with which users can identify themselves as owners of authorized accounts.

Unlike an ATM system, however, computer users are sometimes free to choose not to have passwords or to select passwords that are not very secure. (For example, how secure would you feel if your PIN for your checking account was an easily-guessable *1234* or worse, wasn't even needed to use your bank card?). Choosing a poor password or not having any password at all is a bad idea, and we strongly urge against this practice. It's like playing Russian roulette with your company's data: The single most effective way to foil Internet intruders is to require a password to enter your computer system.

Nevertheless, for reasons that inevitably seem ridiculous after a break-in, users and systems managers frequently ignore or circumvent this important aspect of system security. Others, not realizing the danger, use vendor-supplied passwords that come with the system, choose a password and never change it, or even write down the password and tape it to their computer!

Here are some road-tested tips for choosing passwords that are both easy to remember and secure:

- ■ Use a password that is at least six characters long.
- ■ Use both digits (numerals) and letters.
- ■ Mix upper- and lowercase letters.
- ■ Make sure the password isn't in the dictionary.

- Change passwords at least every sixty days.

- Make sure a password is not a name or word associated with you or the account.

Examples of easily guessed passwords would include your birthday, your social security number, your license plate number, your dog's name, or any word that might appear in a dictionary. Better passwords are those that combine characters and digits in a mnemonic fashion that's easy for you to remember but difficult for intruders to guess. For example, `hi2all` and `2logIN!` are impossible for a program to guess, whereas `linda1` and `XcatX` are okay but could be better.

> **Note:** Don't try to be cute with your passwords. Trust us, many other people have thought of using `letmein`, `hello`, or `password` for their passwords. These are among the first words a wily cracker will try.

In setting up a password security system, it's important to make sure that an intruder who penetrates a single computer can't gain access to your company's entire local area network. Often, all computers at a site are connected, enabling an intruder who breaks into one machine to gain access to all of them.

One protective measure here—although it may inhibit local networking—is to set up each computer on the network with its own password-security procedures. In addition, any computer that houses sensitive corporate data should have its passwords changed frequently.

Fortunately, many security software programs are now available that can assist you in managing passwords and securing your system. For example, Sun Microsystems' ASET program requires the use of uncrackable passwords, and the public-domain COPS software can be used to search a wide variety of UNIX systems for security problems. The Tripwire auditing package from Purdue University in West Lafayette, Indiana, and the Tiger module in the TAMU toolkit (from Texas A&M University in College Station, Texas) can also help you manage individual systems.

Commercial packages, such as Securemax from Demax Software, are designed to both automate the process and collect data from distributed nodes, centralizing these security checks. A small investment of this nature can save considerable headaches and problems later.

For all of these programs and more, we recommend you check with the Usenet newsgroup `comp.security.misc`. Remember that many other people ask questions about these products quite frequently, so scanning through a few days worth of articles should yield the information you seek too.

Firewalls

Like its namesake in firefighting, an Internet firewall is a combination of hardware and software that examines network traffic and allows only approved data to pass through. It creates a controllable gateway between your internal network and the potentially hostile intruders lurking on the Internet.

The simplest form of a firewall uses filters in your network-connection. By programming what's known as the packet *router*, you can tell it to discard any packets requesting information or services that you deem a potential security threat or to funnel requests for a certain service, such as e-mail, to a particular computer. These routers can also be used to divide your networks into segments called *subnets* and to restrict packets passing between those subnets, assisting in internal corporate security and network traffic management.

Another approach to firewalls is to use computers as routers and gateways. Commercial solutions including Digital Equipment Corporation's SEAL product and Eagle Technology's Raptor use workstations to monitor network connections. By using a workstation as the router, not only is there no direct connection between your internal network and the Internet, but all traffic can be carefully monitored, ensuring that potential security problems are detected automatically.

The gateway computer can also be configured to only allow a subset of all Internet services onto (or off of) the local network. Systems like this also create extensive audit trails that are helpful in checking for intruders. Sun Microsystems offers a slightly different approach with its Itelnet, a software-only firewall gateway. There are also public domain solutions, including the Drawbridge portion of the TAMU package.

Security experts warn, however, that there are typically tradeoffs to firewalls in terms of money, access, and convenience. Jonathan Heiliger of the San Francisco Bay Area Regional Research Network (BARRnet) observes, "Firewalls are highly effective only when constructed properly. It's a major capital investment to set up a proper firewall, and there are always tradeoffs and considerations for the users. Usually, the more extreme the firewall, the more difficult or cumbersome it is for users of the system to access the outside world."

Data Encryption

Another important security measure is data encryption. Encryption is important for more than protecting data on the Internet, of course. Even if your system is not directly connected to the Internet, it's important to encrypt it to keep it safe from prying eyes. Once your data is encrypted, intruders can't read it unless they have also stolen the electronic "key" that's necessary to decode it.

Because the Internet is a "nonswitched public network," you have little control over where your data goes once you send it on its journey. It's not so different, actually, from dropping a letter in a mail box; you have no say through which post offices your letter will be routed.

From a security and encryption perspective, there are two main areas to consider—messages in transit and data stored on the disk.

Like other forms of mail, e-mail has some subtle security problems that aren't apparent at first glance. The most important of these, for companies transacting business on the Internet and taking online orders, is verifying the message's sender. To solve this problem, computer scientists have developed a technology known as *digital signatures,* the electronic equivalent of the legally binding signature that lawyers require at the bottom of every purchase order or contract. Unfortunately, there are currently no widely distributed mechanisms for digital signatures in use on the Internet.

Data encryption is vital because it's the only way to ensure that your communications are kept private—especially as wireless pathways (particularly cellular modem transmissions) become more widely used. Encryption works by translating your message into what appears to be gibberish and then sending that data to the recipient. Once the encrypted message is received, the recipient enters either the same key (in the case of *private key encryption)* or a different key (in the case of *public key encryption),* and the gibberish is automatically translated back into readable text or other data. Similarly, encryption can also be used for files and data that you aren't planning to send but prefer to keep private.

Profile: Here's a typical scenario that Dave has encountered more than once with a client: The company has an inexpensive dialup Internet account with a local access provider and would occasionally like to send a company newsletter to its customers via e-mail. To accomplish this, the company wisely maintains its database of e-mail addresses on a local system disconnected from the Internet and transmits a copy of the list of addresses to its Internet account. There it's used to address a copy of the newsletter. Then, rather than left around for prying eyes, the list is encrypted, making it unreadable and secure until the next time the company needs the information.

Several commercial e-mail programs, such as Lotus' cc:Mail, already incorporate encryption; some UNIX-based e-mail programs, notably Elm, offer a simple message scrambling capability. Microsoft's RAS (Remote Access System) and Apple's System 7 offer built in encryption, and most versions of UNIX include the powerful crypt encryption program with the system. Racal-Guardata, Inc. of Herndon,

Virginia, Morning Star Technologies, Inc. of Columbus, Ohio, and UUNET Technologies, Inc. of Falls Church, Virginia all sell hardware for encrypting data before it leaves your site.

Another up-and-coming encryption system is Privacy-Enhanced Mail (PEM), which makes use of digital signatures for security and authentication purposes.

One of the most promising, albeit controversial, encryption programs is *PGP* or *pretty good encryption.* It works by combining two keys to encrypt and decrypt data, permitting secure message transmission.

Here's how it could work for your business: Your company provides a "public key" for customers who want to send you a confidential message—say, a purchase order containing credit card information. In preparing the message, they use both your public key and their own private key. PGP uses a combination of both to encrypt data suitable for transmission through e-mail. When the customer's message arrives in your company's electronic mailbox, your employees decode the message using the public key and your company's private key. This way, your company doesn't need to know the key your customer used and your customer doesn't need to learn your key, either.

> **Tip:** You can learn more about the PGP mail security system by using FTP to connect to `ftp.netcom.com` anonymously, then look in the directory `/pub/gbe` for the five files named `pgpfaq-1.asc`, `pgpfaq-2.asc`, and so on that comprise the PGP frequently asked questions document.

Putting it All Together

No matter which precautions you choose, remember that network security starts at home. Start by making sure that security on your own internal computer system is up to snuff. Experts say that your policy should dictate at least a minimum level of security for all computers attached to your networks and include procedures for checking and maintaining the security of each attached computer. Just as important as any policy, however, is that you regularly *verify* that your account, your password, your system, and your network are all secure.

There's a trade-off to keep in mind as you build a secure system, however. In your effort to make your system secure, don't build a fortress so impregnable that nobody can get in or out. The value of the Internet, after all, is its linkages to a worldwide computer network and the people who access it. Although the security precautions you take must be strong enough to protect your company's computer network, they cannot be so strong that they bar legitimate access by employees, vendors, or customers. Information managers who want to open their networks to their company workers also need to design a security system that is easy to use.

"The key concept in all security, including Internet network security, is to make the cost of attack higher than the value of the asset," says Pat Farrell, senior principal, Pharmaceutical Industry Practice, at American Management Systems in Fairfax, Virginia. "Firewalls, one-time passwords, encryption, etc. simply raise the cost of attack. Nothing will safeguard with certainty."

Emergency Measures: What to Do if a Break-In Occurs

Despite all the Internet security measures now available, break-ins can and do occur. If you have a computer system or local area network on the Internet and have reason to believe that security has been breached, contact CERT immediately at its 24-hour hotline; (412) 268-7090. Be prepared with the following information:

    Names of the computers compromised at your site
    What kind of computer has been compromised, including details on operating system and related software
    Whether security upgrades, modifications, or vendor-supplied patches have been applied to the compromised system or systems; if so, were patches applied before or after the intrusion
    Account or accounts believed compromised
    Other hosts or sites you believe are involved in the intrusion and whether or not you have already contacted those sites about the security violation
    If other sites have been contacted, contact information used for contacting them
    Contact information for other sites that may have been affected so that CERT can contact them directly
    Whether or not any law enforcement agencies have been contacted
    Excerpts from any potentially relevant system logs, including timestamps if available
    What assistance you would like from the CERT Coordination Center

CERT

Because of its pivotal role in Internet security, CERT is worth discussing in greater detail. CERT was created by the Defense Advanced Research Projects Agency (DARPA) in November, 1988, immediately following the Internet worm attack. The attack made it painfully clear that there was no effective way to quickly disseminate security information to the Internet community and, until that time, no agency charged with tracking and maintaining a history of security incidents.

The CERT charter is to work with the Internet community to expedite its response to computer security breaches involving Internet-connected computers, to help raise the community's awareness of computer security issues, and to conduct research targeted at improving the security of existing systems.

CERT products and services include 24-hour technical assistance for responding to computer security incidents, product vulnerability assistance, technical documents, and seminars. In addition, the CERT team maintains a number of mailing lists (including one for CERT advisories) and provides an anonymous FTP server—cert.org—where security-related documents, past CERT advisories, and tools are archived and available for perusal.

In cooperation with a number of leading computer and operating systems vendors, CERT advisories provide information on how to obtain a patch or details of a workaround for known security problems. For obvious reasons, CERT doesn't publish vulnerability information until a workaround or a patch is available. These advisories are published on the Usenet newsgroup, comp.security.announce, and are distributed via the CERT-advisory mailing list. To join the list, send a note to cert-advisory-request@cert.org. However, if you can receive the Usenet group instead, we recommend you use it, thereby easing the load on the CERT computers.

Throughout the year, members of the CERT Coordination Center give presentations at various technical conferences, seminars, and regional network organization meetings around the country. Periodically, special arrangements can be made to tailor the presentation to fit the requirements of the specific site. For further information regarding presentations, contact the CERT Coordination Center.

CERT Contact Information
CERT Coordination Center
Software Engineering Institute
Carnegie Mellon University
Pittsburgh, PA 15213-3890
U.S.A.

Internet E-Mail Address
cert@cert.org
Telephone number
1-412-268-7090 (24-hour hotline)
Fax number
1-412-268-6989

Additional Resources

In this chapter, we've discussed a variety of different approaches to Internet security and, we hope, imparting a sense of the importance of good security. Fortunately, there are many additional sources of information on encryption, public key systems, and Internet security, and timely bulletins on potential security problems and break-ins.

The following text lists some of the best.

Mailing Lists and Usenet Newsgroups

VIRUS-L mailing list is a moderated Internet mailing list with a focus on computer virus issues. Rather than distributing dozens of messages that arrive each day, this mailing list distributes information in "digest" form, compiling the messages into a sort of electronic newsletter. For more information, including a copy of the posting guidelines, use the FTP program to connect to `cert.org` and look for the file `virus-l.README` in the `/pub/virus-l` directory. To be added to the mailing list, send an e-mail message to `listserv@lehigh.edu` with the message body stating `SUBSCRIBE VIRUS-L your name`.

VALERT-L mailing list is a quick way to share urgent virus warnings with other Internet computer users. Any message sent to VALERT-L will also appear in the next VIRUS-l digest. To be added to the mailing list, send mail to `listserv@lehigh.edu`. In the body of the message, type `SUB VALERT-L your name`.

`comp.security.announce` is a Usenet newsgroup formed solely for the distribution of CERT advisories. Must reading for anyone interested in security on the Internet.

`comp.security.misc` is a Usenet newsgroup that offers a forum for the discussion of computer security, especially as it relates to the UNIX operating system. Lots of discussion!

`alt.security` is a Usenet newsgroup discussing computer security and unrelated security issues such as car alarms, locks, and personal security systems.

`comp.virus` is a Usenet newsgroup that focuses on computer virus issues. Much of the information that arrives here copies the messages sent to the VIRUS-L mailing list. It's no surprise that you can obtain a copy of the newsgroup guidelines by using the FTP program to connect to `cert.org` and seeking the file `virus-l.README` in the directory `pub/virus-l`.

`comp.risks` is a Usenet newsgroup about the risks to the public from computers and related systems. One of the oldest newsgroups, it's a terrific place to learn about the latest break-ins and security problems around the world.

Books

There are many books on UNIX and Internet security. We recommend the following for further reading:

Curry, David A. *UNIX System Security: A Guide for Users and System Administrators.* Addison-Wesley Publishing Co., Inc. (ISBN 0-201-56327-4), 1992.

Denning, Peter J., ed. *Computers Under Attack: Intruders, Worms, and Viruses.* ACM Press, Addison-Wesley Publishing Company, Inc. (ISBN 0-201-53067-8), 1990.

Garfinkel, Simson and Gene Spafford. *Practical UNIX Security.* O'Reilly & Associates, Inc. (ISBN 0-937175-72-2), 1991.

Hafner, Katie and John Markoff. *Cyperpunk: Outlaws and Hackers on the Computer Frontier.* Simon & Schuster, 1991.

Stoll, Clifford. *The Cuckoo's Egg: Tracking a Spy Through the Maze of Computer Espionage.* Doubleday (ISBN 0-385-24946-2), 1989.

Wood, Patrick and Stephen Kochan. *UNIX System Security.* Hayden Books, 1986.

Conclusion

What needs to be done to make the Internet safe for business users? Probably the most effective measure would be for all Internet users, whether business or educational, governmental or individual, to tighten security on their own computer systems.

Internet security experts note that even encryption, firewalls, and other security tools available today are still not entirely effective—primarily because not enough people use them. The good news is that many Internet security experts are working feverishly to address this problem. Thanks to them, tomorrow's Internet will be far more secure for you and your customers than placing an order over the phone or handing a credit card to a salesclerk at a local store.

DOING BUSINESS ON THE INTERNET

For many years, the idea of "doing business on the Internet" seemed like a contradiction in terms. Just a few years ago, the Internet consisted of a relatively small population of academics, researchers, government bureaucrats, and some computer companies, but few people actually thought of selling anything through the network.

Now, of course, all that's changing. With the Internet growing at an astounding rate and even small companies looking to electronic mail to link national and international operations, the Internet has become too vast a market and too valuable a communications tool to ignore.

For many companies, the Internet represents little more than a cheap communications link. These days, companies of all sizes are turning to the Internet to connect geographically distant sites, creating their own internetworked environment. The Internet is very well suited to this purpose, and companies of all sizes are stringing together "virtual" wide-area networks that feature all the security and tools typically associated with proprietary networks but at a fraction of the cost.

Then there are the technology companies that see the Internet as a communications channel between customers and vendors. These companies are using the Internet to expand and improve customer support—for example, software developers that transmit code fixes, or patches, to customers in need of immediate help.

Other firms use the Internet to facilitate collaboration with clients. Already, some advertising agencies are not only sending ad page mock-ups over the Internet but also compressed video images and sound bites to clients across town, across the state, or around the globe.

Some of the most interesting companies, however, are those that view the Internet as an inexpensive vehicle for direct sales. Publishers are publishing huge book catalogs on the network, allowing anyone online to search and order desired titles. Catalog merchants are also getting into the act, setting up Gopher sites and World Wide Web versions of their catalogs to showcase product information and take orders electronically.

To be fair, the Internet still has a long way to go before it becomes as commonplace a business tool as the phone, fax, or printed advertisement. For one, the network's infrastructure is still fraught with navigational and security problems. There are also cultural obstacles, such as the Internet community's traditional aversion to anything that smacks of online commerce. For companies desiring to peddle goods and services online, there are other problems, too, such as figuring out how much to charge and how to collect from people who shop in what may be the world's ultimate *laissez-faire* marketplace.

Ultimately, however, one of the biggest barriers to doing business on the Internet has nothing to do with the Internet itself. It's the billions of consumers, businesses, and organizations worldwide that aren't connected to the Internet and lack the equipment, skills, or desire to explore it. Although 20,000,000 Internet users may sound like a big number, it's still a tiny fraction of the global marketplace.

In a sense, this may seem like a fatuous argument. Clearly, no single advertising, marketing, or promotional channel is going to reach 100 percent of the potential market, where the channel is television, radio, print media, or a World Wide Web home page. The reason we mention it is to emphasize that there are some people who are touting the Internet as the "next big thing," the electronic heartbeat of '90s commerce. We advise you to take this hype with a grain of salt while, at the same time, recognizing that the Internet still represents an exciting, new market-place for a wide variety of businesses.

Savvy companies that zero in on niche markets and master the rules of online commerce can do a brisk business on the Internet—many are already.

The purpose of this chapter is to show you the wide variety of creative ways in which companies are using the Internet to enhance their businesses and to show how you, too, can tap the Internet for extra sales and profits.

A Brief History of Internet Commerce

Although Internet commerce has been taking place on a small scale for years, the current commercial free-for-all began in 1991 when the federal government made it known that it no longer intended to limit the network's backbone for use in research.

That policy shift created an incentive for three major Internet access providers—Performance Systems International Inc. (PSI), Uunet Technologies Inc., and General Atomics' Cerfnet—to create their own commercial backbones, allowing them to skirt the government-controlled National Science Foundation NSFNet. These providers, along with nine others, formed the Commercial Internet Exchange (CIX). Today, virtually every form of commercial traffic is allowed to pass through CIX network providers, though unsolicited junk mailings are still frowned on by the Internet community.

In reality, the potential for commercial exploitation of the Internet was always present. Because many large corporations already have TCP/IP networks in place, it's been relatively simple for them to connect computers in distant offices via the Internet. For another, low connection costs provide a cost-effective alternative to building and maintaining expensive proprietary WANs, which also require leasing expensive long-distance lines or hooking up with commercial networks such as CompuServe or MCI Mail.

Also, because companies pay a flat fee for access to the Internet, costs per user are often lower than any of the alternative network connections. How appealing is this? According to the Internet Society, 30 percent of the Fortune 500 is on the Internet, and two-thirds of Internet users work for major corporations.

These days, the Internet's budding commercialization is nurturing entrepreneurial dreams of an information superhighway, with promises of 500-channel cable television, virtual reality, and other forms of high-tech infotainment. Some now view the Internet as a worldwide home shopping network where consumers will ultimately be able to order products displayed via full-motion video, access interactive games, and chat "live" with other users who they see on their computer or television screens. Most of these scenarios envision the Internet as a passive place—a place where users don't add their own channels but flip between the 500 or so that will be in place.

What's more, the Internet's attractiveness to big corporations also makes it quite interesting to direct marketers. Recent demographic studies indicate that the Internet community is affluent and well-educated. Not only do the corporate executives who log onto the Internet have money to spend on goods and services, but so do the college kids who dial up to swap e-mail, research papers, and play games.

Hot Opportunities in Cyberspace

What are the hottest business opportunities on the Internet today? Although hundreds of entrepreneurs are rushing in to set up roadside stands, hoping to sell products and services, long-time Internet observers say the real opportunity lies in building the information infrastructure—the roadways, the on-ramps, even the pit stops—for tomorrow's Internet tourists and travelers.

We believe that there are two key areas that will become more and more important as the Internet continues to grow—companies that can help users find information and companies that can help organize information for providers.

Dave's Internet Mall, a monthly electronic listing of products available through the Internet, offers an interesting glimpse into the growth of commerce on the network. Dave estimates that, during the summer of 1994, one company was added to the Mall every day; now the list includes hundreds of vendors. Over the same period, the volume of users' requests catapulted the Internet Mall to one of the top ten documents sought on the network.

> **Tip:** You can obtain a copy of the Internet Mall for yourself by sending electronic mail to Dave Taylor: send a message to `taylor@netcom.com` with the message subject of `send mall`.

Dave believes that finding information will be the Internet's next big business opportunity. It's no different, he believes, than the friendly gas station in a small town where motorists can stop, ask directions, and find out the quickest route to their destinations.

Communications

Despite the many possibilities inherent in Internet commerce, business communication with customers remains one of the most popular uses of the Internet. Because of its low cost and its universal accessibility, the Internet is complementing and, in some cases, replacing the phone, the fax, and the overnight letter.

Profile: At Lockheed, a Calabasas, California, defense and aerospace giant, roughly 5,000 of the company's 70,000 employees are on the Internet, and the number is expected to grow by nearly 50 percent in 1994. The reason: Lockheed's Internet costs for a T1 line from Advanced Networks and Services, including a router and high-speed modems, runs about $40,000 annually. Add leased-line phone charges and Lockheed's Internet access costs a total of only $10 a user, and that number will decrease as more employees are included.

For Lockheed, setting up a communications hub on the Internet was a matter of survival. Faced with cuts in defense spending, the defense contractor has had to watch costs and find new opportunities fast. Two years ago, Lockheed, a long-time Internet e-mail user, decided to create an electronic infrastructure to enable researchers to share information, synergize, cooperate, and collaborate on research and projects for customers, according to Michael Carroll, manager of advanced computer and software applications for the company.

After several possible network solutions were evaluated, the defense contractor picked the Internet because it already had a TCP/IP backbone in place and was "fairly straightforward to expand," Carroll told *UNIX World* magazine. What's more, public-domain versions of client-server products—such as WAIS, an Internet full-text information-indexing and retrieval program—made it an inexpensive and easy way to build Lockheed's internal Internet databases.

"The price was right," Carroll says. "We had the ability to try [the Internet] without significant investment."

Now, thanks to the company's new Technology Broker System (TBS), a hypermedia search and retrieval environment that bridges the Internet, employees at both Lockheed Missiles in Space in Sunnyvale, California, and Lockheed Advanced Development in Palmdale, California, can search the Commerce Business Daily (via a daily Internet feed) and scan the Lockheed library catalog and a variety of technical and business documents, ranging from manufacturing procedures to management policies to parts catalogs. Lockheed also uses Internet newsgroups to find collaborators on research projects overseas.

"Through the newsgroups and bulletin boards, you can make contact [with] people external to your company and explore a strategic, long-term collaboration," Carroll says.

Real Estate by E-Mail

Internet communication isn't just for large companies such as Lockheed. Even small companies are finding the Internet to be a cost-effective communications solution.

Profile: Alain Pinel Realtors, a Saratoga, California, real estate brokerage firm, shows what a smaller company can do on the Internet. Three years ago, the fledgling real estate firm was struggling to find a competitive edge in the depressed Silicon Valley real estate market. Particularly frustrating was the challenge of trying to keep in touch with the busy engineers, marketing specialists, and sales people who comprised their clientele.

All that changed when Alain Pinel decided to invest in a $180-a-month Internet connection that its agents use to send listings, market analyses, and other information via e-mail to clients as far away as the East Coast, Australia, and England. Once the company saw how easy and effective communication with customers via e-mail was, it set up a wide-area Internet network with its business associates, too.

These days, when Alain Pinel real estate agents need to send escrow information to the local title companies with which they do business, they simply jump on the Internet. In fact, seven title companies were so eager for Alain Pinel's business that they made their own inexpensive Internet dial-up arrangements at a fraction of what the more traditional—private network-based—electronic data interchange solution would have cost. The title companies each pay only $50 a month for Internet dialup access.

> The bottom line: Over the last three years, Alain Pinel has grown from a small firm clawing to succeed in the San Jose, California, region to a flourishing agency with annual home sales of $600,000,000. The firm now employs 200 agents and 30 support-staff personnel and maintains a database that typically includes 500–800 home and property listings, according to *The Wall Street Journal.*

Hooking up to the Internet allows small businesses to deploy resources, access information and communicate with customers in ways that offer a competitive edge to help them spar with larger rivals.

Bob Doyle, director of marketing for SprintLink, an Internet access provider, says that one small bank is using the Internet to exchange interest rates and submit loan applications to the corporate office. A few years ago, KPMG Peat Marwick shelved a proposal to build a proprietary network for the Big Six accounting firm's 200 offices around the world, informing its clients that it'd just be too expensive. Today, the firm is busy recomputing the costs and feasibility based on the new possibilities offered by the global Internet.

The picture isn't completely rosy. In Chapter 3, "Risks and Realities," we discussed problems with Internet reliability and security.

Despite improvements in network security, few in the corporate community have forgotten Robert Morris' worm, which wreaked havoc on the Internet in 1988, effectively shutting down the network for several days.

Today, many companies are trying to assemble secure, reliable networking systems that can co-exist and exploit the global Internet while retaining the key elements of traditional electronic data interchange (EDI) systems—security, reliability, around-the-clock monitoring, and consistent high-speed performance.

Business Services

Companies that provide business services are also beginning to realize that the Internet's combination of price, features, and Internet-connected businesses make the electronic community a promising place to do business.

These companies include consulting, publishing, marketing, and other service firms.

Profile: The Washington law firm of Venable, Baetjer, Howard & Civiletti recently became one of the first law firms to set up its own World Wide Web server, displaying the various services the firm provides, as shown in Figure 4.1. For less than $300 a month, the company can offer in-depth information to potential clients 24 hours a day. The reason why Venable Baetjer can keep its costs so low is because partner Ken Bass set up and maintains the server himself and the firm pays only for its Internet connection.

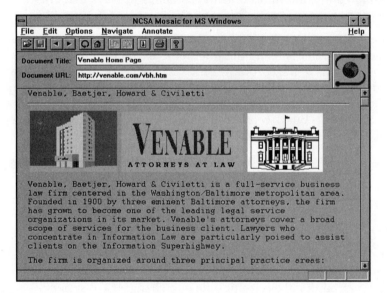

Figure 4.1. The law firm of Venable, Baetjer, Howard and Civiletti is blazing new advertising trails with its Web home page.

Advertising agencies are starting to appear on the Internet. One interesting example is Apollo Advertising, which invites clients to tack up short advertisements on its World Wide Web page for free and charges a modest fee for posting longer ads and other World Wide Web documents. Figure 4.2 shows what an Apollo page looks like.

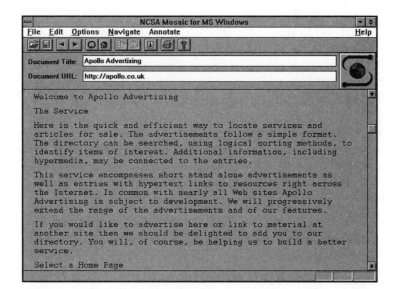

Figure 4.2. Advertising agencies in cyberspace: Apollo Advertising on the Web.

Tip: There are many ways to connect to the various services available on the Internet and just as many ways to express a particular address or connection command. In this book, we try to use the most common ways, including *uniform resource locators* (URLs). A URL address starts with the type of service, followed by the name of the host that offers the service, followed by any other information required by the specific service. For example, you could connect to *Wired* magazine on the World Wide Web using the URL `http://www.wired.com/`. Here you can see that the service type is `http` (HyperText Transmission Protocol) at the host `www.wired.com`.

Other Internet business services include

- Document Center, a hard-copy, document delivery service specializing in government and industry specifications and standards, available through e-mail, Gopher, or World Wide Web. To check it out, send e-mail to `info@doccenter.com`, Gopher to `doccenter.com`, or go to URL://`www.service.com/doccenter/home.html`.

- Infotech Information Technologies, a Charlotte, North Carolina, company, that offers individual and business credit reports, Dunn & Bradstreet information, a Social Security locator service, arrest and conviction records, and other credit-checking information. You can find out more by sending electronic mail to `infotech@fx.net`.

- The Company Corporation, which offers incorporation services for small businesses online. To contact the company by e-mail, send a note to `corp@incorporate.com` or connect to the Web at `http://incorporate.com/tcc/home.html`.

- If your company does business internationally, International Trade Network might be of interest. Daily e-mail messages from the company keep you up-to-date on trade opportunities and import/export trends. Send e-mail to `majordomo@world.std.com` with the subject `info intltrade` for details.

- INFOMARK, a Colorado consulting firm, helps customers develop their own marketing strategies and sells its 900-number resource guide online through Gopher or Web. To check it out, connect to `marketplace.com`.

- National Real Estate Services of Vancouver, Canada, publishes its data-base of over 20,000 real estate listings via the World Wide Web. Check out `http://ww.gems.com/realestate`.

- Computer Literacy offer computer books online. Send an e-mail message to `info@clbooks.com` for more information.

Profile: There's also RealtyNet, an international network of real estate-related computer bulletin boards for brokers and other professionals seeking to do business electronically. RealtyNet is one of several Internet business services launched over the last year by Ted Kraus, president of TKO Real Estate Advisory Group in Mercerville, New Jersey. Kraus's $4,000,000 (sales) company manages 200 shopping centers around the country and publishes a weekly print newsletter and a paper-bound directory about commercial real estate.

Last year, Kraus spent $15,000 to set up a computer bulletin board focusing on commercial real estate, figuring that it would be cheaper and easier to deliver his information electronically than to pay for printing and postage. It wasn't a big success. "We spent the first six months explaining to people what a modem was," he says.

Several months later, Kraus came up with a better idea—starting an Internet discussion group where people can tack up offers to buy and sell properties, without paying to post their listings. Close to 400 people have signed up so far, Kraus says, and soon, he plans to start running online ads. He's also started a discussion group for residential real estate. His cost: $1,000 a month for high-speed Internet access. He says he expects to break even on his ventures within the next two years.

Sales and Marketing

While the Internet is not a mass market—you won't find Coke and Pepsi online slugging it out, for example—a growing number of booksellers, software and computer hardware retailers, and even a florist and gourmet popcorn shop have found it a valuable addition to their current sales strategies.

While retail sales remain a rarity on the Internet, there are some early success stories.

At Computer Literacy, one of the stores described above, four employees help answer Internet e-mail, suggesting a large volume of information requests and, possibly, orders. The Compact Disc Connection has graduated from renting space on an access provider for its one online music store to setting up a sophisticated system of its own with multiple warehouses throughout the United States (`telnet cdconnection.com`). Ceram Inc. sells UNIX workstations through the Internet and puts its Internet-based sales between $3,500,000 and $5,000,000 for 1994.

What kind of businesses are actually using the Internet Mall today? Here's a sampling of Internet merchants culled from the latest issue of The Internet Mall:

- Book Stacks Unlimited, a Cleveland, Ohio, bookstore that specializes in classics such as Shakespeare and Dickens. To connect: `telnet books.com`.

- Moe's Books, Berkeley, California, used bookstore with more than 500,000 titles specializing in rare, antiquarian, remainders, and imported books. Anyone connected to the Internet with electronic mail can seek and purchase books: `moesbooks@delphi.com`.

- Future Fantasy, a bookstore specializing in science fiction, fantasy, mystery and horror, offers an online catalog and the ability for customers to order books directly. To connect with its Web server, use: `http://www.commerce.digital.com/palo-alto/FutureFantasy/home.html`.

- The Online Bookstore sells books in electronic, rather than hard copy, format, enabling customers to download books directly to their computers. Connect to `marketplace.com` with Gopher or a World Wide Web browser such as Mosaic or Lynx.

- Infinity Link Network Services, which offers an online catalog of CDs, video tapes, books, and laser discs. Connect through `telnet columbia.ilc.com` with the login `cas`—or with Gopher, also to `columbia.ilc.com`.

- Softpro Books, a small computer bookstore with shops in Boston and Denver and an online bookstore with a catalog of more than 1000 titles. Send mail to `softpro@world.std.com`.

- Canadian shop Roswell Electronic Computer Bookstore is also an extension of an existing shop, this one in Halifax, Nova Scotia. The online database includes more than 5500 titles. Customers can visit them at `gopher nstn.ns.ca`, through the Web at URL `http://www.nstn.ns.ca/cybermall/cybermall.html`, or via e-mail: `roswell@fox.nstn.ns.ca`.

- JF Lehmanns Fachbuchhandlung is based in Berlin but also accessible via the Internet. The company offers German language technical books and CD-ROM discs through Gopher: `gopher gopher.germany.eu.net` or through the Web with URL: `http://www.germany.eu.net:80/shop/jfl/jfl_kat.html`.

- The Expert Center for Taxonomic Identification in Amsterdam, with funding from UNESCO, makes its Multimedia CD-ROM-based Mac, Windows, and NeXTStep biodiversity disks available via the Internet. For more information about ETI and its products, send e-mail to `info@eti.bio.uva.nl`.

- Planet Earth Management, which sells concert packages complete with tickets and hotel rooms to rock performances by Pink Floyd, The Rolling Stones, and other big-name acts. Information can be obtained via e-mail from `pink@society.com` and `stones@society.com`.

- McCrerey Farm of Pennsylvania, which sells dolls, Santas, handcrafted traditional gifts, natural fibers, and craft supplies. Connect with Gopher to `telerama.lm.com`.

- Grant's Florist and Greenhouse, the Internet's answer to PC Flowers, enables customers to browse its offerings on the World Wide Web. Connect to `http://florist.com:1080`.

- The Programmer's Shop sells software and hardware of interest to computer programmers. For more information, send electronic mail to `progshop@world.std.com`.

- The CERAM Email Marketplace offers weekly price quotes on CPU and RAM chips via e-mail. Send mail to `catalog@ceram.com` for details and a current price quote.

In addition to the online merchants, a growing number of technology service providers also specialize in putting product catalogs and other company products online.

In August, 1993, O'Reilly & Associates, a Sebastopol, California, publishing company specializing in Internet books and guides, introduced the Global Network Navigator, an Internet resource center that enables Internet users to browse product brochures, press releases, and white papers; download demonstration software, and ask company representatives for additional information. Advertisers can submit hypertext advertisements that run in the GNN marketplace or in a general GNN guide to the Internet.

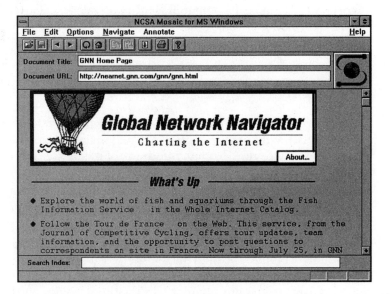

Figure 4.3. Traveling through the World Wide Web with O'Reilly's Global Network Navigator.

Other companies charge a flat fee for posting a company's product catalog or inventory on the Internet. This way, the client company avoids the trouble and expense of setting up an online database or a network connection.

AT&T charges $160 per month for posting databases in the 25- to 50-megabyte range, exclusive of security and access controls. A competitor, Enterprise Integration Technology of Palo Alto, California, will put a company's 30-page quarterly catalog on the Internet for about $15,000 a year, customizing the material to maximize the multimedia possibilities of the Internet. EIT and others exploit Internet capabilities unavailable on other networks such as hypertext from within the

World Wide Web. Like AT&T and other service providers, EIT offers a complete off-site turnkey service, including its own servers, software, and T1 Internet connection.

Despite the Internet's enormous potential as a worldwide marketplace, there are two major drawbacks to Internet retailing today. The first is visibility: Unlike a real-world mall that you might drive by on the way to work or the Prodigy Mall that advertises "specials" on a "welcome" screen that appears when you log on, there's very little on the Internet to direct you to Internet shopping malls or merchants.

There's also a billing problem: Because Internet security is still in its infancy, many customers correctly recognize the potential security threats associated with sending credit card information through the network, forcing Internet merchants to set up 800 numbers and fax services to accommodate them.

Customer Support

Thanks to the Internet, even small companies can stay in touch with customers throughout the world without exchanging international phone calls or staffing offices with on-site service reps. Today, hundreds of businesses offer customer support through the Internet, especially those in the technology field. For many hardware and software vendors, customer support on the Internet is a logical extension of dial-up bulletin boards or support forums set up on commercial online services such as CompuServe and GEnie.

For computer companies, the Internet is especially useful because many of their customers are already online. Through the Internet, customers can ask questions, receive upgrades and bug fixes for their software programs, and sometimes even demonstrate problems to an online engineer, all without leaving the office.

Small software companies have been particularly aggressive in setting up e-mail addresses for problems, questions, enhancement requests, and other messages. Indeed, it's the rare software firm that isn't accessible through the Internet, even if the company also has a presence on CompuServe, AppleLink, or another online service.

Larger computer vendors have also embraced the Internet as a communications tool, particularly those firms whose engineers are already using the Internet for their own purposes. A quick scan of Usenet groups shows Apple employees in Mac-related newsgroups, HP employees in HP groups, Sun employees answering questions in Sun-related groups, and even some Microsoft employees answering questions in the independent Microsoft Word newsletter, distributed through e-mail for free.

Profile: Other companies are offering customer support through the Internet's World Wide Web. One of the most notable is Digital Equipment Corp., where just about everyone is hooked up to the company's internal DECNET network. When a team of engineers at DEC's Palo Alto research facility put up a Web home page at URL `http://www.dec.com/` offering information about the company, thousands of people on the Internet immediately began to explore it.

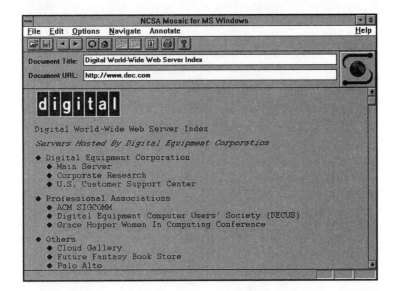

Figure 4.4. Interacting with customers through the World Wide Web: Here you can see the face Digital Equipment Corporation puts on its electronic customer interface at URL `http://www.dec.com/`.

Tip: Here's a handy tip for finding companies that offer support on the World Wide Web: Just type www before the registered domain name. For example, DEC's Web site is `www.dec.com`, Microsoft has `www.microsoft.com`, and IBM has `www.ibm.com`. If you know the domain name of your favorite company, try sticking www in front and then building a URL for a World Wide Web browser:

`http://www.company domain/`

For example, by the time you read this, HP will have its Web server on the Internet, accessible at URL `http://www.hp.com/`.

Profile: Wingra Technology, a 30-employee company based in Minnesota, services a customer base of more than 600 organizations in 33 countries, mostly through communicating via the Internet. Customers send service requests to the firm through e-mail.

Profile: Silicon Graphics, a highly successful manufacturer of high-resolution graphics workstations, has received many kudos from both customers and analysts for its Internet-based customer support plan that includes a set of Usenet newsgroups (`comp.sgi.*`) checked regularly by the company's engineers. Here's a typical response from an SGI engineer to a question posed by an Internet user. Unlike phone and fax support, Internet support costs the customer nothing, and it enables other customers to read and learn from the technicians' responses without filing problem reports of their own:

```
From: aschaffe@holodeck.asd.sgi.com (Allan Schaffer)
Newsgroups: comp.sys.sgi.bugs
Subject: Re: Hardware failure or software problem ?
Date: 7 Jun 1994 20:49:19 GMT
Organization: Silicon Graphics, Inc., Mountain View, CA

vulture@imperial.ac.uk said..
>today my X server on a 4D/25 crashed several times. I got the following
>messages from /usr//adm/SYSLOG:
>
>   carrion unix: WARNING: Gr1PcxSwap: TIMEOUT GE not ready for swap
>   carrion unix: WARNING: Graphics error: base = 0xBF000000  GE PC = 11047
>
>Since this has not happened before in over two years I would like to know
>whether this is likely to be an upcoming hardware failure or a software
>bug or a hack attack.

Sometimes user code can tickle an IRIX bug and cause a pipe crash,
but since you weren't running anything out of the ordinary this is
likely to be flaky hardware.  You might try re-seating the
graphics board.  Also run the diagnostics.  If all else fails (and
the problem continues) call your support folks.

Allan
Silicon Graphics
aschaffe@sgi.com
```

Besides discussion forums, companies can also publish catalogs, product databases, and other information on the Internet, using a variety of electronic tools such as telnet, FTP, WAIS (wide-area information server), Veronica, and Gopher, and more.

Profile: Sun Microsystems offers Sunsolve Online, an Internet support service available to contract customers as an enhancement to Sun's more comprehensive Sunspectrum services. SunSolve provides an FTP database for software patches and almost 250,000 technical documents, complete with full-text search-and-retrieval capabilities.

Profile: DEC offers both FTP and WWW (World Wide Web) hypertext information servers, which allow customers to access an extensive collection of public-domain software, text, Postscript files, product literature, and service information. DEC also offers access to demo Alpha AXP RISC machines over the Internet, giving prospective customers the opportunity to test-drive the AXPs from their desktop computers.

David Flack, editor-in-chief of *Open Computing* magazine, comments in a recent editorial that, by using the Internet, "vendors can offer information products, services, and software for trial use instead of merely hyping them. Customer feedback is enhanced and people can share their opinions of products in ways not possible in the world of read-only advertising."

Research and Development

When you consider that the initial reason for the Internet's creation of the Internet was to facilitate government research and development projects, it should come as no surprise that R&D is still one of the most popular activities on the Internet. Because of its low cost, companies such as Bellcore, GE Medical Systems, Motorola, Intel, and thousands of others are using the network to collaborate on worldwide research efforts.

Thanks to the Internet, researchers can keep abreast of new discoveries, communicate in real-time with colleagues working on similar projects, and even find out about an interesting discovery in an altogether different field. The Internet also links many corporate research divisions directly to supercomputer centers for dedicated research projects.

Some companies use simple e-mail to communicate, others set up internal and external newsgroups to publish and discuss findings, and still others make use of the multimedia capabilities of the Internet to support voice, video, and data. Other companies are using Internet tools such as Gopher and WAIS to set up online libraries to share information worldwide.

Profile: Other researchers tap into the Internet on a less formal basis. At Unocal in Los Angeles, for example, Internet use is flourishing despite the fact that the company isn't particularly pushing it. Unocal engineers frequently traverse the Internet in search of seismic data, satellite maps, and land surveys to use in their search for oil and geothermal energy prospects. They also scan relevant newsgroups on the Internet, exchange mail and files with other researchers and universities, and retrieve new releases, bug fixes, patches, and online technical support from software and hardware vendors. The cost: $12,500 a year for a 56 Kbps Internet connection and a leased line.

Publishing

Newspaper and magazine publishers are also discovering what computer professionals have known for years: hop aboard the Internet and kiss your printing and distribution costs good-bye.

On the Internet, publishers pay a flat monthly fee to publish all the news they want, without paying a penny extra for newsprint, printing presses, or delivery trucks. As a result, the Internet has become a popular hangout for computer-assisted journalists, and close to a dozen newspapers and more than 150 journals and magazines are now publishing online editions on the Internet.

Newspapers

Following their technologically savvy readers, many big-city newspapers, including *The News York Times, The San Jose Mercury News, The Atlanta Journal and Constitution,* and *The Detroit Free Press* are trumpeting deals with America Online, Prodigy, and CompuServe.

However, a small but growing number of newspapers are trying something different—publishing electronic editions on the Internet. Other papers are using the Internet to address publishing's perennial problem of having more information than there's space for in the paper. Their solution is to create stand-alone bulletin boards that are connected, often rather loosely, to the Internet.

For newspaper publishers, much of the Internet's appeal comes down to dollars and cents: Although commercial online services offer market penetration, a centralized infrastructure, and easy-to-use navigational software that would be difficult for a newspaper to duplicate on its own, newspapers typically forfeit all but 10 to 20 percent of the connect-time revenues generated by their publication's online area.

By contrast, publishing a newspaper on the Internet costs very little (apart from the cost of establishing Internet access and setting up a computer bulletin board), and the publisher keeps most of the profits—even after "soft costs" such as staff time, advertising, and billing are deducted.

Two newspapers that publish electronic editions on the Internet are *The Palo Alto Weekly*, a locally owned community newspaper with a twice-a-week circulation of 50,000, and *The News & Observer*, a 155,000-circulation Raleigh, North Carolina, daily.

Profile: Although powerhouse Knight-Ridder, Inc., is betting millions of dollars on Mercury Center, the online edition of its 270,000-circulation *San Jose Mercury News* that it publishes on America Online, the neighboring *Palo Alto Weekly* has opted for the low-cost route by hopping aboard the Internet.

Publisher Bill Johnson says the venture has cost the paper nothing so far—a local Internet access provider has donated its services for free—and resulted in 4,500 people reading the electronic edition within the first two weeks of operation. That's not surprising considering the high number of Internet users in Silicon Valley, the paper's home turf.

Here's how *The Palo Alto Weekly* does it: An editor copies news articles and other text-based content onto a floppy disk after the print edition has been put to bed and then ships it off to Internet Distribution Services, the local access provider. IDS then loads the data onto its computer, and, within a few hours, it's available for the entire Internet community.

For now, the electronic edition is free to anyone with access to the Internet; in Palo Alto's case, that's roughly half the population. The real payoff will come in the near future when the paper begins charging advertisers for classified ads, splitting the revenue with its Internet access provider.

"One of the neat things about the Internet is that a small paper that serves a very focused area can, with minimal effort, offer the community a way to engage in collective dialog," Johnson says. "The appeal of The Internet and its unmanaged chaos just seems so much more appropriate for our newspaper than a commercial online service."

Profile: *The News & Observer*, for its part, demonstrates what a larger newspaper with greater resources can do. Like the *Palo Alto Weekly*, *The News & Observer* is located in a high-tech area where computer and modem use is high—North Carolina's Research Triangle.

The News & Observer publishes two online editions—Nando Land and NandO.net. Both can be accessed through the Internet or by dialing up the computer bulletin board directly. Nando Land, which debuted in February, is a free online service with e-mail, games, reference material, and an electronic edition of the newspaper that's available to every public school in North Carolina during school hours. Teachers can access the service free in the evenings from their home computers; it's also provided at no charge to libraries, not-for-profit groups and the disabled.

On March 1, the paper launched NandO.net, a for-profit, commercial version of Nando Land geared toward its print subscribers. NandO.net users get a specially edited electronic edition that puts greater emphasis on technology news, the full text of U.S. Supreme Court decisions, and other information not included in the printed paper, plus advance access to the paper's classified ads, a legislative bill-tracking system, and unlimited use of the Internet. NandO.net costs $15 a month for readers who already have Internet access; those without Internet access pay $30 a month per household for up to five separate user IDs.

Executive Editor Frank Daniels III says his company spent roughly $500,000 to launch Nando Land. BTI, a Raleigh-based long-distance phone carrier and partner in the project, is donating all school accounts. Although it's too soon to tell how popular NandO.net will be, Bruce Siceloff, the paper's online editor, says he's encouraged by the early results. Less than two weeks after its launch, the system had 1,400 users.

As for the future, Daniels predicts that, "within 10 years, our print edition, as we now know it, will go away. We'll still publish a print edition, but maybe only two editions a week." The paper publishes four daily print editions now; newsroom staff often refer to the online paper as the "fifth edition."

Newsletters

The combination of a large customer base and minimal distribution costs make the Internet an attractive environment for newsletter publishers, too. These days, Internet newsletters are springing up left and right on topics as varied as technology, publishing, and outdoor recreation.

Profile: Hot Off The Tree, or HOTT, as it's known, summarizes more than 100 print publications with an eye toward keeping readers up to speed on technological developments. Circulation is over 31,000 Internet users, all of whom receive the monthly magazine for free.

Publisher David Lewis (d.s.lewis@ieee.org) says his biggest expense is the time it takes him to compile and edit the newsletter. Lewis keeps overhead low by working from home and editing and publishing the magazine himself. Distribution is free because he gets free Internet access through his job. Once he completes an issue, he transfers it from his PC to an Internet-connected computer in San Jose, which transmits directly to the San Diego computer that maintains the circulation database.

Down the road, Lewis hopes to garner revenue from the newsletter by selling advertorials or paid feature stories focusing on specific vendor technologies. "I won't get the recognition of a Stewart Alsop," Lewis notes, "but I really may be able to edit and publish HOTT from the slopes in Montana."

Internet Services

Finding information on the Internet can often seem like the electronic equivalent of searching for a needle in a field full of haystacks. That's why many technology-savvy companies are rushing to provide everything from Internet access to Internet training, consulting, and system design.

Currently, there are hundreds of Internet access providers worldwide, from small companies serving a local customer base such as CyberGate in Deerfield Beach, Florida, to Performance Systems International of Herndon, Virginia, one of the largest Internet access providers in the world.

With Internet access rapidly becoming a commodity, access providers are searching for ways to stand out from the pack. Pipeline in New York and Computer Witchcraft in Kentucky are just two of the growing number of Internet providers offering Windows interfaces to its subscribers. Gateway to the World, an Internet access provider in Miami, offers an Internet menu system featuring on-screen commands in English, Spanish, and Portuguese.

Other companies are hoping to cash in by helping customers find information on the Internet. Because the Internet has no comprehensive "membership directory" or index of centralized services, many companies are racing to provide them. AT&T Business Communications was recently hired by The National Science Foundation, the government agency that built the Internet backbone, to create and publish a "white" and "yellow" pages directory for the Internet as part of its InterNIC program, a five-year project designed to provide public information about the Internet. Nothing is available yet, unfortunately.

Smaller companies such as Aldea Corp. are also publishing Internet directories. Aldea publishes the NetPages, both a "white" and "yellow" pages directory of the Internet, with a focus on business-to-business connectivity. Its first edition, distributed both electronically and in hard copy, debuted in March, with twice yearly editions planned.

Like the traditional phone company Yellow Pages, NetPages divides its listing by subject category—for example, books, computers, magazines, Internet service providers, hardware, and software. The difference is that, along with the traditional contact information, it lists e-mail addresses.

Tip: Learn more about the Internet NetPages by sending an e-mail message to Susan Estrada: sestrada@aldea.com

With all these companies making information available, some businesses are beginning to offer intelligent interfaces, or "filters," with which users can skip information they don't need. One example is the Stanford Netnews Filtering Service, which offers "a personalized netnews delivery service" that searches for and delivers via e-mail only those newsgroup postings that fit a customer's interest profile.

 Tip: To sign up for the Stanford Netnews Filter Service, send an e-mail message to `netnews@db.stanford.edu`. The service is free.

The Internet Group is another model of Internet-related business, providing Internet training and consulting. TIG offers day-long seminars on conducting business on the Internet for $175 per person, with a business-oriented overview of the tools and resources on the Internet.

It also provides participants with an online "tour" of many of the Internet points of interest for new users and provides a guidebook to help participants navigate the Internet on their own. TIG has also assisted O'Reilly, the publisher of the Global Network Navigator, and helped set up an Internet presence for U.S. Judaica, one of the country's largest distributors of Jewish books and religious objects.

The Future of Internet Commerce

The Internet today is a highly effective tool for communications, information-gathering, and multiple-site collaboration, but it still has a long way to go before it gains acceptance as a secure and reliable place to do business. Cultural obstacles also remain, though they're gradually lessening as the Internet community begins to realize that commerce is here to stay.

The biggest barrier to doing business on the Internet today, we believe, is differentiating your message from the tsunami of information that washes over each user every time they come near the network and standing out from the crowd in a way that allows your company to be viewed as a contributor to the growth of the network and online community, not a detractor from its original vision and goals.

Within the next few years, the Internet, or whatever the name the information superhighway takes, will be a busy thoroughfare for all kinds of voice, data, and video traffic. But, because the Internet is not yet a mass market and the technological infrastructure is not fully developed or easy to use, those companies likeliest to profit in the short term are businesses with heavy communications needs and those that sell information products and services, such as publishers, software designers, and online information scouts. At the same time, practically any business can benefit from at least some of the services and information sources available on the Internet today.

How Your Company Can Do Business on the Internet

Now that you've seen how other companies are cutting costs, boosting sales, and interacting with a world of customers and colleagues on the Internet, it's time to take a look at how to harness the power of the Internet to help your company grow.

Here's a checklist to give you some ideas:

- What are our company's communications needs? Do we frequently need to contact customers, employees or colleagues in different cities, states or countries? Do we typically exchange short notes or lengthy documents and files?

- Does our company make frequent use of phone, fax, and overnight mail for long-distance communications? Could the same communications be handled more efficiently via Internet e-mail? How much time and money would we be able to save by making the switch?

- Does our company have an internal e-mail system now? A local-area network or wide-area network? How technologically sophisticated are our employees?

- Do many of our customers, employees, and colleagues have access to e-mail systems? Do the people we most often do business with have accounts with commercial online services or other online networks that are Internet accessible?

- How does our company provide customer support today? Through a toll-free 800 number? A fax-back service? A dial-up computer bulletin board? How fast is our response time? What is the cost per customer of the current strategy?

- Does our company offer a product or service that could be marketed or sold on the Internet? Do we already publish a product catalog? Would our product or service be attractive to the affluent, well-educated users of the network?

■ How does our company share company-wide information resources? Is there a centralized database that could be accessed via a World Wide Web server, Gopher server, or other centralized computer system? How does our company share information with colleagues and research partners at other firms?

■ How does our company gather research and information? Do we have a library staff already in place? How skilled are our library staffers and other employees in searching Internet databases? What training would they require to become Internet experts?

■ What kind of computer system does our company have now? Is it already running TCP/IP-based networks or a compatible network protocol? What kind of network security do we already have in place? How much will we spend to protect our computer system with firewalls, encryption, and other Internet security measures?

It's important to understand that, although the Internet can be a valuable tool, it won't be of much use if your employees, colleagues, and customers are not comfortable using the technology. Sending e-mail over the Internet won't work if your customers rarely log on to check their electronic mailboxes. Likewise, gaining access to the Internet's vast storehouses of information is pointless unless you train your employees how to search them.

It's also important to recognize that any kind of Internet-facilitated business plan contains a hidden cost—education. By this, we mean educating your customers to buy products and ask questions via e-mail, teaching employees to conference online instead of picking up the phone and placing a long-distance call, and convincing colleagues to send reports via e-mail instead of by fax or overnight mail. Like any business tool, the Internet won't be effective until it's easy enough, convenient enough, and available enough for everyone in your business circle to use.

Internet Business Resources

One of the best ways to stay on top of what's happening on the Internet is to subscribe to a few mailing lists or join some of the many business-related Usenet discussion groups. Once you're signed up, it's a simple matter of keeping track of the many online conversations and finding free business ideas as close as your electronic mailbox. There are also a number of Internet business-related newsletters, both online and off, that you can subscribe to for a fee.

Here's where to go to get additional information on doing business on the Internet:

Mailing Lists (Discussion Groups)

■ Com-priv—Sponsored by Performance Systems International, a leading Internet access provider, the com-priv mailing list focuses on the commercialization and privatization of the Internet. To subscribe, send an e-mail message to com-priv-request@uu.psi.com. In the message body, type subscribe com-priv *your full name*.

■ Softpub—This list is a forum for Software Entrepreneurs, including discussion of programming, marketing, and packaging. To subscribe send a message to softpub-request@toolz.atl.ga.us

■ Econ-Dev—The Economics Development project is sponsored by the economic development department in Littleton, Colorado. Littleton's New Economy Project works primarily with small, innovative companies trying to give them the sophisticated tools they need to compete in the new global environment. Instead of "hunting" for distant companies and offering incentives to try to get them to locate in Littleton, the service concentrates on adding value to existing local companies. Services include using commercial databases to provide a variety of strategic information. To subscribe, send subscribe econ-dev to majordomo@csn.org

■ Net-happenings—The "net happenings" list is a service of InterNIC Information Services. The list's purpose is to distribute notices of interest to the Internet community—things like conference announcements, calls for papers, publications, newsletters, network tools updates, and network resources. To subscribe, send an e-mail message to majordomo@is.internic.net. In the message body, type subscribe net-happenings *your full name*.

There is no charge to subscribe to any of these lists.

Newsgroups

■ alt.business.misc—General discussions about managing your business, including how to start a business

■ misc.entrepreneurs—Discussions about operating a small business

■ biz.misc—Miscellaneous postings of a commercial nature

Newsletters and Magazines

■ *The Internet Business Journal*—Published by Strangelove Press, 60 Spring-field Road, Suite #1, Ottawa, Ontario CANADA K1M-1C7. A one-year subscription (six regular issues and six supplements) costs $149 for corporations and $75 for small businesses. The company can be reached at 613-747-6106 or at `mstrange@fonorola.net` on the Internet.

■ *The Internet Letter*—Published by financial writer Jayne Levin, in care of Net Week Inc., P.O. Box 33024, Washington, D.C. 20033-0024. A one-year subscription (12 monthly issues) costs $249. The company can be reached at 1-800-Net-Week (638-9335) or at `netweek@access.digex.net` on the Internet.

■ *The Internet Business Report*—Published by CMP Publications, Inc., can be contacted at 600 Community Dr., Manhasset, NY 11030 or by calling 1-800-340-6485. A one-year subscription costs $279.

■ *Internet World*—published by MecklerMedia of Freeport, CT, Internet World is less a technical or business monthly than a tour guide of the network, with frequent articles explaining how particular services work and what new information is on the net. . E-mail: `meckler@jvnc.net`. Phone: (800)-MECKLER. A one-year subscription costs $24.95.

MARKETING DO'S AND DON'TS

With more than 20,000,000 users throughout the world connected to the network and a growth rate that has been estimated as high as 15 percent a month, selling products on the Internet ought to be as easy as shooting fish in a barrel. If traditional direct-mail marketing typically yields a positive response rate of 2 to 3 percent, blanketing cyberspace with e-mail should result in hundreds of thousands of new sales leads.

Unfortunately for sales-hungry businesses, it doesn't work that way—though that hasn't stopped some entrepreneurs from trying. On the Internet, the traditional rules of sales and marketing are turned upside down. Not only does junk mail fall on deaf ears on the global network, but it often drives away the customers it was meant to attract. Slick ad copy with little or no informational content just doesn't fly, and businesses that send unsolicited advertisements to Internet users are more likely to generate a negative response than any interest in the product. Companies that don't take the hint even risk attack by angry hackers hurling huge payloads of system-clogging data.

Even if you've successfully marketed a product online before, it's important to recognize that what works on CompuServe, America Online, or Prodigy can backfire on the Internet. Just because you know how to drum up business on a commercial online service doesn't necessarily mean you're going to win customers on the Net—in fact, probably just the opposite. While the commercial online services try to restrict overt advertising to the "classifieds" sections of the service, they're typically less picky about what constitutes an ad posted on a special-interest bulletin board. Likewise, people who use commercial online services tend to be more tolerant of thinly disguised sales pitches than some of the purists on the Net.

The bottom line: *Caveat vendor* (Let the seller beware).

On a service like America Online, most groups tend to be fairly autonomous: If you alienate people in one forum by violating a guideline, others on the service are unlikely to hear about it. On the Internet, by contrast, users jealously guard what they view as the last bastion of non-commercial, non-advertising computer space, and a violation in one group, or even on a single mailing list, can often have far-reaching consequences. Worse, you need to be doubly careful because once you alienate users on the Internet, it can be difficult to return to their good graces. Like the proverbial elephant, Internet users have long memories.

No matter how lightly you tread and how religiously you adhere to the tenets of Internet culture, even the most subtly worded commercial message is bound to offend somebody on the Internet. Net-repreneurs who tell you they've never been flamed—attacked by hostile e-mail—are probably lying.

Profile: The first time that Rosalind posted a press release on the Internet about her consulting service for online publishers, she received nothing but positive responses for the first few days. Then, unbeknownst to her, someone forwarded the announcement to a mailing list about computer-assisted journalism. When she joined the list about a week later, she discovered to her horror that her announcement had become Topic A of the discussion and that list members were attacking not only her press release but her credentials and character.

Once the flame war died down, Rosalind began tacking up monthly press releases about her new newsletter, *Interactive Publishing Alert*, on the same list where she'd been attacked—and other lists as well. Though she has received a few flames, she has also received subscription orders from *People*, America Online, *U.S. News & World Report*, Apple Computer, Inc., the Massachusetts Institute of Technology, Ziff-Davis, and dozens of other major media and technology companies around the world.

When Dave's last book—*Teach Yourself UNIX In A Week*—was published, he posted a low-key press release explaining the book, how it differed from others with similar titles, and indicated that he was interested in hearing from journalists and other reviewers who would be interested in a copy of the text. Within 72 hours he'd heard from more than fifty qualified journalists, including writers at *U.S. News & World Report, the Library of Congress,* a German public TV program, *Dallas Morning News,* and the *Charlotte Observer.* Even with distribution across more than fifteen different forums, he never received a single flame or hostile e-mail message.

Without a doubt, posting the press release proved an important element in marketing Dave's book and Rosalind's newsletter and consulting firm.

Films have pivotal moments, musical scores have a key thematic passage, and murder mysteries turn on a particular event. This book is no different, and to us this chapter is the heart of the entire book. If there's only one chapter you read, this should be it. It will not only save you from committing some heinous misstep on the Internet but will also demonstrate a variety of road-tested approaches to marketing your products or services effectively through the network.

The purpose of this chapter is to show you what works and what doesn't in the wild, woolly, and always unpredictable world of Internet marketing:

> You'll find out why the Internet can be a direct marketer's dream come true—and how it can just as easily turn into a nightmare.
> You'll also hear from top marketing gurus and professionals and learn about new marketing strategies and techniques.
> You'll get tips on how to avoid getting flamed plus a glimpse of where Internet marketing is headed in the future.

Internet Marketing: Not Ready for Prime Time?

An analysis of any market begins with its size and demographics. Unfortunately, the Internet is unlike other online community, and quite unlike more traditional marketing venues, in that there is no scientific way to track the number of individuals and organizations that join. Best estimates suggest that about 20,000,000 people have some level of access to the Internet, ranging from e-mail only to a full high speed connection with complete access.

According to a study released in February by The Internet Society, an international organization that promotes cooperation among Internet networks worldwide, the Internet currently reaches over 2,220,000 host computers around the globe. Fifty-three percent of the Internet's smaller "internetworks" are commercial, 27 percent are devoted to research (including commercial enterprises), 9 percent are governmental, 6 percent are defense-related, and 5 percent are educational. Currently, 146 countries are connected to the Internet.

How fast is the Internet growing? No one really knows, and estimates vary widely. Newspapers and magazines, perhaps a bit too gullibly swallowing all the hype about the information highway, have estimated that over 1,000,000 users are joining the network each month. The Internet Society offers a more conservative estimate of one new user each 20 seconds, adding up to a more tranquil growth rate of 133,920 users each month.

We believe that the truth is somewhere in between. Our estimate is around 250,000 new users each month, and even that may be too high. Even if we're close, however, that still adds up to 3,000,000 new users on the network each year.

But that's the future—maybe. Let's look at the Internet today. Despite the network's vast promise, it's still much like the Arctic when it comes to marketing—a giant continent that's mostly under ice. The reason: Most consumers—the people who actually go out and buy the products—are not on the Internet. It's too difficult, it's too costly, and it fails to deliver the information they want in the way they want at the time they want it.

Here's the rub: Everybody is excitedly talking about the capabilities offered through an expensive high-speed Internet connection using powerful workstation hardware, and quoting the number of users who are signing up for cheap dialup accounts. As we've discussed in earlier chapters, a $20-per-month Internet account does not allow you to use a Mosaic browser or to view graphics, and according to market estimates by The Internet Group, inexpensive dialup accounts are by far the fastest growing segment of the Internet community.

Profile: A simple e-mail account and targeted online advertising enables Ceram Corporation of San Diego, California, to generate more than $3,000,000 in Internet-generated revenue for 1994.

Steve Case, president of America Online, spends much of his time debunking the myth of an all-encompassing Internet. At a recent Internet-related conference in Boston, he pointed out that the infrastructure needed for users to take maximum advantage of what the Internet has to offer—that is, a high-powered workstation, a leased line, and hard-to-configure software—is still out of reach for all but the technological elite. "The Internet is harder to use than you think," Case noted, "It's more expensive than you think, and it's smaller than you think."

Though Case's views are a little self-serving—after all, America Online has begun offering a limited array of Internet services through its commercial network— we believe he's got a point. Graphical browsers such as Mosaic can be difficult to install, and as Rosalind knows from her experience in accessing Mosaic through a 486 PC and a 14,400 bps modem, the program can be as slow as molasses when retrieving large amounts of graphics.

The related issue of how many of the millions of Internet users actually are the "technological elite," with sophisticated workstations and high-speed connections to the Internet, is another puzzle with lots of estimates but few solid facts. Case estimates those with full Internet capability at 1 in 10; others have suggested numbers that range from 15 percent to as low as 2 percent.

That's bad news for Internet advertisers who are banking on Mosaic to turn the text-based Internet into the cyberspace equivalent of the Home Shopping Network. Robert Raisch, president of The Internet Company, agrees, noting in a recent Internet posting that "Mosaic is a publishing tool designed by technologists, not publishers. This is a problem. A big one. Mosaic sells well to advertisers until they ask for demographics, to publishers until they ask for presentational control, and to users until they understand the cost." But, just because the Internet has some limitations as an advertising platform, the network can still be a very powerful medium through which to broadcast your commercial message. Think of it this way: If you're selling baseball cards to teenage boys, it wouldn't make sense to take out a full-page ad in The *Washington Post* or the European edition of the *Wall Street Journal.* But it may make sense to post a press release in the `rec.collecting.cards` Internet newsgroup.

For now, companies seeking to market products on the Internet must rely on e-mail messages, postings to Internet discussion groups, and other text-based announcements if they want to reach the widest possible audience. Include snazzy graphics by all means, with the expectation that more and more users will be able to access the World Wide Web with Mosaic and similar tools, but don't ever forget that the majority of your customers will be unable to see it for now.

Profile: Many advertising industry professionals have their doubts about the effectiveness of Internet marketing. Christopher Bonney of Bonney & Co. in Virginia Beach, Virginia, says that, until there's some reliable quantitative or qualitative marketing data about Internet users, few large advertising agencies or their clients will be willing to take a chance on this new medium, Bonney says. Although he finds it encouraging to read reports that publications displayed on the Internet's Electronic Newsstand are receiving 40,000 informational requests a day, Bonney says he wonders how many of these requests translate to revenue for the individual publications.

"Are these inquiries from computer hobbyists asking for info merely to see how the process works?" Bonney asks. "Are they 'tire kickers?' Or are they really good prospective customers, readers, or subscribers? I've seen lots of these kinds of audience claims, but I haven't seen any solid analyses."

From his perspective as an advertising agency president, Bonney sees two fundamental problems with marketing on the Internet:

First, is the audience on the Internet representative of a new group of consumers, or does it merely duplicate an audience reached through other, potentially less-expensive means?

Second, how does a company make its presence known to the Internet's users? Lacking a single, centralized place to search for information, potential customers may not know that your company is online. Bonney foresees a day when advertisers will pay a fee to be listed at popular access sites, and Dave sees the same thing happening today, as companies offer to sponsor the Internet Mall in return for being listed there.

Then there's the big-picture question: "Will the Internet become the information superhighway of the future?" Should a company invest in mastering the cultural and technological intricacies of this medium when it might be made obsolete by another communications technology?

Of course, many concerns about Internet marketing could vanish as more companies achieve commercial successes on the Internet. Think back to the fight that the Home Shopping Channel had in achieving legitimacy; advertising gurus initially ridiculed the idea as appealing only to poorly educated couch potatoes and doubted it would succeed. Then, one night, designer Diane Von Furstenberg went on and sold several millions of dollars worth of clothes in just a few hours.

Is Internet marketing ready for prime time? Probably not. But that doesn't mean that your company should wait until Internet advertising becomes as popular and as costly as a 30-second TV spot on Superbowl Sunday before deciding to test the waters. With the cost of Internet advertising so low and the size of the potential market so huge, it pays to jump in and get your feet wet today.

Rules and Regulations

Before you attempt to market your products or services on the Internet, it's important to understand the rules of Internet commerce.

Unlike TV or radio, no government agency regulates what can and cannot be said or sold on the Internet. In fact, four-letter words are zapped around the network every day with impunity. Nonetheless, there are still parts of the Internet—specifically, the National Science Foundation (NSFNet) backbone—that ban commercial traffic entirely. The NSFNet's Acceptable Use Policy (AUP), which applies to all systems connecting to the Internet through the NSFNet, reads, in part, as follows:

```
NSFNet Backbone services are provided to support open research and education
in and among U.S. research and instructional institutions, plus research arms
of for-profit firms when engaged in open scholarly communication and research.
Use for other purposes is not acceptable.
```

Elsewhere on the Internet, this commercial ban does not apply—though people connecting through university accounts or community free-nets are also likely barred from using the Internet for commerce.

Although many Internet access providers and discussion groups have their own rules governing what's acceptable and what isn't, there's usually a considerable leeway for commercial messages—especially if they combine promotional material with a generous dose of informational content.

Tip: Ask your Internet access provider for a copy of his or her acceptable-use policy, or AUP, and compare it to the NSFNet policy shown previously. Make sure that your intended use of the Internet is acceptable before signing up for an account.

Despite the changes of the last few years, however, the myth that the Internet is a business-averse environment remains prevalent, however. Now, more than 50 percent of the computer systems that comprise the Internet itself are commercial organizations and the commercial Internet—companies hooking their own networks up to the "network of networks"—is the fastest growing corner of the network. Tally the numbers and you'll see that more business users are on the Internet than all commercial online services combined.

As long as you're not bound by academic or non-profit acceptable-use policies, the only real restrictions that you'll face are those imposed by the Internet community itself. That's why it's so vitally important that any advertiser take the time to learn about the multifaceted Internet community, finding out what is and isn't considered acceptable practice and only then beginning to market their products and services.

A Direct Marketer's Dream Come True

Direct marketers are discovering what technologically advanced users have known for years: Hop aboard the Internet and watch your printing and postage costs vanish. On the Internet, your flat monthly fee enables you to blast out all the mail you want to whomever you want without paying a penny extra.

What's more, there's no need to pay thousands of dollars to rent a targeted mailing list. Internet users have already organized themselves into mailing lists and discussion groups focused on a variety of topics ranging from Star Trek to medieval literature, imported cars to cooking, investors to educators.

"Advertisers spend billions of dollars every year to communicate their message to potential consumers," says Internet advertising consultant Michael Strangelove. "Now businesses are discovering that they can advertise to the Internet community at a fraction of the cost of traditional methods...When 1998 rolls around and there are 100,000,000 consumers on the Internet, we may see many ad agencies and advertising-supported magazines go under as businesses learn to communicate directly to consumers in cyberspace."

For small businesses, the Internet can be a tremendous tool for achieving market equity with larger competitors and even for breaking into expensive—but potentially lucrative—foreign markets, markets traditionally reached through personal visits, attendance at international trade shows, or expensive worldwide advertising campaigns.

Thanks to the Internet, you can dial up your local Internet access provider and post a message that potential customers throughout the world will see. Take Rosalind's newsletter as an example. Interactive Publishing Alert now boasts subscribers from Canada, Britain, South Africa, Brazil, and Argentina, most of whom learned about her publication through the Internet itself, an advertising medium that cost Rosalind nothing.

Just as important as the international aspects of the Internet are its capability of leveling the playing field in the domestic market. On the Internet, no one knows how large your company is, so one-person shops can create an advertising and marketing presence in cyberspace that rivals the presence of much larger competitors. If you want to compete with a large multinational in cyberspace, you need merely make your presence known and offer customers an irresistible deal.

Caveat Vendor—Let the Seller Beware

Despite the Internet's enormous potential as a launching pad for grass-roots advertising, marketing efforts face considerable resistance from much of the Internet population.

One barrier is cultural—many Internet users come from academia, the government, and other non-profit environments and vehemently oppose the idea of the Internet being "exploited" for commercial purposes.

Another barrier that's just as important is financial: Not only does Internet "junk mail" sent to users waste their time, but, in some cases, it also costs the user money. CompuServe, for example, charges subscribers 15 cents for every Internet message they receive—whether it's a come-on for a get-rich-quick scheme or a letter from their daughter at college. Internet services that charge by the minute also penalize users who receive unsolicited commercial messages. The more mail a user receives, the more time it takes to retrieve.

Unlike the passive information resource services that we've considered earlier—the Web, FTP archive sites, and the like—active marketing strategies, particularly messages to e-mail lists, cost the receiver, too. Imagine how well advertising on television would be received if everyone watching a show was required to pay a dime for every commercial they viewed!

The fact that mailings cost the recipients money and transgress the implicit privacy of individual e-mail mailboxes is a big reason why companies that violate the cultural restrictions on Internet commerce can face the wrath of the entire community. Although few people bother to fire off a letter of complaint to an advertiser sending a glossy flier into their home mailbox, many Internet users are ready to react with significant hostility—*to flame,* in the lingo of the online community—towards a business they view as an Internet intruder.

Profile: Consider what happened to San Diego-based Magma, a small computer board manufacturer. In 1993, the company sent an advertising blurb to an electronic mailing list, a list with 3,000 subscribers. Though Mesa's direct mail blitz brought in over $30,000 in new business, says Michael Seidel, vice president of sales and marketing, the company was inundated with hate mail from almost 100 Internet users who were outraged that the network was being used for such a blatantly commercial purpose.

"It was as if we had molested their daughters," Seidel noted wryly.

The negative reaction, Seidel says, has not deterred from Magma sending out additional mass mailings, however. Now, the company removes from the list anyone who objects to being on it.

Profile: More recently, a Phoenix, Arizona legal firm called Canter & Siegel violated the cultural mores of the network in a much more blatant fashion, posting an advertisement for their immigration services to 9,000 Usenet discussion groups, most of which had nothing to do with the topic of the law firm's posting. Paying nothing beyond their $30 monthly connection fee, the firm offered to provide legal services to people worldwide who wished to participate in the planned U.S. immigration "green card" lottery.

Although Canter & Siegel may have reached millions of people by spraying electronic graffiti on thousands of cyberspace walls, the Internet community was outraged that the firm had violated the unwritten rules of the global electronic community.

The results of the poorly considered attempt were fast and furious: Not only was Canter & Siegel attacked by thousands of "flames," but the firm immediately lost its Internet access account (and subsequently other accounts with other access providers) and Internet community members quickly spread unflattering information about the firm throughout the network.

When asked about its marketing tactics, the firm told The Wall Street Journal that it has received thousands of inquiries as a result of its posting and more than $50,000 worth of business. The firm's partners say they've been encouraged by the response and plan to send out additional mailings in the future from new accounts on different Internet access providers.

All this raises an interesting question: How important is the good will of the Internet community if in-your-face advertising rings up sales? Canter & Siegel is certainly not the first company to violate cultural mores to make a buck—advertisements featuring barely clad women in computer magazines demonstrate this, too.

In the case of Canter & Siegel, the good will of the entire Internet community may not be too important.

On the other hand, as we've noted before, the Internet community has a long memory and because the distribution system is based on electronic communication, some Internet sites have already taken the violation as a call to arms and added safeguards, or filters, intended to block similar advertising blitzes from entering their systems.

Blitzing the Internet with junk mail isn't the only mistake that marketers can make on the Internet, however. Here are four more to keep in mind before you launch your marketing campaign:

- *Lumping all Internet users together*—With a population of over 20,000,000 users, the Internet is larger than any city in the world and more populous than many states. Although many users are highly educated technological professionals, the Internet also attracts college students, senior citizens, history buffs, sports fans, and just about any other socio-demographic group you can imagine. On the Internet, mass mailings just don't work.

  Instead, think of the Internet as a diverse set of specific markets, small online communities that have distinct histories, posting guidelines, rules, and discussion topics. Directed mailings are much more likely to succeed in this environment: Identify the target subpopulations, learn how the participants interact with one another and how they react to marketing and advertising material, and only then begin to use the group as a channel for your marketing efforts.

- *Tacking up a press release and walking away*—To win credibility on the Internet, you'll do best to join a discussion group and actively participate in the exchange of ideas. It's rarely enough to simply post a press release or product announcement online and never log on again.

  "Presence, not advertising, is the key that will unlock the commercial opportunities of the Internet," says Christopher Locke of Mecklermedia, a Westport, Connecticut, company that recently announced MecklerWeb, a World Wide Web site where businesses can market their wares to Internet customers.

- *Doling out information stingily*—To get something from the Internet, you should give something away, too, preferably for free. Because many users get their Internet accounts at no charge through their university or research institution, the idea of paying for information—something that's taken for granted on commercial online services such as CompuServe, Prodigy, and America Online—is foreign. Supplying a free taste of what you're offering can whet Internet users' appetites for a product or service they'll be willing to pay for later.

■ *Ignoring the Internet culture*—Treating the Internet as just another online service or computer bulletin board will limit your chance for marketing success. Time invested in reading books about the Internet and browsing messages posted on Internet discussion groups can not only teach you how to work with the community but also make you friends and win allies. If you're planning to include the Internet in your long-term marketing plans, make sure you start as a virtual tourist before you settle in for keeps.

Internet Marketing: The Consumer's View

Keeping those caveats in mind, it's educational to hear what Internet users—the consumers being targeted by these online sales efforts—have to say about Internet marketing.

Almost everyone on the Internet believes that crass, overt advertising is inappropriate and shouldn't appear on the network. Consider what Ken Hampton teaches international business and management at Marylhurst College in Oregon, has to say:

In general, I think all-out advertising on the Internet is a bad idea. While advertising can contain worthwhile information, advertising does span the full spectrum from pure scam on one end to genuinely useful information on the other. The Internet is a single channel, unlike commercial television, radio, or billboards. Once an advertiser has your address, as a consumer I do not have the option of changing the channel. Only at some expense and considerable inconvenience to those with whom I want to communicate can I change my electronic address.

Hampton sees some parallels between the prohibitions on overt advertising on public television and a similar cultural limitation on the Internet. He suggests that many of the people who are active Internet users are likely to also enjoy public television, for precisely the same reason—information without advertising clutter.

Internet Advertising: The Marketer's View

Despite the resistance to traditional advertising on the part of Internet users, professional marketers say there are a number of ways to reach Internet users effectively, directly, and inexpensively.

To find out some of the current thinking on the topic, we polled some marketers who regularly participate in a marketing discussion group on the Internet. One of the most interesting responses came from Mark Hornung Sr. of Bernard Hodes Advertising. He says he sees three main advantages to marketing on the Internet, a community he characterizes as upscale, well-educated, and likely to be more highly paid, and to be early technology adapters:

- *Greater participation by the viewer*—A computer requires direct user interaction to move from program to program, whereas a television allows purely passive viewing,

- *The opportunity to present more information*—Unlike an advertisement in a magazine or even an infomercial, the Internet culture encourages vendors to offer significant levels of detail about the product or service being offered. Supporting research, samples, and other means ensure that no questions should be left unanswered.

- *Timeliness*—Unlike the three-month lead time of magazine advertising, or even the weeks-long lead time of television or radio, Internet advertising can be distributed and received by potential customers the same day and in many cases, within the hour.

Here are some of his tips for would-be Internet marketers: "To avoid getting flamed, don't ask for money. Don't send 'junk mail.' And remember that there's no way to completely avoid getting flamed, other than not doing anything remotely commercial."

Hornung, like many marketing professionals, has also spent a lot of time trying to ascertain what kind of products would sell best through the Internet. He believes that the products that can most benefit from online advertising remain those of a technical nature.

One example of a technical service that has become quite popular on the Internet is professional recruitment: With an audience of potentially thousands of qualified technical professionals, the Internet is in many ways a "head hunter's" dream. Indeed, Bernard Hodes Advertising recruits new employees of its own through the network, noting "it's been successful for us because we're not asking users to send money, we're offering them the opportunity to make some."

Marketing Strategies That Work

So far, we've talked about the Internet market as it exists today. But it's important to recognize that the Internet culture is in a state of flux. What works with today's Internet users may not apply tomorrow.

As more private companies pour in and more users join the Internet from commercial online services, the community is rapidly assuming the characteristics of the online world as a whole—less technologically elite and more receptive to business.

For now, however, those who seek to market their products and services on the Internet must still tread cautiously and spend some time learning the in's and out's of this virtual marketplace. It may be better to miss out on a few sales now than to gain a reputation as a virtual carpetbagger, a reputation that could linger for years to come.

Profile: One of the most effective ways to reach today's Internet market is through passive advertising, or corporate sponsorship. One company that has taken this tack is Performance Systems International, the Herndon, Virginia, Internet access provider that sponsors the Internet's com-priv discussion group. Com-priv is an electronic forum focused on topics surrounding the commercialization and privatization of the Internet. Through its sponsorship of the com-priv list, PSI has gained wide visibility and generated considerable good will throughout the Internet community.

Profile: Press releases posted on Internet discussion groups can also be effective—provided that they're worded carefully. Andrew Currie of Cyberspace Development posted an announcement about his company and its services on the net-happenings discussion group in November, 1993. As a result of that one posting, Currie says, the home-based Boulder, Colorado, company received close to 40 sales leads and only three e-mail notes from people who complained. In the firm's release, Currie pledged that Cyberspace Development would post only announcements about the company and its activities that were "informative and of interest to the Internet community" and would "contribute to the quality of the Net's culture by adding free information."

This doesn't mean, of course, that direct marketing is a dead letter on the Internet—especially not if it generates sales. Canter & Siegel, the "green card" law firm, recently told a *New York Times* reporter that it was so pleased with the response to its marketing blitz that its partners are now planning to write a book on how to advertise on the Internet!

Seidel, vice president of the circuit board company that drew scores of flames with its direct mail blitz, told us that he's planning another direct e-mailing on the Internet and doesn't care if he tramples a few electronic toes along the way. The bottom line, he says, is that his company rang up sales of $30,000 from its first mailing without spending a dime to do it.

While there are as many different ways to market products on the Internet as there are products to market, they tend to fall into a number of basic categories.

We've already looked at passive techniques that respect the culture of the Internet, but there are other effective approaches to selling products on the network, too.

Direct Mail

Because each Internet posting contains the "return address" of the sender, it's easy for an advertiser to join a discussion group and build a database of sales leads.

For example, a bicycle manufacturing company could hang out in the `rec.bicycles` newsgroup for a few days, scoop up several hundred names and e-mail addresses, and then send pitch letters promoting its new mountain bike.

Although direct mail may be the most straightforward way to reach Internet users, it's also the most risky—and the fastest way to receive hostile electronic mail, faxes, and other feedback from the very community you seek to sell. Nevertheless, that hasn't stopped some companies from trying it with greater and lesser degrees of success.

Profile: J.S. McBride & Associates of Los Altos, California, has made a lot of money selling collections of electronic mail addresses that it gathers from various online sources, including the Internet. Jim McBride, the company's president, says that his own company sent out an e-mailing last year to about half a million people and got a 35 to 40 percent positive response rate. Because he worded his sales pitch carefully and kept it short and to the point, "my flame rate was only .7 percent. Indeed, when direct mail is used correctly, the number of people offended by it is very small," he says.

At the same time, McBride says, he has suspended selling Internet mailing lists for now because several of his customers have abused them by sending long-winded solicitations that he felt violated the spirit of the Internet culture. However, he says he's continuing to build a demographic database of users, which now has roughly 2,500,000 e-mail addresses.

Despite the impressive success that McBride has enjoyed with his careful direct mail campaign on various computer networks, we counsel all companies to think carefully before trying it themselves. On the Internet, the chance to fire back an angry message is only a keystroke or mouse-click away. The bottom line: If you send a mailing to 1,000 users, you need to be prepared potentially to receive 1,000 hostile responses.

Press Release Postings

Another less offensive technique is to tack up a press release about your product, service, or company on an Internet "bulletin board" (that is, a mailing list or newsgroup).

Mailing lists can be especially effective. By posting a press release to a mailing list—that is, a discussion group about a particular topic or issue—you can broadcast your message to all of the list's subscribers while posting it only once. That's because anyone who subscribes to that mailing list automatically receives a copy of anything that's posted to the group.

The downside, of course, is that, if the members of the list find your posting offensive, you've turned off your entire target market in one fell swoop.

When posting a press release on the Internet, keep two things in mind: the rules (both written and unwritten) of the group you're posting to and the ratio of information to hype that your press release contains.

After you subscribe to a mailing list, you'll sometimes receive a "form letter" containing information about what should and should not be posted there; some groups make FAQ (Frequently Asked Questions) documents available through e-mail. Read these files carefully to determine the nature of the forum and acceptable-use policies.

Don't forget to spend a week or two as a cyber-tourist, watching what kind of topics are discussed and how participants react. If you're not sure whether your posting is appropriate, we recommend sending a brief note to the list moderator, or discussion host, and asking for advice.

Some lists, such as net-happenings and com-priv, are very receptive to new product announcements, conference announcements, and the like concerning Internet-related products and services. Others, such as the Association for Computers & Writing, a potentially excellent place to market word processing and grammar software, are much less so.

> **Tip:** As a general rule, we suggest waiting at least after joining an Internet discussion forum, whether a Usenet group or electronic mailing list, before posting a press release there. We've seen too many people who instantly wore out their welcome by blundering into an existing discussion or immediately subverting an existing group for a new purpose.

Wherever you post your release, it's crucial to keep the informational content high. While there's no hard-and-fast rule, we suggest that the information/promotion ratio should be around 80/20. Let's consider some examples of press re leases that were well received on the Internet.

The first is an announcement regarding the contents of the March, 1994, issue of *Interactive Publishing Alert*, the monthly newsletter that Rosalind publishes. Notice the information to promotion ratio as you read the press release and recall that the target audience for the posting are professional journalists and others associated with newspapers and magazines. Most importantly, this press release didn't generate a single hostile message or response from the Internet community:

```
***

The March issue of Interactive Publishing Alert is now available.

This month's issue contains highlights of last month's Interactive Newspapers
'94 conference, co-sponsored by The Kelsey Group and Editor & Publisher, which
drew more than 600 editors, publishers and consultants from around the world.
The issue includes profiles of Mercury Center, The San Jose Mercury's joint
venture with America On-line, and News in Motion, a full-color multimedia
newspaper published by Todd Chronis of WalkSoft Corp. There are also reports
on audiotex, on-line shopping, database marketing, personal digital
assistants, N11 and interactive television plus a sampling of reader opinion
on Bicycling Magazine On-line, one of America Online's newest electronic
publishing alliances. The issue also contains a roundup of the latest on-line
publishing deals and excerpts of speeches by Interactive Newspapers '94
speakers and panelists.

Here are some of the highlights:

* Donald Brazeal, editor and publisher of Digital Ink, a Washington Post
subsidiary formed to develop and manage the company's electronic products:
"There are some visionaries out there in other industries that ... want to
rent us a hotdog stand in their electronic shopping mall. ... As traditional
publishers, our greatest risk is letting others define us."
```

* Ross Glatzer, president of Prodigy Services Co., the United States' largest on-line service with over two million members : "I believe the marriage of major newspapers and national on-line services makes the most sense. ... The newspaper brings to the table its editorial strengths along with skill in marketing to newspaper readers. The on-line service brings a proven delivery mechanism, knowledge of the intricacies of the information highway, network-management capabilities and skill in marketing to computer users."

* Randolph Charles, director of marketing and new business development, Newsday and New York Newsday: "The move to multimedia for newspapers is an imperative, not an ancillary product opportunity. ... A position you should take is one of placing many small bets, ... [to] try to get your toe in lots of different pots of water as you move into the new world."

* Chris Jennewein, general manager of Mercury Center, an on-line and audiotex extension of The San Jose Mercury News: "This is not a small risk. This is a medium-to-large risk."

Here are some key numbers presented at the conference that publishers ought to consider before venturing into interactive media:

* Newspapers' advertising share is continuing to shrink even as large newspaper chains report hefty profits. While newspapers continue to command the greatest share of U.S. advertising dollars, raking in $31.8 billion last year, according to McCann-Erickson, their share of the advertising market has slipped from 27.6 percent in 1980 to 23.1 percent today, losing ground to direct mail and Yellow Pages.

* Though 33 percent of U.S. households now own computers and 13 percent have modems, on-line services are still far from a mass market. Roughly 4 million people subscribe to the four major on-line services, Prodigy, CompuServe, America On-line and Genie; more than 16 million people read TV Guide.

* Nevertheless, newspapers are betting heavily that interactive media will grow. The number of newspapers offering audiotex, fax-on-demand and/or on-line services has soared from 42 in 1989 to 2,700 today, according to The Kelsey Group.

Interactive Publishing Alert, a monthly on-line newsletter tracking developments in interactive publishing and electronic media, provides hands-on information and advice for editors and publishers thinking about going on-line and for publications that have ventured on-line already. Each issue contains a timely analysis of current trends plus interviews with key managers and decision-makers and case studies of publications that are doing things right (and wrong!). Future issues will explore on-line advertising, Internet storefronts, newspapers on the Net, multimedia, niche marketing, and other topics related to interactive publishing.

Interactive Publishing Alert, is edited and published by Rosalind Resnick, a veteran business and technology writer who specializes in on-line services and consults with newspapers and magazines expanding into interactive media. Ms. Resnick is also the author of Exploring the World of On-line Services (Sybex, 1993). She can be reached on the Internet at rosalind@harrison.win.net.

```
Subscription Info: A subscription to Interactive Publishing Alert is available
for $149 for 12 monthly issues; $79 for six monthly issues; $45 for three
monthly issues, and $15 for single issues. To order this newsletter on-line,
use Gopher to connect to marketplace.com, an Internet information mall, by
typing 'gopher marketplace.com'. Once you see the MarketPlace menu, select the
'Interactive Publishing Alert' menu item. To subscribe via e-mail, send a
message to ipa@marketplace.com. Please include your name, title, company name,
phone number, billing address, credit card number, expiration date, desired
subscription length, and the electronic mail box to which you'd like your
issues sent.

***
```

The second example we'll show is a more succinct message about the release of Dave's previous book: *Teach Yourself UNIX in a Week*. The goal of this press release was to simultaneously announce the book's publication and to differentiate it from the many other UNIX books on the shelf.

The ostensible target audience was book reviewers and educators, but, in fact, the hope was that it would pique the interest of users throughout the community. It was posted to a variety of different Usenet groups and mailing lists, and the response was terrific:

```
From: taylor@Netcom.Com (Dave Taylor)
Subject: New Book: Teach Yourself UNIX In A Week
Date: Sun Mar 13 22:06:28 PST 1994

I'm pleased to announce the publication of "Teach Yourself UNIX In A
Week" from SAMS/Prentice-Hall. This is a new addition to an admittedly
crowded market, but with a few differences that might just pique your
interest...

Most importantly, I have gone to great lengths to include the *output*
of all commands discussed in the book (it's amazing to me how many
intro books show users the command to type, but then don't show what'll
be displayed as a result), and I also focus on the most important and
common flags and commands rather than an encyclopaedic listing of flags
or rewritten man pages: there's no reason to pay for either of the
latter styles of book!

"Teach Yourself UNIX In A Week" is over 700 pages, quite extensive (it
includes a long discussion of Usenet, gopher, and FTP, for example, as
well as a foray into programming and Unix programming tools), and is
widely available at bookstores near you, notably Borders, Barnes & Noble
and all technical bookstores. You can also order it directly from
the publisher by calling (800) 428-5331.

The full citation:

  Taylor, Dave, "Teach Yourself UNIX In A Week", SAMS/Prentice-Hall,
  1994, $28.00 US/$36.95 CAN.  714 pages, including two appendices
  and an extensive glossary. ISBN: 0-672-30464-3  [for both BSD & SVR4]
```

```
Questions? Thoughts? Interested in a review or evaluation copy for
professional purposes? Drop me a note!

Thanks for your time.

                                          -- Dave Taylor
Internet Traveller                        taylor@netcom.com
```

Internet press releases can also be succinct pointers to more extensive information available through the Web, FTP, or even an automatic e-mail respondent. The latter is a strategy we recommend because every one of the millions of Internet users has access to electronic mail, whereas few people can access more sophisticated systems like the Web.

Many Internet shopping mall services offer this service along with their Gopher sites and World Wide Web sites. This way, you can neatly sidestep the risk of a flame war—a series of hostile messages from angry users—by keeping the promotional information out of the press release. Even better, most of the popular automatic e-mail response systems (`filter`, `procmail`, `majordomo`) keep track of who requested information, offering a ready database for future direct mailings.

Here's an example of a press release that takes this approach:

```
InterBEX (Business Exchange) is a commercial information service that
provides a round-the-clock e-mail accessible resource from which Internet
users can request - on demand - 24 hours per day - classified advertising
material and content oriented advertorial e-text posted by individuals,
and by business and professional vendors of products and services.

Access to InterBEX for information retrieval is FREE to all Internet users.
Advertisers can have classified advertisements and advertorial e-text made
available to the global Internet through InterBEX at nominal cost.

InterBEX respects, agrees with, promotes and supports a philosophy of
non-intrusive and non-solicitous commercial use of the Internet. E-mail
advertisements are sent to Internet users only upon request - no unsolicited
ads will be distributed through InterBEX.

        FOR A CURRENT INDEX OF INFORMATION AVAILABLE SEND E-MAIL TO:

                    InterBEX-index@intnet.bc.ca

          (automatic info server - no subject or body is req'd)

For advertising rates and data send e-mail to: InterBEX-FAQ@intnet.bc.ca
(multiple to: addresses and C.C.'s are not processed)
```

Billboards on the Net

A very low-key way to promote your business or service on the Internet is through the signature portion at the end of each message that you send to discussion groups or mailing lists. Think of these "signature files" as bumper stickers that tell passing cars about your firm—or perhaps even vanity license plates—and you'll start to gets the idea. Rosalind calls these "mini-billboards."

We should caution you, however, that blatant or extensive blurbs like "Make Money Fast: Send E-mail!" are sure to raise hackles in any Internet discussion group. Internet users consider it perfectly acceptable, however, to include a line or two about your company and what it does in the signature portion at the end of your message.

It's also perfectly acceptable to include your telephone, fax number, and postal address on business postings. This way, people who see your posting and like what you have to say can call or write if they're interested in learning more about your business.

Here's a good example of what we're talking about from Gordon Cook, publisher of the COOK Report on the Internet. All articles or messages that Gordon sends to mailing lists or Usenet discussion groups include the following few lines at the bottom:

```
Gordon Cook, Editor Publisher:  COOK Report on Internet -> NREN
431 Greenway Ave, Ewing, NJ 08618
cook@path.net                               (609) 882-2572
COOK Report Subscriptions Range in price from $85 to $500.
```

Consultants will also often use the signature space as a spot for some succinct advertising, as this example from Jerod Husvar of Kent State University demonstrates:

```
 / Jerod J. Husvar        \ / Computer Consultant at large.                  \
:> jerodh@mcs.kent.edu   <:> Industrial Hygiene Technician                    <:
:> Kent State University <:> Certified Asbestos Hazard Evaluation Specialist <:
 \ Kent, Ohio  USA        / \ I speak only for myself, thank you.             /
```

Another type of Internet billboard is associated with the Internet *finger* service, a simple way to ascertain whether a user is logged into a system and learn more about that user.

> **Profile:** Jeff Freeman of Front Porch Computers, a mail-order computer retailer in rural Chatsworth, Georgia, says he uses his "signature file" to rake in roughly 60 percent of the company's $4,000,000 annual sales to customers all over the world. Whenever Freeman responds to an Internet user's question, anyone who reads the messages on that board can see the note and contact Freeman if they're interested in what he has to sell. Though Freeman admits he got flamed a few times when he first ventured onto the Internet last year, "now, we don't get any flames at all, probably because there are so many new people who have come on and they have been much more offensive than we have."

All public access Internet services support finger and the key file to create is either called `.plan` in UNIX or `plan.txt` on PCs. Your plan file can contain just about anything you'd like, including information about your company's products or service or your personal credentials; it can even include a price list and other detailed sales and marketing information.

What makes a commercial plan file acceptable on the Internet is that it remains invisible until other users request it using the finger utility. And how does the Internet user know what account to "finger"? Because you've advertised it in your signature. With a plan file, you can be as promotional as you want to be because the Internet user is seeking information from you; therefore, it's not considered unsolicited advertising.

Here's an interesting example from Celestin Company, a Macintosh hardware vendor that supplies cables for high speed modems. Though the company has a brief blurb in Dave's Internet Mall, Internet users can use the finger utility to check out more detailed information on the company's products (`celestin@pt.olympus.net`):

```
IS YOUR STORE-BOUGHT CABLE PROPERLY WIRED FOR YOUR HIGH-SPEED MODEM?

Many Macintosh users and retailers are unaware that high-speed modems, such
as the new SupraFAXModem v.32bis, require a special hardware handshaking
cable for optimum performance. The CompUnite High-Speed Mac Modem Cable
supports hardware handshaking; its support of DTR also makes it compatible
with standard modems as well as software packages such as Appletalk Remote
Access.

The CompUnite High-Speed Mac Modem Cable is a BMUG Choice Product. BMUG is
the largest Macintosh user group in the world. According to the Spring 1993
BMUG Newsletter, "Most high speed modems can take advantage of hardware
handshaking modem cables. They can increase data throughput by up to 20%.
```

```
Generally the cables you get at the store don't support it, and those that
do tend to cost over $25. These [CompUnite] cables work fine with non-high
speed modems as well, and that's cool."

The CompUnite High-Speed Mac Modem Cable is available for only $14.00, and
this includes standard shipping, as well as sales tax for Washington
orders. Customers who for any reason are dissatisfied with their purchase,
can take advantage of our 30-day return privilege. Here is our pinout:


    Mac function      RS-232 function    Mac pin    DB-25 pin
    ------------      ---------------    -------    ---------
    RxD (receive)     Receive Data       5          3
    TxD (transmit)    Transmit Data      3          2
    Ground            Ground             4 & 8      7
    HSKi              CTS                2          5
    HSKo              RTS & DTR          1          4 & 20
    GPi               CD                 7          8


If you are interested in the CompUnite cable, EMAIL the following
information to us:

Yes, I'd like to purchase the CompUnite High-Speed Mac Modem Cable, part
number 7001.

Your Name:
Address:
City:
State:
Zip:
Phone:
Quantity:
Total amount of order (Quantity * $14):
VISA/MC Number:
Expiration Date:
Name on Card:

You may EMAIL your order to any of the following email addresses:

AOL: Celestin
CompuServe: 71630,650
Internet: celestin@pt.olympus.net

Or, FAX your order to 206 385 3586
Or, order via voice at 800 835 5514

Celestin Company, 1152 Hastings Avenue, Port Townsend, WA  98368. 206 385-3767.
```

Relationship Marketing

Another highly effective Internet marketing technique is what MBA programs call
relationship marketing. Instead of—or in addition to—posting a press release
about your company's products or services, you join a discussion group focused

on a topic related to your company or industry and then post messages, answer questions and contribute to the general discussion. While it's hard to market a specific product this way, it's a good way to boost your visibility among customers you want to reach.

If you read trade or industry magazines, you've already encountered this sort of marketing strategy—for example, articles about engine design written by an engineer at an automobile company or a story about new printing technologies from a consultant who works in the printing industry.

Silicon Graphics demonstrates this daily by encouraging its engineers to participate in SGI-related Usenet newsgroups. Freelance writer Kevin Savetz also uses relationship marketing by managing and maintaining the Internet Book List.

Both of this book's authors use relationship marketing, too. Dave specializes in helping companies exploit the Internet to sell products or services in an Internet-friendly manner. To accomplish this, he maintains the Internet Mall, the only free storefront in cyberspace. He accomplishes a number of goals through this project, including an opportunity to interact with most businesses using the Internet for commerce.

More subtle gains result from this strategy too: Through maintaining the Mall, he learns more about which companies are finding the Internet a friendly, lucrative environment, and how they use the various services available. The Mall also serves as an extensive database of companies and services for market analysis. Since launching the Internet Mall in early 1994, Dave has been interviewed by a variety of magazines, most recently *Business Week.*

This approach has also worked quite well for Rosalind. In addition to posting notices about her newsletter on the various journalism and business discussion groups, she also contributes her proverbial two cents on topics being discussed in the various forums. As a result of her high visibility there, she has been interviewed in her capacity as an online publishing expert by *U.S. News & World Report, The Los Angeles Times,* and *The Seybold Report on Desktop Publishing.*

One afternoon, shortly after posting some comments about how newspaper publishers can encourage more women readers to access their online editions, she received a call from a newspaper editor who ordered a six-month subscription to Rosalind's newsletter. The first thing she told Rosalind was that she thought the note Rosalind had written about women online was right on target. Whether or not her posting closed the sale, it certainly didn't hurt.

Profile: Lots of other companies are doing it, too—especially smaller firms that lack the time and resources to network at trade shows and chamber of commerce meetings.

NetPro Computing of Scottsdale, Arizona, has successfully used relationship marketing to win government contracts. By swapping e-mail with government officials on the Internet and CompuServe, the 12-employee software development company has boosted sales to local, state, and federal government agencies to more than 50 percent of its $1,066,000 annual revenues, says Corbin Glowacki, the company's sales manager. Currently, the U.S. Marine Corps is the company's single largest customer followed closely by the Federal Deposit Insurance Corp. and the Resolution Trust Corp.

"Because most of the large government organizations are online, we can go directly to the end users and network administrators and convince them that they have a need for what we offer," says Glowacki, who estimates that his company receives 30 orders a month from government sources. "We usually create the proposal, and we're pretty much a shoe-in for it when the contract is awarded."

Relationship marketing comes naturally to small companies where the president often answers his or her own phone and e-mail, but larger companies accustomed to paying large fees for slick advertising messages broadcast to mass markets may find it more difficult to interact with customers one-on-one.

This requirement of interacting with the community, of bringing some value to the network community, is crucial to success on any long term venture on the Internet. Though some companies have tried to use the Internet as a blanket advertising medium without any interest in contributing to the discussion, we strongly advise against doing that and instead encourage you to think of ways in which you and your employees can help make cyberspace a better place to do business. If you're spending the time, of course, make sure you focus on topics relevant to your business and participate for a while before you look for sales and marketing results.

We take a more in-depth look at relationship marketing and Internet discussion groups in Chapter 6, "The Electronic Schmooze."

Display Advertising (World Wide Web)

Despite the many marketing opportunities available on the Internet today, the Holy Grail of Internet marketing is Mosaic, the popular point-and-click interface to the World Wide Web.

The Web is rapidly growing, not only as a way to access thousands of multimedia information services on the Internet, but as a way to work with the growing World Wide Web, a general-purpose service for hypertext information retrieval that's captured the fancy of businesses, publishers, and advertising agencies around the world.

Once these tools become universally available to the Internet community, advertisers will have the power to lure Internet users to their own colorful, graphical, easy-to-use shopping malls and then present whatever information they desire to the now captive, interested audience.

And, yet, it may take several years before the Web and its graphical capabilities become accessible to the majority of Internet users. Mosaic, for example, is growing at an astonishing rate—more than 2,000,000 copies of the program have been distributed from the National Center for Supercomputer Applications—and the network traffic levels of the Web are also exploding. However, the fastest-growing type of Internet access account is not the multimedia-capable, Mosaic-friendly SLIP or PPP account, but the less expensive, text-based dialup service.

But that's only today. Some consultants believe it won't be long before Mosaic and other multimedia Web browsers take off in a big way.

"I think the problem regarding WWW demographics is a temporary one," says Jeremy Allaire, a Minneapolis consultant specializing in electronic publishing. "Market and technological trends are pretty clear about where things are going—and fast."

Profile: Whether or not the World Wide Web is going to become the pervasive interface to the Internet a few years down the road, many companies are busy creating interactive billboards and information servers on the Internet called *home pages*. One company that has big plans for the World Wide Web is Mecklermedia, publisher of *Internet World* magazine. According to the company's Chris Locke, MecklerWeb's goal is to be "a commercial Internet space in which corporate sponsors and professional associations can cooperatively offer value-added multimedia information to networked communities." MecklerWeb's opening screen is shown in Figure 5.1.

As an example, a drug company could pay an annual fee to join MecklerWeb, allowing it to distribute information to all physicians who access the Meckler system (for free), including graphics and hypertext links to a vast array of documents and data. Instead of bombarding the doctors with a bewildering array of advertisements, drug company representatives could offer advice and information directly to their customers. Advertisers would also be able to include corporate logos to the information they provide, just as IBM and other large firms do at the free art shows and exhibitions they sponsor throughout the world.

Together with partners AlterNet, a major Internet access provider, WAIS, the company that pioneered the Internet search engine that bears its name, and Digital Equipment Corp., a computer manufacturer specializing in UNIX-based systems, MecklerWeb offers businesses the opportunity to showcase their companies and products to professionals in the fields of medicine, law, technology, sports, art, and entertainment. Corporate sponsors will pay $25,000 to market their services on the MecklerWeb; 20 percent of that fee will go to the medical, legal, and other trade associations that bring their members on board to hire a discussion leader for the group.

Although $25,000 is a lot of money to a small business, Locke says, it's a drop in the bucket for the Fortune 1000 companies Meckler is hoping to attract. Many large companies, he notes, can spend a similar sum before they've finished evaluating whether they should advertise on the Internet at all.

Another business-oriented Web experiment is CommerceNet (see Figure 5.2), launched in April, 1994, by a consortium of Silicon Valley companies. Participants include BARRNet, Enterprise Integration Technologies (EIT), and Stanford University's Center for Information Technology (CIT). CommerceNet is operated by the CommerceNet Consortium, a non-profit corporation funded by a $6,000,000, three-year grant from the U.S. government's Technology Reinvestment Project. Matching funds are also donated by the State of California and the various member companies.

In its announcement, CommerceNet said it "seeks to revolutionize the Valley's core electronics, software and information service industries by making interaction between customers, suppliers and development partners as efficient as interactions among internal departments."

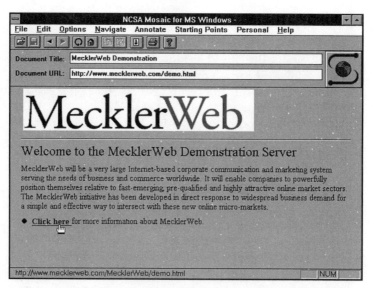

Figure 5.1. The opening screen at MecklerWeb: explore it for yourself by accessing the URL http://www.mecklerweb.com/.

According to the consortium, any individual or organization will be able to offer information, goods, and services on CommerceNet by creating a multimedia "home page" on its server and listing it in appropriate directories on the CommerceNet server, as well as with value-added directories and referral services operated by third parties.

In conjunction with the CommerceNet announcement, EIT, the National Center for Supercomputer Applications (NCSA), and RSA Data Security also announced a plan to jointly develop and distribute a secure version of the Mosaic Web browser. Under the agreement, EIT will integrate its Secure-HTTP software with public key cryptography from RSA into NCSA Mosaic clients and World Wide Web (WWW) servers. The enhancements will then be made available to NCSA for widespread public distribution and commercial licensing.

Although this doesn't make Mosaic capabilities accessible to more people, it does take an important step toward improving the security of Internet commercial transactions. The system is expected to include both public key-based encryption and a digital signature feature, as discussed in the previous chapter. Once proven and widely available, secure Mosaic will expand online commerce as consumers become comfortable transmitting credit card information through the networks.

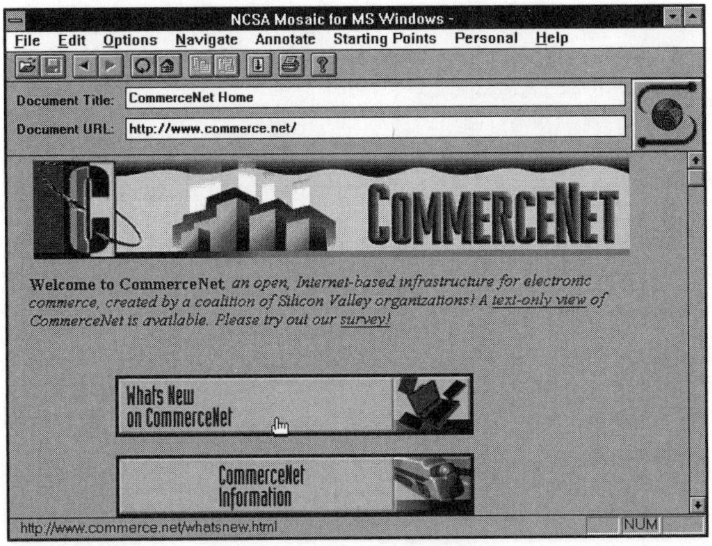

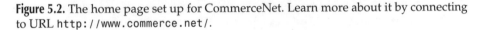

Figure 5.2. The home page set up for CommerceNet. Learn more about it by connecting to URL http://www.commerce.net/.

Jay Tenenbaum, CEO of EIT, observes that "while Mosaic makes it possible to browse multimedia catalogs, view product videos, and fill out order forms, there is currently no commercially safe way to consummate a sale. With public key cryptography, however, one can authenticate the identity of trading partners so that access to sensitive information can be properly tracked."

The secure version of NCSA Mosaic is expected to include a feature whereby users can affix digital signatures to purchase orders and time stamps to contracts. What's more, sensitive information such as credit card numbers and bid amounts will be secure through message encryption. Together, these capabilities should provide the foundation for a broad range of financial services, including the network equivalents of credit and debit cards, letters of credit, and credit checks, enabling Internet users to safely and easily transact business.

Another new addition to Web-facilitated commerce is The Internet Shopping Network (see Figure 5.3), which bills itself as the nation's first electronic superstore on the Internet. Its catalog contains more than 10,000 software and hardware products.

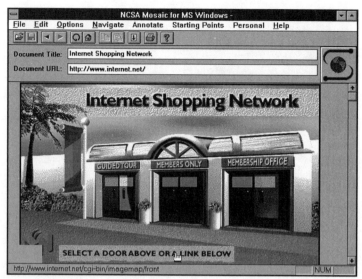

Figure 5.3. A brief trip to the Internet Shopping Network, home of over 10,000 software and hardware products, is as easy as typing the URL `http://shop.internet.net/` into a Web browser.

"The structure of the Internet's World Wide Web, the advent of the Mosaic browser and the introduction of CommerceNet have enabled us to offer users an exciting shopping experience where anyone can browse thousands of computer products and buy them at the lowest prices available anywhere with the click of a mouse," says Randy Adams, president and founder of the interactive shopping network.

We take a more detailed look at the World Wide Web, the Mosaic Web browser, and Internet shopping malls in Chapter 11, "Internet Cybermalls."

The Downside of Internet Marketing—Flame Wars and Worse

In this chapter, we've talked a lot about the importance of tailoring your marketing and advertising tactics to fit the Internet culture. Now, let's take a look at the downside—the kind of response you can expect to receive if you violate the mores of the online community.

Here are some examples:

The first message was posted to the group `biz.comp.services`, a forum that is full of commercial announcements aimed at business-to-business users:

```
Newsgroups: biz.comp.services
Subject: Internetworking Seminar Business - Start Your Own
Date: 7 Jun 1994 21:41:19 GMT

Turn my fully developed and tested seminar into instant profits.  Lots
of people are interested in finding out more about LANs, MANs, WANs,
GANs, Repeaters, Bridges, Routers, Gateways, Media Access Methods, etc.

I cannot believe the success that I have had with this seminar.  I
spent months developing and updating it.  I completed it in June 1993
and immediately made arrangements to teach it at a community college --
once in September and once in December 1993.  In 1994, I ran it
once/month in January, February, March, April, May.  I also have
contracts to teach it once/month in June, September, October, November
and December as well. And this is just at one college.  I have also
picked up contracts to teach it at a computer outlet (training dept)
and for another computer seminar company.

I can supply the original MicroSoft PowerPoint files on a diskette
complete with a copy of the instructor and student manual.  The cost
$275.00 U.S.

Or, I can sell the original Micosoft PowerPoint diskette for $99.00
U.S. and you canprint the manuals out yourself.  The student manual is
simply a copy of the slides, and the instuctor manual is a copy of the
notes.

Either package can be shipped in IBM or MAC PowerPoint file versions.

If interested, please send E-Mail, and I will forward ordering
instructions.
```

The response demonstrates one of the many unusual aspects of the Internet as an advertising medium: If you say something that others find unbelievable, unlikely, or inappropriate, their response can be quite pointed and is distributed just as widely as the original advertisement.

```
Newsgroups: biz.comp.services
Subject: Re: Internetworking Seminar Business - Start Your Own

Yes you to can give seminars on subjects you know little about,
teach people all about WAN's, routers, bridges and network theory
without even once spending a day ever doing it..

yeah right,
```

Interestingly, when we asked the author of the original article if he'd mind our including his name in this book, he declined, but not because he thought his approach was inappropriate:

```
I am sorry but I will not be able to give you permission.  Seems as though
there are lots of people out there that do not want to see Internet used
for business purposes.  I think that if some rules were established, then
there should not be a problem.  I think that some people have their heads
in the sand, however, I really believe that business will succeed in time.
I just don't want to upset anyone.
```

Our second example comes from a Usenet discussion forum called rec.scuba that focuses on topics related to scuba diving. One of the most popular topics of discussion concerns where students can travel to become certified to dive without an instructor. The offensive posting is for a dive shop in Texas.

Note: To explain what's going on here—in any Usenet discussion— any passage that is prefaced by > indicates that it's text from the previous contributor to the discussion, and >> indicates that it's from an even earlier author. In this posting, then, the first three lines are from the original advertisement, and the lines that follow are from two different people who believed the article inappropriate.

```
> > Well its that time of the year when most folks think of water.  We have
> > numerous classes starting up right now and all through the summer.  So
> > what are you waiting for give us a call.

> Now this looks pretty commercial to me!  Before everybody carps on me for
> criticizing commercial posts, remember that it isn't individual posts that
> we're afraid of, but the trend that is going to lead usenet into oblivion!
> Remember Canter and Siegel (the GREEN CARDS?)  Well, I haven't checked
> lately, but at my last reading ( c.a. a mo ago) they were planning to write
> a book on how to advertise and spam on usenet!

This post also hit a bit at my 'commercial-o-meter.'  It is not
horrible-it is in the right group, for example, but it does not contain
anything except 'come dive with us.'

If the post had contained a bit of information about Texas diving,
followed by a low key plug I think it would have been fine.  I do want
information from commercial services as well as private individuals, but
I agree with you that spam attacks are bad form.

Any comments?
```

The original article violated two cardinal rules of Internet advertising: 1) It had no informational content and 2) it reached an audience much wider than intended. Here you'll also note the use of the expression *spam attack*. This newly coined phrase appeared on the Internet in the wake of the blanket postings by Canter & Siegel.

Tips on Avoiding Flame Wars

The best way to avoid Internet flame wars—apart from never posting a commercial message—is to spend some time getting to know your target market instead of just diving in with a commercial message. Explore the current conversations, paying particular attention to what your potential customers want, how they like to interact, and what level of seriousness, professionalism, or information is most apt.

It's a good idea to keep your message short. Otherwise, you'll almost certainly be accused of chewing up valuable bandwidth and wasting Internet users' time and money. We recommend postings no longer than 45 lines of text.

Remember that you can always end the message with "for more details, send e-mail to" or some other pointer to further information.

Perhaps the most common problem with Internet advertising is the tendency of marketing types to sensationalize their message. Because the Internet community prefers information to hype and experiences the Internet as streams of plain text rather than in full-color as on the World Wide Web, traditional ad copy with its generous helpings of style, metaphor, image, and hype is likely to fall flat.

Michael Strangelove offers a few ideas about avoiding this pitfall: "Couch your message within a commentary on industry trends, create an electronic newsletter that provides a range of related information, or enter into dialogue with the forum about surrounding issues."

The Contrarian View: In-Your-Face Marketing

Although we've spent the better part of this chapter advising you how to market your products on the Internet without stepping on any toes (or, at least, as few toes as possible), it's only fair to tell you that in-your-face Internet advertising can work—provided you're willing to wade through the hostile responses of the community and find alienation of the majority acceptable in the interest of finding customers.

We've already discussed the law firm of Canter & Siegal with its attempt to find business through posting an advertisement to thousands of Usenet newsgroups, but there are other examples. One Internet marketer who is successfully bending the rules is Michael Beatty, Director of Special Projects at Communications Systems International in Colorado Springs, Colorado.

Profile: Beatty first dipped a toe in the Internet three years ago. Itching to test the Internet's potential as a marketing tool, Beatty teamed up with a U.S. vitamin distributor seeking to sell to China and posted a note on an Internet discussion group called China-net. Unbeknownst to Beatty, the group to which he'd posted his note was for Chinese computing experts, few of whom were interested in vitamins.

The next day, Beatty discovered 50 messages waiting for him in his e-mail box—but not the kind he was looking for.

"The first one said, 'Pour the gallon of gas over your head, you ignorant jerk, light the match. Whatta you have?

What do you have? Flames!,'" Beatty recalls. "Of course, I'm loosely paraphrasing, but that was the essence of probably 80 percent of the responses."

Toning down his sales pitch a bit, Beatty pressed on. Using the same techniques, he successfully peddled low-priced computers over the network; then he found out about a company selling "dial-back, long-distance" service, a way of placing international phone calls to the United States on the cheap by taking advantage of the lower U.S. rates. Before long, Beatty was posting ads on the Internet trying to drum up customers worldwide for the long-distance carrier.

"My system was to offer as extensive of an explanation of the concept of dialback as the discussion group would bear, without attracting too much negative reaction, and briefly mention the name of the company," Beatty says. "Then, if after getting that far without bullets or flames, follow up by developing a relationship with the interested party through e-mail messaging."

Beatty says he did so well marketing dial-back long distance on the Internet that the long-distance carrier—Communications Systems International of Colorado Springs, Colorado—offered him his current job. Now that the Internet is rapidly becoming commercialized, Beatty says, his postings slip by with nary a flame.

Future of Internet Marketing

What does the future hold for marketing products and services through the Internet?

One indisputable fact is that there will be more of it; there's clearly no going back. The Internet's high-income demographics, its low cost, and its huge size and fast growth will make the Internet irresistible to any marketer. The *Wall Street Journal* put it this way in a January 11, 1994, article about the new breed of online "techno-savvies" being targeted by big-time advertisers such as Ogilvy & Mather.

"How much advertising the Techno-Savvies will tolerate isn't known," The *Journal* wrote. "Users of the Internet are famous for responding to electronic sales pitches with vitriolic screeds. But advertisers say some of the more recent entrants into cyberspace won't be so irritable."

In the future, marketers predict, the question won't be whether to market products on the Internet but how. We expect that more and more mechanisms for advertising will appear, ranging from support for direct mail (and remember that direct mail that hits its target audience is rarely disliked) to cyberspace billboards through Gopher, the World Wide Web, and even some Usenet groups. Mailing lists will spring up to channel particular types of advertising for interested parties; an obvious possibility are the many multi-level marketing schemes that frequent Usenet newsgroups.

Some companies are already moving in these directions: Macmillian Computer Publishing is setting up a World Wide Web site to promote its many technical book titles as well as offer software, information, and other products and services, with an online discount for customers that purchase the book directly from the publisher. Other firms, notably O'Reilly & Associates, also offer a discount for online users. It's not too much of a leap for companies to make electronic product coupons available through the network to encourage cyber-shoppers to shop at particular stores and eat at specific restaurants.

Five years from now, predicts Mark Hornung of Bernard Hodes Advertising in San Francisco, the Internet will be "much more a mainstream medium than it is today. The collapse of the Bell Atlantic/TCI and Cox Broadcasting/Southwestern Bell alliances indicate that the RBOCs have discovered that 500-channel utopia is just not around the corner, and it'll cost a fortune. The Internet exists, its architecture allows easy and rapid expansion, and it's low cost."

Visions of the future inevitably hit the obstacle of interfaces and access capabilities, with vendors dreaming of a world where everyone has a high-speed SLIP or PPP connection, so they can run Mosaic or other graphical browsers. The reality, however, does not yet support this dream, but it may before too long.

Another possibility is government regulation of Internet commerce—just as the Federal Trade Commission (FTC) oversees real-world business dealings today. Bonney, the Virginia Beach marketer, warns that, although today's abusive Internet marketers are unofficially regulated by angry users hurling flame letters, tomorrow's Internet police could well be the FTC wielding cease-and-desist orders.

"The Net's simply too public a medium and too underwritten by federal dollars for this not to happen," Bonney says. "Also, as more and more commercial interests and transactions take place on the Net, there'll be no excuse for the FTC to not take a more active role."

It's impossible to say what will happen in five years, of course, but we believe it's safe to bet that there will continue to be commercial activity on the Internet, that entrepreneurs will start making serious money in cyberspace, and that larger businesses will become more interested and more involved in the network. As with any new marketing venture, take the sales pitch of service providers with a grain of salt and make sure you work with the Internet community to achieve the best possible results.

THE ELECTRONIC SCHMOOZE

One of the most effective ways to market a product or service on the Internet is to join a discussion group and interact directly with current and potential customers.

What we call *the electronic schmooze* is really no different from passing out business cards at your favorite trade shows—except, instead of talking, you're typing. Because Internet discussion groups are as close as your computer, you can schmooze anywhere, anytime—from home, from the office, even at 2:00 a.m. when you're wearing just your pajamas—without taking the time to shower, dress, or drive somewhere. And because the Internet is closely monitored by journalists, reporters, and editors from major newspapers and magazines, maintaining a high profile online is also an effective and inexpensive way to get your name out in the media.

Electronic schmoozing can take many forms such as the following:

> You can tack up a virtual press release about your company or your products; just remember to include more information than hype.

> You can also showcase your expertise and contribute to your industry by taking part in online discussions; not only are contributions of this nature less likely to result in strong negative responses—in other words, flames—but they're also part of what makes the Internet such an interesting community to join.

> Another way to network online is by answering questions, offering advice to other discussion group members and joining in topical conversations.

Whichever way you choose, Internet schmoozing can be a great way to drum up business, network with professional colleagues, even find a job or start a business.

As with any marketing approach, of course, there are some drawbacks. There's no guarantee that your comments and insights will be well received by the other members of the group. Worse, in some groups, any unintentional mistake that you make in your contributions, be they typographical or lapses in logic, will be speedily transmitted throughout most of the world.

Another drawback is that, if you join a busy discussion group or two, you might find dozens to hundreds of messages cluttering up your electronic mailbox every morning, with content running the gamut from pearls of wisdom to a waste of electrons. Even with powerful electronic mail-reading software and Usenet browsers, you'll end up investing quite a bit of time.

The purpose of this chapter is to demonstrate how to use Internet mailing lists and newsgroups to "network" with customers and colleagues worldwide. We'll show you how to pick which discussion groups to join, how to join them, and how to post and respond to notes.

We'll also show you how to create your own mailing list—in case none of the thousands of discussion groups available fit your needs.

No discussion of online interaction would be complete without a discussion of network etiquette—*netiquette,* as it's known, so we'll also equip you with our own road-tested guidelines based on more than a decade of using the Internet and other online services. Along the way, you'll see how other companies are turning Internet discussion groups into powerful sales and marketing tools.

At the end of the chapter, you'll also find an annotated list of some of the Internet mailing lists and Usenet newsgroups of interest to specific businesses and professions.

Choosing a Discussion Group to Join

By now you're familiar with the oft-used metaphor of the *information superhighway*. In many ways, the Internet is quite unlike any real world highway, but in other respects, it's a fairly accurate analogy.

Imagine a highway system connecting thousands of towns and cities but without any signs marking which is which and without any AAA roadmaps and you're starting to get an inkling of one of the biggest problems on the Internet today. There's no centralized index to consult if you want to find a list of discussion groups about medicine. Worse, with more than 8,000 mailing lists and more than 6,000 Usenet discussion groups available, even learning about a small subset of the potential lists on the Internet can be a challenge.

The good news is that there are some fairly painless ways to find out about Internet discussion groups. Perhaps the best way is to ask colleagues which groups they find most valuable. Another is to find one appropriate group and post a question asking for pointers to others. Before you do that, however, take the time to check for a Frequently Asked Questions document available through that discussion group or on an FAQ server. These documents can often point you in the right direction.

Dozens, if not hundreds, of books purport to offer navigational guides to the Internet. Most of them provide considerable help with lists of mailing lists and Usenet groups; browse them in a bookstore to find one you'll like. We recommend the book *Navigating the Internet* by Richard Smith and Mark Gibbs, published by SAMS. Another valuable reference, if a bit specific, is *Internet: Mailing Lists* (Prentice Hall, 1993), edited by Edward T.L. Hardie and Vivian Neou. This guide, compiled and maintained by the Network Information Systems Center at SRI International in Menlo Park, California, contains names, descriptions, and subscription instructions for more than 800 Internet mailing lists—from opera and chess to engineering and library science.

This being the Internet, it shouldn't surprise you that you can obtain lists of discussion groups online, though it can be a bit tricky. The best-known list of Internet mailing lists, maintained by SRI International, is called the *List of Lists*. Although *Internet: Mailing Lists* is essentially a nicely formatted printout of that list, the online version is always more up-to-date. To obtain a copy of the List of Lists via the Internet, send an e-mail message to `mail-server@sri.com`. In the body of the message, type `send netinfo/interest-groups`.

Another set of mailing lists, often more academic in nature, are hosted on BITNET, a large academic network that comprises part of the Internet itself. Unfortunately, these lists include only brief descriptions—often, ten words or less—but you can join a list without any human intervention. To obtain the complete list of BITNET lists, send an e-mail message to `liserv@bitnic.bit.net` with the message body containing the phrase `list global`.

Obtaining a list of Usenet newsgroups through electronic mail is a bit more difficult. The easiest way is to ask your Internet access provider for a list of the "newsgroups" file (or you can look for it yourself; it's called `/usr/lib/news/newsgroups`) or other document listing the groups received by the local site you log onto. You can also check out the long list of newsgroups that is frequently posted to several Usenet newsgroups, including `news.lists`, `news.groups`, `news.announce.newusers`, `news.announce.newgroups`, and `news.answers`. These lists are usually posted around the beginning or middle of the month.

A list of active newsgroups, many including descriptions, is available via FTP from `ftp.uu.net:/networking/news/config/newsgroups.Z`.

> **Tip:** If the filename ends in .Z, as in the preceding, then you'll need to uncompress it before downloading to your own computer: type uncompress *filename* where *filename* is the name of the specific file. Once you've downloaded an electronic copy of a discussion group list, use your word processor to open it as a text file. This way, you can do a keyword search for the topics you're interested in instead of scrolling through the file manually or printing it. Remember to look for synonyms, too. One list might discuss *medicine*; the next may discuss *doctor*, *hospital*, or *clinic*.

Joining and Participating in a Discussion Group

Once you've decided which Internet discussion group or groups look interesting, it's time to take the plunge. There are two kinds of discussion groups: mailing lists and Usenet newsgroups. Joining a newsgroup is easy: follow the instructions we provided in Chapter 1, "Putting the Internet to Work for You," to select or deselect any newsgroups you desire.

Most Internet mailing lists, including the thousands of BITNET lists, use a software program called a *list server,* in e-mail parlance a LISTSERV. To join any mailing list that uses this software, you simply send a note to the `listserv` program on the host machine requesting a subscription.

> **Tip:** Never send a message to the list itself requesting a subscription; your request will be forwarded to hundreds or thousands of subscribers and doubtless provoke some flames!

Let's take a closer look at a list that both Rosalind and Dave subscribe to—net-happenings. The net-happenings list is hosted by an Internet organization called *Internic,* and mail to the list is sent to the e-mail address `net-happenings@is.internic.net`.

To join the list, simply replace the name of the list with `majordomo` (which is the software package that processes subscription requests). So sending a mail message to `majordomo@is.internic.net` will do the trick. The body of the message should contain your specific request: list shows which mailing lists are maintained by the list server on that computer, subscribe adds you to the list, unsubscribe drops you from the list, and help shows you the many other options available. To join a specific list, send a message to the list server list indicating which list you would like to subscribe to followed by your first and last names: Rosalind signed up for the net-happenings list by sending the message subscribe `net-happenings rosalind resnick` to `majordomo@is.internic.net`.

Once you join a Usenet newsgroup, there will probably be a small number of articles waiting for you. Your newsreader program (rn, tin, nn, or any of the others) displays them automatically. When you join a mailing list, it generally takes a few hours before the first message appears in your mailbox. Either way, here's rule number one for any discussion group:

> **Tip:** Always read a discussion group for a minimum of a week before joining in any conversation or starting any new discussion topics.

Once you're ready, participating in an Internet discussion group involves two activities—reading messages and posting messages. The technicalities of doing this vary depending on the kind of news and mail reading software you or your Internet access provider uses (see Chapter 1, "Putting the Internet to Work for You," for an overview of the software available.)

With a mailing list, you can treat the articles you receive just like any other e-mail messages—read them, respond to them, delete them, or store them in a folder for future reference. One important tip: Train yourself to be sensitive to the return address on messages: Some groups are set up so that your response goes only to the author of the original message; others will send your mail to the entire list unless you change the return address!

That's why, if you want to post your reply to the group as a whole, it's important to make sure that your posting is addressed to the list's address. Conversely, if you want to keep your reply private, address your note to the e-mail box of the individual who posted the note. The same applies when posting a note of your own.

With a newsgroup, you typically don't get postings delivered to your mailbox (although some programs, such as WinNET Mail, have that capability). Instead, you log onto your Internet account and use a newsreader such as nn to access them. For example, to read the postings on the `misc.entrepreneurs` newsgroup, an nn user would type `nn misc.entrepreneurs` at the prompt. This displays a list of subject headings to help you decide which postings to read and which to ignore.

With a newsgroup, as with a mailing list, you can reply to and post messages of your own. The difference is that more people might see your postings on a newsgroup because there's no need to subscribe; on the other hand, there's no guarantee that the colleagues or customers you're trying to reach will see them because your postings aren't delivered to their e-mail boxes.

The Fine Points of Netiquette

The nuts and bolts of joining Internet discussion groups are pretty straightforward, all in all. Far more difficult is mastering the unwritten rules of network etiquette, or *netiquette*, the unwritten code of conduct that every good Internet citizen is expected to follow.

If you're a business user trying to win acceptance for your company and its products, you'll want to be doubly sure to follow these guidelines, but a mastery of netiquette is also important for anyone wanting to cruise the information highway, hoping to make friends, business connections, or just find a good conversation or two.

Just as in the offline world, where it's considered bad manners to talk with food in your mouth or to interrupt someone in the middle of a sentence, a whole list of things are widely held to be unacceptable on the Internet—everything from typing your postings in all capital letters (that's considered shouting) to posting a reply that says, "Me, too!" (that's considered to be a waste of bandwidth).

Here are ten rules of Netiquette to keep in mind when posting or replying to an Internet discussion group:

If you don't have something interesting to say, don't say it. There's no better way to turn off fellow discussion group members than to gain a reputation as being a "me-too" kind of poster. Remember: Talk is cheap, bandwidth is not.

Brevity is the soul of wit, so be brief. The Internet is not a courtroom, a soap box, or a podium. If you feel you can't say what you want to in less than 100 lines, try to condense it— or break it up into separate messages. Though with many Internet news and mail reader programs you have the ability to "capture" the text of the posting you're responding to and include it with your follow-up note, it's rarely necessary to include more than a few lines of the previous posting in your reply.

Don't post anything you wouldn't want seen around the world. The Internet may seem like a cozy, little place when you're typing on your home PC at 2:00 a.m., but it's important to recognize that your little posting may well be excerpted, re-posted, archived, stored on CD-ROM, published in a newspaper, and read by millions of people all around the world today, tomorrow, and years after you posted it. Although private e-mail is confidential, mailing list postings are also considered by many journalists to be fair game.

Be considerate. No matter how angry those other discussion group members have made you or how inaccurate you think (or know) their postings to be, remember that the people on the other side of the computer screen are human beings. Stick to the issue at hand. Don't stoop to personal attacks. If you'd rather not be flamed, don't light a match under somebody else.

Post your message once and only once. Don't send along a follow-up message to make sure that everybody got your first one.

Title your posting clearly. Label your posting with a header that describes in a couple of words the contents of your message. There are few things more annoying than getting a posting entitled, *Your Message* or *Hello*.

Respect others' privacy. Re-posting a private e-mail message to a public discussion group without the sender's permission is inappropriate and rude. Some lawyers also suggest that it may be a violation of U.S. copyright law.

Post only relevant material. If you're participating in a group for IBM PC users, don't launch into a discussion about the Macintosh. If you're not sure what's appropriate to post, take a look at the group's FAQ (Frequently Asked Questions) list.

Say what you mean. Online, nobody can see you smile and it's hard to tell whether somebody's joking. As a result, what you may consider to be wry wit can frequently come across as obnoxious and offensive. If you want to convey humor or ironic intention, flag it with a "smiley," a sideways smile that looks like :-) or :), or a "grin" that looks like <g>.

Keep your signature short. With many Internet mail and news readers you can set up online "signatures" that are included at the bottom of any message you send. Typically, these "sig files" contain your name, address, company, and a line or two of other pertinent information. However, some people have turned them into a minor art form complete with "sketches," sayings, witticisms, and other electronic graffiti.

In short, be polite on the Net and keep it a pleasant place for everyone.

The Rules of Netiquette

If you keep these points in mind, you'll find it easy to participate in Internet discussions like an Internet veteran. But just to give you an idea of what not to do, we've included some excerpts from a funny piece called "Emily Postnews" that was written by Brad Templeton. Besides being a witty guy, Templeton is president of the ClariNet Communications Corp. of San Jose, California, an Internet newspaper that carries news and features ranging from Reuters to Miss Manners. The full Emily Postnews document is regularly posted on the news.newusers.questions newsgroup.

```
"Dear Emily Postnews"

        Emily Postnews, foremost authority on proper net behaviour,
        gives her advice on how to act on the net.


Dear Miss Postnews: How long should my signature be? -- verbose@noisy

A: Dear Verbose: Please try and make your signature as long as you
can. It's much more important than your article, of course, so try
to have more lines of signature than actual text.

Try to include a large graphic made of ASCII characters, plus lots of
cute quotes and slogans. People will never tire of reading these
pearls of wisdom again and again, and you will soon become personally
associated with the joy each reader feels at seeing yet another
delightful repeat of your signature.

Be sure as well to include a complete map of USENET with each
signature, to show how anybody can get mail to you from any site in
the world. Be sure to include Internet gateways as well. Also tell
people on your own site how to mail to you. Give independent
addresses for Internet, UUCP, and BITNET, even if they're all the
same.
```

Aside from your reply address, include your full name, company and organization. It's just common courtesy -- after all, in some newsreaders people have to type an entire keystroke to go back to the top of your article to see this information in the header.

By all means include your phone number and street address in every single article. People are always responding to Usenet articles with phone calls and letters. It would be silly to go to the extra trouble of including this information only in articles that need a response by conventional channels!

Q: How can I choose what groups to post in?

A: Pick as many as you can, so that you get the widest audience. After all, the net exists to give you an audience. Ignore those who suggest you should only use groups where you think the article is highly appropriate. Pick all groups where anybody might even be slightly interested.

Always make sure follow-ups go to all the groups. In the rare event that you post a followup which contains something original, make sure you expand the list of groups. Never include a "Followup-to:" line in the header, since some people might miss part of the valuable discussion in the fringe groups.

Q: How should I pick a subject for my articles?

A: Keep it short and meaningless. That way people will be forced to actually read your article to find out what's in it. This means a bigger audience for you, and we all know that's what the net is for. If you do a followup, be sure and keep the same subject, even if it's totally meaningless and not part of the same discussion. If you don't, you won't catch all the people who are looking for stuff on the original topic, and that means less audience for you.

Q: What sort of tone should I take in my article?

A: Be as outrageous as possible. If you don't say outlandish things and fill your article with libelous insults of net people, you may not stick out enough in the flood of articles to get a response. The more insane your posting looks, the more likely it is that you'll get lots of followups. The net is here, after all, so that you can get lots of attention.

Q: What is the measure of a worthwhile group?

A: Why, it's Volume, Volume, Volume. Any group that has lots of noise in it must be good. Remember, the higher the volume of material in a group, the higher percentage of useful, factual and insightful articles you will find. In fact, if a group can't demonstrate a high enough volume, it should be deleted from the net.

Tapping into Internet Discussion Groups for Fun and Profit

Now that you've learned the rules of communicating in Internet discussion groups, it's time to take a look at how your participation can benefit you and your company. As we discussed earlier in the chapter, online networking is a great way to "work the room" without actually being there. Here are four ways in which a business can use an online discussion group to its advantage:

> Sales and marketing
> Trend-watching and information-gathering
> Customer support
> Employee recruitment

Sales and Marketing

Blatant advertising is a no-no on Internet discussion groups; however, subtle advertising that contains a healthy dose of information interesting to the list can slide by with no problem.

With that in mind, there are three ways to advertise your products on a discussion forum:

- Post a press release announcing the formation of your company or the availability of your product or service.

- Assist other discussion group members by answering their questions or pointing them to information.

- Include a few lines of advertising information (such as a brief description of your business or the price of an annual subscription to your newsletter) in the signature file at the bottom of your posting.

Here's an example of a posting on the subject of Internet trademark searches. The author is a Washington lawyer looking to snag some clients.

```
While I obviously have a built in bias, there is no substitute for having a law
yer do a full trademark search for you. The following is not meant to be an ad
but for information purposes. At my firm, we can do a database search
inexpensively (approx. $35 per name) to identify any obvious problems. Once a
client has  narrowed down the list of possible names to a few, we usually hire
a tm search  firm to do a full search. These pick up federal registrations,
state registrations, and common law usages. The fee depends on how fast you
want the results, but $250 is average. We do not mark up our costs for these
services. Rather, we  charge our regular hourly rates to review the results
```

and advise the client about whether they can safely use a mark.
Is this more expensive than CompuServe? Sure. Will it be cheaper in the long
 run? I think so. Intellectual property is an asset; sometimes the value of a
mark is a company's most valuable asset. You should treat it as such.
I expect the usual flames, lawyer jokes etc. about how expensive lawyers can be
. My experience is quite the opposite. You need to look for a lawyer that is a
little hungry and values long term relationships.
Lewis Rose
Arent Fox Kintner Plotkin & Kahn
1050 Connecticut Avenue, N.W.
Washington, D.C. 20036-5339
(202) 857-6012 (voice)
(202) 857-6395 (fax)
lewrose@netcom.com (internet)
Expertise in Advertising and High Tech Marketing Law

As you can see, Rose keeps his posting brief and to the point. He discusses the advantages of hiring an attorney to handle a trademark search and then plugs his own firm's service and prices. He also attempts to ward off flames by publicly stating that he expects them. And finally, he includes a signature file that lists his name, firm's name, address, phone number, fax number, Internet address, and professional expertise. When we talked with Rose about his posting, he told us that not only hadn't his note generated any flames, but it prompted a request from a prospective client for a more detailed fee proposal.

"The name of the game is to increase your referral network," says Rose, who participates in a variety of newsgroups and mailing lists and spends several hours a day on the Internet. "The days when you say, 'I'm from XYZ law school' and you wait for the phone to ring are gone."

By contrast, here's an example of a posting, really more of a "chain letter," purportedly by a Dave Rhodes, that's been re-posted to newsgroups all over the Internet in a none-too-flattering light.

Dear Friends,
My name is Dave Rhodes. In September 1988 my car was reposessed and the bill
collectors were hounding me like you wouldn't believe. I was laid off and my
unemployment checks had run out. The only escape I had from the pressure of
failure was my computer and my modem. I 3longed to turn my advocation into
my vocation.
This January 1989 my family and I went on a ten day cruise to the tropics.
I bought a Lincoln Town Car for CASH in Feburary 1989. I am currently
building a home on the West Coast of Florida, with a private pool, boat slip,
and a beautiful view of the bay from my breakfast room table and patio. I
will never have to work again. Today I am rich! I have earned
$400,000.00 (Four Hundred Thousand Dollars) to date and will become a
millionaire within 4 or 5 months. Anyone can do the same. This money making
program works perfectly every time, 100% of the time. I have NEVER failed
to earn $50,000.00 or more whenever I wanted. Best of all you never have
to leave home except to go to your mailbox or post office.

In October 1988, I received a letter in the mail telling me how I could
earn $50,000 dollars or more whenever I wanted. I was naturally very
skeptical and threw the letter on the desk next to my computer. It's funny
though, when you are desperate, backed into a corner, your mind does crazy
things. I spent a frustating day looking through the want ads for a job
with a future. The pickings were sparse at best. That night I tried to
unwind by booting up my computer and calling several bulletin boards. I
read several of the message posts and than glanced at the letter next to
the computer. All at once it came to me, I now had the key to my dreams.
I realized that with the power of the computer I could expand and enhance
this money making formula into the most unbelievable cash flow generator
that has ever been created. I substituted the computer bulletin boards in
place of the post office and electronically did by computer what others were
doing 100% by mail. Now only a few letters are mailed manually. Most of the
hard work is speedily downloaded to other bulletin boards throughout the
world. If you believe that someday you deserve that lucky break that you
have waited for all your life, simply follow the easy instructions below.
Your dreams will come true.

Trend-Surfing on the Net

Thanks to the Internet, you don't have to spend time and money subscribing to
industry trade publications to keep track of what's going on in your industry—
though you have to sort through a daily stack of e-mail. Two of the most widely
followed business-oriented lists are com-priv, which focuses on the commercialization and privatization of the Internet, and net-happenings, which distributes
notices of interest to the Internet community—conference announcements, calls
for papers, publications, newsletters, network tools updates, and network resources.

Here's an excerpt from an announcement that was posted recently to the
Kidsphere educational mailing list and then re-posted to the net-happenings
newsgroup. The message announces the latest version of Mosaic, the University
of Illinois' popular Internet navigational software package:

We are happy to announce the release of NCSA Mosaic for Microsoft Windows
Version 2.0alpha3. NCSA Mosaic is a network navigational tool that will
allow you to easily access networked information with the click of a button.
Mosaic is capable of accessing data via protocols such as Gopher, World Wide
Web, FTP and NNTP (Usenet News) natively, and other data services such as
Archie, WAIS, and Veronica through gateways. NCSA Mosaic was designed to
provide its user transparent and seamless access to these information
sources and services. There are now two versions of Mosaic. The most
common version is wmos20a3.zip, it was created for Windows 3.1, Windows
for Workgroups, and Windows NT(80X86). The other version, decmosa3.zip,
was compiled for DEC alpha's running Windows NT.
NCSA Mosaic for Microsoft Windows is a WinSock client program. It requires
network (TCP/IP) access through the WinSock DLL interface. If you are using

```
Windows NT, this is built in. If you are using Windows 3.1, you need to
obtain a WinSock and install it on your system. If you are running a
commercial TCP/IP stack, such as FTP Software, Novell, PCNFS, etc., you
will need to obtain that vendor's winsock.dll. If you need a winsock.dll
and you would like to obtain a shareware product called the "Trumpet
Software International Winsock", you can find the latest version at
ftp site, ftp.utas.edu.au. The file winsock.zip is in the pc/trumpet/winsock
directory.
```

Industry announcements are frequently posted to newsgroups as well. There's even a newsgroup for conference announcements: `news.announce.conferences` (this group was created by co-author Dave Taylor for those trivia buffs reading this!) Announcements can show up anywhere, however, and we found the following conference announcement on the `news.announce.conferences` newsgroup:

```
From: rmutton@superior.ccs.carleton.ca (Ross Mutton)
Newsgroups: news.announce.conferences
Subject: Association for Media and Technology in Education in Canada
Date: 31 Mar 1994 14:07:46 -0600
Organization: Carleton University

    Association for Media and Technology in Education in Canada

                      Annual Conference

                      June 12 - 15/94

                   University of Lethbridge
                 Lethbridge, Alberta, Canada


----------------------------------------------------------------
    AMTEC, Canada's national association for educational media and
technology professionals is holding its annual conference at the
University of Lethbridge in Lethbridge, Alberta, Canada.  This
year's theme is "The Winds of Change", looking at changing the way
we think, changing to a digital environment and changing the way we
work.
```

The real value of Internet discussion groups is not only to read announcements, some of which, in fact, you may read about in *The Wall Street Journal, The New York Times,* or your industry trade journal, but to ask questions to a worldwide group of high-level professionals in your field. Especially if your work involves computers or technology, the Internet can be a treasure chest of free information. And because Internet discussion groups tend to be more specialized than those on commercial online services, you can go straight to the experts instead of hoping that someone knowledgeable happens to drop by.

How specific can your questions get? Consider this example from the computer programming group `comp.lang.asm370`, focusing on assembly language for the IBM 370 computer system:

```
hi all,

a friend of mine is working for a large company. he has to deal with very ugly
assembler programs (e.g., self-modifying), developed since about 1970. it
would be extremely helpful to use tools which help to analyse, restructure
and redesign such applications. i only found some tools which handle fortran
or cobol sources (e.g., Delta). any hints to assembler level tools are welcome.

thanks in advance
        timo
```

Customer Support

Businesses also use Internet discussion groups to offer customer support. Sometimes the companies drop in on groups discussing topics of interest to their customers (for example, technical support staffers at a financial-software company might hang around a discussion group about investments or personal finance); other companies set up their own discussion groups and invite customers. We'll talk more about how to start your own discussion group later in the chapter.

Providing online customer support is an inexpensive way to deal with customers' complaints and problems while getting your company's name out in a positive way. This can take the form of responding to customers' questions or posting useful information such as the following FAQ posted by Digital Equipment Corp. on the `comp.sys.dec` newsgroup focused on the equipment and products released by DEC:

```
D3. How can I make an RZxx disk spinup on power-on?

In order to conserve power, the builtin disks on VAXstations,
DECstations, and Alpha workstations do not spinup when the power is
turned on, but do so under software control. If you need to change this
to use an RZxx disk on another system, there are several ways to do it:

1) On ULTRIX, use "rzdisk -c ask"
2) Move a jumper. The location of this varies from drive to drive.
3) Use the SCSI console diagnostics on a DECstation.
4) Use the VAXstation service diagnostics (tricky)
5) On a Macintosh, use the "Silverlining" program.
6) On a DOS PC, use the shareware program SPINUP.

The drives do respond to the START UNIT command.
                        [William Jackson, jackson@pravda.enet.dec.com]
                        [David Burren, davidb@otto.bf.rmit.oz.au]
```

Employee Recruitment

Many businesses find Internet discussion groups useful for another reason: They provide a quick and effective way to recruit employees without paying a headhunting fee. That said, there are plenty of recruiters who place ads on discussion groups as well. Internet users don't usually object to such postings because, after all, the advertiser is offering them money, not asking for it. In fact, there are a number of newsgroups, including `misc.jobs.wanted`, `misc.jobs.announce`, `misc.jobs.resumes`, and `misc.jobs.contract` in the mainstream Usenet hierarchy, and `biz.jobs.offered` in the biz hierarchy, that consist of job listings, resumes, and discussion about finding a job.

Here's a recent posting on `misc.jobs.offered` from recruiting company Bluestone Inc. of New Jersey:

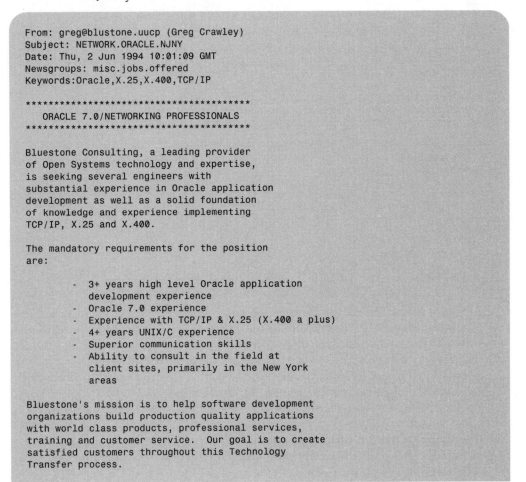

```
From: greg@blustone.uucp (Greg Crawley)
Subject: NETWORK.ORACLE.NJNY
Date: Thu, 2 Jun 1994 10:01:09 GMT
Newsgroups: misc.jobs.offered
Keywords:Oracle,X.25,X.400,TCP/IP


*******************************************
    ORACLE 7.0/NETWORKING PROFESSIONALS
*******************************************

Bluestone Consulting, a leading provider
of Open Systems technology and expertise,
is seeking several engineers with
substantial experience in Oracle application
development as well as a solid foundation
of knowledge and experience implementing
TCP/IP, X.25 and X.400.

The mandatory requirements for the position
are:

        - 3+ years high level Oracle application
          development experience
        - Oracle 7.0 experience
        - Experience with TCP/IP & X.25 (X.400 a plus)
        - 4+ years UNIX/C experience
        - Superior communication skills
        - Ability to consult in the field at
          client sites, primarily in the New York
          areas

Bluestone's mission is to help software development
organizations build production quality applications
with world class products, professional services,
training and customer service.  Our goal is to create
satisfied customers throughout this Technology
Transfer process.
```

```
Fax:    (609) 778-8125
Phone:  (609) 727-4600 X103

Correspondence may be sent to:

    Greg Crawley
    Bluestone
    1000 Briggs Road
    Mt. Laurel, NJ 08054
```

Here's an Internet "want ad" posted in biz.jobs.offered by PRT Corp. of America, a New York technology consulting firm:

```
From: p0064@psilink.com (Edward D. Lawler)
Subject: SYBASE, UNIX C DEVELOPER WANTED
Newsgroup: biz.jobs.offered
Date: Tue, 12 Apr 94 17:41

PRT Corp. of America, one of the countries fastest growing technology
consulting firms, specializing in the emerging technologies, has an
opening for:

A person to develop and build a Unix C Compliance Procedure System.
SYBASE, UNIX C, and SUN systems with financial background required.
Experience with General Counsel, Legal or regulation issues preferred.

Long term position in Greater New York Metropolitan Area.

Respond to:

Edward Lawler
PRT Corp. of America
342 Madison Avenue, Suite 1104
New York, NY 10173

TEL (800) 853-JOBS
FAX (212) 922-0806
INTERNET p0064@psilink.com
```

Just how effective are these Internet job listings? We asked Edward Lawler, the account manager at PRT, who told us that his company has been receiving two to three resumes a day since posting its first job notice on the Internet a month earlier. Seventy percent of the responses, Lawler says, "have come from very skilled people." In the past, he says, PRT has filled jobs through traditional methods such as word-of-mouth, networking, computer user groups, and unsolicited resumes. By advertising on the Internet, PRT doesn't have to spend money to take out a classified ad in a newspaper or to pay a recruiter a finder's fee. At no extra cost, the company also can use the Internet to advertise its positions to programmers around the world, an important capability now that PRT is expanding its operations overseas.

"The Internet gives us access to untapped talent both at home and abroad," Lawler says. At the same time, he cautions, "you have to be careful how much you disclose so that you don't give away your plans to your competitors."

Creating Your Own Discussion Group

As we've already observed, there are thousands of discussion groups on the Internet, with topics ranging far and wide. Nonetheless, there's a chance that none of them may meet your needs. That's why some companies start their own discussion groups.

On the Internet, unlike most commercial online services, you don't need anyone's permission to start a new group; you just do it. By creating your own discussion area, filtering out irrelevant or inflammatory postings, and providing leading-edge information about your products and your area of expertise, you can establish a relationship with current and potential customers without risking getting tarred with the "advertiser" tag.

> **Profile:** A Palo Alto, California, restaurant called Country Fare uses an Internet mailing list to distribute Menu Mailers, an electronic newsletter that informs subscribers of upcoming daily specials. (You can sign up by sending a message to `listserv@country-fare.com` with the message `subscribe menu your name`.) The idea is to whet customers' appetites for the restaurant's food and beverages.

If you decide to create your own electronic mailing list, circulate an announcement about the group to Internet discussion groups that your customers might read, inviting them to sign up.

Don't forget to include information about the forum in your other promotions, too. If there's a high demand for the group and it becomes quite active, you can apply to have it changed to a Usenet newsgroup. In Appendix B, we include instructions for creating your own newsgroup, but we recommend against creating such a group immediately because a mailing list is easier to maintain and might be exactly what you desire.

Once you set up your own group, you can send all the promotional material you want, and, instead of being viewed as an Internet despoiler, you'll be viewed as a welcome builder of the Internet community. Remember, however, that if there's nothing of value to the subscribers—your potential customers—everyone will rapidly "unsubscribe" from the group. Again, be careful not to exceed the information-to-hype ratio that applies to all postings on the Internet.

Realize, too, that, once you've created either a Usenet newsgroup or an open mailing list in which every submission is automatically forwarded to all subscribers, any customer complaints will also become public knowledge.

In fact, once customers discover that your company has launched its own discussion group, some may decide to post some fairly hostile notes. Consider this example from the Usenet discussion forum, `biz.zeos.general`, a general discussion group for users of ZEOS PC-compatible laptop and personal computers:

```
From: faust@access.digex.net (Doug Linder)
Subject: Why I am returning my Pantera
Newsgroup: biz.zeos.general
Date: 13 Apr 1994 13:43

Fernando Medrano (medrano@fraser.sfu.ca) wrote:

: My god, this place is starting to read more like the Gateway
: newsgroup. Though I am fairly satisfied with my Zeos so far,
: this story does not bode well for what could happen in the
: future. Does any out there have any recommendations for good,

This seems to be the way things work in mail-order.  They start small,
then get huge by providing great customer service and beating out the Big
Guy.  Then, when they get big themselves, one day they wake up to find
they've lost their coveted high honors in PC Magazine's readers survey.
In the next issue, you see a letter from them apologizing, and promising
to do better.  After that, they slide into mediocrity.  Zeos will soon take
its place next to Dell and Gateway, and some up-and-coming young turk will
take their place for a while with lower prices and better support.


--------------------------------------------------------------------
Doug Linder                          Beware the man of one book.
faust@access.digex.net                  Proud to be an atheist.
-------- It's not illegal to be a straight, white male...yet. --------
```

As you might expect, computer and technology companies have been in the forefront of launching Internet discussion groups, but other companies are starting them now as well. In April, *The Seattle Times* set up a local Seattle newsgroup called `seatimes.ptech` to enable the newspaper's editors, reporters, and readers to interact online. In its announcement, the paper said it plans to use the newsgroup to solicit reader responses that will run in the paper's weekly Personal Technology section as part of a regular feature called The Electronic Neighborhood.

"The idea is to allow readers to more than send us 'letters,' but also to exchange ideas and viewpoints among themselves, just as they would in any neighborhood," says Mark Watanabe, the technology section's editor.

Other companies are creating mailing lists. Ted Kraus, president of TKO Real Estate Advisory Group in Mercerville, New Jersey, manages two Internet mailing lists, one about commercial real estate, the other about residential properties. On Kraus' lists, brokers are allowed—even encouraged—to tack up offers to buy and sell properties without paying to post their listings. Close to 400 people have signed up so far, Kraus says, and he plans to start running online ads soon.

Kraus acknowledges that selling advertising on his mailing list may prove controversial, but, he reasons, it's his list and he can do with it as he pleases. Subscribers who don't like getting ads in their e-mail boxes can simply cancel their subscriptions and leave the list.

"Before everyone starts flaming, let me say this," Kraus wrote in a recent posting to the HTMARCOM high-tech marketing communications discussion group. "I run the list, I promote the list, I pay for the list, I'm the owner of the list. Nothing complicated to understand about that. No one is forced to receive the list. If they want to continue to receive the benefits of the lists, they accept the ads. If they don't want to see the ads, they can unsubscribe."

Another mailing list owner is Steve Outing, an El Cerrito, California, electronic publishing entrepreneur who runs the online-news and online-newspapers mailing lists. Outing's list began as a spinoff of the CARR-L computer-assisted journalism list and now has attracted close to 500 subscribers all over the world. Though he doesn't make money from operating the list, Outing says it's a good way to stay on top of developments in the electronic publishing industry and a valuable way to get his name before the media.

"My business requires that I stay on top of developments in electronic newspapers," Outing says. "The list is my best source of what's going on in my field. Often, I'll hear about something important on the list before it hits *The Wall Street Journal* or the trade press. It's my most valuable source of news for electronic newspaper developments."

Outing says his expenses are minimal because his lists are kept on a server operated by his partners at Cyberspace Development, a Boulder, Colorado, company that sets up Internet storefronts. Most of the time he invested in the project occurred at the beginning when he was signing up his initial subscribers, he says. The return on his efforts, he notes, has been substantial.

"Within the first couple months of running the list, I got several requests for interviews from reporters doing stories on electronic newspapers," he says. "By virtue of being the owner of these lists, all of a sudden I was perceived as an expert in this field. The downside is that owning a list can take up a lot of your time. I often have to spend an hour a day plowing through and answering my e-mail. I get upward of 100 messages a day during the week. The online lists account for about half of that, including lots of failed-delivery reports. I use the Delete key a lot."

We encourage all potential mailing-list owners to keep two things in mind: 1) Don't assume that you can dump anything you want on your list without risking an unfavorable reaction and 2) Keep the discussion public so that you can work through problems with customers openly, letting other customers and potential customers see how your company resolves problems.

How to Start Your Own Mailing List

Starting a mailing list doesn't require any special permission or authorization, though you will need to work with the system administrator at your local Internet access provider if that's how you're connected to the Internet. Any individual or company with free time, a computer connected to the Internet (or account on an Internet system), and the storage capacity to handle a mailing list can set one up at any time. To find out whether your system can handle a mailing list, check first with your system administrator. We also recommend that you use either the Listserv or majordomo software packages. Both are available for free through the Internet. Listserv software is available via anonymous FTP in the `/pub/listserv` directory on `cs.bu.edu`. Majordomo software is available via anonymous FTP at `pub/majordomo.tar.Z` from `ftp.GreatCircle.com`.

Before you decide to create a list, however, you'll need to spend some time thinking about the topic of your new discussion forum. What will be the central topic of discussion? Will you moderate the list or allow discussion to flow freely? Do you want to use a digest format (a list in which messages are gathered by the moderator and then sent out as a group)? Do you want to maintain archives of the discussions so that you or your subscribers can access them for future reference? (Two mailing list digest programs are DIGEST and DLIST, which are both available via anonymous FTP from `Simtel20.Army.Mil. RFC 1153`.)

Once you've decided what kind of list you want to create, the next step is to write a mission statement that includes a description of the topics your list will cover, the policy guidelines for the types of messages that are appropriate for the list, and whether you plan to keep archives or an FAQ for the list and where and how subscribers can retrieve them. Once everything is in place, you can announce your list's existence to the Internet community by sending a message containing the list's description to `interest-groups-request@sri.com` and to `new-list@vmi.nodak.edu`.

Conclusion

As we've seen in this chapter, the Internet can be a great place for electronic schmoozing—"working the room," so to speak, without actually being there. Whether you decide to join a discussion group or create your own, the Internet can be a great place to expand your network of professional contacts, find new customers and pick up the latest industry information. Of course, the Internet can also be a way to broadcast your company's foibles and follies if you fail to observe the rules of "netiquette" or create a discussion group that serves to anger customers rather than entice them.

But person-to-person interaction isn't the only thing the Internet has to offer businesses—there's also a wealth of free information available for the taking. In the next chapter, "Dialing for Data," we'll show you how to use Internet tools such as Gopher, Archie, WAIS, FTP, telnet and Veronica to mine the Internet's motherlode of electronic information for tips, trends and statistics that can give your company an edge over the competition.

Business-Related Discussion Groups

Here's a sampling of business-related mailing lists and newsgroups to get you started.

Business-Professional Interest

Computing

Adv-Info on *LISTSERV@UTFSM.BITNET*

This mailing list publicizes the latest advances in computing technology. To subscribe, send the following command to LISTSERV@UTFSM.BITNET via mail or interactive message. SUB ADV-INFO *yourfullname* where *yourfullname* is your real name, not your login I.D.

Electrical ENGINEERING

Adv-Eli on *LISTSERV@UTFSM.BITNET*

A mailing list where electrical engineers share information about advances in their field. To subscribe, send the following command to LISTSERV@UTFSM. SUB ADV-ELI *yourfullname*.

Entrepreneurs

misc.entrepreneurs

Newsgroup for discussions about running a business.

Journalism

alt.journalism

Newsgroup for discussions of issues of interest to journalists.

Law

misc.legal

Newsgroup for discussions of legal topics and issues.

Mechanical Engineering

MECH-L%UTARLVM1.BITNET@CUNYVM.CUNY.EDU

This mailing list covers topics pertinent to the mechanical engineering community. To subscribe, send the following command to LISTSERV@UTARLVM1: SUB MECH-L *yourfullname*. Non-BitNet users can subscribe by sending the text: SUB MECH-L *yourfullname* in the body of a message to LISTSERV%UTARLVM1. BITNET@CUNYVM.CUNY.EDU.

Media

MEDIA-L%BINGVMA.BITNET@MITVMA.MIT.EDU

Media professionals use this mailing list to share information or ask questions about educational communications and technology issues. To subscribe send the following command to `LISTSERV@BINGVMB` (non-BitNet users send mail to `LISTSERV%BINGVMB.BITNET@MITVMA.MIT.EDU`) `SUBSCRIBE MEDIA-L` *yourfullname*.

Medicine

MEDCONS%FINHUTC.BITNET@VM1.NODAK.EDU

This is a medical mailing list used by physicians and investigators on a voluntary basis to consult on diagnoses. BitNet users can subscribe by sending the following command to `LISTSERV@FINHUTC`: `SUBSCRIBE MEDCONS` *yourfullname*. Non-BitNet users can join by sending the above command in the text/body of a message to `LISTSERV%FINHUTC.BITNET@VM1.NODAK.EDU`.

Museum Professionals

MUSEUM-L on LISTSERV@UNMVM.BITNET

Museum professionals and others interested in museum-related issues share ideas and information regarding new methods of interpreting information for visitors, both high-tech and low-tech. To subscribe, send a one-line message to `LISTSERV@UNMVM.BITNET`: `subscribe MUSEUM-L` *yourfullname*

Oil and Gas Exploration

OIL-GAS@PAVNET.NSHOR.NCOAST.ORG

This is an electronic newsletter for the serious oil and gas investor and discusses current oil and gas industry issues, problems, events, and opportunities. Included are day-by-day oil prices. The newsletter is published monthly, with periodic "Extra" updates or additional coverage. Subscription contact: `nshore!pavnet!oil-gas-request` OR `oil-gas-equest@pavnet.nshore.ncoast.org` (Please use `SUBSCRIBE` or `UNSUBSCRIBE` as the subject).

Veterinary Medicine

AAVLD-L on LISTSERV@UCDCVDLS.BITNET

Mailing list for veterinary diagnostic laboratories and members of the AAVLD to discuss topics such as test standardization, fees, diagnostic information assistance, animal health surveillance, and reports on conferences and symposia. To subscribe to the list, send the following command to `LISTSERV@UCDCVDLS` via interactive message or in the BODY of e-mail: `SUBSCRIBE AAVLD-L` *`yourfullname`*

Geographic

Australia

soc.culture.australia

Newsgroup for discussing Australian culture.

Canada

CANADA-L on LISTSERV@VM1.MCGILL.CA or LISTSERV@MCGILL1.BITNET

Mailing list for political, social, cultural, and economic issues concerning Canada. To subscribe to CANADA-L send a message or e-mail to `LISTSERV@VM1.MCGILL.CA` or `LISTSERV@MCGILL1.BITNET` with the body containing the command `SUB CANADA-L` *`yourfullname`*

India

INDIA-L%UTARLVM1.BITNET@VM1.NODAK.EDU

Mailing list for topics of interest to people living on the Indian subcontinent. BitNet users may subscribe by sending the following command to `LISTSERV@UTARLVM1`: `SUBSCRIBE INDIA-L` *`yourfullname`*. Non-BitNet users can join the list by sending this command as the only line in the text/body of a message to `LISTSERV%UTARLVM1.BITNET@VM1.NODAK.EDU`.

Japan

AJBS-L@NCSUVM.CC.NCSU.EDU or *AJBS-L@NCSUVM.BITNET*

Mailing list operated by The Association of Japanese Business Studies (AJBS), an international association of scholars, students, government and business researchers, and executives interested in the Japanese economy and business systems. To subscribe, send mail to `LISTSERV@NCSUVM.BITNET` or `LISTSERV@NCSUVM.CC.NCSU.EDU` with the body containing the command `SUB AJBS-L` *yourfullname*.

Korea

soc.culture.korean

Newsgroup for discussing Korean culture.

Malaysia

soc.culture.malaysia

Newsgroup for discussing Malaysian culture.

Mexico

MEXICO-L@TECMTYVM.MTY.ITESM.MX

MEXICO-L@TECMTYVM.BITNET

Mailing list for people wanting to know more about Mexico's cities, customs, cultures, and tourist attractions. BitNet users can join by issuing the following command: `TELL LISTSERV AT TECMTYVM SUBSCRIBE MEXICO-L` *yourfullname* or the equivalent for sending messages, if your operating system is not VM/SP. Non-BitNet users can join by sending a message to `LISTSERV@TECMTYVM.MTY.ITESM.MX`, with the one-line command `SUBSCRIBE MEXICO-L` *yourfullname* in the body of the message.

Russia

Russia@IndyCMS.IUPUI.EDU or Russia@IndyCMS.BITNET

Mailing list for the exchange and analysis of information regarding Russia and her neighbors. To subscribe, send e-mail to either `LISTSERV@INDYCMS.BITNET` or `LISTSERV@INDCMS.IUPUI.EDU` (Internet) with the body (text) of the mail containing the command `SUB RUSSIA` *yourfullname*.

Vietnam

soc.culture.vietnam

Newsgroup for discussing Vietnamese culture.

Company, Product, User Groups

3Com Products

3COM-L%NUSVM.BITNET@CUNYVM.CUNY.EDU

3COM-L on LISTSERV@NUSVM.BITNET

Mailing list for topics related to 3Com products, such as 3+ Network, 3+Open LAN Manager, 3+Open TCP, 3+/3+Open Mail, NDIS, MultiConnect Repeater, LanScanner, 3Com Ethernet Cards, and so on. To subscribe, send the following command to one of the preceding addresses: `SUBSCRIBE 3COM-L` *yourfullname*.

IBM 9370 Computers

9370-L%HEARN.BITNET@MITVMA.MIT.EDU

Mailing list for topics specific to the IBM 9370 family and the VM/IS packaging system, and the special opportunities/problems of those products. To subscribe send the following command to `LISTSERV@HEARN` (non-BitNet users send mail to `LISTSERV%HEARN.BITNET@MITVMA.MIT.EDU` with the command in the message body): `SUBSCRIBE 9370-L` *yourfullname*.

Intel 80386-Based PC Computer Users

386USERS@UDEL.EDU

Mailing list for Intel 80386 topics, including hardware and software questions, reviews, rumors, and so on. All requests to be added to or deleted from this list, problems, questions, and so forth, should be sent to 386USERS-REQUEST@UDEL.EDU.

Intel Computer Systems

comp.sys.intel

Newsgroup about Intel systems and parts

Macintosh

comp.sys.mac.announce

Newsgroup containing important notices for Macintosh users.

Multimedia

comp.multimedia

Newsgroup about multimedia hardware and software, all platforms.

NeXT Computers

NeXT-L%BROWNVM.BITNET@MITVMA.MIT.EDU

Mailing list for discussion of the NeXT Computer. To subscribe, send a message to LISTSERV AT BROWNVM: SUBSCRIBE NEXT-L *yourfullname*. Non-BitNet users send a message to LISTSERV%BROWNVM.BITNET@MITVMA.MIT.EDU.

OS/2

comp.os.os2.announce

Newsgroup featuring announcements related to OS/2.

DIALING FOR DATA

What's the fast-growing city in the Pacific Northwest?

What's the hottest foreign market for fax machines?

How many shares of stock have the officers and directors of Sun Microsystems sold this year?

Gathering up-to-the-minute market intelligence is vital for any business, and businesses hooked into the Internet know that it's available through the network—for free—anytime you want it.

Unlike commercial online services and database providers that charge as much as $200 an hour to tap into specialized business and financial databases, the Internet offers millions of files from libraries, universities, and government agencies worldwide for nothing more than the cost of an Internet account, and you can search and retrieve information from all these files.

Of course, you don't get something for nothing. Unlike commercial services that offer easy-to-use menus and navigational tools, finding information on the Internet can be time-consuming and difficult.

Another problem is information overload—there's so much available on the Internet that trying to keep track of it all can be overwhelming, especially if you're new to the network. And while the Internet offers unparalleled access to government data, library card catalogs, and university research, many of the best sources of business information are still available only from commercial services like Dialog, Mead Data Central, and CompuServe. (You can access these services via the Internet, but you'll still have to pay to use them.) If you're looking for real-time stock quotes or full-text articles from *The Wall Street Journal*, there's nowhere else to get them except Dow Jones News/Retrieval.

The good news is that there's more and more business and financial information becoming available on the Internet every day, and the Internet tools required to find it are becoming much easier to use. Another plus is that many leading commercial services are beginning to provide gateways for Internet users—you still have to pay to access their information but this way, you don't have to log on and off every time you want to search a database on CompuServe, Nexis, or Newsnet.

In this chapter, we'll teach you the basics of finding information on the Internet, searching through various different Internet databases for information that can help your company grow and prosper.

You'll get an overview of the government, university, business, and financial databases that can be accessed through the Internet—Commerce Business Daily, the Federal Register, the Library of Congress catalog, the U.S. Department of Commerce's Economic Bulletin Board, and many more—and learn the fastest and easiest ways to use them.

We'll also revisit in more detail some of the Internet tools first introduced in Chapter 1, "Putting the Internet to Work for You," including FTP, telnet, Gopher, Veronica, WAIS, and the World Wide Web.

Infomania on the Internet

Until online databases became popular, up-to-date business and financial information was difficult to find and frustratingly slow to retrieve.

Gathering government export statistics, for example, often meant trekking to far-away libraries and sifting through huge volumes filled with tiny print. Compiling postal mailing lists required manually combing obscure trade association directories and other hard-to-find books. And doing market research to find out which part of the country buys the most cellular phones or which company is expected to emerge as the leader in the global aerospace industry by the year 2000 could take weeks—not to mention dozens of expensive long-distance phone calls.

These days, all you need is a computer and a modem to instantly access the kind of business and financial information that once was available only to Wall Street professionals and Fortune 500 companies.

With ready access to everything from the number of chocolate truffles consumed in Peoria, Illinois, to the number of satellite dishes hooked up to households in Singapore, you can quickly and easily target new markets and boost business with customers you already have.

You can also find out about trademark availability, credit information, and sometimes, your competition's marketing plans.

The trouble is, getting information from commercial services can cost a lot of money, especially if you're not a professional information-hunter or you've never searched a database before. On the Internet, much of the same data is available for free—if you know where to look.

Bargain-Hunting on the Internet

Here's a scenario for you to consider: Two companies send you fliers advertising fax paper. One is free, but only if you drive to their shop, about two hours out of town, to pick it up. The other company is a toll-free phone call away, with overnight delivery, but charges $20 for the same product. That afternoon you bump into a colleague at a local cafe, and she tells you that the free fax paper is great, but the proprietor of the store is a bit forgetful and sometimes closes the shop without notice in the middle of the day. That's because she doesn't stock a lot of the paper so that sometimes she has to drive to get some, closing her shop until she returns. Which would you choose—the free fax paper or the $20 fax paper with fewer hassles?

The Internet is much like the free fax paper store of this analogy: There's a lot of information available, but you have to figure out where it is, and even then, it might not be quite what you were hoping for. On the other hand, it's free, and when compared to the expense of major commercial business data services, that can be quite appealing. On the other hand, many time-pressed entrepreneurs and executives prefer to pay a commercial service in return for greater ease and convenience.

Librarian Blake Gumprecht discusses the pros and cons of Internet information-hunting in his forward to *Internet Sources of Government Information*, an electronic guide to Internet information available from local, state, federal, and international government agencies.

Although Internet resources are often more up-to-date than their paper counterparts, more easily searchable, and provide information that's not available in more traditional formats, Gumprecht writes, what's available one minute on the Internet may not be available the next. System addresses, source directories, and filenames are often changed without notice. Sometimes a remote system may be temporarily out of commission.

> **Tip:** You can obtain your own copy of the *Internet Sources of Government Information* by sending e-mail to mail-server@rtfm.mit.edu with the message body containing two commands: send usenet/news.answers/us-govt-net-pointers/part1 and send usenet/news.answers/us-govt-net-pointers/part2.

Here's another scenario. You're head of a major corporation and are curious about the assets of a competitor. Indeed, you're wondering whether it would make sense to buy the company outright. If you had access to a commercial service, you might simply click an "investment forum" icon and immediately be able to choose between S&P data, Disclosure II, Dun's Market Identifiers, and more.

Instead, you figure it's a great opportunity to explore the Internet to see what information you can glean from the public networks. On the Internet, you can find the same information, but what are the tradeoffs? The first is immediately obvious: There's no centralized Internet index to tell you where to find the information. Worse, you realize that unlike paid commercial services, there's no guarantee that the computer housing the information will be in service, and even if it is, no guarantee that the information will be timely and accurate.

Fortunately, finding information on the Internet is easier than it appears—once you know what you're doing! We'll show you strategies for actually tracking down and finding information on the Internet later in this chapter. Before we get there, however, we'd like to whet your appetite with a free sample of Internet information—two free business and financial databases available on the Internet for which you'd otherwise have to pay to access through a commercial online service provider.

EDGAR

One of the best financial freebies on the Internet today is brought to you by the Securities & Exchange Commission, the federal agency with which every publicly traded company must file financial results on an annual and quarterly basis.

The SEC recently started an experimental electronic data-gathering, analysis, and retrieval system known by its acronym, EDGAR. Sponsored by a grant from the National Science Foundation to the New York University School of Business, the EDGAR database makes available for free to Internet users the records of all SEC-required corporate filings.

The EDGAR database is huge—and so is the demand for the information it contains. Carl Malamud, an NSF subcontractor and president of the Internet Multicasting Service, another participant in the project, estimates that roughly

14 gigabytes of data—the equivalent of 14,000,000 pages of information—were sent out in a single month—March, 1994. More than 32,000 documents from thousands of different companies are available, each with a digital signature to guarantee authenticity.

To get similar information on a pay service like CompuServe, you'd have to access the service's Disclosure database and pay $11 per report plus connect-time charges. To be fair, we will note that EDGAR is still a new system, with considerably less historical data than Disclosure. Although the commercial database offers historical financial data dating back years, EDGAR today offers only 1994 electronic filings that are publicly available. Financial reports by companies that do not file electronically and filings that are not available to the general public cannot be accessed through EDGAR. And because the project is experimental, the data is provided as-is with no guarantee as to its accuracy.

Tip: Access EDGAR yourself: Send an e-mail message to mail@town.hall.org with the body of the message containing the single word HELP.

State Department Travel Advisories

Thinking of scouting the local market for tractor parts in Colombia? Better check with the State Department first. You'll want to know how safe it is before you get on that plane.

The State Department's Travel Advisories database provides the full text of U.S. Department of State reports that give travel information and travel advisories for countries around the world. Arranged by country, the files include current conditions, country descriptions, entry requirements, embassy and consulate locations, information about registration, medical facilities, drug penalties, crime, and more. They can also be searched by keyword.

Tip: You can connect directly to the State Department database of travel advisories by typing gopher gopher.stolaf.edu at the system prompt.

Exploring the Internet with a Map

Now that you're beginning to get an idea of the information that's out there, let's press ahead. Like preparing for any expedition, it's a good idea to take a map.

Because the Internet isn't a centralized system, you can't type GO INDEX and have a list of databases pop up on your screen. And because new computer systems are hooking up to the Internet every day and bringing their databases along with them, there's no way of knowing exactly what information is on the Internet at any given moment. In fact, even Internet experts are continually stumbling on rich repositories of data they didn't know were there.

Fortunately, there are a number of excellent Internet books and directories available and a number of comprehensive online resources as well. One of the most useful we've found is *Internet Sources of Government Information*, compiled by Blake Gumprecht, formerly documents librarian at Temple University in Philadelphia. The latest edition lists more than 325 different sources, two-thirds of which weren't listed in the first edition, along with their Internet locations. The guide is available for free: send e-mail to send usenet/news.answers/us-govt-net-pointers/*.

Another useful guide is *Business Resources on the Net* (BRN), compiled by Leslie Haas, Business Reference Librarian at Kent State University Libraries and Media Services, with assistance from information-hunters throughout the Internet. The BRN guide is organized by subject and includes sections on finance, economics, management, personnel, and statistics. Each section is a separate file available via anonymous FTP from ksuvxa.kent.edu in the /library directory. BRN is also available via Gopher at refmac.kent.edu.

There's also a guide called *Government Sources of Business and Economic Information on the Internet* by Terese Austin and Kim Tsang, available at a variety of sites, including Sam Houston State University in Texas. You can obtain your own copy by pointing your Gopher program to Niord.SHSU.edu. The guide lists many of the same databases included in Gumprecht's guide plus a valuable list of business-related mailing lists and newsgroups.

Once you know the name and location of the database you're seeking, the next step is to log onto the Internet and find it. Fortunately, there are a number of excellent search and retrieval tools available, from straightforward e-mail to menu-driven Gopher to the hypertext-based World Wide Web. In fact, many Internet information sources may be searched using any number of different tools, such as e-mail, telnet, FTP, and Gopher, or some combination thereof.

Stock-Picking with EDGAR

Let's say you're trying to track down the latest quarterly financial report filed by Sun Microsystems. You've just read an article about the company in *The Wall Street Journal* and think that now might be a good time to invest. You don't want to call your stockbroker, however, before you've had a chance to analyze the company's latest financials.

It's a perfect time to try out EDGAR, the free SEC database you learned about earlier in the chapter. EDGAR can be accessed several different ways—e-mail, FTP, Gopher, and the World Wide Web—depending on what's most convenient for you.

Assuming that you're like many Internet users these days and all you have is e-mail access to the network, you can simply send an e-mail message to mail@town.hall.org and type the words, SEARCH EDGAR Sun Microsystems in the body of the message. Within a few minutes, the system will respond with the results of your query:

```
=> Search: EDGAR Sun Microsystems

Result(s) of EDGAR search

Company Name            Form Type       Date Filed       File
------------------------------------------------------------------------
SUN MICROSYSTEMS INC    10-Q            (02/08/1994)     edgar/data1/709519/00008
91618-94-000031.txt (58659 Bytes)
SUN MICROSYSTEMS INC    10-Q            (05/10/1994)     edgar/data1/709519/00008
91618-94-000111.txt (44294 Bytes)
SUN MICROSYSTEMS INC    8-K             (04/01/1994)     edgar/data1/709519/00008
91618-94-000092.txt (6566 Bytes)
SUN MICROSYSTEMS INC    8-K             (04/07/1994)     edgar/data1/709519/00008
91618-94-000095.txt (6860 Bytes)
SUN MICROSYSTEMS INC    SC 13G          (02/10/1994)     edgar/data1/729057/00007
29057-94-000076.txt (6122 Bytes)
SUN MICROSYSTEMS INC    SC 13G          (02/11/1994)     edgar/data1/732812/00009
50150-94-000300.txt (12283 Bytes)
SUN MICROSYSTEMS INC    SC 13G/A        (02/14/1994)     edgar/data2/888002/00008
88002-94-000087.txt (43756 Bytes)

Your message has been processed.

Server general info:

 - Commands are case-insensitive, files are case-sensitive.  Be aware of this.

 - The files available through this mail server are the same files
   that can be retrieved via anonymous ftp to town.hall.org.

 - If you are looking for information on EDGAR, issue the following
   command:
```

```
For example:  send edgar/general.txt


 - "help" will yield a document with more info on how to use
   the server.

Mail Server finished.
```

You can see from the bottom of the message how to retrieve the various available documents, but what if you don't want to wait and instead would like to be able to search interactively? After all, when it comes to the stock market, time is money.

One quick and easy way to get your hands on that filing is to access the EDGAR database using Gopher, a software tool with a menu-based interface to a wide variety of Internet information resources. There are two ways to work with Gopher: You can wander around until you find the information you seek, or you can connect directly to the site you desire.

To access EDGAR's Gopher site, log onto your Internet access provider and type gopher gopher.town.hall.org at the prompt or enter gopher.town.hall.org in your Gopher client program. Here's what you'll see:

```
Internet Gopher Information Client 2.0 pl10

                  Root gopher server: gopher.town.hall.org

 --> 1.  Welcome to the Internet Town Hall.
     2.  Federal Reserve Board/
     3.  General Services Administration/
     4.  SEC EDGAR/
     5.  U.S. Patent and Trademark Office/
```

Selecting menu item 4 (SEC EDGAR/) takes you to the next menu, where you can choose Search EDGAR Archives to look for information on Sun Microsystems. Choosing the search option results in your being prompted for a search pattern. From there, you can type Sun Microsystems to search EDGAR's archives.

A minute or two later, you're presented with a list of documents that are related to the company and are in the database. As you probably know, quarterly financial results are called *10Q* filings and you can quickly extract the data you need from the search results menu, as shown here:

```
Internet Gopher Information Client 2.0 p15

                Search EDGAR Archives: sun microsystems

-->  1.  SUN MICROSYSTEMS INC  10-Q     (02/08/1994).
     2.  SUN MICROSYSTEMS INC  10-Q     (05/10/1994).
     3.  SUN MICROSYSTEMS INC  8-K      (04/01/1994).
     4.  SUN MICROSYSTEMS INC  8-K      (04/07/1994).
     5.  SUN MICROSYSTEMS INC  SC 13G   (02/10/1994).
     6.  SUN MICROSYSTEMS INC  SC 13G   (02/11/1994).
     7.  SUN MICROSYSTEMS INC  SC 13G/A (02/14/1994).
```

If you're a harried executive, you're probably too busy to wait for the results of a search. Additionally, you've already done an e-mail query and found out the exact name of the file you want. Through the Internet's FTP program, you can connect directly with the EDGAR database and extract the specific document you seek. At your Internet account shell prompt, you connect by typing `ftp ftp.town.hall.org` and logging in as anonymous using your electronic mail address as your password. (For example, Rosalind would use `rosalind@harrison.win.net` as her password.)

Once you've entered the database, you double-check the filename specified in the e-mail message from EDGAR and see that the file in question is called `/edgar/data1/709519/0000891618-94-000031.txt` This means that you'll want to change to the `data1/709519` directory and then retrieve the specified file. We recommend cutting and pasting rather than trying to type the string of numbers correctly!

Using a text-based FTP interface, here's what you'll want to type and how it will look on the screen:

```
ftp> cd edgar
250-
250- Welcome to the Internet EDGAR Dissemination project. Get the
250- file named general.txt for an introduction to this data archive.
250-
250-This project is funded by a grant from the National Science Foundation
250-to the New York University School of Business in conjunction with the
250-Internet Multicasting Service. Additional support for this project
250-has been provided by Sun Microsystems and UUNET Technologies.
250-
250-
250 CWD command successful.
ftp> cd data1/709519
250 CWD command successful.
ftp> get 0000891618-94-000031.txt
200 PORT command successful.
150 Opening ASCII mode data connection for 0000891618-94-000031.txt (58659 bytes
).
226 Transfer complete.
local: 0000891618-94-000031.txt remote: 0000891618-94-000031.txt
```

```
59816 bytes received in 10 seconds (5.7 Kbytes/s)
ftp> quit
221 Goodbye.
```

Suppose that you didn't know where the EDGAR Gopher site was located. All you knew was that you wanted to find financial data—and you had a hunch that it was on the Internet somewhere. That's where Veronica can prove handy. With Veronica, an acronym for Very Easy Rodent-Oriented Net-wide Index to Computerized Archives, you search by keyword through all the items listed on all the Gopher servers in the world. Here you could search for, say, edgar and sift through the 2,200-plus Gophers that exist worldwide, looking at all the entries that match the specified keyword. You'd have to do a little digging, but, eventually, you'd find what you're looking for. The other nice thing about Veronica is that, once you select a choice from the menu, you're instantly whisked away to the Gopher server that's holds the data you seek.

Here's an example of what you might see on your screen if you used Veronica to search the NYSERNet information system computer in New York, one of several Veronica servers available to the public:

```
           Search gopherspace (veronica) via NYSERNet: edgar

  -->  1.  Edgar Knapp (knapp@cs.purdue.edu)/
       2.  Knapp, Edgar (knapp@cs.purdue.edu) <Picture>
       3.  How to access SEC's EDGAR database online.
       4.  SEC'S  EDGAR SYSTEM.
       5.  net.edgar/
       6.  SEC and EDGAR.
       7.  SEC and EDGAR.
       8.  EDGAR (SEC 10-K Reports) from town.hall.org/
       9.  The Liberals and J. Edgar Hoover: Rise and Fall of a Domestic Inte...
      10.  94-0003 EDGAR Database.
      11.  John Edgar Wideman to Speak at UMass Commencement May 22.
      12.  04/29:  EDGAR on the Internet -- Making Government Data Freely.
      13.  April Colloquia: Preseus Project and EDGAR Database.
      14.  Bronfman (Edgar M.) East-West Fellowship Endowment.
      15.  Bronfman (Edgar M.) East-West Fellowship Endowment.
      16.  04/29:  EDGAR on the Internet -- Making Government Data Freely.
      17.  1994-04-29 (Fri): EDGAR on the Internet.
      18.  EDGAR FTP Access/
      19.  EDU.SPE.Williams,_Ed.D.,_Edgar.txt.
      20.  EDGAR Project (Electronic SEC Filings)/
      21.  EDGAR (Electronic SEC Filings by ftp)/
      22.  EDGAR-from-TAP.
      23.  SEC EDGAR Database "on-line".
```

To read the blurb about how to access the EDGAR database online, you'd type 3 and press Return or move the arrow down to the third entry and press Return.

Globe-Trotting with Telnet

Now that you've made a killing in the stock market (the Internet doesn't yet offer online brokerage services—though it will soon), let's take a look at how you can use the Internet to help your company crack overseas markets.

The database we're talking about now is the U.S. Commerce Department's Economic Bulletin Board, an electronic warehouse containing thousands of files, more than 700 of them updated daily. The board offers in 20 general subject areas information about current economic conditions, economic indicators, employment, monetary matters, and more. One of the most valuable files is a list of trade leads from other countries—overseas purchasing requests for everything from footwear to computers.

Commercial users without Internet access dial up the Economic Bulletin Board directly, at a cost of $45 a year plus per-minute connection charges. And that's not including the long-distance phone charges you'll pay if you live anywhere other than Washington, D.C.

That's where Internet users have an advantage. By accessing the bulletin board through the Internet, you can log on for free and download a wide variety of files, all without incurring a single charge. The Internet access tool that you use to do this is called *telnet*. To use telnet, connect to your local Internet account and then enter the electronic address of the computer you seek. Here the computer is called `ebb.stat-usa.gov`, so the command you'd enter is `telnet ebb.stat-usa.gov`. Once you log in as `guest`, you can use the bulletin board to select menu items and download files, just as if you had dialed it directly.

Let's say your company makes and distributes personal computers and peripherals. You've heard that demand for computers is exploding in Latin America, and you're looking for some sales leads. You log onto your Internet account by typing `telnet ebb.stat-usa.gov` at the prompt and entering the Economic Bulletin Board as `guest`.

Here's what you'll see on your screen:

```
            THE ECONOMIC BULLETIN BOARD (R)
                       of the
          UNITED STATES DEPARTMENT OF COMMERCE

               RONALD H. BROWN, Secretary

          Operated by          | Data lines:  300/1200/2400 202-482-3870
  the Office of Business Analysis |             2400/9600 bps 202-482-2584
                                |              9600 bps      202-482-2167
Director (acting):      Ken Rogers | Telnet access:        ebb.stat-usa.gov
EBB Manager:       Forrest Williams |
System Operator:     Bruce Guthrie | Orders and info:         202-482-1986
```

```
The Economic Bulletin Board is a registered Trademark of the Dept. of Commerce

           Subscribers:  use your account number as your User ID
           Nonsubscribers:      please use GUEST as your User ID

User ID? guest

TBBS Welcomes GUEST
Your last time on was 06/14/94 21:23
You are authorized 20 mins this call

June 13, 1994  Foreign Assets Control Files Updated

  The Office of Foreign Assets Control have updated their files on Haiti
  including banking restrictions.  See File Area 17 for details.

June 10, 1994  Historical Bank Credit (H.8)  ***NEW***

  Weekly and monthly historical Federal Reserve Board Bank Credit (H.8)
  data from 1988 to the present is now available on the EBB.  BCDETAIL.EXE
  is located in File Area 8 and will be updated weekly.

May 27, 1994  Software International articles   ***NEW***

  Software International is a series of articles prepared by the U.S.
  Department of Commerce's (DOC) Office of Computers and Business
  Equipment in conjunction with other DOC offices.  These articles
  discuss upcoming DOC trade promotion events, intellectual property
  rights, export licensing, and other issues related to exporting
  computer hardware and software.  Their primary goal is to provide
  U.S. vendors with information that will facilitate international
  sales.  These articles are available to GUEST users in file area 3
  or as a subscriber in file area 23.




           You have a GUEST status on this board.  As a result, you will have
only
limited access to many of the options in these menus.

ECONOMIC BULLETIN BOARD     Local time in Washington DC: 21:39 on 06/14/94
======== ======== =====     Connect time for this call: 00:00:27
      MAIN MENU             Port: 10   Speed: 9600
      ==== ====
<B>ulletins          View or list system bulletins
<F>iles              Download or search for files on system
<T>rade Promotion    Export promotion files and resources
<P>residential       Presidential Announcements (including US Budget)
<N>ews               New files and updates expected this week, news flashes
<R>egister           Sign up for EBB
<U>tilities          Set default download protocol, change keyword, etc
<C>omments           Send comments to EBB staff or read response from same
```

```
<L>ogon again     Logon again using another userID

==><G>oodbye   <?>Help!!

Command:
```

Type f for *files* at the command prompt to get into the files directory. Then download the bulls.exe file (the one containing the most recent trade leads) using your communications software. Once you've opened that self-extracting file, you can search for computer-related trade leads using the search command in your word-processing software. Unfortunately, this program only works on IBM-compatible PCs.

You can also use telnet to get free legal information for your company. Suppose that, for example, you run a home business and you've just released a new antivirus program that's selling like crazy on the local computer bulletin boards where you've uploaded it. One day, when you're online poking around, you notice another antivirus program. After downloading it and checking the code, you see some unsettling similarities between that program and the one you just wrote. Instantly, you reach for the phone to call your lawyer—but then you put it down when you remember how much he charged you the last time you called.

Instead, you connect to your local Internet access provider and telnet to the Cornell Law School Legal Information Institute and bone up on a little copyright law, so you won't waste time asking dumb questions that rack up big legal bills. While you're there, you might also want to dip into West Publishing Company's online legal directory; maybe there's an attorney who's better (and cheaper) than the one you're using now.

Tip: Connect to the Cornell Law School through telnet by requesting the host fatty.law.cornell.edu. For example, from a dialup account, you would type telnet fatty.law.cornell.edu at the system prompt. No password is required.

Finding Your Way with Wide-Area Information Servers

Another helpful tool for finding information on the Internet, albeit one that many people find confusing, is Wide-Area Information Servers (WAIS).

Like Gopher, WAIS simplifies hunting for data sources on the Internet. Unlike Gopher, it actually does the searching for you. Currently, more than 420 databases are available through WAIS servers, including a fair amount of information on business-related topics. Searches completed through WAIS are easy to work with because the program ranks matched documents based on the number of search words that occur, putting the most relevant document on the top of the pile.

Here's what popped up when we did a keyword search for business on the WAIS server at Thinking Machines Corp. (telnet to the system with telnet quake.think.com, logging in as wais.):

```
SWAIS                                  Search Results                        It
  #    Score    Source                     Title                          Lines
001:  [1000]  (directory-of-se)  Health-Security-Act                        296
002:  [ 778]  (directory-of-se)  ersa                                        55
003:  [ 667]  (directory-of-se)  ANU-Australian-Economics                    99
004:  [ 667]  (directory-of-se)  ANU-CAUT-Academics                          80
005:  [ 667]  (directory-of-se)  ANU-CAUT-Projects                           84
006:  [ 667]  (directory-of-se)  ANU-SSDA-Australian-Census                 106
007:  [ 667]  (directory-of-se)  ANU-SSDA-Australian-Opinion                114
008:  [ 667]  (directory-of-se)  ANU-SSDA-Australian-Studies                126
009:  [ 667]  (directory-of-se)  ASK-SISY-Software-Information               34
010:  [ 667]  (directory-of-se)  IAT-Documents                               33
011:  [ 667]  (directory-of-se)  National-Performance-Review                 62
012:  [ 667]  (directory-of-se)  academic_email_conf                         61
013:  [ 667]  (directory-of-se)  agricultural-market-news                    23
014:  [ 667]  (directory-of-se)  cerro-l                                     23
015:  [ 667]  (directory-of-se)  journalism.periodicals                      58
016:  [ 667]  (directory-of-se)  usda-csrs-pwd                               47
017:  [ 667]  (directory-of-se)  world-factbook                              21
018:  [ 667]  (directory-of-se)  wu-wien-phonebk                             20


<space> selects, arrows move, w for keywords, s for sources, ? for help
```

There are actually quite a few more matches to our search, but here we're presented with the 18 highest scoring entries. Notice that the first entry seems a bit unlikely: Health-Security-Act scored 1,000, the best possible score. Therein lies one of the problems with WAIS: it's a primitive keyword search program, so this reflects that the word we specified—business—was found more times in that document than any other, regardless of its context. One explanation for this document bubbling up to the top of our search list is that it's considerably longer than the others in the match list, as you can see from the information in the last column.

If we decided to explore the second match, we would press the Down Arrow on the keyboard, moving the highlight bar to the second entry, and then press the Spacebar to select the specified item. Pressing Return after selecting one or more items will display those items on your screen, one after the other.

The way to think about WAIS is to imagine it as a database of databases, or to use a metaphor, it's like the section of a library that contains books specifying where other books can be found there. Once you've searched, you need to search a second time within the databases matched—the reference books—to actually find the information you seek.

If this seems complex and confusing, don't despair: WAIS is still a complex tool for finding information in databases and is evolving at quite a fast pace to become more friendly and easy.

Who's on First? (Tracking Down Internet Names and Addresses)

One of the biggest problems on the Internet is finding e-mail addresses for people you want to contact.

Even though there are a number of firms compiling Internet "yellow" and "white pages," it's still easier to call somebody on the phone than search the network for an e-mail address. The reason: with 20,000,000 people on the Internet, it's impossible to keep an up-to-date directory. What's more, people come and go all the time, especially students, and some users don't want to be found.

But what if you can't make that phone call? Perhaps the person you're trying to reach lives in another country, many time zones away, a place where a long-distance phone call would be time-consuming and expensive.

Fortunately, there's a Gopher site at the Texas Tech University Computer Science Department that might have just what you're looking for. Type `gopher gopher.cs.ttu.edu` and you'll get a menu that looks like this.

```
-->      1.  Search Netfind for E-mail addresses <?>
         2.  Search Netfind for Internet Domain addresses <?>
         3.  Search for a Country's Top Level Internet Domain Code <?>
         4.  Verify Someone's Internet E-Mail Address <?>
         5.  Inter-Network E-mail From-To Information/
         6.  Country Specific E-Mail Information/
         7.  Netfind - (Internet-wide E-Mail address searches)/
         8.  Phone Books at Other Institutions/
         9.  USENET E-Mail Addresses/
        10.  WHOIS Gateway/
        11.  X.500 Gateway/
        12.  U.S. Zip Code Directory <?>
        13.  U.S. Postal Codes Directory <?>
        14.  U.S. Telephone Area Code Directory <?>
        15.  U.S. Geographical Information by City or Zip <?>
        16.  Local Times Throughout the World/
        17.  CIA World Factbook, 1993 edition <?>
        18.  World Telephone Area Code Directory/
        19.  Search US State Department Travel Advisories <?>
```

From there, you can access a wide variety of Internet tools and databases that can help you find the person you're looking for. The Texas Tech Gopher also contains some other nifty features. For example, it searches U.S. postal zip codes plus telephone area codes in both the United States and overseas, separating foreign area codes by country instead of zone.

Is Company X on the Internet?

One recurring question that might pique your interest now and again is whether a particular firm is connected to the Internet. The best way to answer this is through a simple little program called *whois*, a program that can search for users, computers, or even tell you information about any hostname on the network.

Is Prentice Hall, the publisher, on the Internet? To find out, type whois prentice-hall and here's what you'll see on the screen:

```
Prentice-Hall Legal & Financial Services (NET-PHLFS)
   15 Columbus Circle
   New York, NY 10023

   Netname: PHLFS
   Netnumber: 165.160.0.0

   Coordinator:
      Sangiorgi, Adelaide  (AS18)  [No mailbox]
      212-373-7565

   Record last updated on 24-Jun-93.
```

That's not right, so we try again without the hyphen and see a completely different result:

```
Prentice Hall (PRENHALL-DOM)
   Route 9W
   Englewood Cliffs, NJ 07632

   Domain Name: PRENHALL.COM

   Administrative Contact:
      Reichlin, Seth  (SR146)  BOOKS@PRENHALL.COM
      (201) 592-2358
   Technical Contact, Zone Contact:
      Jenkins, Colin  (CJ2)  JENKINS@PRENHALL.COM
      (201) 461-7091

   Record last updated on 01-Sep-93.
```

```
Domain servers in listed order:

HYDRA.PRENTICE.COM          192.251.132.3
NS.UU.NET                   137.39.1.3
```

With many Internet services, it's worth trying something with a slightly different tactic if your first attempt fails to yield the results you seek.

> **Tip:** You can use *whois* to find out about one of the authors: try whois Taylor,Dave.

So Many Databases, So Little Time

Now that you've got a sense of how to search for free information on the Internet, it's time to find out what's out there for you and your company.

As you might expect from a computer network that was spawned by the federal government, there's lots of government information available. Besides the SEC and the Commerce Department, government data available on the Internet includes information from the Census Bureau, the Patent Office, the Federal Deposit Insurance Corp., the Federal Communications Commission, and the Bureau of Labor Statistics, just to name a few.

State governments from New York to Michigan to California make their data available, too. More and more foreign governments and intergovernmental agencies are also making their information available to Internet users.

These days, you can even use the Internet to send e-mail to the President, and enactment by Congress last year of the Government Printing Office Electronic Information Access Improvement Act ensures an increasing role for the U.S. government in distributing information electronically. A variety of other proposals suggest that in the future, more and more information produced by state, local, and international governmental organizations will also be available online, sometimes exclusively, predicts Gumprecht, the librarian who compiled the Internet government information sources list.

The Internet is an excellent example of free enterprise at work. Entrepreneurs and universities have rushed in to offer government information on the network when the agencies have been slow to join the information highway directly. Indeed, if you scan back over some of the references we cite earlier in this chapter, you'll quickly notice how many of them live on non-government computer systems.

It's also worth noting that one of the reasons private parties can offer government information in this way is because the majority of government documents cannot be copyrighted by law.

What kind of information is available on the network? Here's a useful document we recently retrieved from the Census Department's Gopher site at gopher.census.gov, the kind of information that can help your business decide which new markets to target for future products, offices, and campaigns:

```
housing "New Housing Data on Salt Lake City Revealed" (06/01/94)

        EMBARGOED UNTIL:  JUNE 1, 1994 (WEDNESDAY)


Public Information Office                    CB94-H.08
301-763-4040
301-763-5668 (TDD)

Ed Montfort
301-763-8551

        NEW HOUSING DATA ON SALT LAKE CITY REVEALED
             BY U.S. CENSUS BUREAU AND HUD

    In the Salt Lake City metropolitan area, about 30 percent of
the householders rated their neighborhood a perfect "10" (on a
scale of one to 10) and 33 percent reported that their home was
the best place to live.  Even so, 7 percent of the householders
living in neighborhoods reported problems with crime, 10 percent
reported traffic problems, and 6 percent had problems with litter
or housing deterioration, according to a report released today by
the Commerce Department's Census Bureau and the Department of
Housing and Urban Development (HUD).

    Information collected in the 1992 American Housing Survey,
sponsored by HUD and conducted by the Census Bureau, "reveals a
mixed bag for area residents," said Ed Montfort of the bureau's
Housing and Household Economic Statistics Division.

    The following is some additional information about the
Salt Lake City metro area:

    The area had 383,800 housing units in 1992, of which 366,500
    were occupied, (68 percent by owners and 32 by renters).

    Single-family homes at 75 percent of all occupied units are
    the predominant housing type in the area.

    The median age of area homes was 43 years for the city
    of Salt Lake City, compared with 20 years for the
    remaining area.

    Homes in the area had a median of 2.8 bedrooms.
```

Of area homeowners, 24 percent had central air conditioning,
94 percent had clothes dryers,
75 percent had dishwashers, and 77 percent had garbage
disposals.

Homes in the area had a median of 2.6 persons per unit, with
a median of 6.2 rooms per unit.

Fifty-three percent of the single detached and mobile homes
had at least 2,000 square feet of living area,
with the median being 2056. About 69 percent of these
homes had at least 500 square feet per person, with the
median being 678.

Eight percent of the owner-occupied homes were located on an
acre or more.

Three percent of the occupied units had moderate or severe
physical problems with upkeep, or with the plumbing,
heating, or electrical systems.(more)

Nineteen percent of the homes were on streets in need of
minor or major repairs.

Five percent of the metro area occupied homes had open
cracks or holes some place inside the home.

Of all area homeowners, approximately 90 percent had a
porch, deck or patio, 90 percent had a garage or carport,
and 60 percent had a usable fireplace.

During the two years prior to the survey, 26 percent of the
owner-occupied units with repairs, improvements or
alterations had roofs replaced, and 18 percent had kitchens
remodeled or added.

Five percent of the homeowners spent $100 or more per month
during the previous year on routine maintenance.

Ten percent of the owners and less than 1 percent of the
renters had monthly housing costs that were
$1,000 or more.

Thirty-seven percent of the householders had incomes of less
than $25,000.

The 1992 median household income for area homeowners was
$39,200, compared with $20,400 for renters.

Renters had median monthly housing costs that represented
25 percent of their current income compared with 18
percent for owners. Monthly housing costs include
mortgage payments or contract rent, utilities, fuels,
insurance, real estate taxes (for owners), and other
housing-related expenditures.

```
    Six percent of the homeowners had yearly real estate tax of
    $1,800 or more.

    Median value of homeowners' residences in 1992 was
    $75,300, down 10 percent from a 1992 constant-dollar figure
    of $83,300 for 1988.

    Forty-six percent of the 14,300 owner-occupied homes built
    since 1988 cost $100,000 or more; 40 percent of the owners
    in new homes used savings or cash on hand for their down
    payment.

    Fourteen percent of the homeowners with a mortgage had a
    current interest rate on their mortgage loan of less than
    8 percent in 1992.

    Salt Lake City was one of eight metropolitan areas surveyed
    from July to December 1992.  This was the sixth visit to the
    area, which was first surveyed in 1974.  Altogether, 44
    metro areas are involved in the survey, a subset of which is
    interviewed each year.  Eight areas were interviewed in
    1992.

    Data are also shown separately in this report for units with
African American householders.

    Since data in this report are from a survey, they are
subject to sampling variability.

                            -X-
```

Universities throughout the world, for their part, provide access to everything from library card catalogs to course catalogs and free software. The Library of Congress and The New York Public Library are among the hundreds of private libraries available through the network, too. You can't read or check out books through the network—yet—but being able to search the world's top libraries for reference works can be an invaluable strategic resource.

And there's more! These days, dozens of private companies, Internet access providers, and commercial online services are making business-oriented databases available to Internet users. The World, for example, offers a Gopher menu that provides a gateway to 15 commercial online services providers, including CompuServe, Datastar, Delphi, Dialog, and Dow Jones News/Retrieval. Though you still have to pay to use them, you can access them for the cost of a local phone call without logging off to dial each one of them separately. Here's what you would see if you chose Commercial Services via the Internet after using Gopher to connect to the World in Boston, MA (use gopher gopher.world.com):

```
            Commercial Services via the Internet
 --> 1.  Information about the Commerical Services menu.
     2.  BRS (Bibliographic Retrieval Service) [McLean, VA] <TEL>
     3.  BioTechNet - +1 508 655 8282 <TEL>
     4.  Compuserve // via hermes <TEL>
     5.  Datapac information +1-800-267-6574 // via hermes <TEL>
     6.  Datastar <TEL>
     7.  Delphi <TEL>
     8.  Dialog [Palo Alto, CA] <TEL>
     9.  Dow Jones News/Retrieval [Princeton, NJ] <TEL>
    10.  EBSCONET <TEL>
    11.  LEXIS/NEXIS (Mead Data General) [Dayton, OH] <TEL>
    12.  Legi-Slate Info Service <TEL>
    13.  Newsnet // via hermes <TEL>
    14.  OCLC <TEL>
    15.  Research Library Information Network (RLIN) [Stanford, CA] <TEL>
    16.  WLN - Western Libraries Network (free til 1 Oct 1992) <TEL>
```

The Financial Economics Network (FEN), an Internet mailing list where subscribers can swap via e-mail information about banking, accounting, stocks, bonds, options, small businesses, corporate finance, and emerging markets, delivers a daily report to its members that provides a market summary of 29 indices and averages. The free report includes the Dow Jones industrial average and the Standard & Poor's 500 stock index and a list of the most actively traded stocks and changes in foreign currency prices.

Tip: Join FEN by sending mail to either editor Wayne Marr (marrm@clemson.clemson.edu) or John Trimble (trimble@vancouver.wsu.edu).

Microsoft Corp. recently debuted a public database containing financial information about the company, enabling Internet users to download Microsoft's 10-K annual and 10-Q quarterly reports and recent press releases free of charge. Bell Atlantic has done the same. You can connect to these services through FTP at ftp.microsoft.com and bell-atl.com.

Tip: Curious about whether your favorite firm has publicly available information? Use *whois* to see whether they're on the network and then try connecting to their site with several different Internet tools. For FTP access, try ftp.*their domain name*, for Gopher, try gopher.*their domain name*, or just connect to their server directly.

> For example, here's how we could search for public information that's available from Cisco Systems: Step one would be to log in to our Intenet access account and type `whois cisco`. This reveals that the company has a registered domain name of `cisco.com`. Armed with that information, we could explore what information is available by typing `ftp cisco.com` or `ftp ftp.cisco.com` at the system prompt to see if either lets in anonymous users (log in with `anonymous` to find out) or by typing `gopher cisco.com` or `gopher gopher.cisco.com`. We could even try connecting to a Web server by using the generic URL `http://www.cisco.com`. There's no guarantee it'll work, of course, but this time we found out that the company has a variety of information available to the public through FTP and the Web.

In summary, the Internet can be a wonderful place to find free information—as long as you're aware of its limitations. Although the information available through the network won't cost you money, it may end up costing you plenty in terms of your valuable time. Therefore, we advise you to go in with your eyes open and to carefully weigh the pros and cons of retrieving information through the free-form Internet versus the more costly and more convenient commercial services. At the same time, we caution you not to get discouraged if you get a little lost on the Internet the first time you go dialing for data. The time you invest in learning your way around the Internet can pay big dividends later.

Business Databases on the Internet

To help you get started, we've compiled a list of business-oriented databases available for free on Internet-connected computers. Many of them are listed in Gumprecht's guide; others come from recent postings on net-happenings—the Internet mailing list devoted to spreading the word about new Internet resources—and many are those we stumbled across in various searches, discussions, and articles in the media.

As a rule of thumb, we encourage you to always skim any article you see about the Internet or information highway for news of additional Internet resources. You never know what you'll find!

General Reference

FedWorldNational.   Technical Information Service system provides access to more than 100 U.S. government computer bulletin boards, many of them previously accessible only by modem. Also includes full text of select U.S. government publications, statistical files, federal job lists, satellite images, and more. The system is often difficult to access because the number of available connections is limited. Connect with `telnet` `fedworld.gov`. The full text of select documents is also available from FedWorld's FTP archive. Try `ftp ftp.fedworld.gov` with user `anonymous` and your e-mail address as the password.

Library of Congress Information System.   Provides access to the Library of Congress online catalog, U.S. government copyright files, databases containing current information about federal legislation and foreign law, a catalog of sources available in Braille or audio format, a national directory of organizations, and more. Connect with `telnet` `locis.loc.gov`.

Library of Congress Marvel.   One-stop source for a multitude of government material taken from a variety of sources—census data, Congressional information, White House documents, crime statistics, State Department reports, and more. You can use either `gopher` `marvel.loc.gov` or `telnet marvel.loc.gov` (login as `marvel` if you telnet).

National Trade Data Bank.   A comprehensive business and economic site on the Internet. More than 300,000 documents, more than 130 information programs from 20 federal sources, including the Department of Commerce Foreign Trader's Index, the Export Yellow Pages, the Trade Opportunities Program, and Market Research Reports. Other agencies will also release data, including the White House and the Departments of State, Treasury, Defense, Agriculture, Labor, Transportation, and Energy. Other major sources of information include the Central Intelligence Agency, the U.S. International Trade Commission, the Export-Import Bank of The U.S., the Federal Reserve Board, the Overseas Private Investment Corporation, the Office of the U.S. Trade Representative, the U.S. Trade and Development Agency, the U.S. Agency for International Development, the U.S. Small Business Administration, and the Social Security Administration. You can connect by three methods: `ftp ftp-stat-usa.gov`, `gopher.stat-usa.gov`, or from a Web browser like Mosaic: `www.stat-usa.gov`.

SunSITE Archives.   This University of North Carolina system is the best first source for the full text of important new government reports. Also provides access to White House documents, NATO information, North Carolina Supreme Court decisions, full text of the North American Free

Trade Agreement, and much more. Use gopher sunsite.unc.edu or telnet sunsite.unc.edu with the log in of gopher. Either way, choose worlds of sunsite to get started.

U.S. Government Gophers.   Provides one-stop access to nearly 100 U.S. government Gopher systems. Connect with your favorite gopher client program to gopher peg.cwis.uci.edu and then navigate through: individuals' information sources, cjboyer, gophers and finally United States government gophers.

U.S. Government Publications Index.   Provides keyword access to citations for U.S. government publications issued through the Government Printing Office since 1976. Connect using the main system of the Colorado Alliance of Research Libraries (CARL) with telnet by typing telnet database.carl.org and then choosing carl systems library catalogs, carl systems libraries - western u.s., carl, library catalogs, government publications.

Zip Codes.   Database of U.S. zip codes, searchable by keyword. The data is made available through the University of Oregon for Gopher and telnet access: gopher gopher.uoregon.edu and then choose Desktop Reference, Geographic And Travel Information. To access the data through telnet, type telnet gopher.uoregon.edu and log in as gopher.

Demographics and Market Research

Census Information.   Provides one-stop access to a broad range of Bureau of the Census-compiled data through Rice University in Texas. Connect with Gopher: gopher riceinfo.rice.edu and then choose Information By Subject Area, Census.

Census of Population and Housing 1990.   Census data available in text and Lotus 1-2-3 spreadsheet formats for U.S. cities, counties, metropolitan areas, states, and the nation, with comparisons from 1980. This information is housed at the University of Missouri. Access it by typing gopher bigcat.missouri.edu and then look in Reference And Information Center. (For an archive of historical Pennsylvania Census data, see the listing for the *Economic Development Information Network* in the *Economics and Business* section.)

Public Opinion Item Index.   Though not government information, public opinion polls provide valuable insight into the American public's view on a variety of topics, including views on the government, its officials, and policies. This University of North Carolina system allows users to search an archive of data from polls conducted by *USA Today*,

Louis Harris, *The Atlanta Journal-Constitution*, and others. Get to it with `telnet uncvm1.oit.unc.edu` and then log in as `irss1` with the password `irss`. Once there, look in IRSS for the section labeled `Public Opinion Item Index`.

U.S. Department of Agriculture Economics and Statistics Gopher.
USDA-Cornell University system provide access to statistics on a wide variety of agricultural topics—consumer food spending, milk and dairy sales, ozone levels, meat consumption, fertilizer use, and more. Most data can be downloaded in Lotus 1-2-3 format or as text. Connect with the command `gopher usda.mannlib.cornell.edu` or try `telnet usda.mannlib.cornell.edu` with the password `usda`.

Technology

High Performance Computing and Communications: Toward a National Information Infrastructure.   This site offers the full text of the federal government's report on the proposed National Information Infrastructure, the formal name of what we know today as the *information highway*. Use Gopher to connect: `gopher gopher.hpcc.gov` and then choose `HPCC-Toward A National Information Infrastructure`.

Information Infrastructure Task Force Gopher.   Provides access to task force directories, press releases, calendars, and committee reports, as well as the full text of speeches, documents, and select legislation relevant to the National Information Infrastructure. Connect with Gopher: `gopher iitf.doc.gov`.

National Information Infrastructure Agenda.   Full text of a Clinton administration report describing the role of government in promoting the development of the telecommunications and information infrastructure by the private sector. Again, use Gopher to find this information: `gopher ace.esusda.gov` and then step through `Americans Communicating Electronically`, and `National Policy Issues` to find the information.

Merit Network Information Center.   The Michigan-based MERIT consortium provides information about the Internet, NSFNet, and MichNet, including General Accounting Office reports, Office of Management and Budget reports, National Research and Education Network activity, conference proceedings, newsletters, statistical reports, policy statements, user's guides, and more. Use: `gopher nic.merit.edu`.

Economics and Business

Basic Guide to Exporting.   Full text of a U.S. International Trade Administration introduction to exporting through Gopher: `gopher umslvma.umsl.edu` and then choose `the library, government information`.

Commerce Business Daily.   Full text of the 10 most recent issues of the Commerce Business Daily, a U.S. government publication that invites private bids on projects proposed by federal agencies. You can also search the information here by keyword to find if there are any bids invited for a specific product or service. Connect with `gopher cns.cscns.com` and select `Special-Commerce Business Daily`.

Country Reports on Economic Policy and Trade Practices.   Full text of detailed U.S. Department of State reports describing the economic policy and trade practices of individual countries around the world. Connect to the University of Missouri at St. Louis: `gopher umslvma.umsl.edu`, `The Library, Government Information`.

EconData.   University of Maryland archive of economic time series statistics prepared by U.S. government agencies. Data from this site must be downloaded and reformatted on your own computer; they provide downloading instructions and tools. The path: `gopher info.umd.edu` and then `educational resources, economic data`. Through telnet: `telnet info.umd.edu`.

Economic Bulletin Board.   The Department of Commerce offers easy access to thousands of data files, more than 700 of them updated daily. Includes information about current economic conditions, economic indicators, employment, foreign trade, monetary matters, and more in 20 general subject areas. Connect with `telnet ebb.stat-usa.gov` and log in as `guest` or use the University of Michigan Gopher server: `gopher gopher.lib.umich.edu` and then `social sciences resources, economics`.

EDGAR Securities.   New York University continues with the Securities and Exchange Commission to make a wide variety of stock and corporate information available to Internet users. Current data only encompasses information on companies that file reports electronically. Try `gopher vaxvmsx.babson.edu` and then look in `business resources`. Alternatively, use FTP—as shown earlier in this chapter—with `ftp town.hall.org` and a login of `anonymous` and your own e-mail address as the password.

Empowerment Zones and Enterprise Communities.   This site provides information about a new government program to designate up to 9 empowerment zones and 95 enterprise communities for the purpose of helping to create jobs and improve conditions in the nation's poorest urban neighborhoods and rural areas. Learn more with Gopher: `gopher ace.esusda.gov` and then choose `americans communicating electronically`.

The Financial Economics Network (FEN).   FEN is an Internet discussion group where subscribers swap information via e-mail on banking, accounting, stocks, bonds, options, small business, corporate finance, and emerging markets. FEN delivers Holt's Stock Market Reports, also by e-mail, to subscribers. The daily report provides a market summary of 29 indices and averages, including the Dow Jones industrial average and the Standard & Poore's 500-stock index. It also lists the most actively traded stocks and changes in foreign currency prices. To sign up, contact editor Wayne Marr (`marrm@clemson.clemson.edu`) or John Trimble (`trimble@vancouver.wsu.edu`).

General Agreement on Tariffs and Trade (GATT).   Full text of the final version of the GATT agreement, incorporating all changes made at the Uruguay round of negotiations. An executive summary written by the U.S. trade representative is also available. Connect to `gopher ace.esusda.gov` and look in `americans communicating electronically, national policy issues`.

Gross State Product Tables.   U.S. Bureau of Economic Analysis tables estimating the value of goods and services for 61 industries in 50 states. Use: `gopher gopher.lib.umich.edu` and then `social sciences resources, economics (2/94)` or connect with telnet: `telnet una.hh.lib.umich.edu` and log in as `gopher`.

Industry Profiles.   Full text of a series of Small Business Administration reports that describe the trends and opportunities for small businesses in select industries. This one is at the University of Missouri, St. Louis: `gopher umslvma.umsl.edu` and then look in `the library, government information, small business administration industry profiles`.

International Business Practices.   Full text of a Department of Commerce reference work that provides overviews of import regulations, free trade zones, foreign investment policy, intellectual property rights, tax laws, and more for 117 countries. Try `gopher umslvma.umsl.edu the library, government information`.

Labor News.   Department of Labor bulletin board provides access to labor statistics, daily news releases, OSHA information, abstracts of articles in the Monthly Labor Review, and more. Via telnet: `telnet fedworld.gov` and then choose `gateway system` and connect to `gov't systems`.

LabStat.   Bureau of Labor Statistics system provides access to current and historical employment and unemployment data, occupational injury and illness rates, consumer and producer price index figures, as well as other labor and economic data. Only available through FTP directly from the Bureau as follows: `ftp stats.bls.gov` and then log in with `user anonymous` and your e-mail address as the password. Start with directory `pub`.

Massachusetts Institute of Technology Experimental Stock Market Database.   Stock prices are updated daily, and there are charts tracking price and volume performance on 315 stocks and several mutual funds, including Fidelity Magellan and the Janus Fund. You'll need access to the World Wide Web for this one: use URL `http://www.ai.mit.edu`.

National Export Strategy.   Full text of a report to Congress by the Trade Promotion Coordinating Committee outlining 60 actions designed to strengthen U.S. export promotion efforts. Available through FTP: `ftp sunny.stat-usa.gov`, log in as anonymous with your e-mail address as the password. Start in `pub/export`.

North American Free Trade Agreement.   Full text of NAFTA and related documents, available through two different Gopher sites: `gopher ace.esusda.gov` and then `americans communicating electronically, national policy issues (2/94)`, or, if that doesn't seem to work: `gopher umslvma.umsl.edu, the library, government information`.

Occupational Outlook Handbook.   Full text of a U.S. Department of Labor annual publication that provides detailed information about more than 300 occupations, including the nature of the work, working conditions, training and education requirements, job outlook, average salaries, and more. Connect with `gopher umslvma.umsl.edu` and then look in `the library, government information`.

Overseas Business Reports.   Full text of U.S. International Trade Administration reports describing the economic and commercial climate in individual countries around the world. At the University of Missouri, St. Louis: `gopher umslvma.umsl.edu` and then `the library, government information`.

President Clinton's Economic Plan.   Full text of A Vision of Change for America, a summary of the President's economic plan. Connect with Gopher: `gopher wiretap.spies.com` and then search in `government docs` for `clinton's economic plan`.

QuoteCom.   Plans to offer delayed quotes on stocks, bonds and futures contracts; historical data on stocks and futures contracts, and closing quotes and United Press International business news, also fed on a

15-minute delay. The service is free for limited usage. Subscribers who want to check more than five stock quotes during the day will be required to register at a cost of $19.95 a month. You can send QuoteCom a list of up to 20 ticker symbols, and it automatically updates the value of your portfolio, sent daily to your electronic mailbox. For more information about QuoteCom, send e-mail to `info@quote.com`.

Regional Economic Information System (REIS).   This Department of Commerce system offers statistics on employment by industry, income and earnings by industry, and transfer payments for states and counties. Try: `gopher sunny.stat-usa.gov` and then choose `economic conversion information, regional statistics`.

State Small Business Profiles.   Full text of a series of Small Business Administration reports that provide statistical overviews of the economy in each of the 50 states, focusing on the small business sector. Connect with: `gopher umslvma.umsl.edu, the library, government information, small business administration state profiles`.

Uniform Commercial Code.   Full text of the Uniform Commercial Code, including a keyword search system, available at Cornell University. Connect through telnet by typing `telnet www.law.cornell.edu` with the login `www`.

U.S. Industrial Outlook.   The Department of Commerce annually examines recent trends and provides five-year projections for the top 350 industries in the United States. Connect with Gopher: `gopher gopher.lib.umich.edu` and then look in `social sciences resources, economics, industrial outlook`. Alternatively, try: `telnet una.hh.lib.umich.edu` with the login of `gopher`.

Government Regulation

Ambient Monitoring Technology Information Center.   This Environmental Protection Agency system provides information and the full text of regulations concerning ambient air quality monitoring. Use: `telnet ttnbbs.rtpnc.epa.gov` with the login of `amtic`.

Americans with Disabilities Act.   The full text of the 1990 Americans with Disabilities Act is available through Gopher from the University of California at Santa Cruz. Connect with `gopher scilibx.ucsc.edu` and then look in `the library`, for `electronic books`.

Clean Air Act Amendments Bulletin Board System. EPA system provides access to information relevant to 1990 Clean Air Act Amendments, including full text of the act. Connect: `telnet ttnbbs.rtpnc.epa.gov` with the account `caaa`.

Clean Water Act. Full text of the Clean Water Act, as taken from the U.S. Regulatory Code. Use Gopher: `gopher sunny.stat-usa.gov` and then search in `economic conversion information exchange`, `adjustment programs and laws`.

Clearinghouse for Inventories/Emission Factors (CHIEF). This EPA system provides information about air emission inventories and emission factors and provides access to tools for estimating emissions of air pollutants and performing air emission inventories. Use: `telnet ttnbbs.rtpnc.epa.gov` then log in as `chief`.

Environmental Protection Agency. The EPA system provides access to a directory of environmental information resources, a database containing information about environmental regulations governing the closure of military bases, proposed new rules for the pulp and paper industry, pesticide regulatory information, and more. Use: `gopher gopher.rtpnc.epa.gov`.

National Air Toxins Information Clearinghouse. EPA system provides access to a directory of government air toxins control officials, descriptions of regulatory programs, emissions guidelines and inventory data, and more. Connect with `telnet ttnbbs.rtpnc.epa.gov` and then log in as `natich`.

Food and Drug Administration Bulletin Board System. Full text of FDA news releases, enforcement reports, import alerts, drug and product approval lists, Federal Register summaries, agency publications, articles from FDA Consumer, and more. Use: `telnet fdabbs.fda.gov` with a login `bbs`.

Food Labeling Information. This FDA database provides information about new food labeling regulations and activities related to the Nutrition Labeling and Education Act. Use Gopher to connect: `gopher zeus.esusda.gov` and then look in `usda and other federal agency information` for `food labeling information`.

Health Care Reform Information. Full text of the Clinton administration's health care reform proposal, a detailed section-by-section explanation of the Clinton plan, along with related reports and press releases. Connect: `gopher ace.esusda.gov` and then look in `americans communicating electronically`, `national policy issues` for `health care reform agenda`.

Occupational Safety and Health Administration Regulations.   Full text of current OSHA standards and regulations, as taken from the Federal Register and Code of Federal Regulations. Use Gopher to connect: `gopher stellate.health.ufl.edu` and then choose `OSHA`.

TOXNET.   You can use this system at the National Institutes of Health to access a database with information about the toxicity of hazardous chemicals. It's being built as we write this, and in the future is also expected to offer a variety of other databases, including the Toxic Chemical Release Inventory (TRI), the Registry of Toxic Effects of Chemical Substances (RTECS), and the Chemical Carcinogenesis Research Information System (CCRIS). Try connecting `gopher tox.nlm.nih.gov`.

International Trade

Background Notes.   Full text to a series of U.S. Department of State reports that provide brief overviews of the people, history, government, economy, and foreign relations of individual countries around the world. Use `gopher umslvma.umsl.edu` and then choose `the library` and `government information`.

Country Studies and Area Handbooks.   Full text of select Army Area Handbooks, such as *Japan: A Country Study*, which present in-depth discussion of the political, economic, and social conditions of countries around the world. This is accessible through Gopher: `gopher umslvma.umsl.edu`. Choose `the library, government information` then `army area handbooks`.

International Organizations.   Provides access to general information about more than two dozen major international organizations, from the Food and Agriculture Organization to the World Bank. Connect to the University of Vermont through Gopher `gopher mirna.together.uvm.edu` and then choose `united nations, UN organizations`.

State Department Travel Advisories.   Full text to a series of U.S. State Department reports that provide travel information and travel advisories for countries around the world. Arranged by country, files include current conditions, country descriptions, entry requirements, embassy and consulate locations, information about registration, medical facilities, drug penalties, crime, and more. Use Gopher: `gopher gopher.stolaf.edu` and then choose `internet resources, us-state-department-travel-advisories`.

World Bank Public Information Service.   Full text of World Bank policy papers, environmental reports, project information documents, country economic reports, publications catalogs, and more. Try: `gopher gopher.worldbank.org`.

Law

Code of Federal Regulations.   Users can use commercial systems to browse the Code of Federal Regulations or search it by keyword. Access to the complete CFR is not yet available. The system places limits on the amount of information non-subscribers can retrieve. Use Gopher to connect: `gopher gopher.internet.com`, and then choose `counterpoint publishing (2/94)` or through telnet: `telnet gopher.internet.com` with a login as `gopher`.

Computer Law.   Australian FTP archive includes a variety of files containing information on computers and the law, including the text of many U.S. state laws. Use FTP to access the files: `ftp sulaw.law.su.oz.au` and then login as `anonymous` with your e-mail address as your password.

Copyright Information.   The Library of Congress allows users to search a database of information about works registered in the U.S. Copyright Office since 1978. Also includes files that provide general information about copyright. Connect: `telnet locis.loc.gov`.

Cornell Law School Legal Information Institute.   Uses the World Wide Web to search and retrieve information from numerous legal texts, including the U.S. Copyright Act, Supreme Court decisions, and the Uniform Commercial Code. Use Mosaic or another Web browser to connect with URL `http://www.law.cornell.edu` or `telnet fatty.law.cornell.edu`.

Internet Patent News Service.   List of all U.S. patents issued during the previous week, available by free subscription via electronic mail. To sign up or to find out more information about the mailing list, send e-mail to `patents@world.std.com`.

Patent and Trademark Office Bulletin Board System.   Provides access to Official Gazette notices, information about new patents, patent and trademark fee schedules, agency directories, full text of PTO news bulletins, press releases, brochures, and more. Use: `telnet fedworld.gov` then `gateway system, connect to gov't systems`.

Patent Office Reform Panel Final Report. Full text of a U.S. Patent and Trademark Office report recommending that U.S. patent procedures be changed to follow policy held by most industrialized nations. Try: `gopher wiretap.spies.com` and then look in `government docs`.

Supreme Court Decisions. High court decisions updated nightly and available through the World Wide Web. Use the URL `http:// archive.orst.edu:9000/supreme-court`.

Venable, Baetjer, Howard & Civiletti. Washington law firm specializing in information law. One of the first law firms in the country to offer a World Wide Web server. See what they have to offer the Internet with URL `http://venable.com/vbh.htm`.

CONNECTING THE WORLD WITH INTERNET E-MAIL

As local markets evolve into a global marketplace, businesses large and small are searching for a quick, easy, and inexpensive way to communicate with employees, customers, and colleagues worldwide.

These days, global networking often means patching together a hodge-podge of long-distance phone, fax, data-transmission, videoconferencing, and overnight courier services and trying to integrate it all with the company's communications network back home—a complex and costly process. Even for giant multi-nationals, the cost of setting up a wide-area network to move voice, data, and video traffic around the world can often be prohibitive.

That's why the Internet is so attractive. With the Internet, your company pays a flat monthly fee to hook up to the network, enabling you to send all the e-mail, documents, graphics, audio, and video you want virtually anywhere in the world. Unlike commercial online networks, Internet doesn't charge by the byte or by the hour. With the Internet, you can forge ahead into new international markets confident that your profits won't sink in a sea of long-distance phone bills.

Of course, price isn't the only issue—especially for business. If it were, Federal Express would have gone out of business long ago!

As we discussed in previous chapters, doing business on the Internet carries some risks; in terms of communications, these risks involve reliability, security, flexibility, and integration with local-area networks (LANs). Although Internet e-mail may be a low-cost way to reach out on a global scale, it's also a dicier way to go when your data absolutely, positively has to be there overnight (if not sooner).

The purpose of this chapter is to show you how to use the Internet to exchange messages, documents, graphics, video, and other files with employees, customers, vendors, and colleagues worldwide. We'll consider the pros and cons of Internet e-mail versus commercial network providers such as AT&T, MCI, Sprint, and CompuServe. We'll also discuss some of the challenges involved in integrating the Internet with your existing local-area network, showcasing solutions for small, medium, and large companies that are looking to set up Internet mail gateways.

Around the World with Internet E-Mail

For companies doing business internationally, Internet e-mail offers three key advantages:

- It's available all over the world
- It's easy to use
- It's a lot cheaper than the commercial alternatives

According to the University of Wisconsin's Larry Landweber, who compiles a list of Internet-connected countries, 146 countries now have Internet connectivity, from France, Spain, Germany, and Italy to China, the Dominican Republic, and Zimbabwe. With more and more countries hooking up all the time, the Internet is fast becoming the Esperanto of electronic communications systems. (For a list of Internet-connected countries, see the chart in Appendix C, "The World According to the Internet.")

With Internet e-mail, you can use a wide variety of text- and graphics-based interfaces to send an electronic letter to one person or thousands of people. You can send text files and binary files. You can distribute memos, product announcements, brochures, job postings, and electronic magazines—all for a lot less than you'd pay for postage or long-distance phone service. You can even send messages to people on online networks for which you don't have an account; for example, if you're a CompuServe subscriber, you can send a message to someone on America Online or vice versa.

Of course, Internet e-mail isn't just useful for international businesses. Companies that do business locally can benefit, too. For example, Copytech Printing of Canton, Massachusetts, uses the Internet to swap messages with customers and vendors and to receive files for printing. Technical manager Jeff Weener says the Internet gives his company a competitive edge. "We're in the demand print business where lead times are short," Weener says. "Internet helps with delivery and makes it easy to get files."

In Kansas City alone, Internet e-mail users include the following companies:

AlliedSignal Inc. is using the network to periodically update databases in five remote locations and send electronic mail. The company fields questions about machine tools through a toll-free telephone number and then sends out answers to its customers via the Internet.

Sprint Corp., the nation's third largest long-distance carrier, is hooking its internal computer networks to the Internet so that all its departments can communicate through the system. Sprint employees can now tap into Internet newsgroups to discuss professional development or telecommunications topics. Sprint has also used the Internet to set up an electronic information booth for employees featuring a variety of information about the company and its benefits.

Marion Merrell Dow Inc. has a pilot Internet project in place. Researchers access the network to search for the latest studies and doctoral dissertations in their fields. They also use external e-mail to communicate with fellow researchers throughout the world.

Olathe-based Ruf Corp. employees use the Internet to send e-mail to customers and talk with computer and statistics experts on Internet newsgroups.

In Pennsylvania, Internet e-mail users hail from industries as diverse as health care to petroleum. Students at Hahnemann University medical school in Philadelphia who are doing rotations at the hospital can use the Internet to tap into Hahnemann Automated Library and find out what's going on at their school. Buckeye Pipeline Co. in Emmaus, Pennsylvania, uses the Internet to communicate with the American Petroleum Institute and other trade groups.

Profile: In Rosalind's home-based publishing business, she's used the Internet to communicate with business associates as far away as Australia and as close as those down the street. Several weeks ago, after posting a press release about her newsletter, an editor from South Africa's *Weekly Mail & Guardian* requested a subscription.

Thanks to the Internet, she was able to exchange a series of notes with him without resorting to expensive long-distance phone calls. What's more, she doesn't have to charge him extra for overseas postage because she distributes the newsletter through e-mail—incurring the same low cost for subscribers down the block as those across the globe.

With a busy travel schedule and full-time school, Dave also relies on Internet e-mail to keep in touch with his friends, colleagues, and clients throughout the world; it's common for a client to contact Dave through electronic mail, for them to hammer out a contract online, and the materials to be delivered, all without a single piece of paper changing hands. Even invoices are distributed electronically. Clients in England or Japan can collaborate as easily as those in the same town.

Internet E-Mail Versus the Rest of the Pack

Although there are a number of commercial networks that offer worldwide connectivity—AT&T, MCI, Sprint, and CompuServe, to name some of the major ones, the Internet is far less expensive and more widely available. These days, even large corporations that rely on commercial networks are discovering the advantages of using the toll-free Internet instead, swelling Internet usage by about 15 percent a month.

As we saw in Chapter 4, "Doing Business on the Internet," companies as large as Lockheed, which pays $40,000 a year for a leased line to connect 5,000 of its 70,000 employees worldwide, to businesses as small as Alain Pinel Realtors, a California real estate brokerage that pays $180 a month to connect its 200 agents with local customers and vendors, are finding the Internet to be a cost-effective solution to their communications needs. Almost all of the major auto manufacturers are now utilizing the connectivity strengths of the Internet, too, including Toyota, Honda, Chevrolet, Ford, and Chrysler.

Cost isn't the Internet's only attraction for corporate users. Unlike many of the commercial e-mail products on the market today, the Internet was designed to handle large numbers of users and incorporates an addressing system that makes that possible. The Internet's simple yet sophisticated addressing format divides each address into two parts—the name and the location. Locations always have an assigned domain portion—commercial, educational, military, and the like. SRI

International, a government-funded organization in Menlo Park, California, maintains the Internet directory, making sure all names are unique.

By contrast, local-area network software packages such as cc:Mail and Microsoft Mail use a single, flat directory structure for addressing messages. There's no hierarchical organization; if there are two Joe Smiths, one has to use a different name. This type of addressing works fine for 100 or even 1,000 users. But what about a 1,000,000? 20,000,000?

If you work for a large company, you may have heard of the X.400 messaging system, an internationally endorsed computer standard for addressing and building e-mail messages that is language and transportation-system independent. It has some definite advantages over Internet e-mail, notably its support for foreign languages, but it's suffering from the chicken and egg problem and too few sites use it for us to recommend your choosing it as a basis for your corporate e-mail.

The Internet's addressing system also offers advantages over the widely used X.400 protocol. Unlike the not-for-profit Internet, X.400 is the commercial approach, currently used by more than 200 public networks worldwide, including mail systems from MCI Communications Corp. and AT&T EasyLink Services. X.400 services are more functional, more complex, and far more expensive a route than the Internet and are at heart a commercial system, with many features designed specifically for the business of moving messages. Were it not for the Internet, X.400 would be the only real choice for worldwide e-mail.

If you decide to use a different carrier to access the Internet, you generally don't have to change your e-mail address. With X.400, you must include your carrier identification as part of your address. That's like having to change your telephone number every time you switched long-distance carriers.

The Internet also boasts another advantage: It's a single interconnected network. Once connected, you can send e-mail to anyone without restriction. By contrast, X.400 is made up of separate networks managed by different organizations. Each of these networks is called an Administration Management Domain (ADMD). Usually a long-distance carrier or a government-owned telecommunications company owns an ADMD. ADMDs must bilaterally agree to be connected to one another, and not all ADMDs are interconnected, restricting your reach to those with X.400 connections.

Because of the Internet's low-cost, widespread use, and addressing versatility, many experts now are touting the Internet as a one-stop shopping mall for corporate telecommunications needs. Within a few years, the prediction of Tom Lunzner of SRI International might be true: "The Internet will replace the now-ubiquitous fax machine."

How Internet E-Mail Works

To understand how Internet e-mail works, it's time to revisit the highway metaphor. As we noted in the introduction, the Internet is not a centralized system like CompuServe or America Online but a decentralized "network of networks," a collection of thousands of small regional networks connected by phone lines, cables, even satellites. The Internet's high-speed links carry a wide variety of data, including chunks of files (FTP), commands (telnet), discussion (Usenet), and even pictures (the Web).

What makes all this Internet traffic possible is a set of common traffic laws called Transmission Control Protocol/Internet Protocol (TCP/IP), a language that all Internet-connected computers share.

The best way to understand how the network works is to think of it all as a variety of layers, each protocol building atop the previous. At the bottom of the stack, serving as the foundation of the highway, is the Internet Protocol (IP), a specification that details how to send specific packets of information—called *datagrams*—across multiple networks. IP features a packet-addressing method that allows any computer on the network to forward a packet to another computer that is closer to the final destination. (At least, it is usually closer. On the Internet, routes can change at a moment's notice depending on computer loads, competing demands on the network, and other factors.) Another IP feature is the capability to break a datagram into small chunks, which is necessary because different networks may have different packet sizes.

It's important to recognize that, unlike Federal Express and other commercial carriers, IP is a "best efforts" packet delivery protocol. There's no method within the IP "layer" for verifying that a given packet arrives intact at its destination—or at all. In addition, IP routes each packet separately. Different packets, even within the same message, may traverse the network along different paths and may arrive at their final destination out of order.

Both of these problems are resolved by a high-level protocol—in this case, the Transmission Control Protocol (TCP). TCP exists to ensure reliable transportation of messages across Internet-connected networks. It handles the error-checking of IP packets and, if necessary, requests retransmission of damaged or missing packets. It also handles the resequencing of out-of-order packers and discards any duplicate packets that may occur when too many packets are retransmitted. If IP is the concrete foundation of the information highway, TCP is the set of rules that allow specific lanes to be delineated, on- and off-ramps to be designed, and signs to be built.

The information highway isn't very useful without traffic of some sort—let's call these cybercars—and one important, and popular, type of cybercar is e-mail traffic. Unlike real cars, however, these e-mail messages travel by zooming from gas station to gas station, parking for seconds, minutes, or even hours at each stop. In computer parlance, this is called a *store-and-forward* network, and it means that your e-mail message isn't sent immediately or even directly to the recipient but is driven down the highway en route. The rules that govern the driving of these e-mail cybercars is called the Simple Mail Transfer Protocol (SMTP). It details the explicit steps one computer must make to connect to another computer and transmit an electronic mail message. Usually SMTP is built atop TCP/IP (that's the layering we discussed earlier) but can use alternate means as appropriate such as as SLIP. Thanks to SMTP, a universal e-mail protocol, highly dissimilar machines to exchange electronic mail without fuss or translation.

How does Internet e-mail compare to the U.S. Postal Service? Actually, it's much the same. People who use Internet e-mail don't exchange messages directly any more than the postal service picks up a letter from the mail box outside your office and carries it directly to the office park across the state.

Like the postal service, your Internet access provider takes your electronic letters, trucks them to the nearest Internet "post office," sorts them and distributes them.

It may distribute them to your neighboring office park (because both buildings are in the same neighborhood and use the same post office), but, more often, your e-mail message will stop at five or six Internet "post offices" along the way—just as if you mailed a postal letter from Tallahassee, Florida, to Sioux City, Iowa.

And like postal mail, the recipient has to check his Internet electronic mail box to retrieve your letter, a letter courteously, if silently, delivered by the electronic Internet postman.

All postal mail carries the postmark of the post office that first received the letter, and often, if it's been routed through multiple post offices, it will bear one or two postmarks on the envelope.

An Internet e-mail message not only carries the postmark of the original computer post office receiving the message but also includes information about each of the systems en route that forwarded the mail. On the Internet, these postmarks can be easily seen in each message by examining all the headers.

Here's an example of this from an Internet message Dave recently received from a colleague at the Virginia Department of Education. Take a close look at the "Received:" lines:

```
From jhammond@vdoe386.vak12ed.edu  Sun Jun 19 08:02:19 1994
Return-Path: <jhammond@vdoe386.vak12ed.edu>
Received: from virginia.edu by mail.netcom.com (8.6.8.1/Netcom)
     id IAA02029; Sun, 19 Jun 1994 08:02:17 -0700
Received: from vdoe386.vak12ed.edu by uvaarpa.virginia.edu id aa25289;
```

```
         19 Jun 94 11:01 EDT
Received: by vdoe386.vak12ed.edu (5.65/1.34)
         id AA05854; Sun, 19 Jun 94 14:56:46 GMT
From: "D. Jon Hammond" <jhammond@vdoe386.vak12ed.edu>
Message-Id: <9406191456.AA05854@vdoe386.vak12ed.edu>
Subject: Help
To: taylor@netcom.com
Date: Sun, 19 Jun 94 10:56:45 EDT
X-Mailer: PENELM [version 2.3.1 PL11]
```

Notice how the mail was received by the original host, vdoe386.vak12ed.edu, at 14:56 GMT and then routed to uvaarpa.virginia.edu, which received it at 11:01 EDT (which is 15:01 GMT). Then the message was forwarded to mail.netcom.com at 08:02:07 PST (GMT plus seven hours, which is also 15:02:07 GMT). Despite the stops along the way, total transit time was less than five minutes from Virginia to California.

Internet E-Mail Software

Unlike e-mail systems on many commercial online services, there's no single way to send Internet e-mail. It all depends on the type of computer system and software you're using; there are dozens of DOS, Windows, Macintosh, and UNIX-based programs available for sending Internet e-mail.

All Internet e-mail programs share certain features, however. They all prompt you to fill in the recipient's address (the To: prompt) and the message header (the Subject: prompt) and then allow you to enter the message itself, known as the "body" or text of the message. With many programs, you also can include other documents, or even audio, as attachments.

Now, let's complicate the picture a bit. Internet e-mail is handled by two kinds of programs—clients and servers. Don't panic: The post office works the same way; there are letter carriers who show up at your home and handle specific mail transactions such as delivering and picking up mail, and there are the faceless thousands who work at central routing and delivery facilities throughout the world.

Clients are the programs that you see when you work with e-mail; servers are the lower-level systems that take care of routing and delivery through the network. Good client programs offer a complete facility for managing your electronic mail, including address books, message folders, and more. Server programs queue your messages in a pile and periodically send them on electronic "trucks" to other computers on the Internet.

There are a wide variety of client programs, particularly for UNIX systems. Among the best are Mail (also known as Berkeley Mail), the Elm mail system, Pine, and

Mush. All text-based, these programs all handle the basics of e-mail messaging and often can be invoked by typing their names when you log onto your Internet access provider; Dave, who authored the Elm program in (date), is partial to Elm for his UNIX accounts. Graphical programs include ZMail, XMH, and MailTool for UNIX systems. Lots of Mac and Windows clients are popping up, too: Eudora runs on DOS and Macintosh systems, and Pipeline and WinNET Mail are both software-server combinations that provide an easy-to-use Windows interface. Rosalind uses WinNET Mail on her PC.

Berkeley Mail is one of the most widely available Internet e-mail programs for dialup access, but also one of the most basic. It can be started by typing `mail` at the UNIX command prompt once you log onto your Internet access account, or if you specify an e-mail address when you start the program, it will let you compose and send a message to the designated recipient, as shown in this simple example:

```
% mail bill@tyler.win.net
Subject: Still on for lunch?
Bill,
Just checking in with you to confirm our lunch at Monty's in Miami today.
Send me a note if you need to change our plans.
Thanks,
Rosalind
.
Cc:
%
```

Here the mailer prompted us to type a summary of our message after `Subject:`. We encourage you to always use succinct, meaningful subject lines for all your messages. Once you've typed the subject line, you can write as many lines as you like. The very last line of the message is indicated with a `.` by itself. Once that's entered, the program asks whether you would like to send copies of the message to any other recipients. In our case, there were none, so we pressed Return at the `Cc:` prompt and sent the message to Bill. Once we sent our message, the client program handed off the message to an e-mail server for delivery, probably using a program called *sendmail*.

There are other, easier programs for working with e-mail if you're on a UNIX account. Both Elm and Pine offer more control over handling and filing your messages. With the Elm Mail System, each summary line indicates when the message was sent, who sent it, how long it is, and what the message is about. To act on the message, you simply scroll the selection bar up or down to highlight the message and then press the appropriate key. Pressing `d`, for example, deletes a highlighted message; by pressing `r`, you can reply to the message.

Here's what Dave's incoming mailbox looks like when he uses Elm:

```
       Mailbox is '/usr/spool/mail/taylor' with 29 messages [ELM 2.4 PL23]


 --> 1   Jun 17 Rosalind Resnick    (74)    Internet Business Guide — Book Cover
Info
      2   Jun 17 Kim Patch          (37)    a request...
      3   Jun 17 Rosalind Resnick   (25)    Business Guide cover art?
      4   Jun 17 Martha E. Anderson (43)    updated information
      5   Jun 17 Optel@aol.com      (27)    questions
  D   6   Jun 17 Rosalind Resnick   (114)   FEDGOVT> National Trade Data Bank vi
      7   Jun 17 Rustici@aol.com    (31)    Re: Information on the Internet Mall
      8   Jun 17 Robert Wachtel     (119)   Possible listing or assistance
      9   Jun 16 Scott L. McGregor  (25)    How about a proposal for GATT/NII?
     10   Jun 15 LukeDuff@aol.com   (28)    Your book is great!


       ¦=pipe, !=shell, ?=help, <n>=set current to n, /=search pattern
 a)lias, C)opy, c)hange folder, d)elete, e)dit, f)orward, g)roup reply, m)ail,
   n)ext, o)ptions, p)rint, q)uit, r)eply, s)ave, t)ag, u)ndelete, or e(x)it

Command: Quit
```

Pine is similar to Elm—indeed, it's an acronym for Pine Is Not Elm—and is available in DOS, Windows, and UNIX versions, as is Elm, it provides an easy-to-use menu interface that enables you to issue commands with the touch of a key. Press c, for example, and you can compose a message. You can also use Pine to create folders in which you can organize your messages and maintain an electronic address book to store e-mail addresses.

Here's what the Pine main screen looks like:

```
PINE 3.87   MAIN MENU                         Folder: INBOX  2 Messages


        ?    HELP              -  Get help using Pine

        C    COMPOSE MESSAGE   -  Compose and send a message

        I    FOLDER INDEX      -  View messages in current folder

        L    FOLDER LIST       -  Select a folder to view

        A    ADDRESS BOOK      -  Update address book

        S    SETUP             -  Configure or update Pine

        Q    QUIT              -  Exit the Pine program
```

```
       Copyright 1989-1993.  PINE is a trademark of the University of Washington.
                       [Folder "INBOX" opened with 2 messages]
     ? Help                  P PrevCmd                        R RelNotes
     O OTHER CMDS L [ListFldrs] N NextCmd                     K KBLock
```

Although text-based programs such as mail, Elm, and Pine are widely available (and they're almost always free because they're already installed on your Internet access provider's computer), you may prefer a graphical interface, especially if you're a Mac or Windows user and don't like typing commands at the system prompt. Not only can these graphically-based e-mail programs be easier to use, but you can also cut and paste between applications, so you can create a letter or document in your word processing package and then paste the text onto your e-mail message.

An even newer category of software is software-server combination packages, offered by Internet access providers such as Netcom, Pipeline, and PSI. Pipeline, for example, puts a pretty face on a full range of Internet services, including e-mail, newsgroups, Gopher, and even an Internet guide, and also provides a dialup server. WinNET Mail offers an easy-to-use front-end for Internet e-mail and newsgroups only. With WinNET's mail editor, you can maintain an off-line address book, create folders for managing your mail and newsgroup messages, and compose and file messages offline. WinNET Mail does not yet offer FTP, Gopher, or telnet access. Figure 8.1 shows what the WinNET Mail "in box" looks like.

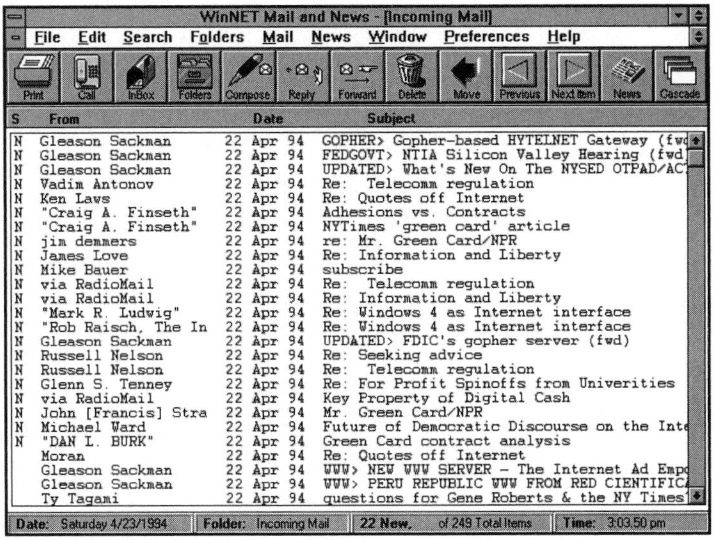

Figure 8.1. WinNET Mail's In Box, which displays new messages.

Internet Addressing

As we discussed in Chapter 1, "Putting the Internet to Work for You," Internet addresses have three parts—the user I.D., the name of the computer system, and the domain, or type of network. As a shortcut, think of addresses having the format *user@host.domain* (pronounce this as *user at host dot domain*.). Usually the user portion of an e-mail address is a login address such as `taylor` or `ldunlap`, but actually, it can be anything that the receiving machine understands such as `cedric.higgins` or `the-boss`. It can be composed of any combination of letters, numbers, and punctuation characters such as a dot, dash, or underscore.

Domains are the most interesting part of the address and are built from right to left, with the rightmost item indicating the top-level Internet domain. For example, `com` means a for-profit commercial enterprise like Apple Computer, Prentice Hall or CompuServe; `net` is a network; `edu` is an educational site, `gov` is a government site, `mil` is for military facilities, and `org` is for nonprofit and other private organizations.

For example, if you were on CompuServe, you could reach Rosalind by sending mail to `71333,1473`. But let's say you had an America Online account rather than a CompuServe account. Instead of sending your e-mail to `71333,1473`, you would send it through the Internet to `71333.1473@compuserve.com`. By adding a domain specifier, you tell the AOL mailer that the recipient is on another system. The `.com` high-level domain indicates that it's a commercial address and `CompuServe` specifies which of the more than 60,000 registered commercial domains is your intended destination. Note that, when sending mail through the Internet, CompuServe's commas (,) must be changed to periods (.).

Here's how you would send Rosalind an e-mail message via the Internet if you wanted to contact her on one of the online networks on which she has accounts:

Prodigy: `vbtj94a@prodigy.com`
CompuServe: `71333.1473@compuserve.com`
America Online: `rosalindr@aol.com`
GEnie: `rosalindr@genie.geis.com`
Delphi: `rosalindr@delphi.com`

She also has two accounts with Internet access providers—Computer Witchcraft in Louisville, Kentucky, the company that developed WinNET Mail, and CyberGate in Deerfield Beach, Florida, a local Internet access provider. Her WinNET Mail address is `rosalind@harrison.win.net`, and her CyberGate address is `rosalind@gate.net`.

Tip: The best place to find the Internet addressing formats for other online networks, such as Bitnet, BIX, Easylink, Fidonet, and MCI Mail, is Scott Yanoff's *Internetwork Mail Guide*. It's available via anonymous FTP at `csd4.csd.uwm.edu`. Connect with `ftp csd4.csd.uwm.edu`.

Internet Directory Assistance

Although sending e-mail through the Internet is quick and easy, tracking down people's Internet addresses can often be a time-consuming and frustrating experience. Unfortunately, there's no comprehensive membership list as there is on CompuServe, MCI Mail, and the other commercial networks, and there's no Internet "white pages" or "yellow pages" directory that you can open to find somebody's e-mail address (although several enterprising net-repreneurs are now attempting to put this sort of thing together).

For now, probably the quickest way to find somebody's e-mail address is to call by phone and ask—not very high-tech, we admit. Nevertheless, there are several Internet "directory assistance" tools that you can try before you spring for that long-distance call.

As you learned in Chapter 1, "Putting the Internet to Work for You," there's a program called *whois* in which you type a person's name and find a directory listing for the person you're looking for. The whois services lists approximately 70,000 Internet users, though, with 20,000,000 people now on the network, the odds are not good that the person you're looking for will be listed there.

An alternative way to try and find an e-mail address is to use a program called *netfind*. Netfind is a white pages service that automatically searches through a variety of e-mail databases for you, though it is a bit tricky to use. Try it for yourself by connecting to the University of Colorado: `telnet bruno.cs.colorado.edu`.

There are a few other alternatives, including *finger*, which is of assistance in confirming addresses (try `finger taylor@netcom.com` to confirm that's the e-mail address of one of the co-authors). In addition, most university computers maintain a *ph*—phone number—database that contains information on people who have Internet accounts at that site. There's also a Gopher site at Texas Tech that can point you in the right direction (see Chapter 7, "Dialing for Data," for details).

The Pitfalls of Using Internet Mail

By now, you're probably thinking, "If the Internet e-mail is so great, why doesn't everybody just ditch their accounts on commercial networks and climb aboard?" The fact is, many businesses are. At the same time, the Internet has some major drawbacks that are likely to keep CompuServe, MCI, and AT&T in the e-mail business for quite some time. The three biggest stumbling blocks to Internet e-mail are

> Reliability
> Versatility
> Compatibility

Let's take a look at them one by one.

Reliability

Although the Internet provides a good, low-cost electronic mail alternative for routine business communications such as memos, press releases, and product brochures, it's a risky bet for mailings requiring high levels of security and immediate delivery.

Although most Internet messages are delivered within minutes, others can take days to deliver if a computer along the route is down for maintenance or because of other problems. And unlike CompuServe, the Internet has no easily accessible "return receipt" function to make sure that the person on the other end actually got your mail.

What's more, with the Internet in the midst of a population explosion, the huge volume of message traffic is beginning to result in delays in delivery, the online equivalent of traffic jams. And because the Internet is a collection of separately managed networks instead of a centralized commercial service, there's no control over the routing of data traffic and no way to tell what happens to your data once it's transmitted.

For now, many management information systems professionals—a group that tends to be conservative in its adoption of new technologies and perhaps a bit anxious about some of its authority being usurped by a shared information highway—remain skeptical of the Internet as a corporate communications tool.

Versatility

The Internet excels at sending text files—ASCII documents that don't contain any formatting, graphics, or embedded audio or video.

When it comes to transporting binary files, however, the Internet's e-mail system falls short. To send a program, graphics, or other kind of binary file over the Internet, you first have to encode it—translate the binary information into text—using a special tool called *uuencode.*

The typical steps involved are uploading the file to the Internet host, feeding the file to uuencode, e-mailing the uuencoded file to someone, and hoping they can unencode it with *uudecode.* On the receiving end, the recipient must save the message as a file and then feed the saved message through uudecode to convert it back to the original format.

There are various utilities available that can uuencode and uudecode files (or otherwise encode and decode files) without leaving your Mac or Windows system—notably StuffIt Deluxe for the Mac or a freeware program called Wincode for Windows—but that only eases a single step. You still have to encode the file, upload it, and then e-mail the uploaded file.

> **Note:** WinNET Mail, the software-server program we described previously, has an automatic encoding and decoding feature built into the program that makes sending and receiving binary files a snap.

Receiving mail in this format is a bit easier, but it's still a weakness of Internet use. While writing this book, we gave up swapping screen shot graphic files through Internet e-mail, given the challenges of finding compatible formats and the complexities of uuencode and uudecode. Rosalind used CompuServe to send her screen shots to our editor, Mark Taber, who also has a CompuServe account, thereby eliminating the need to encode and decode the files.

On the other hand, as Dave finished his chapters, he would uuencode the Microsoft Word text files directly on his Macintosh using UUTool, a shareware program, and then e-mail them to Mark directly via the Internet. It may have been a bit awkward, but it was considerably faster—and cheaper—than sending floppy disks via postal mail.

Sending messages that include graphics, audio, or video clips through the Internet is also a problem, though the gradual acceptance of the Multipurpose Internet Mail Extensions (MIME) protocol is helping.

MIME specifies a multiple media format for electronic mail messages in a way that is compatible with the Simple Mail Transfer Protocol (SMTP), allowing it to coexist with current mail systems. Current Internet e-mail systems do not provide the framework required for sound and video technologies; the MIME protocol offers the support these technologies require and provides future extensibility.

Integration

Another big drawback to Internet mail—and one of the most serious for business users—is the difficulty of integrating the Internet mail system into a local-area network.

If your company is like most businesses, you aren't running a TCP/IP based network currently, but rather one based on NetWare, Vines, AppleTalk, or similar software. If you're running a software package like these, hooking up your internal network to the Internet can be much more difficult than you might imagine.

Part of the trouble is that each LAN e-mail package uses a different addressing scheme, as does the Internet. Currently, there is no universal translator or common e-mail directory scheme, though many vendors have proposed their own systems as universal, trans-network standards.

Incompatible addressing is only one of many problems destined to confront corporate network administrators attempting to bring the Internet "in-house." They must also attempt to balance cost, performance, reliability, compatibility, consistency, security, and support, while the array of solutions available changes constantly.

That's because LAN-based e-mail systems have ignored worldwide standards, such as the Internet's SMTP protocol, in order to include sophisticated functions such as workflow processing, integrated scheduling, and the compression of attached files. The price has been the inability to work with each other and the rest of the e-mail world.

Profile: How hard can it be to get the different systems working together gracefully? Network consultant Kevin Angus described the battle he waged in integrating cc:Mail with the Internet, in a December, 1993, article in *LAN Times*. UUCP, in his article, is a primitive store-and-forward protocol for slow phone lines, allowing files to be automatically copied from one UNIX system to another.

"When I set out to install my first Internet gateway, for a client using cc:Mail, I thought it would be a snap: simply fork over $495 and install cc:Mail's cc:Mail Link to UUCP," Angus wrote. "The nondeterministic nature of the Internet's store-and-forward message delivery made testing and troubleshooting the setup quite a challenge. Sending a message between the same two points takes from 10 minutes to two days—if it gets there at all. If one of the Internet post offices crashes, any mail stored in that post office and awaiting forwarding can be lost."

> Because he was working with UUCP-based e-mail, he also discovered to his chagrin that some older Internet post offices truncate messages longer than 1 kilobyte, drop attached files, or disallow node names of more than six characters. Because his client wanted to use an eight-character company name, that became a problem. He also had to wade through dozens of pages of incomprehensible UNIX instructions.

Les Kent, who wrote an article about the problem recently for *InfoWorld*, compares connecting a LAN-based electronic mail system to the Internet and other networks to "trying to stop the fighting in Bosnia."

"As anyone who builds e-mail solutions that try to bridge the gap between LAN and public services quickly discovers, the landscape is a battlefield of trade-offs," writes Kent. "The one certainty is that any e-mail solution deployed today will be a temporary fix."

As a result, creating transparent interoperability between all e-mail systems so that every user, regardless of location, hardware, operating system, or e-mail application, can easily send electronic messages to anyone else is often a challenging and elusive goal.

Although it's possible to send mail from one LAN to another over the Internet, it's never simple. Messages can be garbled, attachments sometimes get dropped, and improperly formatted text in messages is ignored. Ironically, the very features that make LAN-based e-mail programs so attractive are the prime reasons these programs have difficulty working with the Internet, CompuServe, and other public access networks.

E-Mail Solutions

Although it can be difficult to get a private mail system on a local network to interact gracefully and reliably with the Internet, it's also true that savvy network administrators are finding creative solutions to get things up and running.

Although dialup Internet connections for the PC and Mac are beginning to appear, leased lines are usually the best bet for heavy Internet users. Alternatively, if you have a UNIX mail server at your site, you can set up a connection—a bridge—directly to the Internet. Once you have a leased line to the Internet, you can use an SMTP gateway to get from your LAN e-mail system to the rest of the world. Every major LAN-based e-mail system has a vendor-supplied SMTP gateway; ask yours for more information but take any claims of easy connectivity with a grain of salt.

Another hassle-free way to connect your system with Internet e-mail is through a value-added network provider such as CompuServe, which requires a Novell Message Handling Service gateway, AT&T Mail, or MCI Mail.

Be warned: Although this method is more reliable and secure, it can also be quite costly. CompuServe, for example, charges 15 cents for each Internet message received in addition to connect-time charges for time spent retrieving them. Imagine a dozen people at your company joining a busy set of Internet mailing lists, and you're looking at shelling out some serious money.

On the other hand, if you're a small company and you're looking for some sort of Internet connectivity without too much fuss, connecting through CompuServe or a similar service can be a viable solution. This allows a simple Internet connection, plus relatively inexpensive message costs. If your firm sends a large volume of e-mail internationally, you may find the expanded international X.400 connectivity of a dialup service provider, such as AT&T or MCI, a better fit.

Once your firm grows beyond a certain size, paying the per-message charge through a commercial service can quickly add up to much more than a dedicated Internet connection, and it's a sure bet that this expense will grow as your staff learns about the many riches available on the network. As a result, we strongly recommend that companies of any significant size connect to a public network carrier.

Nevertheless, hooking a LAN to the Internet will continue to be a challenge until a new generation of LAN e-mail front ends and message server back end programs become available from Microsoft, Lotus Development Corp., and Hewlett-Packard later this year. Even then, however, expect to spend a fair amount of time getting everything to work the way you want it.

For now, many smaller firms are taking a middle-of-the-road approach when it comes to Internet connectivity, using the Internet to supplement rather than replace the commercial networks they're using.

Profile: Peter Stephenson, who recently wrote an article for *LAN Magazine* called "E-mail on a Budget," describes the compromise he struck. His LAN program, Lotus Development Corp.'s cc:Mail, incorporates an MCI Mail gateway.

"I travel the world so I need a service that covers the world and connects to my private system," Stephenson wrote. "One such service—the Internet—provides this capability, but in many cases, it's awkward to use directly. When I'm in China, I can access the Internet. More importantly, people I work with can access the Internet. But not everyone does. So, for me, the Internet is necessary but not sufficient as a public carrier. Within the United States,

> another large system serves most of my colleagues who do not use the Internet. That service, also available in many other countries, is MCI Mail." Making this an even better solution, users of the Internet can send e-mail directly to an MCI Mail account, and people hooked up through MCI Mail can also send messages to Internet users.

The Future of Internet E-Mail

Despite the highlighted drawbacks and difficulties, the Internet, and particularly Internet e-mail, is receiving lots of attention from software developers and network architects around the world, each of whom is working on trying to more fully integrate the Internet into existing applications, systems, and platforms.

Graphical Interfaces

One promising trend is the growing number of *graphical interfaces* that make Internet e-mail quicker and easier to use. One interesting example, albeit one that doesn't work for simple dialup connections, is Eudora, a popular shareware program developed by Qualcomm, Inc. of San Diego and used by more than 100,000 Internet users. Qualcomm recently introduced a commercial version with many more features, capabilities, and a higher level of reliability.

The commercial version of Eudora includes mail filters and mail-management functions with which you can automatically download and sort Internet e-mail. This way, you can set up folders for each of your mailing lists and Eudora will filter your messages according to their headers. You can also read, create, and edit messages off line.

What's more, Eudora supports common Mac and UNIX file transfer protocols like unencode, binhex, and Apple Computer's proprietary message formats. Eudora is also one of the first Mac mail programs to support MIME. In the future, Eudora users will be able to correspond electronically with users of Microsoft Mail, Lotus Development Corp.'s cc:Mail, or any other mail system that connects to TCP/IP networks. Qualcomm is shipping Eudora for Apple Macintosh users as we write, with a Microsoft Windows version scheduled to ship by the end of the year.

Interoperability

The second trend is *interoperability*—the breaking down of barriers that now exist between the Internet and other networks.

One group that's working on improving the capability of Internet services to interact with PC and Mac systems is the Internet Engineering Task Force (IETF). The IETF is developing its first standard protocol for accessing and manipulating electronic mail, a draft specifying an Internet message access protocol (IMAP), which covers commands for retrieving messages and manipulating mailbox activity in TCP/IP networks.

IMAP will provide standard methods for creating, deleting, renaming, and checking the status of individual mailboxes on TCP/IP-based e-mail servers. The draft also specifies mechanisms for manipulating Internet mail messages and messages composed in MIME format, providing a way for TCP/IP networks to handle e-mail from different kinds of networks.

Meanwhile, private access providers are also busy trying to solve many of these interoperability problems. Gordon Bridge, president of AT&T EasyLink Services, notes that "the Internet is influencing all of us to build more TCP/IP capability. EasyLink's InterSpan interconnect service, popular among Fortune 500 businesses, provides the largest public e-mail interconnect service in the world. That service includes a way of connecting to the Internet. The InterSpan offering, which is multimedia-based, focuses on establishing business-to-business connections, such as electronic message backbones and gateways to LANs."

PC-based Internet access is also becoming easier and better integrated with commercial e-mail programs. If your company uses the popular Lotus Notes package, for example, you can add access to Usenet newsgroups by using News Link, from Corporate Software in Canton, Massachusetts. If you're a Windows user, you can buy Usenet news reader software from several TCP/IP providers, including Spry of Seattle, Washington. One Internet access provider, NovX InterServ, also in Seattle, offers a service called MS Mail that connects Microsoft Mail users directly to Internet mail using a dial-up router.

Multimedia

The third trend is toward easier *multimedia* transmissions. Last fall, Unipalm Ltd. announced Mail-It 2.0, a $700 tool for sending multimedia files over the Internet. The Windows-based program is compatible with any UNIX-based electronic mail package via SMTP and supports both MIME and Microsoft Corp.'s Messaging Application Programming Interface (MAPI). Mail-It is designed to appeal to users frustrated by the limitations of local-area network e-mail and who want to take advantage of the worldwide wide-area links provided by the Internet. The program eliminates the need for expensive and difficult-to-manage gateway technologies, but does require that you know what kind of mail system the recipient is using.

The MAPI feature allows e-mail to be sent while users work in a Windows application. MIME allows nontext attachments to be sent across the Internet from a desktop computer. In MIME, the user can send multiple attachments in a single message. When Microsoft ships Windows 4.0, which will include the TCP/IP software needed for full Internet connectivity, Microsoft Mail users will be able to use Mail-it to communicate directly between Microsoft Mail and the Internet. UNIX-to-UNIX Copy (UUCP) users can use Mail-it Remote, which comes with an extra program that enables sending and receiving e-mail over remote serial links to the UNIX mail host.

Mobility

The fourth trend is *mobility*. The new Simple Network Paging Protocol (SNPP) will enable users to connect their electronic mail systems to paging networks through the Internet for time-critical message transmissions.

Adoption of the protocol by vendors would allow software developers to create applications that route important messages to pagers through the Internet, which is already used by many organizations to connect e-mail systems with gateways based on SMTP. SMTP does not support message acknowledgment or immediate notification, however.

With SNPP, users connected to the Internet can page mobile recipients with an urgent message and receive an acknowledgment from the paging network, according to Allen Gwinn, who wrote the protocol specifications. However, SNPP requires separate gateways and clients, an obstacle to its wide acceptance by the mobile paging industry.

Meanwhile, the Internet Anywhere Consortium has established a joint venture to develop a software and hardware systems solution to allow wireless access over Morbitex to the Internet, CANet news, mail, and data transfer services. Companies involved in contributing technologies and performing research and development efforts include Mortice Kern Systems Inc. (MKS), the Information Technology Research Center (ITRC), and Research in Motion Limited (RIM).

Whether all of these projects and programs succeed, it's clear that the trend is for Internet e-mail to be more pervasive, more easily integrated into your existing local-area network mail system, and easier to access from throughout the world. The Internet already connects much of the world, as you can see if you check Appendix C, "The World According to the Internet."

In summary, the pros of using Internet e-mail far outweigh the cons. Internet e-mail's worldwide connectivity, low cost, and ease of use make it an ideal way to reach customers and colleagues all over the world. But it's also important to recognize that Internet e-mail has its limitations—namely reliability, versatility, and compatibility with your internal e-mail network. So before you junk your company's wide-area network or pull the plug on your account on a commercial online service, keep in mind that Internet e-mail is a useful tool but not a panacea for business communications needs.

CUSTOMER SUPPORT

No matter what product or service you sell, it pays to cultivate your customers; even they don't know that they're your customers yet.

If customer support is a priority for your business, as it is for most, the Internet can offer you an unparalleled opportunity to build and strengthen your customer relationships. Through inexpensive means, you can offer present and future customers easy access to your sales and development team, free updates and information sheets, and even extra copies of documentation or technical notes, all with minimal fuss and practically no expense.

No matter what your business, customer service is the name of the game. Provide high-quality service on a consistent basis, and customers will make a beeline to your door. Let the ball drop or start treating customers like credit card numbers and those customers—along with potential new ones—will defect to your competitors all too quickly.

The Internet makes customer service easy. By putting product and technical information on a Usenet newsgroup, a Gopher server, a World Wide Web, or an FTP site, even the smallest company can stay in touch with customers and provide up-to-the-minute technical assistance without costly international phone calls or overseas offices.

Through the Internet, customers can ask questions, receive upgrades, and bug fixes for their software programs, demonstrate performance problems to an online engineer, and offer ideas for future enhancements and future products—all without ever leaving their offices or picking up their telephones.

It's no surprise that today hundreds of businesses offer customer support online. For many hardware and software vendors, high-tech hand-holding on the Internet is a logical addition to their dial-up bulletin boards or the forums these firms maintain on commercial online services like CompuServe, America Online, and GEnie.

Digital Equipment Corp., Sun Microsystems, Hewlett-Packard, Wingra Technology, and Silicon Graphics are all busily using the network to interact with customers. High-tech companies might seem a logical fit for the network, but even non-computer-related businesses are starting to exploit the Internet for customer support, businesses such as bookstores, newspapers, even an underwear manufacturer.

At its most basic, the Internet offers companies the advantage of worldwide access to customers, but there's more. Through the Internet, companies can use search-and-navigation tools such as e-mail-based servers, WAIS, Veronica, and Gopher to provide customers access to information about products and other business information, or even a database of frequently asked questions and answers.

This chapter will show you how a wide variety of companies, both big and small, are using Internet tools to provide customers service and support in a cost-effective manner. We'll also take a look at the costs involved in setting up a customer support site on the Internet and discuss how you can integrate Internet support with the support that you already offer via phone, fax, and, if you're a technologically-based firm, computer bulletin board.

Evaluating Customer Support Options

Most companies today offer customer support in one of four ways: telephone, fax, postal mail, or a computer bulletin board (either direct dial into the corporate office or through a commercial online service). Many companies rely on some combination of all four methods.

Each delivery method has its advantages and disadvantages.

> Phone support, often via a toll-free number, gives customers direct access to live technicians with whom they can discuss problems voice-to-voice until the problems are resolved. The disadvantage is that, at a busy

company, phone support often results in busy signals, lengthy waits on hold, and a high degree of customer frustration. It can also be expensive—for the customer if it's a toll call, for your company if customers dial in on your 800 line.

Fax support, in which customers write short summaries of their problems and fax them to the customer service center, can take even longer than phone support to resolve problems. It may also be less effective because the suggestions customers receive by fax may not solve their problems completely.

Postal mail is slower than either phone or fax, though it's often a less costly way to provide documents or computer files that are not time-sensitive. Most software firms distribute upgrades through postal delivery, for example, a strategy we'll consider later in this chapter.

Computer bulletin boards can be the ideal customer service solution—especially for technology companies whose customers are knowledgeable about computing. By logging onto a computer bulletin board, customers can tack up notes any time of day or night and receive a response within hours. Large companies such as Microsoft and IBM assign paid technical support staffers to answer questions on their forums on CompuServe and other commercial online services. Customers can also go online to download software upgrades and bug fixes and to search technical documentation.

There are a number of disadvantages for companies that select an individual commercial service or offer their own dialup BBS. One problem is that the burden of dealing with the complexities of the technology is placed on the customer. For many customers, configuring modem settings is no easy task.

Another problem is that, unless the customer subscribes to the commercial service where the company has located its technical support forum, the customer can't gain access to the information without joining the service and paying a fee. Many customers find it frustrating to purchase a product and then be expected to fork over even more money to get the information they need to make the product work.

The Internet, for its part, offers all the advantages of a computer bulletin board and more plus the convenience of a support strategy that can be integrated smoothly and seamlessly with the way your customers already work.

There's more to customer support than answering users' questions, of course. Frequently, your next great product idea will come from a customer suggestion. Think of it this way: have you ever said to yourself, "If they'd just make a few changes, this would be a great product?" Have you ever taken the trouble to write a letter to the company telling them your idea? With Internet e-mail, these kind of ideas routinely flow in to businesses actively promoting their Internet connectivity, offering a "virtual" focus group that costs the company nothing to set up.

Providing technical support through the Internet can also be far less expensive than any of the other support options, particularly if large amounts of information are involved.

> **Profile:** In August, 1993, Sun Microsystems, a Mountain View, California, workstation manufacturer, launched a program called *SunSolve* to answer its customers' technical questions through Internet e-mail and to distribute software fixes through the network. Previously, the company had relied on a toll-free number for questions and a staff of technicians who packaged, addressed, and mailed CD-ROM updates to each customer.
>
> In the year since SunSolve was introduced, use of the toll-free telephone support line has dropped by over 90 percent, and the company has cut support costs by $1,000,000 a year. What's more, Sun has also managed to offer more information to more customers, increasing customer satisfaction, a critical gauge of the success of a support strategy. Even better from a company perspective is that this higher level of support requires the services of fewer people because their time and resources are better allocated.

Of course, just because you're offering customer support through the Internet doesn't mean that you should pull the plug on your toll-free hotline or scrap any other customer-support options. Because many customers—even customers of computer companies—are not yet hooked up to the Internet, it's vital to maintain phone, fax, computer bulletin board, and postal mail options.

No matter which support options you choose, your goal should be to make it as easy as possible for your customers to interact with you—even if it means more trouble and expense for your business. Although we believe that the Internet can save you money on customer support, cost savings should not be the only factor you consider when choosing a customer support strategy.

Net Results: Why Internet Support Is Good Business

A growing number of companies are discovering another advantage to offering customer support through the Internet; it's excellent public relations.

Profile: InterCon Systems, a Herndon, Virginia, company that develops Internet software for PCs and Macs, has used the Internet masterfully for this very purpose. Through its aggressive use of the Internet, InterCon Systems has developed a worldwide reputation for providing top-notch customer support. Typically, InterCon developers spend several hours a week reading Usenet newsgroups covering computer-related topics. They respond to any posted query they can answer, whether or not it has anything to do with InterCon products.

Developer Amanda Walker, known around the office as the Net Goddess, has even begun to get fan mail from Internet users who rave about the calm, smart, and non-technical way in which she pens her postings. One man liked Walker's style so much that he said that he'd even want to read her description of how to boil an egg. The end result: New customers for InterCon's products.

Getting Feedback with E-Mail

Providing customer support through the Internet can be as simple as letting your customers contact you through e-mail.

These days, many newspapers and magazines are soliciting letters to the editor via Internet e-mail—*The Boston Globe, The Sacramento Bee, The San Jose Mercury News, Business Week, The New Republic, Playboy,* and *Wired* are all on the Internet. *Newsweek,* NBC, and National Public Radio are also accessible by e-mail. In fact, *Newsweek* just added a new page called *Cyberscope,* complete with an e-mail address for tips. Other media organizations have e-mail addresses on commercial online services, which Internet users can reach through gateways.

Not only does the Internet funnel reader letters more quickly to the publications, but it also eliminates the need to have them typed into the computer for layout. What's more, by creating an Internet mail-server, the publication can automatically send each reader an acknowledgment—at far less cost than stuffing an envelope and paying for postage. The convenience of Internet e-mail also frees readers from the bother of sitting down to write a letter and rooting around for a stamp, thus encouraging a larger and more diverse group of readers to write.

To give you an idea of how this works, here's the automatic message that The Boston Globe sends in response to the e-mail it gets:

```
This is to confirm that your electronic mail message to The Boston
Globe has been received.  Thanks for taking the time to write to us.
Although we cannot respond individually to all the messages we
receive, we encourage you to watch the appropriate spot in the
paper if you have submitted a letter or question to a Globe editorial
department.
For your reference, here are the other e-mail addresses at The
Globe:
  news@globe.com
      story ideas, suggestions
  circulation@globe.com
      circulation requests/problems, vacation stops, subscription info
  classified@globe.com
      information about placing a classified ad
  letter@globe.com
      letters to the editor (please include full name and address)
  voxbox@globe.com
      submissions to the Living section's "Voxbox" column
  ombud@globe.com
      comments on our coverage (to Globe Ombudsman)
  ask@globe.com
      submissions to "Ask The Globe"
  list@globe.com
      event listings for Thursday's Calendar section
  howwhy@globe.com
      Health and Science section
  chat@globe.com
      submissions to "Confidential Chat"
  ciweek@globe.com
      City Weekly section
  religion@globe.com
      religion editor
  arts@globe.com
      arts editor
When sending e-mail to the Globe, please include your full name,
address and phone number.  Thank you.
```

Some companies even answer their Internet e-mail manually. You might think, for example, that a clothing manufacturer is an unlikely candidate for electronic customer support, but Joe Boxer Corporation, a California designer underwear manufacturer, has ditched its toll-free phone line for an Internet e-mail box in an attempt to reach the twentysomething market that cut its teeth on the Internet. Joe Boxer's billboards and advertisements all now read, "Contact us in underwear cyberspace; Internet `joeboxer@jboxer.com`." The company says it gets 15 to 20 messages a day, each of which receives a personal response.

"It's pretty hard to live in San Francisco and not be aware of things cyber," says Denise Slattery, the company's marketing director. Though she says she doesn't know how many of the online inquiries result in sales, providing customer support through the Internet "positions our company as very forward thinking."

Spreading the News with Usenet Newsgroups

As InterCon's experience shows, companies can successfully offer customer service through the Internet simply by responding intelligently to messages posted on Internet discussion groups. However, many businesses prefer to stay within Usenet newsgroups focused on their own products, the Internet equivalent of the bulletin boards and forums offered on commercial online services like CompuServe, Prodigy, and America Online.

One company that closely monitors Usenet newsgroups focused on its product line is Mountain View, California-based graphics workstation manufacturer Silicon Graphics. Silicon Graphics participates in eight different Usenet newsgroups under the `comp.sys.sgi` newsgroup umbrella, including `comp.sys.sgi.applications`, `comp.sys.sgi.hardware`, and `comp.sys.sgi.tech`, focused on applications, hardware and technical discussions, respectively.

What kinds of discussion are found there? Here's a partial list of recent messages posted in `comp.sys.sgi.hardware`, a newsgroup focused on hardware problems and solutions:

```
ATM boards for SGI?
Advice on Contem Cyber, Periph Sol?
Archiving Devices
Are there any DSP boards for the Indy's?
BIT3 VME-VME Adaptor
Bezels for drive sleds?
Block to inode-number
Brand New Fuji 8mm Exabyte $7 each
Causes of Exabyte servo failure?
Composite or separate H/V syncs on an RGB monitors??
DAT vs. QIC..
Disabling Indy power button
E&S dialboxes
EISA FDDI card?
EXABYTE HOWTO FOR SGIs
Exabyte 8505 on Indigo2 with IRIX 5.2
Experience with VME-based reflective memory on Challenge?
Fast Ethernet : WHEN & WHAT ??
Filming a monitor
Galileo board installation
HP 2.1 GB disk in 4D/25
HP 35450A 4mm DAT tape drive on Indigo 2
HP DAT drive problem on indy
```

Notes posted to the company's newsgroups come from customers all over the world. This note posted by a Silicon Graphics customer in Japan is fairly typical:

```
From: ysuzuki@u-tokyo.ac.jp (SUZUKI Yuzuru)
Subject: Question: Serial Port Connection
Date: 23 Apr 94 05:44

I want to connect a 3D digitizer to Indy via Serial Port (RS232C).
Unfortunately the digitizer is designed for IBM PC and we got no
information about how to connect it to Indy.
The only information that I could find in Indy's manual is a document
about the pin arrangement of the serial port connector.
Can anybody tell me where I can find more information, how to write
programs to read/write data via Serial Port and so on?
Your help will be much appreciated.
--
Yuzuru SUZUKI
-----------------------------------------------------
ysuzuki@u-tokyo.ac.jp
The University of Tokyo,  JAPAN
```

By responding to newsgroup postings, Silicon Graphics assists not only the customer who posted the note, but also other customers who may be encountering the same problem. Here's a response from Silicon Graphics' Dave Olson to a question posted by a customer from Denmark:

```
From: olson@sgi.com (Dave Olson)
Subject: Re: HP35480 on Indy - Having problems
Date: 24 Apr 1994 19:27

Ottmar Roehrig (or@silicon.hanse.de) writes:

>       wd93 SCSI Bus=0 ID=4 LUN=0: SCSI cmd=0x8 disconnected \
>       on non-word boundary (addr=c0044402, 0x7bfe left), can't DMA.\
>       Resetting SCSI bus

This means the 'no disconnect during data phase' DIP switch isn't
set.  I have heard that the DIP switches for this might be different
with different model or firmware revs, with no further info.  I think
your best bet is to call your distributor for the drive, and try to get
an answer as to which DIP switch.  If you are successful, please
let us know.  You might also ask (including the firmware rev) on
comp.periphs.scsi, as some of the HP Bristol folks responsible for DAT
often answer questions there.

(The firmware rev should be displayed as part of the inquiry by 'mt stat').
Also, since bru seems to work, you could try dropping the i/o size from
64K (last member of struct) to 32K or 20K (bru uses 20K), and see if that
Also, since bru seems to work, you could try dropping the i/o size from
64K (last member of struct) to 32K or 20K (bru uses 20K), and see if that
works around the problem, or explicitly give something like 'tar cb 64'
when making tapes.
--
The most beautiful things in the world are       |   Dave Olson
those from which all excess weight has been       |   Silicon Graphics
removed.  -Henry Ford                             |   olson@sgi.com
```

Newsgroups are only one facet of the customer-support services that Silicon Graphics provides on the Internet. Research and development manager Jennifer Cantele, who heads the Silicon Surf team that recently put up a company World Wide Web server, says Silicon Graphics also offers customers the ability to send questions to technical support staffers via e-mail.

Through the company's new *customer profile* service, also available via the Internet, Silicon Graphics customers can continually update information about their locations, their e-mail addressess, and the computer system they're responsible for, and they can automatically receive the appropriate software from the company.

The future, as Cantele sees it, is the company's new Web server, which customers can use to browse through information about the company and its products as well as to use hyperlinks to explore its FTP archives and other data. The server, operational since March of 1994, and shown in Figure 9.1, has already been accessed 20,000 times. (You can check it out yourself if you've a Web client program such as Mosaic. Use the URL `http://www.sgi.com`.)

"As the Internet has opened up to what we feel is more commercialization, we see this as the perfect opportunity to use it to provide support to our customers," Cantele says. "We've really just scratched the surface."

Figure 9.1. Silicon Graphics' World Wide Web server.

Anticipating Questions with FAQs

In addition to answering individual customers' questions, many companies post FAQs, or Frequently Asked Questions lists, on the Internet. Companies can post FAQs on their own newsgroups or on newsgroups discussing related topics. The idea is to anticipate general questions that customers may have before they ask them, thereby freeing the customer support staff to focus on solving less common problems.

Long-time computer manufacturer Digital Equipment Corp. (DEC) produces two FAQ documents for its customers throughout the world, accessible through electronic mail, FTP, or by reading the Usenet newsgroups `comp.unix.ultrix`, `comp.sys.dec`, `comp.unix.osf.osf1`, `news.answers`, and `comp.answers` newsgroups. Here's a snippet from that document:

```
S1. How can I get lots of free software for ULTRIX and OSF/1?
The main FTP server for DEC is gatekeeper.dec.com, which maintains a
large selection of sources from the net in general, as well as public
code for ULTRIX, such as "monitor", "top" and other system-specific
tools.  /pub/DEC has sources for several packages written by employees
at Digital (though they are not supported Digital products), as well
as some programs that required special changes to port to ULTRIX. None
of these sources or utilities are "supported" by anyone other than
their authors.  The directory /pub/DEC/Alpha/apps has several programs
to have been ported to Alpha OSF/1.
In addition, Digital's "European UNIX Competency Circle" produced a
CDROM of free software for UNIX.  To get a copy, speak to a local
person from Digital.  For questions or suggestions about it, except
about availability, write to
freeware@uniriv.vbo.dec.com
Because the disk is in ISO 9660 format, it can be mounted and used
n almost any UNIX system and many proprietary systems, including ULTRIX,
OSF/1, Solaris, DOS, and VMS.
Answer A1 in the OSF/1 FAQ says how to order the Alpha OSF/1 Freeware CD.

S4. How do I play music CDs on DEC CD-ROM drives?
Music CDs can be played through a speaker jack on RRD42 CD-ROM drives,
which is the one contained in the DECstation 5000/{120,125} box.
The are three different programs available. A command line version and
a Motif-based version can be found in:
gatekeeper.dec.com or decuac.dec.com
in /pub/DEC:
                cdp.c[.Z]          /* command line version */
                xcd_source.tar.Z   /* Motif version. */
                   [Timothy Williams, williams@nvl.army.mil]

M6.**NEW** How do I contact Digital Customer Relations?
If you are having a problem dealing with Digital that you cannot
satisfactorily resolve through your local Digital office, please contact
US Customer Relations at:
     Internet: response@mkots3.enet.dec.com
     Phone:    800-DEC-INFO or 603-884-0915
```

```
FAX:     603-884-4692
Mail:    US Customer Relations
         Digital Equipment Corporation
         Digital Drive, MKO2-2/D15
         P.O. Box 9501
         Merrimack, NH 03054-9501
```

If you decide to provide an FAQ for your products and services—a strategy we highly recommend—follow these guidelines:

- Keep the questions and answers succinct.

- Include a summary of all questions at the top of the document.

- Be sure to include valuable information.

Currently, there are over 2,200 FAQ documents available throughout the Internet on a wide variety of topics, and the Internet community considers them a valuable source of information. It's also a good idea to set up a mail reflector that automatically sends your company's FAQ document to any customer who requests it via e-mail. We suggest faq@*yourcompany*.

Finally, don't let your FAQ information become stale. Try to include up-to-date information about product release schedules, software upgrades, and contact information for current corporate executives and product specialists within the firm.

Do-It-Yourself Support with FTP Sites

One of the most common problems for software companies today is distributing fixes, patches, and updates to a large and diverse customer base. Many companies rely on product registration cards and then charge customers from $20 to more than $150 to purchase an upgrade—an upgrade that usually includes nothing more than a stack of floppy disks.

With the Internet, the cost of providing these updates can be eliminated. The customer database can then become an electronic mailing list (useful for sending company newsletters, press releases of new products and the like), the cost of disk duplication vanishes, and even printed manuals can be offered online for free.

By setting up your computer as an FTP site, your customers can access a library of software programs and documentation with almost no effort. Customers connect to the site's Internet location, search the directory for the appropriate text or file, and download it to their own computer.

DEC, which operates one of the largest FTP sites on the Internet, makes over 9,000 company documents and software programs available to Internet users plus more than 300,000 public domain software programs. Russ Jones, the company's Internet program manager, estimates that Internet users access more than 20,000 documents a month from DEC's archives.

Here's a partial listing of the kinds of files, documents, and programs available in the contrib (user-contributed software and information) directory of the FTP archive at gatekeeper.dec.com:

```
Alpha/          VMS/            database/       micro/          sf/
BSD/            X11/            doc/            misc/           standards/
DEC/            X11-contrib/    editors/        multimedia/     sysadm/
Digital/        athena/         forums/         net/            text/
GNU/            case/           games/          news/           usenet/
Mach/           comm/           graphics/       plan/           usenix/
NIST/           conferences/    mail/           published/
UCB/            data/           maps/           recipes/
```

Though DEC has been hooked into the Internet for more than 10 years, Jones says that the company started aggressively using the network as a way to reach customers only two years ago. "So many of our customers are on the Internet that it just became very obvious that the time was ripe to do it," Jones says.

Prior to the DEC Internet customer support system, the company required customers to use their modems to dial one of the many DEC bulletin boards around the world to download software updates and technical documentation. Now, DEC customers can obtain the same support through the company's FTP site on the Internet without needing special hardware or software other than the existing Internet connection.

Like Silicon Graphics, DEC participates in company-related Usenet newsgroups. Current estimates suggest that more than 80,000 people read the discussion in the Usenet group comp.sys.dec, the main Digital newsgroup. Digital's new World Wide Web server, launched in October, 1993, attracted more than 9,000 visitors in its first four months in operation. (Its Internet address is URL http://www.digital.com/home.html.)

DEC also operates what it calls *The Electronic Connection,* an online ordering service that customers can access through telnet. (Type telnet order.sales.digital.com at the system prompt.) Since DEC opened the service on February 15, 1994, the company's monthly online order rate has increased by $1,000,000 a month.

Here's an example of what you'll see if you enter DEC's online "store":

```
List               Net  Days Lead
   Model No    Description                  Price  Disc    Price   Time
1.     QT001-3M FORTRAN-20,SOURCES MT9 1600  1404 10.00   1263.60
2.+    QT001-3Z FORTRAN-20, SVC RTC UPD       468 10.00    421.20
3.     QT001-8M FORTRAN-20,SOURCES MT9 1600  2244 10.00   2019.60
4.     QT001-9M FORTRAN-20,SOURCES MT9 1600  4572 15.00   3886.20
5.     QT001-DZ FORTRAN-20,SRC LICENSE ONLY  2100 10.00   1890.00  30
6.     QT001-IM FORTRAN-20,SOURCES MT9 1600   760  0.00    760.00
7.     QT001-NM FORTRAN-20,UDP MT9 1600      2678 10.00   2410.20  30
8.     QT001-NZ FORTRAN-20, RT TO COPY        599  0.00    599.00  30
9.     QT001-XM FORTRAN-20,SOURCES MT9 1600 12075 10.00  10867.50  30


       + fast ship product              Total of   9 model numbers found
-----------------------------------------------------------------------
   Type a selection number or command letter, then press <RETURN>:

Commands:   Order   Help   Back   Main   Quit
```

In an interesting marketing move, DEC also allows customers to test-drive its OSF/1 AXP server directly by logging in through the Internet. The system, in place since September 1, 1993, receives roughly 360 logins a day, or one every four minutes. The AXP test drive program has been so successful that the company has expanded it to include an OpenVMS AXP server and an Alpha AXP Workstation Farm.

"What we're trying to do is use every mechanism on the Internet to reach customers," Jones says. "We don't care if the customer has access to a newsreader, telnet, or a Web browser. We want them to be able to reach our information no matter which tools they're using."

We heartily endorse and applaud DEC's savvy strategy of using a variety of Internet tools to disseminate, distribute, and circulate information about the company and its products.

Publishing Information with Gopher and WAIS

Thanks to the Internet, companies can publish large databases of technical information in searchable format by using Internet tools such as Gopher and WAIS. Some companies are now setting up World Wide Web servers so that customers can use the popular Mosaic graphical interface to browse support information more easily.

Sun Microsystems is a pioneer in using the Internet to provide customer service. Sun operates SunSITE, an Internet server at the University of North Carolina that serves as a repository, not only for information about Sun products, but also for public domain software, White House papers, and other data.

Usage of the system has reached as high as 100,000 transfers a day. Additional SunSITE "mirror" servers have been set up in Tokyo and London, and four more sites are slated to go online this year. By locating document archives around the world, Sun hopes to help its overseas customers reduce the long waits to access data from the North Carolina server.

Here's a sampling of the many SunSITE offerings available:

```
-->   1.  SunSITE Sustainable Agriculture Information/
      2.  Sunsite Political Science Archives/
      3.  Worlds of SunSITE -- by Subject/
      4.  What's New on SunSITE/
      5.  Music - The American Music Resource - Via Sunsite Gopher Server/
      6.  Sunsite Gopher Server/
      7.  Poetry - Poetry and Creative Writing - Via Sunsite Gopher Server/
      8.  National Information Infrastructure Information (from sunsite)/
      9.  National Health Security Plan (from sunsite)/
      10. Pictures - White House Pictures - Via Sunsite Gopher Server/
      11. Sustainable Agriculture Information - Via Sunsite Gopher Server/
      12. Welsh Language and Culture Archive - Via Sunsite Gopher Server/
      13. GNU Software (Sunsite)/
      14. University of North Carolina at Chapel Hill  (Ogphre..site archives)/
      15. SunSITE gopher/
      16. Sunsite Gopher Server/
      17. Russian coup information on sunsite.
      18. Usage stats from sunsite.unc.edu.
      19. sci.econ.research Archives (from sunsite.unc.edu)/
      20. Virtual Reality - Via Sunsite Gopher Server/
      21. Multimedia - University of North Carolina SUNsite/
      22. Pictures - Univ. of N. Carolina SUNsite White House Pictures/
      23. New files on sunsite.unc.edu.
      24. Re: Patches removed from sunsite.
```

Here's what you'll see when you log onto the main menu of the SunSITE Gopher server at the University of North Carolina (to access it, type gopher sunsite.unc.edu at the system prompt).

```
                   Root gopher server: sunsite.unc.edu
-->  1.  About Ogphre/
     2.  Sun and UNC's Legal Disclaimer.
     3.  Surf the Net! - Archie, Libraries, Gophers, FTP Sites./
     4.  Internet Dog-Eared Pages (Frequently used resources)/
     5.  Worlds of SunSITE -- by Subject/
     6.  SUN Microsystems News Groups and Archives/
     7.  NEWS! (News, Entertainment, Weather, and Sports)/
     8.  UNC Information Exchange (People and Places)/
     9.  The UNC-CH Internet Library/
     10. UNC-Gopherspace/
     11. What's New on SunSITE/
```

To access customer information about Sun, select menu item 6. Here's what you'll see on your screen:

```
 -->  1.   About Sun Microsystems Archives.
       2.   Browse Sun Related Information And Archives/
       3.   SUN Flash product announcements (1989 - present)/
       4.   SUN related news groups/
       5.   Search  Postscript copies of Sun Technical White-papers <?>
       6.   Search  SUN Spots Archives <?>
```

To round out its Internet offerings, Sun launched its own Web server in April. If you have a Web browser, you can see what the firm has done by connecting to URL http://www.sun.com. By utilizing the technology underlying the World Wide Web, customers can simply click SunSITE and access the server from there. Though Mosaic does not yet permit access to newsgroups and lacks the universal search capability offered within Gopher, Mosaic's graphical interface and hyperlinks to other documents make it an ideal browsing tool.

Point-and-Click with Mosaic and World Wide Web

Like Silicon Graphics, Digital Equipment Corp., and Sun Microsystems, many companies are looking to the World Wide Web to give their customers an easier way to browse through technical information.

Hewlett-Packard, for example, recently added a World Wide Web service to its HP SupportLine electronic support services. Through the new Web server, customers can resolve software problems quickly and easily by searching up-to-date support and problem-solving information, browsing news and current announcements, and subscribing to mailing lists that automatically deliver the latest Hewlett-Packard support information to their electronic mailboxes.

Doug Levitt of Hewlett-Packard's Response Center Lab in Mountain View, California, says HP SupportLine began providing customer support over the Internet in 1991—before the Web even existed. The first thing the group did, he says, was to set up an FTP site where customers could download software patches. Prior to that customers had to call the Response Center by phone and order a disk through the mail. That was not the optimal solution: "When you're a large company and you want to deliver software to thousands of customers, the costs can become prohibitively expensive."

After getting its FTP site up and running, Hewlett-Packard set up an Internet mail link to enable customers to obtain software patches by requesting them via e-mail. The company also launched a group of eight mailing lists to disseminate information to existing and potential HP customers. Though Levitt says it's hard to estimate how many people read the mailing lists (because many people subscribe and then pass them on), "we believe that this is a cost-effective way to distribution information to our customers."

Down the road, Levitt says, Hewlett-Packard is looking at offering Internet support involving multimedia—giving customers the ability to communicate through voice instead of clicking buttons on a screen or typing commands on a keyboard. (See Chapter 13, "The Future of Internet Business.")

For now, however, HP SupportLine's World Wide Web service is state-of-the-art. Here's how it works:

At the HP home page (URL `http://support.mayfield.hp.com`) customers click one of a number of buttons pictured in Figure 9.2 to read news and announcements, search problem-solving databases, browse software patches, subscribe to electronic digests, and select other options.

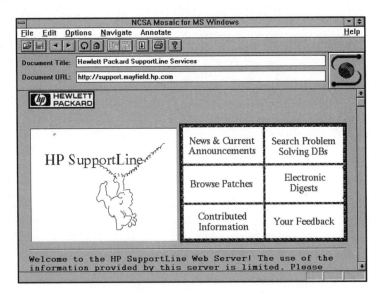

Figure 9.2. Hewlett-Packard recently added a World Wide Web service to its HP SupportLine electronic support services.

Clicking the News & Current Events Announcements menu displays a hyperlinked menu (pictured in Figure 9.3) that connects customers to documents containing information about new products, HP discounts, promotions, technical tips, and other information.

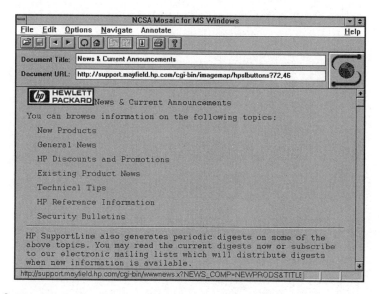

Figure 9.3. Hewlett-Packard uses the Web's hyperlinks to provide a variety of product support and information to its customers.

By accessing HP's problem-solving database, customers can find the answers to their technical questions at their leisure. A technical document is pictured in Figure 9.4.

HP's Web setup also makes it easy for customers to subscribe to a variety of HP mailing lists to keep them informed about new products, technical tips, security, and general news. In the Web page pictured in Figure 9.5, customers are prompted to fill in their e-mail addresses and select which HP mailing lists they'd like to subscribe to.

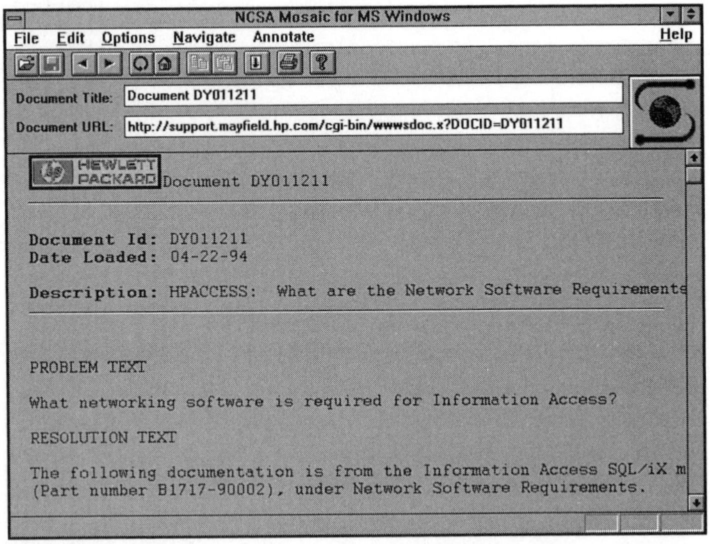

Figure 9.4. An example of a technical document available through Hewlett-Packard's Web server.

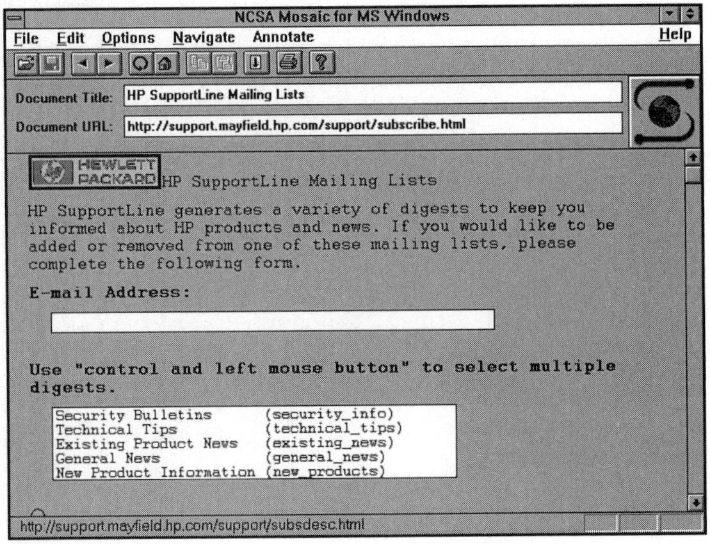

Figure 9.5. Through the company's Web server, Hewlett-Packard customers can sign quickly and easily subscribe to a variety of Internet mailing lists to meet their particular needs.

Customers can also browse contributed information, such as these documents supplied by Ohio State University and pictured in Figure 9.6.

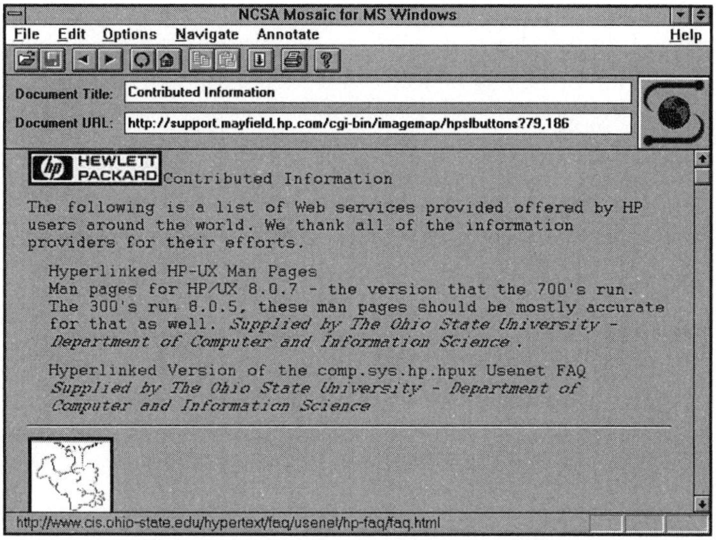

Figure 9.6. Through the company's Web server, Hewlett-Packard customers can access relevant information contributed by other research organizations.

The Bottom Line: the Cost of Providing Customer Support on the Internet

How much does it cost to provide customer support over the Internet? Some customer support options, such as responding to customer queries via e-mail or setting up newsgroups and mailing lists, cost practically nothing—apart from the cost of obtaining Internet access, which your company may have already. You also have to factor in the time that your technical support personnel must spend interacting with customers electronically, though this may actually result in a time savings if your company had previously been providing support by phone, fax, or postal mail.

The cost of setting up Gopher databases and FTP archives on the Internet is likely to vary depending on how much information your company has in electronic format already. If you already have a computer bulletin board up and running, offering that information on the Internet can be as simple as establishing a telnet link to your company's computer system or uploading the data to an Internet-connected server.

Indeed, many FTP and Gopher servers are so simple to set up that you can drop all the files you want to offer in a single directory, point the server to that directory, and start advertising the new capability. More sophisticated organization isn't much more difficult, either. Divide the information into categories (as shown earlier in our Gopher examples), assign each category a subdirectory in the main server directory, and make sure you include mnemonic names.

If you have the resources, remember our advice about offering free information to the Internet community: If your firm sells modems, for example, it may be a good idea to set aside some space on your server for publicly available telecommunications information such as FAQs plus free or low-cost software programs.

A few dozen megabytes of disk space can mean the difference between the Internet community viewing you as just another vendor hanging tech sheets on the wire and people pointing others to your site as a source of valuable information. On the Internet, good will goes a long way.

The most expensive means of offering customer support via the Internet is by setting up a Web server. Sun, for example, has dedicated a $50,000 SparcCenter 1000 UNIX server to the project plus several full-time employees, says Eric Schmidt, the company's chief technology officer. The projected cost is $150,000 to $250,000 a year.

But don't be scared away by those large numbers! Even regular dialup accounts can be used to distribute information to your Internet-connected customers. Netcom Communications Services, for example, allows all dialup users five megabytes of space in its anonymous FTP archive site to use as they see fit. If you have a few spec sheets, press releases, and an FAQ you want to put there, that should be plenty of space.

Another alternative is to configure an inexpensive PC with a dedicated 14.4 Kbps connection, perhaps through SLIP. From our earlier analysis in Chapter 2, "Getting Connected: Your Ticket to Ride," you saw that the cost of this connection is approximately $160 a month and dropping rapidly. Add the appropriate modem, phone-line lease, and your cost is about $500 for setup and $200 monthly.

Take a quick glance at any computer publication and you'll see that you can easily find a 486-based PC with up to a gigabyte of hard disk space for under $2,500. The server and communications software you'll need is free—and probably available directly from your Internet access provider, too. Total setup may run you about $3,000 with operating costs of roughly $200 a month. Compare that to the cost of a single postal mailing to your customer base and you'll soon see why so many companies are rushing to provide customer support on the Internet!

The Keys to Good Customer Support

There are two important ideas in this chapter that you need to keep in mind if you're going to consider setting up a customer support site through the Internet, or even supplement your existing system with network connectivity:

- Offer your support information through a variety of Internet tools so that all customers can access your information.

- Add value to your information archives to encourage those who aren't customers to visit.

In this chapter, you've seen how a wide variety of companies are using the Internet to enhance their customer support offerings, gaining customers and good will along the way. We believe that the best way to show your customers that your company is serious about riding the information highway is to reach out your hand and invite them along for the ride!

THE VIRTUAL CORPORATION

The Internet can revolutionize how companies interact with customers through global online customer support, as you learned in the previous chapter. Hooking up to the worldwide network offers a further enticement for businesses—the opportunity to create virtual corporations.

Through the Internet, executives, engineers, scientists, and researchers throughout the world are collaborating on new products and services without ever meeting face to face. Once the exclusive domain of Fortune 500 companies with powerful computers and dedicated wide-area networks, global networking is now available to any company with e-mail access to the Internet. Through the network, companies large and small are setting up "offices without walls" and team members swap messages, documents, software programs, and audio and video clips—all for the price of basic Internet access.

Recent interest in virtual corporations hasn't sprung from technological advances alone; economic trends are also encouraging companies of all sizes to explore distributed workforces. These factors include the continued downsizing of corporate America; the declining federal budget for defense, space, and other technical programs; layoffs in the U.S. aerospace industry; the rapid growth of home-based businesses; greater demand by employees for job sharing, flex-time, telecommuting, and other flexible workplace arrangements; the decentralization of American corporations, and the continuing shift from an economy based on manufacturing to one based on information.

At the same time, a number of bugs remain in the virtual corporation concept—both from a business and a technological standpoint.

For one, many companies have not yet gone online, relying instead on the communications and information-gathering methods of the past. Though Internet e-mail provides the least expensive communications link available, postal mail remains more common than e-mail, and fax machines are still more popular than modems at companies worldwide. For many business owners who grew up before the computer generation, it's easier to dictate a letter to a secretary or scribble a note and stick it in the office fax machine. Executives like these often prefer to communicate in person or by phone rather than by sending electronic messages; they also like to shake hands before signing a contract.

From a technological perspective, the Internet is also limited in its effectiveness as a communications tool. Though the network is widely used by businesses for exchanging letters—employees at Sun Microsystems, for example, send and receive more than 1,000,000 e-mail messages a day—Internet audio- and videoconferencing are still at a very early stage. (See Chapter 8, "Connecting the World with Internet E-Mail.")

What's more, many developing countries have slow e-mail-only access to the Internet, making it difficult for international colleagues to share data. Others have no Internet access at all. Another problem is Internet security; because companies must build firewalls to protect their proprietary data from network hackers and insist on encrypted data transmissions, researchers can find it difficult and time-consuming to exchange data with colleagues at other sites.

This chapter will take a look at how companies such as IBM, General Electric, Intel, and Motorola are using Internet tools such as e-mail, telnet, and newsgroups to facilitate and lower the costs of research and development. You'll also find out how entrepreneurs are using the Internet to create global marketing and consulting networks and how to avoid the technological and legal pitfalls of doing business online.

The Rise of the Virtual Corporation

For companies seeking to do business internationally, the chief obstacle has always been cost—the cost of travel, long-distance phone calls, overnight courier services, and overseas offices.

Thanks to the Internet and other online networks, the cost of entry into the global marketplace has diminished dramatically, especially in technology-related industries. These days, collaborative networks link hundreds, thousands, even tens of thousands of people together at very low cost. From design to development, manufacture to marketing, international virtual corporations are working well today.

By hooking up electronically, businesses can form and dissolve relationships at a moment's notice and create new corporate ecologies to meet customer demand. Whether a company's "virtual workers" are in Singapore or Cincinnati no longer makes a difference when they can dial into the company's database and access customer records online. As a result, geographically scattered workers can operate as if they were all at company headquarters.

"Imagine that, of all your suppliers and strategic partners, there are 40 important ones with whom you do business digitally," writes Robert Weber, a consultant at Boston's Northeast Consulting Resources, Inc., in a recent article posted on the Net.

"Let's say you exchange engineering and design information. Today, it's likely that corporate security requires a separate point-to-point network link for each of these 40 partners. Many companies require that all data on each link be encrypted so that, even if the link were tapped, the message contents could not be deciphered easily."

What Weber is describing here is the precursor to a true data highway: Individual roads linking individual buildings together. For security reasons, each of these roads requires guards, walls, and other measures to ensure that information which must remain private doesn't fall into the hands of unscrupulous competitors.

The Internet offers an inexpensive alternative—a single highway system that each company can hook into, share, and use for intra-company and external communications. The potential savings of constructing a single on-ramp to an existing—and growing—highway system are immediately apparent, and encryption and other techniques can guarantee data security. The best part of building an Internet-based virtual corporation, of course, is that you can add new clients with minimal work: Once you're on the network, it's just a matter of adding their network address to your distribution list.

R&D on the Internet: From Medical Imaging to Oil and Gas

Research and development is an especially hot area for virtual collaboration over the network. These days, companies are using the Internet to collaborate on research and development projects in fields as diverse as medical imaging and diagnostic techniques, oil exploration, and oceanography.

Brigham and Women's Hospital

At Brigham and Women's Hospital in Boston, Massachusetts, for example, there's a project underway to transform the output of magnetic resonance imaging systems into three-dimensional maps of the human brain.

To assist with the project, a research partner at the Cancer Research Institute in Heidelberg, Germany, uses the Internet to access the hospital's computers in Boston. Meanwhile, colleagues in Switzerland collaborate on the segmentation of various structures in the brain and exchange data with Dr. Ron Kikinas of the Boston lab over the network.

Dr. Kikinas' collaborators also include the research scientists at the General Electric Research and Development Center in Schenectady, New York, one of the world's largest suppliers of diagnostic imaging equipment. Bill Lorensen, a GE graphics engineer who works with Dr. Kikinas on the project, credits the Internet for reducing the time lag between research teams in different locations starting a project with a new idea and turning it into a finished application. Over the network, GE scientists can try different approaches to data analysis, generating software to create three-dimensional images or rotating images to see whether the new look will help with diagnosis, Lorensen says.

Before the research partners began using the Internet, they used to exchange tapes containing huge data files—an inconvenient and time-consuming process given the fact that each "slice," or image, weighs in at half a megabyte and GE researchers typically transfer 25 megabytes of data to Dr. Kikinas' lab each week. Now, the GE researchers use the Internet's telnet feature to log in remotely to the Boston lab—though file transfers can still take as long as 3 hours depending on the volume of data.

At the same time, there are some drawbacks to swapping files over the Internet. Because of GE's security concerns, the company has set up a firewall to buffer its computer system from problems on the network. As a result, Lorensen can't access Dr. Kikinas' computer system directly: He must first telnet to the GE firewall and then telnet to the hospital's computer. When using the Internet's FTP function to retrieve a file, he must first transfer it to GE's firewall and then transfer it a second time to GE's computer system.

Another problem they face is the Internet's incapability of supporting high-speed videoconferencing. Though various tools and applications are available, they're all too slow for true conferencing and the network itself has difficulty keeping up with the megabytes of information being zapped from site to site.

Global Basins Research Network

The oil industry is another hotbed of Internet-facilitated research and development activity. Through the Global Basins Research Network, scientists are developing and testing new methods for locating huge underwater oil fields based on computer visualizations of all seismic, geophysical, and geochemical data gathered over time from a likely deposit site.

As large amounts of data are gathered into databases at different locations, computer models track the movements and interactions of key elements used to predict the location of oil. Finally, the computerized results are put to the test with on-site drilling to confirm whether oil will indeed be found where the computer models predicted.

From the start, the Project has involved close collaboration among universities, corporate participants, and the federal Department of Energy. University researchers from Columbus, Louisiana State University, Penn State, and the University of Colorado have joined forces with geochemists from the Woods Hole Oceanographic Institute and Texas A&M's Geochemical and Environmental Research Group through the Internet. Twelve oil companies including Amoco, Chevron, Mobil, and Texaco are also providing support in addition to a number of high-tech companies, including Advanced Visual System, Inc., Landmark Graphics Corp., and Sun Microsystems.

Monterey Bay Aquarium Research Institute

In Northern California, the Monterey Bay Aquarium Research Institute is also using the Internet to facilitate its R&D efforts. Its goal is to fully map the underwater terrain and life of the Monterey Bay to help understand the complexities of the oceans.

The setup is fascinating: MBARI has a research vessel that runs a remotely operated vehicle on the end of a tether in the bay; the ROV, as they call it, has a number of onboard computers that work with similar systems on the boat. A line-of-sight microwave relay transmits all visuals and other data directly to the MBARI research facility onshore, directly to systems that are connected to the Internet.

Other oceanographic research facilities, including Scripps Institute of Oceanography 450 miles south in San Diego and Woods Hole Oceanographic Institute across the United States, can tap into the video signal as it's transmitted up from the ROV, and through a set of custom software applications, the remote researchers can actually manipulate the instruments on board the research vessel itself. All this is done through the Internet, and all without additional network hookups or other expensive equipment.

Big Business on the Net

Like General Electric, many of the companies using the Internet to facilitate worldwide research and development projects are members of the elite Fortune 500. IBM, General Electric, Motorola, Sun Microsystems, and Intel rank among the network's power users, companies sending the greatest volume of traffic through the NSFnet backbone.

Motorola

At Motorola, more than 13,000 employees are engaged in research activities throughout the company—and many of them require access to the Internet.

Some of Motorola's earliest users belonged to its computer and semiconductor groups, who tapped into the Internet to participate in scientific far-flung research projects. For example, Motorola scientists researching chip design and working on other projects requiring high-level visualization and simulation resources had to have access to the supercomputer at the University of Illinois at Urbana-Champaign, an Internet-connected machine.

These days, Motorola researchers use the Internet for purposes as varied as downloading files, communicating with overseas colleagues via e-mail, and participating in Internet newsgroups. But, like GE, Motorola uses a firewall to protect its computer system from Internet predators—and that firewall limits its researchers' activity on the Internet. John Byrns, a principal staff engineer at the company, says the Motorola gateway is set up to permit one-way telnetting to remote computers without compromising security; however, nobody from the outside can telnet into Motorola's system without a password and a "smart card." Motorola researchers who want full Internet access must first connect to the company's firewall computer.

Sun Microsystems

Sun Microsystems has a similar strategy for its thousands of researchers at its Mountain View, California, headquarters. A single system—sunbar—offers full connectivity to the Internet for employees, though individual workstations cannot directly interact with external systems. If you're a Sun customer, ask for a copy of the firewall-modified applications; they're free as of this writing. Hewlett-Packard, Silicon Graphics, and many other major corporations on the network have similar security systems in place.

As companies like Sun have recognized, the fundamental strategy is to understand that, although there are dangers and threats on the Internet, they can be managed through intelligent planning and deployment of resources. No hacker can break into your computer if your gateway to the network doesn't allow external data packets to enter the local-area network.

Creating a central connection point—a single machine through which all traffic to and from the Internet routes—lets Internet experts within your company monitor external data traffic to spot intruders before they breach company security. (Clifford Stoll's book, *The Cuckoo's Egg,* tells how he spotted and helped catch an intruder this way at Lawrence Berkeley Labs.)

The challenge is to set up your firewalls and other security measures in a way that doesn't prevent your own company from reaping the riches of an Internet connection. Recall, too, that a simple dialup connection to an off-site Internet access provider still offers much of this shared R&D and virtual corporation capability without many of the security headaches.

Finally, data transmissions of a sensitive nature should always be encrypted; if you're working with other companies throughout the United States, you can both use a DES or RSA encryption package. There's another more subtle advantage to shared encryption: Once you call or fax your colleagues to let them know your encryption keys (you never want to send these through e-mail), successfully decoding their messages enables you to be reasonably sure that the information really comes from your project partners. See Chapter 3, "Risks and Realities," for more details about Internet security considerations. Remember that an ounce of prevention can save you from a potential nightmare.

Linking Small Businesses Worldwide

Large corporations aren't the only ones using the Internet for remote collaboration. Small businesses are getting into the act as well. Thanks to the Internet, a small company with big ideas but limited staff and resources can find partners around the world with complementary skills, interests, and contacts.

Like worldwide accounting and consulting firms, a global network of small businesses can project an image to potential customers of a large, unified organization when, in reality, it is an amalgam of different firms with each partner responsible for his or her own profit and loss.

A virtual corporation like this typically requires an affiliation agreement among the members, a common corporate name or identity, and a set of standards that ensures the consistency and quality of the group's services and products. The final component is a communications link with the capability of facilitating the rapid transfer of information worldwide.

That's where the Internet comes in.

KnowledgeNet: a Corporation in Cyberspace

One organization that's using the Internet to create a virtual network of small businesses is KnowledgeNet, a worldwide consulting firm with more than 100 member practices in 16 countries. All the group's members fall under the umbrella of professional services, engaging in activities as diverse as systems analysis, accounting, technical writing, sales and marketing, project management, and software development.

KnowledgeNet is the brainchild of entrepreneur David Boone, who heads D.L. Boone & Company, an international systems and management consulting firm in Vienna, Virginia, that coordinates the activities of the worldwide network. Prior to founding KnowledgeNet, Boone served as a management consultant within the federal government and with the Federal Services Group of KPMG Peat Marwick in Washington.

Boone's goal is to put together a world-class consulting firm composed of small firms and individuals who are being driven from the corporate world by the current economic climate and then market the firm's services under a single internationally known trademark.

Because D.L. Boone & Co. is a "virtual corporation," it maintains no fixed facilities and keeps only those permanent employees essential for corporate operations. Each of KnowledgeNet's affiliate offices—called *Associates*—contributes to the financing of the company's operations and shares in its profits, if any.

Boone anticipates that KnowledgeNet's major clients will be governments, corporate entities, international public and private organizations, and non-profit organizations. The company also plans to zero in on the small business market, which accounts for a substantial proportion of job creation in today's economy.

To recruit Associates quickly and cost-effectively, Boone has posted notes on commercial online services such as CompuServe and America Online and also on the Internet's `misc.entrepreneurs` and `alt.business.misc` newsgroups.

There's also an added benefit. As he points out, "The subscribers to these services are generally well-educated, computer-literate professionals. They know how to use a computer, have an understanding of telecommunications, and more importantly, have an understanding of the reality and the potential of remote collaboration and distributed workforces."

Boone also uses online networks to distribute copies of his business plan to consultants interested in joining. KnowledgeNet's business plan can be retrieved from CompuServe's Working From Home Forum and Entrepreneurs Forum, America Online's Microsoft Small Business Center or by sending e-mail through the Internet to `info@knowledgenet.com`. Associates who link up with KnowledgeNet use the Internet and other networks to communicate via e-mail. Boone says half the Associates have Internet accounts; the other half use commercial online services. Boone himself has accounts on CompuServe, America Online, Prodigy, and the Internet.

So far, however, KnowledgeNet has been slow getting off the ground. Operational since August, 1993, the company has won only two contracts—a small job from KPMG Peat Marwick, Boone's old firm, and another small contract from Computer Sciences Corp. Other proposals are pending, and the virtual corporations' board of directors is optimistic about the future.

The Pros and Cons of Being a Virtual Worker

Although the vision of having an office set up at home and an Internet line poking out of the wall is an attractive one for some, working at home without the daily interaction of colleagues and peers is perceived by many as a significant obstacle to virtual employment.

One business owner who views working in a separate facility as a problem is KnowledgeNet Associate David Habercom. The virtual corporation concept, he says, "actually does not appeal to me very much at all. I much prefer to work with people I can see, touch, and go to lunch with. The noise of people walking by, laughter down the hall, a meeting with sleeves rolled up and intense, face-to-face debate, in my mind at least, is half of what makes work satisfying."

On the other hand, experts like Habercom don't deny that the idea of building a consulting group where each member brings complimentary skills to the table is an appealing one. Further, by sharing expertise and resources with partners, he believes he can reach—and work with—clients whom he could never manage alone.

Another fundamental problem that any virtual corporation faces is the problem of bringing everyone together face-to-face for meetings with potential clients. Many executives are unaccustomed to and distrust the idea of computer-mediated interaction; for them, the inability to call an all-hands meeting with the corporate staff can be unsettling. As Habercom puts it, "Most executives are like me and prefer doing business face-to-face. When something goes wrong, I want to be able to get my hands around the other guy's throat; that and knowing he can do the same to me helps keep us honest."

Nevertheless, there are some ways to avoid the pitfalls of work-alone business. KnowledgeNet Associate Ankur Lal works in an office in New Delhi, India, with nine other engineers. Lal and his team have helped American and Canadian companies develop software applications in India for the last five years and work in an Indian facility linked via e-mail to overseas clients. By going online, the group can send and receive specifications, code, and messages through their computers.

"I am sure the virtual corporation idea will pick up more and more with people able to work wherever they are and give it their best," Lal says. "With the information superhighway, distance will be [only] a psychological barrier since the quality of work would be the same in one's own office or 10,000 miles away. So good business sense will mean using the best services at the most economical cost anywhere in the world. The virtual corporation is very much here to stay and will take the world by storm."

Virtual Transactions: Where Do I Sign and How Do I Pay?

Despite the promise of the virtual corporation—and the experiments being tried today, consummating business deals and purchasing products online is not yet a reality. Even technologically, problems remain.

One important problem is security; another is authentication. Contracts, credit card purchases, and other business documents typically require signatures; that way, if a dispute arises later on, there's something tangible to show a mediator or judge. The trouble with e-mail is there's no way of knowing—yet—if the person who sent the message really is who he says he is or just some hacker playing a practical joke.

Although digital signatures could move significantly toward resolving this problem (see following section), the technology is not widely distributed or used, and no legal precedent has been set for the binding nature of electronic communications. For an in-depth look at these problems, see Chapter 3, "Risks and Reality."

Is an e-mail-based contract legally binding? The expert opinion is split. Attorney Victor Cosentino observes that "under legal rules governing evidence and contracts, it's hard to prove the existence of a contract based on e-mail; fabricating an e-mail message is just too easy."

Other lawyers believe that e-mail contracts probably are enforceable, though no e-mail contract has yet been contested in a lawsuit. Texas lawyer Benjamin Wright argues that, if used carefully, electronic communication can confidently be used for legal transactions.

Although the Uniform Commercial Code states that a contract for the sale of goods priced at $500 or more is not enforceable unless it is put in writing, Wright believes that an e-mail contract should be able to qualify. However, Wright cautions in his book, *The Law of Electronic Commerce* (Little, Brown & Co. 1991), absent sufficient security controls, electronic documents can be altered and electronic signatures can be forged—putting the validity of the contract in question.

Wright's advice: Both parties to a transaction should include a provision in their contract stating that "a properly transmitted message is deemed 'written,' and a designated symbol(s) or code(s) within the message is deemed a 'signature.'"

Digital Signatures

The crux of the issue is whether an electronic document is considered "signed." Though contracts can be written such that any e-mail sent from one user to another is considered binding, that doesn't necessarily alleviate problems of electronic fraud, particularly with regard to online purchases.

Unless a computer system is very secure, electronic signatures can be compromised. As we discussed in Chapter 3, Internet connections provide a relatively easy way for crackers and other intruders to break into company computers. Once the company's system is breached, intruders possessing the requisite equipment can intercept passwords, e-mail, files, and other network data.

That's where encryption comes in, particularly a "signature" that is encrypted per-message and can only be unencrypted by using a key specific to the recipient: the encrypted (scrambled) signature will look different on each message you send, so it couldn't be duplicated. Proponents of these digital signatures, which rely on public-key encryption technology, claim that they're even more secure than paper signatures, which can be forged.

With a digital signature, supporters claim, you can prove beyond the shadow of a doubt that a given document was signed with a given signature. Because there is no way to forge or alter a digital signature, such a signature is, for all practical purposes, absolutely secure. If a dispute arises later on, the contractors or purchasers cannot claim that the signature is not theirs.

The issue of electronic signatures comes into play not only in business-to-business contracts but also in retail credit card transactions.

Here's an example of how a company can use digital signatures to facilitate mail-order purchases: The order is prepared in a machine-readable form, such as a text file, an electronic mail message, a text document, or a spreadsheet. The order is then digitally signed by the person making the order, who sends it to the merchant via the Internet.

One advantage to digital signatures is that they do not require a secure communications network because the signature itself cannot be cracked. If a digital signature is attached to a purchase order, the presence of that signature guarantees that whoever owns the signature signed the order.

An important feature of a digital signature is that it is generated both from the document being signed and from the private key provided by the signer. This is in contrast to a paper signature, which is created manually by the signer and does not depend on the document being signed.

For example, if you sign page four of a four-page contract, the first three pages can be significantly modified without a trace. Not so with a digital signature. Any change in the text of the signed document—even so much as adding a space, a comma, or changing a letter from uppercase to lowercase—will invalidate the signature. That's why, with a digital signature, you get a guarantee that the signed document has not been modified in any way and that it corresponds in every detail to the document signed by the author. The signer cannot claim later that it was modified after he signed it, because modification is impossible.

Here's an example of a digital signature created using PGP encryption software:

```
##SIGNATURE##
----BEGIN PGP SIGNATURE----
Version: 2.4
iQB1AgUBLcdMbJ81eg63LALlAQFoZwMArkMpjzwfTuF9YdOFpPzVsPzAp/m/dlOJ
moEGrWlwrctHnfhKHdioTlo6fz3KxSXJa7e9W4YuSHTfP6gFbZkaUU/c8yPMcBq3
IunJjn+M8JeUBnGGvAs5STw6PLbvet2B
=RSu1
----END PGP SIGNATURE----
```

The block of text that appears to be gibberish contains a "digest," or digital summary, of the actual message, encrypted using the private key of the sender. If you were to change even one word in the message body, it would produce a different digest so that it would be apparent that the message had been altered after it was signed.

Although one block of gibberish looks much like another, the program that produces a signature of this type can also perform the calculations to determine whether a signature on another message is correct. Further, it's impossible to cut the signature off one message and tack it onto the end of another: The digital summary would be different, and verification software would indicate the mismatch.

It's also worth noting that you can affix a digital signature to the end of an encrypted document to be doubly sure that it survives the trip and has been sent by the person who purportedly sent it. For an extra layer of security, add a digital signature to the unencrypted document, encrypt both the document and the signature, and then add a second digital signature to the encrypted block of text. The recipient who unencrypts the document can be quite confident that the text he reads is exactly as transmitted, character for character.

Digital Currency

Although digital signatures address the problem of verifying that a message comes from a specific sender, firewalls and other mechanisms ensure messages' security. The next obstacle that Internet commerce must overcome is digital currency, both for large transactions (which is relatively easy with message encryption and digital signatures) and small.

In other words, there's no generally accepted electronic money that your customers can use to pay for products purchased through the network. That's where commercial online services such as CompuServe and Prodigy have an edge over the Internet; on commercial networks, subscribers can and do order software, flowers, plane tickets, and other items online, secure in the knowledge that their credit card information won't be compromised. As we noted in Chapter 3, "Risks and Realities," commercial networks tend to be more secure than the Internet because most message traffic remains within the proprietary system. One Internet-based solution in the offing is a secure version of Mosaic scheduled to be released late summer, 1994, by CommerceNet. (See Chapter 11, "Internet Cybermalls.")

Already, however, several companies are offering piecemeal solutions to the Internet's digital currency crunch. SoftLock Services of Rochester, New York, for example, sells an automated credit card processing service targeted primarily at shareware authors, independent software developers who post their programs online and let customers "try before they buy."

Currently, shareware authors must rely on the honor system because they have no way of knowing who has downloaded their programs or how many copies they have made. SoftLock's technology allows developers to try a different strategy: adding a "lock" on certain advanced features that are inaccessible until the user pays a specific registration fee.

When a user tries to access one of those features, the program displays a message similar to the following:

```
In order to access the advanced features of this
program in their full capacity, just...

1. Contact SoftLock Services any time, day or night, by
telephone, modem, electronic mail, or fax.

2. Tell them you want a password for Product Number
87654321

3.  Tell them the unique ID for that product on your
computer is 12345678

4.  Give them your credit card number (or SoftLock
Voucher Number)

And within 30 seconds, they'll give you a password
that will unlock the advanced features, on this hard
drive, forever!
```

"SoftLocking can be used to strike the appropriate balance between free sample and purchased product, all the while preserving the user's ability to backup, copy, and pass on to others the entire SoftLocked application or document," says Jonathan Schull, the company's president. For more information, send e-mail to IntroLong@SoftLock.com.

Virtual Liabilities

The possibility of a forged or unenforceable contract is not the only risk facing companies attempting to conduct business in a virtual environment. Because the law surrounding Internet issues is unclear, disputes are starting to appear regarding legal issues as diverse as copyright claims and libel laws.

For example, does someone who posts a note to an Internet mailing list or newsgroup own the rights to his work? Can a newspaper or magazine reprint it without asking the author's permission or paying a royalty? Can a harshly worded Internet "flame" be considered the online equivalent of telephone harassment? Can the recipient of a flame attack sue the author of the message, claiming damages as the result of libel?

To keep things in perspective, remember that, although the Internet may seem at times like a comfortable corner café, many of its discussion groups have a readership that far exceeds that of most daily newspapers. Washington lawyer Victor Cosentino observes that "while no newspaper editor would publish a blatantly defamatory article, Internet users do so with apparent impunity; there are no laws covering such online behavior. It's possible, however, that laws pertaining to its off-line equivalent could be stretched to fit."

There has also been quite a bit of discussion in digital and print media about copyright and trademark law and how it relates to Internet addresses. For example, does Apple Computer have the exclusive right to use "apple" as its domain name—or could a bunch of apple growers band together and do the same thing? Because domain names aren't really names, but addresses, some argue that they can't be protected by federal trademark law—just as Delta Airlines couldn't stop a startup airline from listing its address as "Delta Street."

Libel on the Internet

Legal issues such as these are far from theoretical. In March, a Washington journalist named Brock Meeks, who works by day as a reporter for *Communications Daily* and publishes an Internet newsletter called *Cyberwire Dispatch* on the side, distributed a harshly worded critique of a company called the *Electric Postal Service* that was peddling a deal Meeks suspected was too good to be true: Make money by volunteering to receive direct-mail solicitations sent to your electronic mailbox.

Meeks decided to check it out. On responding to the offer, Meeks says he received a direct-mail ad for a $159 book-and-software package that promised to make him rich. Meeks then published a muck-raking article calling the direct-mail offering a "scam" and characterizing Benjamin Suarez, president of the company that sent out the circular, a "slick, direct-mail baron," court papers say.

Suarez didn't just get angry; he filed a libel suit against Meeks, claiming lost business, seeking damages, and demanding an injunction to block Meeks from ever again writing about him or his company on the Internet. The lawsuit, pending in Cuyahoga County court in Ohio, is one of the first U.S. defamation suits to arise from an article published on the Internet.

If Suarez wins the case, some legal experts predict it will spawn other lawsuits—accelerating the pace of Internet-related litigation. According to the May 12, 1994, issue of *Computer Weekly*, Canadian professor Laurence Godfrey issued a libel writ in London against a Geneva-based academician, claiming he was defamed by a bulletin board message posted on an Internet newsgroup.

"The golden age of cyberspace is drawing to a close," says I. Trotter Hardy, a College of William & Mary law professor who leads an Internet discussion group for lawyers interested in debating cyber-related issues, "but the golden age for lawyers is just dawning."

Internet Legal Tips

Despite the legal risks involved, we believe that businesses can steer clear of trouble if they take proper precautions. If you're planning on doing any business on the Internet, here are some legal tips offered by intellectual property lawyers:

- **Get it in writing.** Unless you're using a digital signature system, ask your customer or contractor to send you a signed paper original or a fax. Because of security and authentication problems, e-mail should not be used to create a contract. In the case of Rosalind's' newsletter, for example, her bank has recommended that she ask her credit card subscribers to fax a signed letter confirming their order rather than her just keeping a copy of their e-mail message on file.

- **Watch what you say (type, that is).** As matter of law, it usually doesn't matter which medium was used to transmit allegedly defamatory material. Even letters and telegrams have been considered sufficient, says Hillary Miller, an attorney who participates in CompuServe's Legal Forum. "There is every reason to include electronic media within the scope of those media capable of use for the commission of a tort of defamation, particularly given the potential for immediate and widespread dissemination of information to a targeted audience where substantial harm can be inflicted," Miller says. Translation: Post something really nasty online and prepare to be sued.

- **Recognize that the laws that apply in the real world will probably be applied to cyberspace as well.** This is particularly true of laws involving copyright infringement, wire fraud, legal malpractice, and misappropriation of trade secrets. Although an e-mail message may not be enough to sustain a contract, it may be more than enough to land you and your company in court over a legal dispute. Says Miller: "The propensity of businessmen to memorialize their wrongful conduct in business records is a plaintiff's lawyer's dream."

- **Know your rights.** Although electronic forgeries may be difficult to prevent, companies that spot them have recourse under federal law. According to Wright, there is a wide range of civil and criminal penalties for misconduct that arises under state and federal law. For example, the federal wire fraud statute (18 U.S.C. Section 1343) covers the transmission of fraudulent electronic records over the interstate telephone system. Other statutes cover false and fraudulent entries in the books and records of federal banking institutions and almost any electronic dealings with the government, including electronic filings and electronic contracting with the government. The Computer Fraud and Abuse Act of 1986 (18 U.S.C. Section 1030), the Electronic Communications Privacy Act of 1986 (18 U.S.C. Section 2701), and statutes in many states protect against unauthorized use of or access into computers as well as the unauthorized alteration or destruction of data.

Additional Reading

If you would like to know more about virtual corporations, here are some useful books and magazine articles to check:

Books

Butman, John. *Flying Fox: A Business Adventure in Teams and Team Work.* Published by AMACOM. ISBN-0-8144-5099-7.

Davidow, William and Michael Malone. *The Virtual Corporation.* Published by Harper Collins. ISBN-0-88730-593-8.

Goldman, Steven. "Co-operating To Compete from Alliances to Virtual Companies." *CMA The Management Accounting Magazine.* March, 1994.

Harrington-Mackin, Deborah. *The Team Building Tool Kit.* Published by AMACOM. ISBN-0-8144-7826-3. (American Management Association, 135 West 50th Street, New York, NY 10020).

Rheingold, Howard. *The Virtual Community.* Published by Addison-Wesley. ISBN-0-201-60870-7.

Wright, Benjamin. *The Law of Electronic Commerce.* Little, Brown & Co. 1991. ISBN-0-316-95632-5.

Magazine Articles

Bleecker, Samuel. "The Virtual Organization." *The Futurist Magazine.* March, 1994.

"Computers as Metaphors." *Wired Magazine.* February, 1994.

Davidow, William and Michael Malon. "Virtual Corporations." *Forbes*. December 7, 1992.

"How We Will Work in the Year 2000." *Fortune Magazine*. May, 1993.

"Making High Tech Work for You." *Fortune Magazine*. Autumn, 1993 (Special Issue).

"Plugged In! How To Use a Personal Computer To Bring the World to You." *U.S. News & World Report*. December 6, 1993.

"The Virtual Corporation." *Business Week*. February, 1993.

"The Virtual Entrepreneur." *Success Magazine*. June, 1993.

"There Will Be No Info Highway." *Wired Magazine*. February, 1994.

"Videoconferencing Changes the Corporate Meeting." *Management Review*. February, 1994.

"Virtual Reality." *Upside Magazine*. June, 1993.

"Virtual Realities." *Inc Magazine*. August, 1993.

"Washington Confronts Part-Time America." *Management Review*. February, 1994.

"Wired World." *Maclean's Magazine*. January 17, 1994.

"Will the Delta Clipper Turn Deep Space into Cyberspace?" *Wired Magazine*. February, 1994.

INTERNET CYBERMALLS

Whenever a new highway comes to an area, retail shops and malls spring up to provide goods and services to the burgeoning population.

The information superhighway is no exception.

These days, retailing is becoming big business on the Internet, and storefronts, shopping centers, and cybermalls are springing up on virtually every electronic street corner. Book stores, software companies, incorporation services, auction houses, florists, newspaper publishers, law firms, and even restaurants are displaying their wares on the Internet, and customers are making their purchases online.

One of the driving forces behind this retailing boom is Mosaic-World Wide Web technology, which enables merchants to create full-color displays that enable shoppers to browse for products with the click of a mouse. Through the Web, Internet shoppers can also use hyperlinks to access information and product descriptions located elsewhere on the network.

These days, national retail chains such as KinderCare, LensDirect, and Gymboree are setting up shop on the Web. The Washington law firm of Venable, Baetjer, Howard & Civiletti recently became one of the first law firms to put up a Web server.

The goal of this chapter is to give you an overview of the Internet retailing options now available and to show you how companies are successfully using the Internet to attract new customers, ring up sales and, in some cases, even deliver electronic merchandise directly to the customer's computer.

We'll also take a look at the technologies that make Internet retailing possible, from the simplest option—e-mail—to telnet, Gopher, Mosaic and the World Wide Web. You'll find out how to set up your own Internet cybermall and how to negotiate the best deal on "mall space" from an Internet landlord.

Internet Shopping Malls

Internet stores run the gamut from tiny boutiques to sprawling retail complexes. On the Internet, a storefront can be as simple as an e-mail address on a Gopher server. Such an address automatically responds with a catalog or a menu item to messages, and potential customers can read a blurb about a company and order a product online.

A larger store may take up an entire Gopher server, and shoppers can telnet to the site and select from hundreds or thousands of books, magazines, CDs, software programs, or other items.

A *cybermall* built on a World Wide Web server offers Internet merchants the ability to showcase their stores and products by using formatted text, a colorful company logo, and graphics images and sounds. Through an Internet storefront, merchants can display their wares, take customer orders, and in the case of software programs and electronic books and magazines, even fulfill them online.

In the following section, we'll look at examples of the following four kinds of Internet stores that exist today:

- The company mailbox
- The storefront
- The store
- The cybermall

The Company Mailbox: Information Researchers

On a network where it seems as though anyone and everyone can find information of value just by wandering the Internet for a few hours, selling custom research services can be daunting.

Information Researchers, a company working out of the University of Illinois at Urbana-Champaign, has years of experience working on the Internet. The company knows that when a customer is seeking a specific piece of information, the right tools won't necessarily help them find what they seek. That's why the company offers a broad range of custom research such as company and industry profiles, literature and database searches, and bibliographies. Through the Internet, a company can also deliver electronically the results of queries and searches.

An initial consultation is arranged by sending mail to info@uiuc.edu. Here's what you receive in return:

```
From: Cindy Kehoe <kehoe@alexia.lis.uiuc.edu>
Subject: Information Researchers
Date: Thu, 23 Jun 1994 14:58:05 -0500 (CDT)

800-643-2807
info@uiuc.edu

INFORMATION RESEARCHERS (IR) is a full-service, professional
information broker offering custom research, online database
searching, and document delivery. IR has been in operation since
1976 as a cost recovery unit of the Graduate School of Library and
Information Science at the University of Illinois,
Urbana-Champaign.

Products and Services
Information Researchers offers rapid, convenient document delivery
from a wide variety of sources, and provides a broad range of
custom research on any topic, including: retrieval of specific
facts and statistics; literature and online database searches;
custom bibliographies; company and industry profiles; written
reports, from brief summaries to extensive papers; custom mailing
lists; and custom-designed projects.

Clients
Information Researchers serves individuals and organizations in
business, industry, education, and government, in fields such as
manufacturing, law, environment, health sciences, and small
business.

Resources
IR provides copies of almost any published documents, from the
collections of the University of Illinois (the third largest
academic library in the nation), as well as most other libraries in
the United States, the British Library, commercial document
suppliers, publishers, and government agencies.
```

Information Researchers also subscribes to the major database vendors, such as DIALOG, NewsNet, OCLC and LEXIS/NEXIS, which allows access to thousands of databases. In-house CD-ROM and other databases are also available.

IR staff includes professional information specialists with Master's degrees as well as college-educated writers and researchers.

For more information, or a free initial consultation and estimate, contact Information Researchers at: University of Illinois, 501 East Daniel Street #215, Champaign IL 61820-6212. Telephone: 800-643-2807, 217-333-6202; Fax 217-333-9361; E-mail: info@uiuc.edu.

Ask Information Researchers for:

Journal articles	Books
Conference papers	Technical reports
Government documents	News and trade articles
Names and addresses	Biographical information
Lists of companies	Standards and specifications
Technical data	Government regulations
Custom bibliographies	Technical and scientific research
Literature searches	Fact-finding
Electronic clipping service	Export opportunities
Government contract leads	Demographic data
Market research and forecasts	Company profiles
Product information	Competitor activities

Note: Businesses that are connected to the Internet through commercial services such as America Online are limited to sending out information via e-mail as opposed to letting users access it via Gopher, World Wide Web, or other Internet information servers.

Two companies on Dave's Internet Mall list are also taking this approach: The Chinook College Funding Services of Tucson, Arizona, which helps college students find financial aid, and Myers' Gourmet Popcorn of Colorado Springs, Colorado, which offers a range of gourmet popcorn products in its catalog and accepts orders through electronic mail.

Tip: Connect to Chinook College Funding Service by sending mail to CllgFunder@aol.com. Learn more about Myers' Gourmet Popcorn by sending e-mail to mgp@aol.com.

Some sites are fully connected to the Internet but function as simple storefronts aimed at the largest possible target audience, basing their information services on e-mail only. The Virtual Mall at Calpurnia Communications of Ontario, Canada, is just one of these services, distributing a wide variety of mail-order company catalogs through electronic mail. All e-mail requests are handled by the Virtual Mail e-mail server, which routes all mail to `vmall@hookup.net`.

Here's a sampling of the food companies affiliated with the Virtual Mall: Rogers Chocolates (the subject of the message should read, `send rogers catalog`), Murchies Tea and Coffee (`send murchies catalog`), River View Herbs (`send rvherbs catalog`), and Watson's Barrels and Wine Making Supplies (`send watson catalog`).

The River View Herbs gourmet herb and spice mail-order catalog, received within seconds of sending e-mail to the Virtual Mall, contains more than 60 pages of material. Here's what the first page looks like:

```
From: vmall@hookup.net (Grant Rowson)
Subject: Re: send rvherbs catalog
Date: Fri, 24 Jun 1994 02:57:56 -0400


-------------------------------------------------------------------
   {} {}   {}
 {}  {}  {}
   {}  {}   {}
    {}  {}
       )
      (
@@@@@@@@@@@@@
  @@ RIVER @@              RIVER VIEW HERBS
  @@@ VIEW @@                 HERBS AND SCENTED GERANIUMS
   @ HERBS @
   @@@@@@@@@                              Page 1
-------------------------------------------------------------------


INTRODUCTION

MAITLAND GREENHOUSES, located in Hants County, Nova Scotia,
overlooks the mouth of the Shubenacadie River where it flows
into the Bay of Fundy. Established in 1988 from the former
River View Farm, it operates year round producing fresh cut
culinary herbs for sale to restaurants, hotels and grocery
stores. These fresh herbs are available to anyone residing in
the Atlantic Provinces, Southern Quebec and Ontario.

Recently we have opened two retail garden centre outlets, one
in Maitland and the other in downtown Halifax.

In addition, we now produce seasonally 350 varieties of herb
and scented geranium plants that are sold by mail order. These
can be delivered anywhere in Canada. Delivery commences in
early May.

All plants are grown in pots 2.5 inches square and 3.5 inches
deep. Although it contributes extra to the shipping cost as
```

```
compared to the standard 2.5 cm pot, it produces a much more
robust, vigorous plant better able to withstand the rigors of
shipping and transplanting.

Plants are carefully packed in a carton designed to withstand
mistreatment in shipping and we guarantee their delivery in
good condition. However, we do not ship basil, fennel, dill,
coriander, summer savory or arugula plants... only seed.
Shipping is by courier service. For areas where normal courier
is not available, alternative delivery will be found.

Herb seed is also available for selected varieties.

All the herb products in this catalogue are sold under the
registered trademenk RIVER VIEW HERBS.
```

The Storefront: Harmony Games

The next step up in connectivity, one that requires a slightly higher investment but offers greater and more immediate interaction with customers, is making information on your service available through a Gopher server.

One company that's "renting space" on a Gopher server is Harmony Games, an online game store that sells hard-to-find board games from small companies. Many of the games that Harmony sells aren't often seen in local game shops because the manufacturers don't have enough advertising clout to make the titles big sellers.

By putting up a storefront on the Internet, board-game designer Scott Harmon can market these games at low cost and enable customers to ask questions, open the box (so to speak), read what other players think of them, and purchase whatever strikes their fancy. Cyberspace Development, Harmony's "landlord," charges tenants setup fees of $250 to $2,500 depending on the complexity of the job; monthly fees range from $100 to $500 depending on the level of service desired by the customer. Cyberspace Development also takes commissions of 20 to 30 percent of its tenants' sales.

Here's the opening screen that shoppers see when they log onto marketplace.com, the Gopher server operated by Cyberspace Development. (To have a look for yourself, type gopher marketplace.com at the system prompt.)

```
        Root gopher server: marketplace.com
-->  1.  About MarketPlace.com - The Internet Information Mall
     2.  Online Bookstore/
     3.  The Maloff Company (Internet Reseller Market Report)/
     4.  Information Law Alert/
```

```
    5.  Interactive Publishing Alert/
    6.  *Alternative-X*/
    7.  INFOMARK - International Telecom Information/
    8.  Harmony Games/
    9.  How to open a storefront in Marketplace.com
    10. Commercial Internet Directory/
    11. Cyberspace Development: Builders of Internet Storefronts
    12. Frequently Asked Questions about Internet Commerce
Choosing Harmony Games (menu item 8) brings you to the menu pictured below:
                              Harmony Games
  -->  1.  Welcome!
       2.  What's New?
       3.  BATALO (R): A Delicate Balance of Power/
       4.  CORPORATION (TM): The Game of International Trade/
       5.  MAGE WARZ (TM)/
       6.  How Do I Order?
       7.  Coming Attractions
       8.  Opportunities/
       9.  Send all inquires to harmony@marketplace.com
Choosing menu item 4, for example, shows you a description of Corporation (TM):
The Game of International Trade.
What is CORPORATION (TM)? B(1k)                                    73%
+------------------------------------------------------------------+
    CORPORATION (TM)--the board game that combines skill and luck.
It's filled with suspense, intrigue, cooperation, strategy and
exitement every time you play. Play CORPORATION (TM) and test
your business skills. Bid, buy, sell, and trade your way to the top of
international trade.
    Successfully bid for manufacturing companies. A role of the dice
lands you in cities where raw materials are available. Aquire millions
in revenue by selling raw materials to other manufacturing
companies. Outwit opponents' corporate raids and stock takeover
attempts. Buy corporate headquarters worldwide and win the game!
Build your corporate empire and span the globe. The world can be
yours.
Ages: 12 to Adult
Number of Players: 3 to 6
Approximate Playing Time: 3 Hours
Game Components:
- One three-fold full-color Gameboard
- two six-sided dice
+------------------------------------------------------------------+
```

To order the game, you return to the main Harmony Games menu and select item 6 (How Do I Order?).

```
How Do I Order? (0k)                                              99%
+------------------------------------------------------------------+
Prices include shipping and handling charges.
All games have a 30-day money back guarantee. Return game(s) in
original shipping materials to HARMONY GAMES for a full refund.
BATALO (R) $13.95 each
CORPORATION (TM) $34.95 each
```

```
MAGE WARZ (TM) $27.95 each
Specify which games and how many of each you are ordering.
Send check or money order for total amount to:
      HARMONY GAMES
      1085 14th St. Suite 1043
      Boulder, CO 80302
Include your name and shipping address. (We cannot ship to P.O. Boxes.)
Allow two weeks for delivery.
+-----------------------------------------------------------------------+
```

The Store: The Electronic Newsstand

An example of a larger cyberstore is The Electronic Newsstand, an Internet magazine rack through which shoppers can browse more than 100 publications on topics ranging from computers and technology to business, foreign affairs, the arts, travel, medicine, sports, and politics at no charge.

To entice readers to their publications, magazines and newspapers offered on The Newsstand—or Enews, as it's commonly known—post the table of contents and several articles from each current issue on the newsstand's Gopher server. After perusing the free samples, shoppers can then subscribe, either online or through a toll-free number.

To give you an idea of how Enews works, we connected with gopher internet.com and found the table of contents posted by *Business Week*, one of the magazines displayed there. Here's a snippet:

```
Magazine:  Business Week
Date: 06/27/94
Title:  BW Table of Contents

***Cover Story***

56  BILL GATES'S VISION
Microsoft may be king of desktop software, but its chairman
is worried. With networks poised to shift the computer
industry's center of gravity away from the desktop, Gates
wants to make sure Microsoft isn't left behind. So he's
taking his company for a risky ride onto the Information
Superhighway

60  STRUGGLING WITH SERVERS
Can Microsoft fix Windows NT?

62  WHERE BILL PUTS HIS PENNIES
Gates's stakes in startups

***Top of the News***
```

```
22  MERCK FINALLY GETS ITS MAN
The drugmaker taps outsider Ray Gilmartin, CEO of Becton
Dickinson, to succeed P. Roy Vagelos

26  IBM'S PC COMEBACK IS GONE
After a promising start, the year looks like a washout

27  AUCTIONING OFF ZIFF'S EMPIRE
Can it command top dollar--or will the sale reflect the
company's stall?

28  A BATTLE FOR THE GOP'S SOUL
Moderate Republicans wake up to an attack from the religious
right

29  WELFARE-REFORM MOM
Representative Lynn Woolsey has her own plan to remake
welfare

32  EXIT AT SIMON & SCHUSTER
Chairman and CEO Snyder is shown the door by parent Viacom

32  THE METLIFE/TRAVELERS DEAL
Now, they must rush to beef up their combined health-care
business

34  BALL OR STRIKE?
The baseball owners' salary-cap plan could mean empty
stadiums

36  A "HOMECOMING" FOR SATURNS
The car company throws a party for its fanatical customers

38  IN BUSINESS THIS WEEK
Exxon's exposure, Service Corp., USAir/British Airways,
reversal for GM, Tartikoff, GE, video wars
```

Through The Newsstand, Internet users can order single copies or full-year subscriptions to the printed (or electronic) versions of any of the publications displayed by sending an e-mail message or calling a toll-free number (1-800-40-ENEWS).

Launched in July, 1993, by The Internet Company and *The New Republic,* Enews is now accessed more than 40,000 times per day and has sold subscriptions in 18 different countries, including Australia, Canada, England, France, Hong Kong, India, Italy, and the Republic of China. Rosalind, who began advertising her newsletter there in June, recently received a subscription order from the Associated Press.

Enews typically charges publishers an annual set-up fee ranging from $1,000 to $5,000 depending on the circulation and frequency of the newspaper or magazine plus a percentage of their online subscription sales (usually about 10 percent).

To check out Enews for yourself, type `gopher internet.com` at the system prompt and select `The Electronic Newsstand` from the menu; you can also type `telnet internet.com` and log in as `enews` if you don't have Gopher at your site.

Here's what you'll see when you pull up The Electronic Newsstand's main menu:

```
                    The Electronic Newsstand(tm)
 -->  1.  Introduction to the Electronic Newsstand/
      2.  Notice of Copyright and General Disclaimer -- Please Read
      3.  Sweepstakes -- Win Two Round-trip Air Tickets to Europe!/
      4.  Best of the Newsstand/
      5.  Titles Arranged By Subject/
      6.  All Titles Listed Alphabetically/
      7.  Business Publications and Newsletters/
      8.  Electronic Bookstore/
      9.  HeadsUp: A personalized daily news service from INDIVIDUAL, Inc./
      10. The Electronic Showroom(tm)/
      11. Lufthansa Takes Off.../
      12. Titles In Development -- Hardhats Required/
      13. Search All Electronic Newsstand Articles by Keyword  <?>
```

Choose menu item 6, and you can view The Newsstand's titles listed alphabetically:

```
                    All titles listed alphabetically
 -->  1.  10 Percent/
      2.  American Demographics/
      3.  American Journal of International Law/
      4.  American Quarterly/
      5.  Arthritis Today/
      6.  Automatic I.D. News/
      7.  Best Friends/
      8.  Bio/Technology/
      9.  Blue & Gold Illustrated - Notre Dame Football/
      10. Body Politic/
      11. Business Week/
      12. CD-ROM World/
      13. Cadalyst Magazine/
      14. California Mining Journal/
      15. Canoe & Kayak/
      16. Christopher Street/
      17. Colloquium: A Digest for Investment Managers/
      18. Computerworld/
```

Because Enews is a Gopher site, the standard Gopher search tools can be used to find articles containing a particular keyword or phrase. Here's the result of choosing `search all articles by keyword` from the main Enews menu and then entering `Italy` as the keyword:

```
           Search All Electronic Newsstand Articles by Keyword : italy
 --> 1.  October 1993 -- THE OBSOLESCENCE OF CAPITAL CONTROLS? Economic Mana..
     2.  September 20, 1993 - THE GODMOTHER By Martin Jacques
     3.  April, 1994 -- Recent Changes in German Refugee Law: A Critical Ass..
     4.  Issue Date: SUMMER 1994  -- The Migration Challenge: Europe's Crisi..
     5.  August 9, 1993 -- THE TREMOR by Chalmers Johnson
     6.  April 2, 1994 -- Table of Contents
     7.  August 9, 1993 -- AIDEED IT MY WAY by S.J. Hamrick
     8.  September 13, 1993 -- CORRESPONDENCE
     9.  October 4, 1993 - Robert Brustein on Theater: All's Well That Ends ..
    10.  December 13, 1993 -- OF KINGS AND DIVAS
    11.  December 27, 1993 -- UNITED COLORS
    12.  April 11, 1994 -- REDFELLAS
    13.  January 1994 -- The Frescobaldi Brothers
    14.  January 22, 1994 -- Table of Contents
    15.  MArch 19, 1994 -- Table of Contents
    16.  November 27, 1993 -- Table of Contents
    17.  December 11, 1993 -- Table of Contents
    18.  January 31, 1994 -- ON FILMS: Fellini, Farewell
```

Is this form of Internet advertising limited to magazines, newspapers, newsletters, and other publications? Certainly not! In fact, the Electronic Newsstand recently signed the German airline, Lufthansa, as a client. Here's what you'll see when you choose Lufthansa Takes Off from the main Gopher menu:

```
                         Lufthansa Takes Off...
 --> 1.  Information about this Section
     2.  Destination of the Month
     3.  Hot Offers
     4.  Lufthansa News
     5.  Did You Know? (more fun facts)
     6.  Reaching us by electronic mail
```

Select menu item 3 (Hot Offers), and the following information appears on your screen:

```
Discover Europe at prices you can't believe!
Imagine yourself uncovering the mysteries of Europe's greatest cities,
the history, the tradition.  Now imagine yourself doing all this, at
discounted rates.
Just purchase your Lufthansa, Finnair or Lauda Air ticket in the USA for
transatlantic travel to Europe, on any published, Economy Class
round-trip fare.  Now you can take advantage of our Discover Europe
fares within Europe.  Buy a minimum of 3 flight coupons for $125 each,
good for travel to any one of over $100 destinations in Europe.
Purchase up to six additional coupons for $105 each.  Each Lufthansa,
Finnair or Lauda Air flight you board within Europe requires one flight
coupon.
See Europe at your own pace and price!  Seats are limited and
restrictions apply, so make your reservations today.  Call your travel
agent or Lufthansa at 1-800-645-3880 for details.
```

Electronic Newsstand shoppers can also contact the airline via e-mail; details are provided further down in the same document.

Of course, you don't need to contract with a service provider such as The Electronic Newsstand to offer your company's information through a Gopher server. However, you do need a 24-hour connection to the network—a SLIP or PPP connection at a minimum, ideally a 56 Kbps or faster connection. The Gopher server software for Macs, PCs, or UNIX systems is freely available from Gopher's developers at the University of Minnesota, and it's quite easy to set up if you're already on the Internet: just point it to your "home" Gopher server (which can be done by typing a hostname), and it'll remember from then on.

Tip: Gopher server and client software packages can be downloaded from the University of Minnesota computer system. Use FTP to connect to `boombox.micro.umn.edu` and then look in the `pub/gopher` directory.

The Cybermall: Internet Distribution Services

Although Gopher servers can be an excellent way to distribute promotional literature and even sell products, they lack the visual appeal and ease of use of a World Wide Web cybermall accessed through Mosaic or other Web browsers.

The tradeoff here between the Web and a simpler service such as Gopher is akin to the difference between advertising in *Fortune* and *Forbes* rather than *TV Guide* and *People*—you get a smaller but more select audience.

Internet Distribution Services, run by Marc Fleischmann of Palo Alto, California, is one of a growing number of cybermall operators who rent space on their World Wide Web servers. In addition to the Web, clients can use IDS to post their information on Gopher servers and deliver it via e-mail through mailing lists, thereby making the information available to the many Internet users without high-powered network connections.

Fleischmann's clients include The Document Center, a document-delivery service; The Company Corporation, a worldwide incorporation service; *The Palo Alto Weekly*, a local newspaper that publishes an online edition; Country Fare, a local restaurant; The Auction Directory & News, a nationwide auction information service, and The Technology Board of Trade, a trading floor for companies seeking and/or providing reusable software technology.

Any site that runs a World Wide Web server has a base, or "home" page to help orient people and highlight important or interesting new additions. IDS' home page features many of its clients. Figure 11.1 shows how it looks.

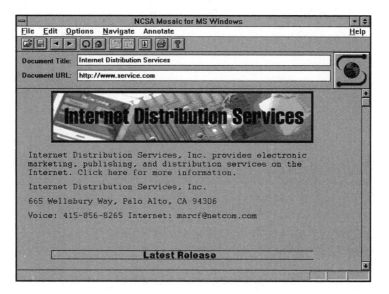

Figure 11.1. Internet Distribution Services is one of a growing number of cybermall operators "renting space" on World Wide Web servers.

Tip: To check out the IDS World Wide Web server for yourself, connect to the URL `http://www.service.com`.

Recognize, however, that IDS is only one of hundreds of commercial Web sites. Another company that has taken the idea of a distributed environment for graphics and text and turned it into a successful small business is the National Real Estate Services of Vancouver, B.C., Canada, which publishes its database of more than 20,000 real estate listings on a Web server. Figure 11.2 shows what we saw when we connected to URL `http://www.gems.com/realestate/`.

Other companies offer storefronts with a theme: The Avid Explorer, a Web server provides information on travel destinations around the world. Besides providing convenient links to the wealth of travel information on the Internet, The Avid Explorer (see Figure 11.3) presents information of interest to travelers interested in scuba, skiing, diving, and other sports plus information on cruises, tours, and domestic vacations. (Use URL `http://www.explore.com`.)

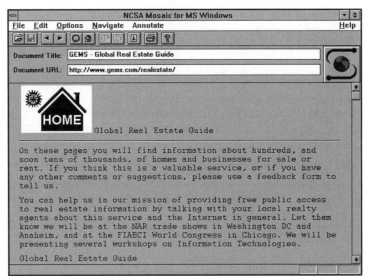

Figure 11.2. The National Real Estate Services of Vancouver, Canada, advertises home and business listings through its *Global Real Estate Guide*.

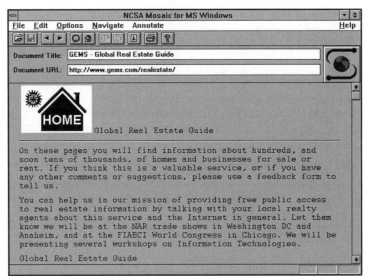

Figure 11.3. Even travel companies like The Avid Explorer are using Web servers to advertise on the Internet.

The cost of a Web connection, whether leased or through a connection of your own, is considerably higher than any other Internet options. Fleischmann's clients, for example, pay a setup fee of $2,500 to $15,000 plus monthly maintenance fees of $500 to $2,500, depending on the quantity of data. Others charge less. Branch Information Services of Ann Arbor, Michigan, charges $960 a year to rent a single page on its Web server plus $500 a year for online ordering capabilities. Additional pages cost $720 to $820 a page depending on the number of pages desired. (For more information about the Web and how it works, see the next section, *Surfing the Web with Mosaic*.)

Many World Wide Web sites indicate that they're satisfied with the sales produced through the Web. When customers at Softpro Books in Burlington Massachusetts, started asking owner Rick Treitman whether he could respond to e-mail queries, he opted to go onto the Internet. Two years later, he says that setting up shop on a Web server is yet another way to reach potential Internet customers. The storefront cost the company $2,000 to set up plus $20 a month for an e-mail hookup.

Some shoppers visit the Web site to preview books before coming by the store in person; others place their orders online. Significantly, Trietman says "the Internet is more effective as a marketing channel than as a sales channel," a claim that many more technologically-oriented vendors, such as Ceram Corporation of Colorado, which sells multimillion dollar UNIX workstation sales by e-mail, might dispute.

Let's look at some other companies and how they're using the Internet and the Web to sell products. Grant's Florist and Greenhouse (URL `http://florist.com:1080`), an Ann Arbor, Michigan, company that's been in business since 1947, has seen its sales blossom thanks to its presence on the Web.

Co-owner Larry Grant says his store received 40 orders for Mother's Day bouquets through the Internet, compared to 45 from the international FTD network. Currently, the company receives two to five orders a day via the Internet, and the number is steadily growing. Grant's Florist "rents space" on the Web server operated by Branch Information Services and pays no fee except for a small sales commission for every Internet order received. Grant says he was able to snag this favorable deal because he was one of Branch's first customers; other businesses that advertise on the Web server pay close to $1,000 a year for the service. Jon Zeeff, Branch's president, says he is no longer offering percentage deals.

Interestingly, Grant himself does not yet have an Internet account; the shop receives online orders via a fax connection with Branch. Zeeff compares the arrangement to advertising in a publication you don't read. "You don't have to be a subscriber to advertise," he notes. Figure 11.4 shows the shop's Web page.

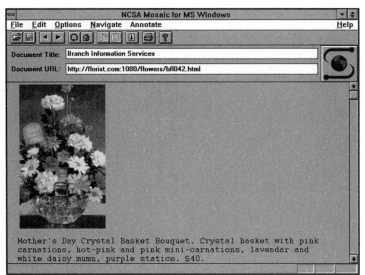

Figure 11.4. Grant's Florist and Greenhouse of Ann Arbor, Michigan, gets two to five orders a day from its Internet cybermall.

The Document Center, a hard-copy document delivery service in Belmont, California, which has set up shop on the IDS server, also reports encouraging results from the Web, Gopher, and WAIS servers on which it posts its information. Since launching its Internet storefront in October, The Document Center has attracted 1 to 2 e-mail queries a day and approximately 3,000 Internet browsers a month. The company says it paid less than $10,000 to set up the storefront and pays under $1,000 a month for space on the Web server, the ability to transfer files from its minicomputer to the server, and maintenance and improvements to its online offerings.

"For now, the Internet is a very small percent of sales; we just do a lot of traditional business," says company president Claudia Bach, who is trying to persuade her existing customers to go online. "The Internet has not been a mass-media before, and there will be something of a transition period, which may be unpleasant at times. It is not secure, reliable, and does not meet my quality standards."

Nevertheless, Bach says, "I am learning to live with its limitations because the pros are so compelling. To be on the Internet right now is to be trying something really different. It is a completely new medium, unlike any other medium we know of. And it will really be fun as multimedia hits. I think the sky's the limit."

Surfing the Web with Mosaic

If you're used to accessing the Internet through a UNIX shell or other text-based program, you're in for a surprise the first time you start Mosaic. Seen through a Mosaic browser, the Internet becomes colorful and exciting, its virtual "streets" lined with World Wide Web cybermalls that users can browse with a click of their mouse.

But there's more to Mosaic than a pretty interface. Because Web software provides hypertext and hypermedia links to other document sources throughout the network, Internet shoppers can click a word or a picture on a Web page to access product information housed on a computer thousands of miles away.

> **Note:** Hypertext works like a footnote—a pointer to other text within the same document or another. Hypermedia works the same way except that, instead of pointing to words, it points to images, sound, or even animation. Through these hyperlinks, documents can be linked to other documents on other computers anywhere on the Internet, transforming the Internet into a giant relational database that's transparent to the user.

Here's an example: Open up to the Avid Explorer's home page (URL `http://www.explore.com`) with a Web browser, click the words, `Dr. Fun`, and you'll be immediately transported to the section of the University of North Carolina's SunSITE server that contains information about Doctor Fun, a single-panel cartoon distributed every day over the Internet. Click an item there, and you leap instantly to Japan or Germany. Another click might move you to Mexico or Canada.

To work with the World Wide Web, you'll need a *browser*. A browser both reads documents and fetches them from other sources. Though there are many different Web browsers, Mosaic, developed by the National Center for Supercomputer Applications, has become the most popular.

The Web embraces more than just words and graphics, however. Inventive programmers have designed interfaces to a wide variety of information services on the Internet. Here's a list of the types of information available through the Web in addition to hypermedia documents:

- Anything served through Gopher
- Anything served through WAIS
- Anything on an FTP site

- Anything on Usenet

- Anything accessible through telnet

- Anything in Hytelnet

- Anything in the form of man pages

World Wide Web sites are typically referred to by their Uniform Resource Locator (URL) address, an awkward but useful format for specifying an information object on the Internet, such as a file or newsgroup. All URLs indicate the type of object, a colon, and then the address of the object and any further information required. All Web documents are accessed through a protocol called the *hypertext transfer protocol*, so Web server URLs all begin with `http:` .

Here are some examples of URL addresses:

```
file://wuarchive.wustl.edu/mirrors/msdos/graphics/gifkit.zip
http://info.cern.ch:80/default.html
news:alt.hypertext
gopher://tyrell.net
telnet://dra.com
```

The first address specifies a file at Washington University, the second is a hypertext pointer to a Web server in Switzerland (CERN is the organization that invented the World Wide Web), the third is a Usenet newsgroup URL, the fourth points to the Gopher server at Tyrell Corporation of Kansas City, Missouri, and the last denotes a telnet connection to the Data Research Associates in St. Louis, Missouri.

If you're running Mosaic on your computer, whether it's the Macintosh, Windows, or UNIX version, it's easy to enter URLs to hop around; click the File menu and you'll see an item called `Open URL`. Select it with your mouse and type a URL. Figure 11.5 shows us the screen as we're about to use Mosaic to connect to the Internet Distribution Services.

Tip: Type URL addresses carefully. Mosaic and other Web browsers are very picky about slashes, colons, and commas!

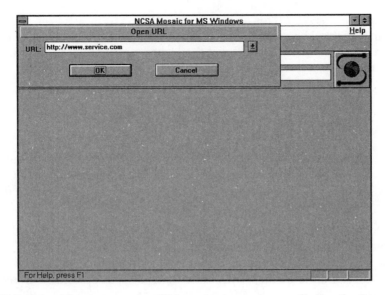

Figure 11.5. Using Mosaic to access a Web server is as easy as selecting the Open URL command and typing its Internet address.

If you or your customers don't have a high-speed Internet connection and are unable to use a graphics Web server such as Mosaic, don't despair! There are a variety of text-based client programs Internet users can use to access the Web's textual information while omitting the graphics. There are also several public-access Web browser sites that you can try. Your Internet access provider might also have a text-based Web browser installed. One popular UNIX-based browser is called *Lynx*.

A list of public access Web sites is available through the Web, though that isn't going to help much if you can't connect to the Web in the first place. To leap this hurdle, check out any of the following sites. On these sites, you can telnet to a Web browser. For the full list check out the URL `http://info.cern.ch/hypertext/WWW/FAQ/Bootstrap.html`).

> `ukanaix.cc.ukans.edu`. Connect to the University of Kansas system with `telnet ukanaix.cc.ukans.edu` and log in as www. No password is required. You'll need a vt100 terminal emulator for best results.
>
> `www.njit.edu`. Connect with `telnet www.njit.edu` and log in as www to use this full-screen Web browser located at the New Jersey Institute of Technology.
>
> `info.cern.ch`. Connect with `telnet info.cern.ch`. No password is required. This system is located in Switzerland, however, so U.S. users may achieve faster results by using a closer browser.

`vms.huji.ac.il`.   This dual-language Hebrew-English Web site offers a line-oriented browser. Connect with `telnet vms.huji.ac.il` and then log in as www. This site is located at the Hebrew University of Jerusalem in Israel.

Mosaic: The Internet's "Killer App"?

Spend ten minutes with a text-based Web browser, and you'll realize that it's pretty hard to use. The National Center for Supercomputer Applications (NCSA) at the University of Illinois thought so, too, so a group of researchers there developed Mosaic, a multi-platform hypermedia browser.

With its flashy graphics and easy connectivity, Mosaic has caught the popular imagination. According to Joseph Hardin, director of the group that developed Mosaic, more than 50,000 copies of the program are being downloaded monthly from NCSA's public server—with more than 300,000 copies distributed overall.

Businesses have been quick to jump on the bandwagon, too. Five companies have already signed licensing agreements with NCSA and announced plans to release commercial products based on the program. Also underway is development of a so-called "secure" Mosaic to protect confidential data, such as credit card numbers, and to make sure that customers making purchases online really are who they claim to be.

Special Uses of Mosaic

Apart from the enthusiasm that Mosaic has generated as a graphical interface for Internet shopping, Mosaic has also caught the attention of newspaper and magazine publishers seeking alternatives to commercial online services such as Prodigy, CompuServe, and America Online. To date, *The Palo Alto Weekly* and *The* (Raleigh) *News & Observer* are the only commercial U.S. newspapers that have published online editions using Mosaic and the Web.

However, Learned Information, Ltd., a European publisher based in London, recently launched an Internet document server, The Learned InfoNet, which is accessible via both World Wide Web and Gopher. Learned Information intends to use the Internet to publish notices of its upcoming conferences, exhibitions, and Internet training sessions as well as selected highlights from current issues of Learned Information's periodicals, such as *Information World Review, Electronic Documents, The Electronic Library, Expert Systems,* and *Online & CD-ROM Review.* (Try it yourself by connecting to URL `http://info.learned.co.uk/`.)

Other publications are also experimenting with Web-based publishing. *Gazeta Wyborcza*, Poland's largest daily newspaper, says it's planning to publish its entire contents on the Web by the end of the summer of 1994. All articles are in Polish. To view a prototype of Gazeta online, log onto the Internet and use a Mosaic or lynx browser to view `http://info.fuw.edu.pl/gw/0/gazeta.htm`. *Mother Jones Magazine* published its July/August issue on the World Wide Web. To view it, log onto the Internet and go to `http://www.mojones.com/motherjones.html`.

To give you an idea of how Web-based publishing works, Figure 11.6 shows what you see when you connect with the *Palo Alto Weekly* at URL `http://www.service.com/PAW/home.html`.

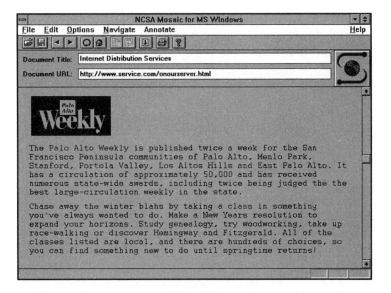

Figure 11.6. *The Palo Alto Weekly* is one of the first commercial U.S. newspapers to publish an online edition on the World Wide Web.

Figure 11.7 shows the menu of stories and other features that appear when you click the highlighted words, `The Palo Alto Weekly`.

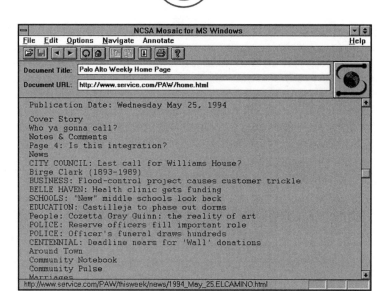

Figure 11.7. Internet users click highlighted headlines from the menu to access stories and other features from the online edition of *The Palo Alto Weekly.*

Click on Movie Times to access local theater listings (Figure 11.8).

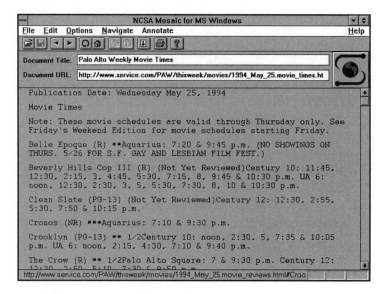

Figure 11.8. Not only are *The Palo Alto Weekly's* news stories available but also its movie listings are accessible to readers through the World Wide Web.

Although Mosaic has advocates in the publishing world, it also has some detractors. Critics note that there are some important limitations as a publishing tool—the fact that Mosaic can't make a newspaper look like a newspaper—and that the high-powered Internet connection necessary to run Mosaic makes it inaccessible to the majority of Internet users.

Essentially, the debate breaks down like this: Mosaic's fans argue that once publishers make the decision to publish on the Web, they need to accept that they are giving readers flexibility, both in how they access the information and in how it's presented. Mosaic's detractors respond that the program takes too much control away from the publishers and puts too much in the hands of the reader. Not only is Mosaic too limited in its layout capabilities, they contend, but once a publisher creates an attractive layout, there's no way to guarantee that it will look the same on every reader's computer. What's more, different versions of Mosaic might not necessarily display information the same way.

To understand the problem, let's take a brief look at the programming language used to construct Web documents. Known as *hypertext markup language* (HTML), it's actually a subset of *standardized graphic markup language* (SGML), a complex, sophisticated way of modifying and marking online documents.

The problem is, although SGML has considerable power, HTML is a very simple tool without much flexibility. With HTML, you can't specify typefaces, type sizes, or even which items should be where. Rather, you are constrained to work with a primitive text-based language where `<bigger>` specifies a larger type size and `<b> </b>` indicates that you want the passage between the two marks typeset in boldface.

Even visual elements such as the color used as a document hyperlink highlight is defined by the reader, not the publisher, so you can't specify, for example, that blue words will get you help and red words lead to more products.

Mosaic's proponents, however, believe that the individual reader's ability to define the contents of the document and its presentation is exactly what's so exciting about the entire technology. Steve Auerweck of the *Baltimore Sun* points out that "hypertext makes it easy to present headlines and summaries of a large number of stories compactly, and you can flip to the jump page without dragging the front across the butter dish."

Drawbacks to Using Mosaic

Both fans and critics of Mosaic point to five major weaknesses in the program:

- ■ **Accessibility.**   Only Internet users with high-speed connections can use the program. Right now, that's only about two percent of the Internet population. The number is growing rapidly, but the fastest growing portion of Internet use remains the simpler dialup connections.

- ■ **Speed.**   Though Mosaic runs fairly quickly over the high-powered 56 Kbps and T1 lines installed at many large companies, individuals, and small business owners using 14.4 Kbps modems must often wait as long as several minutes for Mosaic images to be downloaded to their computers. It's like being able to get 500 channels on your TV but having to wait up to five minutes between each station flip for the picture to fully resolve on your screen.

- ■ **Security.**   Although Mosaic may be ideal for showcasing products online, the current version has no mechanism for protecting credit card numbers and other sensitive information from Internet thieves. As a result, Mosaic's value for handling purchases and other transactions is limited—at least for now.

- ■ **Authentication.**   Mosaic lacks a password system that would enable Internet merchants to verify that their customers really are who they say they are. For businesses, this could result in uncollectable debts and charge-backs.

- ■ **Search tools.**   The current design of the hypertext markup language is such that there's no easy way to index Web documents without creating a database of all words in all Web documents through the network. Without helpful search tools, precious few of which are available today, users are forced to "wander the Web" searching for information, a drawback for Internet users who don't have time to spend browsing.

Despite the limitations of Mosaic and the World Wide Web, an attractive Web server can nonetheless serve as a popular waystation on the Internet. Put up lots of interesting, useful, and eye-catching information, add links to other servers, and your electronic billboard could quickly become a traffic-stopper.

Technical wizard Eric Schmidt of Sun Microsystems sums it up this way: "I personally believe that Mosaic is the 'lighthouse' of killer applications in the 90s. It 'shows the way.' There will be many commercial efforts to enhance or replace Mosaic, and Web servers will evolve, but their real legacies are the protocols. The protocols will be here forever."

Owning Versus Leasing: Setting up Your Own Web Server

Now that we've filled you in on the pros and cons of Mosaic and Web, you may decide that you'd like to give the new technology a try. The next decision you need to make is whether to set up your own server or to rent space on somebody else's.

Though new Web servers are going up every day and the cost of renting Web space is dropping, there are a number of technical and business issues to consider. Does your company have a technician on staff capable of setting up and maintaining the server? Do the potential sales and marketing benefits justify the expense of setting up your own?

How much does it cost to set up your own Web server? Here's how some Web operators say the costs break down:

UNIX Workstation (server):	$5,000 to $10,000
Internet Access:	$500 to $1,000 a month
Phone line installation for 56 Kbps or T-1 line:	$2,500
Routers:	$5,000 to $6,000 a year
Full-time programmer:	$100,000 a year (benefits included)
TOTAL =	$150,000

Of course, there are more modestly priced solutions as well. We estimate that you can get your own Web server up and running for roughly $14,500 in setup fees and $1,000 a month in operating costs. Here's how these costs break down: $2,500 for a high-powered PC or Macintosh computer, $500 to $1,000 a month for a 56 Kbyte Internet connection and a $2,000 initial setup fee, and $10,000 for a consulting firm to set up the server, design your Web home page, and help distribute announcements of its existence to the Internet community.

If your company's technical expertise is limited to PCs or Macs, training them to use a UNIX workstation can involve considerable expense. However, if you already have UNIX experts in-house, a similarly priced PC running UNIX will offer more server capability—particularly the ability to serve more simultaneous users—for the same investment.

The key question is whether you want to set up your own Web server or whether you want to rent space elsewhere.

As we noted above, "renting space" in an Internet landlord's cybermall can cost less than $1,000 a year but will typically run about $10,000 if you want multiple Web pages. Note, however, that prices vary dramatically from city to city. It's also possible to negotiate a lower upfront fee if you agree to turn over a certain percentage of your company's Internet-based sales to your online landlord.

If you want to focus on building and selling your product as opposed to managing the technical aspects of advertising it online, your best bet may be to contract with a firm like IDS, Branch, The Internet Group of Pittsburgh, or any of the other cybermall operators.

If, on the other hand, you want to retain control over your Web server, adding information, fiddling with layouts, and incorporating slick graphics and dazzling audio and video, the convenience of having the server in-house may more than justify the expense.

Whether you decide to set up your own server or rent space in a cybermall, be sure to check out Appendix D, "Working with the World Wide Web: Tips and Tools." There you'll find everything you need to create your own HTML documents and find out more about Mosaic and the Web."

The Future of Internet Retailing

What's the future of Internet retailing?

In three words, *World Wide Web.* Although Gopher sites will continue to exist, we believe that the trend is rapidly shifting in favor of an easy-to-use graphical interface similar to those offered by commercial online networks like Prodigy, CompuServe, and America Online.

Though Web-based cybermalls still suffer from serious drawbacks such as inaccessibility and lack of security controls, we believe that, as more and more people learn about their advantages and gain access to faster Internet connections, text-based information servers will eventually fall by the wayside.

We also recognize, however, that savvy retailers operate in the present, not the future, so again we strongly encourage businesses selling products on the Internet to offer multiple ways of distributing information to the Internet community. Although the Web may be the wave of the future, it's important for your company to provide the same information through text-based tools such as e-mail and Gopher for those Internet users who lack high-powered connections and access to graphical tools.

Here are some other Internet retailing trends on the horizon:

> **More and bigger cybermalls.**   Thanks to the popularity of Mosaic, more and bigger cybermalls will continue to pop up on the Internet. Because the cost of "renting space" on a Web server is so much less than opening an online store on Prodigy, CompuServe, or GEnie, a growing number of companies will give Internet cybermalls a try. (Wondering exactly how much it costs on CompuServe to set up shop? In the next chapter, we

examine the commercial networks in depth.) Large companies will probably want to set up their own Web servers for reasons of cost and control; smaller businesses will probably want to rent space on servers operated by cybermall operators.

> **Tip:** Many Internet access providers that aren't cybermall operators can still offer you a place on the Web. Netcom Communications, for example, will help set up a Web home page for your business even if all you have is a simple dialup Internet access account.

Greater accessibility and variety.   With new versions of Mosaic in the works, Internet users with regular dialup connections and 14.4 bps modems are likely to gain fast, reliable access to Mosaic/Web servers by the end of 1995. The rapid growth of the Internet population will encourage more merchants to set up shop on the Internet, too.
Secure transactions.   With the demand for Internet retailing heating up, dozens of companies are working to develop new software tools that will provide security and authentication for online transactions. Once these tools are released, Internet customers will feel more comfortable about typing their credit card numbers at a Gopher screen, Web site, or in an e-mail message, and Internet merchants will feel more comfortable accepting their orders.

> **Note:** One promising development in the area of security is an effort to create a secure version of Mosaic. This project is a joint venture of Enterprise Integration Technologies, the National Center for Supercomputing Applications, and RSA Data Security. The announcement was made in conjunction with the launch of CommerceNet, a large-scale market trial of electronic commerce on the Internet. The planned Mosaic and Web server enhancements will be made available to NCSA for widespread public distribution and commercial licensing.
>
> This secure Mosaic, slated for release in September, 1994, would allow users to add digital signatures to messages and time stamps to contracts so that they become legally binding. In addition, sensitive information such as credit card numbers and bid amounts can be securely exchanged with automatic data encryption. Together, the companies hope that these capabilities can provide the foundation for a broad range of financial services, including the network equivalents of credit and debit cards, letters of credit, and checks.

> CommerceNet will certify public keys on behalf of member companies and will also authorize third parties such as banks, public agencies, and industry consortia to issue keys. Such keys will often serve as credentials, for example, identifying someone as a customer of a bank, with a guaranteed credit line.
>
> Significantly, all the transactions involved in making routine purchases from a catalog can be accomplished without requiring buyers to obtain public keys. Using only the server's public key, the buyer can authenticate the identity of the seller and transmit credit card information securely by encrypting it under the seller's public key. Because there are far fewer servers than clients, public key administration should be greatly simplified.

The ultimate question about Internet retailing, of course, is not whether the majority of Internet users will be able to access Mosaic but whether businesses can convince consumers to buy online instead of browsing through a printed catalog, picking up the phone, and ordering through a toll-free number. Despite a few highly publicized success stories, online merchants on commercial networks have traditionally had a hard time attracting customers. (We'll revisit this problem in Chapter 12, "The Commercial Online Services.") Although the Internet has proved successful in facilitating business-to-business transactions, it remains to be seen whether the Internet can attract the mass market of home computer users.

THE COMMERCIAL ONLINE SERVICES

12

When you hear the term, *information superhighway*, it's quite likely that you think *Internet.* Although we believe that the Internet is clearly the best choice for international network commerce, there are other online options that may be better suited to your business' needs. Like the Internet, these commercial networks offer different—and possibly more appropriate—venues for your marketing, customer support, or information-hunting needs.

Though smaller than the Internet, the five largest U.S. commercial online services—CompuServe, Prodigy, America Online, GEnie, and Delphi—boast a combined membership roster of almost 5,000,000 subscribers and that number is growing at a rapid rate. By 1997, predicts market research firm SIMBA Information and Communications Trends, close to 10,000,000 people throughout the United States will subscribe to commercial online services.

For businesses, the commercial networks offer several advantages over the Internet—at least for now. One big plus is ease of use. The four largest services—CompuServe, Prodigy, America Online and GEnie—offer free or inexpensive graphical front-ends so that users can bypass the confusing text-based interfaces that bog down so much of today's Internet usage. Delphi, the smallest of the Big Five commercial networks, is a text-based service but currently has a graphical interface in development. The commercial services also feature directories of databases, bulletin boards and members, making them far easier than the Internet to search and navigate.

Another advantage for businesses is the capability of setting up online shopping malls on the networks and to transact business there. Unlike merchants who set up shop on the Internet's cybermalls, vendors on commercial online services don't have to worry as much about security risks; what's more, they can advertise their presence on the services' welcome screens and, in the case of Prodigy, full-color display ads that run across the bottom of subscribers' screens. Unlike on the Internet, all this is visible to users with connections as slow as 1200 bps.

The third advantage to using commercial online services is cultural. Although the commercial online services try to restrict blatant advertising to the "classified" sections of their services, they're typically less strict than Internet newsgroups and mailing lists as to what constitutes an ad. Likewise, the people who use commercial online services tend to be more tolerant of thinly disguised sales pitches than some of the purists on the Internet. As a result, flame wars are far less common there.

So what's the catch? The biggest drawback to doing business on the commercial online networks is financial; commercial online services are far more expensive than the Internet. In the commercial world, online time is metered, there are often fees for sending e-mail, and many databases are steeply surcharged. After all, the commercial networks are private-sector companies that are in it to make a profit—though not all of them are running in the black.

As we wrap up this book, we believe it will be useful to consider the five largest commercial online service providers and compare them with the Internet. We'll also consider what each service offers for businesses and analyze the strengths and weaknesses of each. You'll find out how much the networks charge for e-mail, advertising, storefronts, and other services and learn how to craft a successful online marketing and communications strategy that combines the best of what both the Internet and the commercial online services have to offer.

And that's the bottom line—finding the online solution that's best for your business, no matter what kind of product or service you sell.

Commercial Online Services Versus the Internet

Like the Internet, commercial online services provide e-mail, file transfer, discussion group, and sales and marketing capabilities. Both types of networks can be accessed through modems and local-area networks. Both reach an international user base.

But that's where the similarities end. Here are some of the key business differences between the Internet and its commercial cousins:

- **Demographics.** The commercial online services, with the exception of CompuServe, attract primarily home computer users, not business owners, government officials, or academics. Unlike the Internet, the commercial networks also tend to reach a predominantly domestic subscriber base; CompuServe, the online service with the biggest international presence, has only 600,000 subscribers outside the United States.

- **Culture.** As noted previously, subscribers to commercial online services tend to be less adverse to advertising and solicitations than Internet users. As a result, advertisers on commercial services can put up display ads and storefronts and, in some cases, send targeted mailings to subscribers who express interest in their products.

- **Infrastructure.** Because commercial networks provide a ready-made infrastructure complete with mainframe computers, a nationwide (or worldwide) network of local-access phone numbers, a well-advertised market presence, hundreds of bulletin boards, and the capability of setting up a gateway to databases, there's no need to set up a Gopher or World Wide Web server. The downside is that commercial networks typically take a hefty cut of the online revenues generated by their business partners (see below).

- **Pricing.** Unlike Internet access, which typically offers users unlimited access to e-mail and other services for a flat monthly fee, subscribers to commercial networks pay based on actual usage. CompuServe, for example, charges $22.80 an hour for 9,600-bps access, though frequent users can cut costs by paying $8.95 a month for a flat fee plan that provides unlimited access to basic services such as news, sports, and weather, a generous allotment of e-mail, and a discount on hourly rates charged to access bulletin boards and other features.

- **E-mail.** Unlike the Internet, where users pay a flat fee for the ability to send an unlimited number of e-mail messages, the two largest commercial networks, CompuServe and Prodigy, levy per-message surcharges after the subscriber has exceeded his monthly allotment of "free" e-mail. Although that allotment may be more than sufficient for individual users, businesses that rely on e-mail as their primary communications tool may be in for an unpleasant surprise when they receive their online services bill at the end of the month.

■ **Discussion groups.** Commercial networks offer computer bulletin boards, similar to Internet newsgroups, on thousands of topics from pet care and scuba diving to small business and computing. In fact, many leading hardware and software companies provide technical support bulletin boards on the commercial services. However, commercial services lack the equivalent of the Internet's mailing lists—discussion groups through which companies can automatically distribute postings, press releases, brochures, and product announcements to colleagues and customers.

■ **Databases.** Although the Internet offers a wealth of free government, university, and technical information, the commercial services offer gateways to the world of pay-as-you-go information sources such as Dow Jones News/Retrieval, S&P Online, Disclosure, Predicasts, and Ziff-Davis' Computer Database Plus.

■ **Walls.** Unlike the Internet where you can telnet from one computer to another to order a book or download a file, you can't travel freely from one commercial service to another. If you're a CompuServe subscriber, for instance, you can't access an America Online bulletin board, and vice versa. Likewise, you can't search a CompuServe database if you're a Prodigy subscriber or read the latest electronic issue of *Time* magazine on America Online. The "walls" that exist between the commercial services for competitive reasons also make it impossible for a company to make a single media "buy" that reaches all commercial-services subscribers.

Making Money on the Commercial Networks

There are a variety of ways for businesses to use the commercial online networks to promote, advertise, and sell their products. In fact, there are many more options than on the Internet right now. Here are seven of them:

■ **Networking.** Just as you can post notes on Internet newsgroups or mailing lists, you can also tack notes on commercial network bulletin boards, which can be an excellent way to market your products and boost company awareness. If you sell software to mail-order vendors, for example, you might want to put a note on CompuServe's Entrepreneur's Forum. If you sell baby gifts, you might want to post a note on Prodigy's Homelife Bulletin Board. It's important to keep your postings more informational than promotional, however. Posting a list of "10 Ways to Save Money on Your Taxes" will go over a lot better than a blatant ad for your accounting firm.

> **Tip:** Cultures vary in cyberspace, but, as a general rule, users respond more favorably to advertisements that contain useful and interesting information than empty hype.

■ **Targeted e-mail.** Some commercial services permit—and even encourage—targeted mailings to subscribers based on interests or demographic criteria. This means that you can send an ad for your new pet food to anybody who belongs to the service's Pet Lovers Bulletin Board. It also means that you can send reminder notices a week before Mother's Day to all the people who placed an order at your online flower shop within the last year. True, you could do the same with an Internet flower shop, but it's impossible to know who subscribes to a particular Usenet newsgroup.

■ **Advertising.** All the major commercial networks—except Delphi—offer classified advertising, the same as you would find in the "Classifieds" section of a daily newspaper. Prodigy is the only commercial network that offers full-color display advertising similar to ads in magazines. Commercial networks also allow advertisers to post notices on the welcome screen that appears when the subscriber logs on; choosing the number next to it automatically transports the user to the vendor's online area.

■ **Online storefronts.** Prodigy and CompuServe feature large online shopping malls with hundreds of merchants hawking everything from computers to CDs to flowers. Subscribers can browse merchandise, find out pricing and product information, and order it online by typing their credit card numbers. However, the price of setting up shop can be pretty steep, as we'll show you later in the chapter.

■ **Sponsorship.** Commercial networks also offer companies the opportunity to "sponsor" an online area, a less obtrusive form of advertising that enhances the company's online presence without peddling a specific product. Microsoft, for example, sponsors the Microsoft Small Business Center on America Online.

■ **Joint ventures.** These days, dozens of newspapers, magazines, and other media companies are hooking up with commercial networks to publish online editions. *Time, Road & Track, The San Jose Mercury News, The Chicago Tribune, The Atlanta Journal and Constitution, U.S. News & World Report*, and *The Detroit Free Press* have all joined forces with commercial networks within the last few years. Typically, the print publication gets a 10- to 15-percent share of the revenues generated by the online area through users' connect-time charges, though revenue guarantees are coming into vogue as the online services compete to sign up print publishers and lure their large subscriber base. Once they're online, the newspapers and magazines can sell subscriptions to their print publications, books, software, and other products.

- **Database gateways/publishing.** As noted previously, the commercial networks offer gateways to specialized databases containing financial, research, travel, directory, and other information. Typically, the database provider receives a share of the revenues generated by the online service's subscribers.

The World of Commercial Online Services

Just five years ago, fewer than 1,000,000 Americans subscribed to commercial online services. Prodigy was in its infancy. Today, the IBM-Sears joint venture is one of the nation's largest online services with more than 1,000,000 subscribers. The total number of people online with the various commercial services is approaching 5,000,000 with the likelihood that the number will double within the next four years. And that's not counting the tens of thousands of people who dial up the more than 50,000 independently owned bulletin board systems (BBSs) nationwide.

Other demographic trends are also encouraging. According to Link Resources' Annual Home Media Survey, 31 percent of U.S. households now own personal computers, 39 percent of personal computer owners have modems, and 46 percent of modem users log onto online services. If we assume that there are 258,000,000 people in the United States, there are 80,000,000 home PCs and 31,000,000 modems, and 14,030,000 people are logging on somewhere or other. Though these numbers may be a bit high, they clearly illustrate that the online marketplace is no futuristic fantasy.

CompuServe

CompuServe Information Service, a unit of H&R Block, is the most business-oriented of the commercial online services.

An information treasure chest that doubles as one of the world's busiest online communications hubs, CompuServe offers access to more than 1,700 databases, including newspaper and magazine libraries, stock market and financial data, an online stock brokerage, an online shopping mall and an online travel agency, plus communications links with the Internet, MCI Mail, AT&T Mail, the NetWare MHS Local-Area Network, and fax and Telex machines around the world.

By entering key words or phrases, CompuServe's Executive News Service subscribers can "clip" news stories from Associated Press, United Press International, *The Washington Post,* Reuters Financial, World, European Community, and Sports reports, and OTC NewsAlert, an information service on over-the-counter stocks.

CompuServe enjoys an especially strong following among the small business and entrepreneurial crowd. It's also the most cosmopolitan of the commercial services, with 1,400,000 subscribers in the United States and Canada, 400,000 subscribers in the Pacific Rim, 120,000 in Europe, and 80,000 in the rest of the world.

Profile: Jeff and Mary Freeman have used CompuServe to build their home-based business, Front Porch Computers, into a $4,000,000-a-year computer mail-order company. By spending less than $200 a month to run a classified ad on CompuServe, the Chatsworth, Georgia, couple has attracted customers from as far away as Europe, South America, and Asia. Without his CompuServe link, Jeff Freeman says, his booming business would be "nowhere." That's because Chatsworth, population 5,000, is 100 miles north of Atlanta, and his computer store is the first and only one the town has ever had—and is ever likely to.

With a store in a town like this, you may sell one computer at a time, but on CompuServe you may meet somebody who wants to buy multiple computers for his business," Freeman says. "Our store is a small thing here, but with CompuServe I can reach the world.

In addition to the standard online staples of news, weather, sports, and computer games, CompuServe also offers hundreds of special-interest bulletin boards called "forums" where its close to 2,000,000 members gather to discuss everything from quilt-making to fantasy baseball to computer programming, and to download free and low-cost software. CompuServe's forums also provide free technical support for most major hardware and software vendors, and its CB Simulator chat area provides a forum for real-time conversations among CompuServe members worldwide.

Until recently, CompuServe had two main drawbacks—ease of use and cost. For novice users, the service's complex command structure and text-based interface can be difficult to navigate; its connect-time charges of $12.80 an hour for 2,400 bps access and $22.80 an hour for 9,600 bps access are far higher than its competitors.

These drawbacks have been mitigated in recent years, however. CompuServe Information Manager (CIM), a graphical front-end program for DOS, Windows, and Macintosh platforms, makes the service much easier to navigate. Subscribers can click icons, pull-down boxes, and other on-screen options with a mouse instead of typing commands at the system prompt. On CIM, subscribers can compose mail and set up file transfers before logging on, saving time and money.

CompuServe has also taken steps to bring its pricing more in line with the rest of the pack by introducing an $8.95-a-month flat fee plan that includes unlimited access to many of its basic services. Though CompuServe still charges by the hour for accessing its bulletin boards, the service recently reduced its bulletin board rates for flat-fee subscribers by 40 percent to a more affordable $4.80 to $9.60 an hour, still sufficient to run up a substantial bill at the end of the month, however.

Business Opportunities

Advertisers in CompuServe's Electronic Mall pay $15,000 to $20,000 up front to set up a store online plus a 2-percent commission on each sale. For $10,000, advertisers can test The Mall but do not receive promotion in CompuServe Magazine and other vehicles. Figure 12.1 shows a Father's Day gift that can be ordered from The Postsmouth Trading Co., an online merchant.

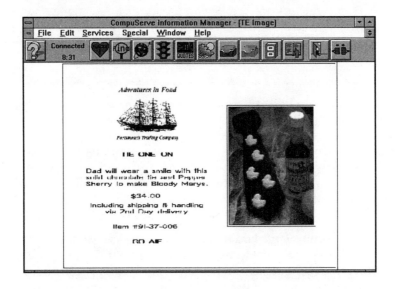

Figure 12.1. With CompuServe's Electronic Mall merchants can display photographs of their products online.

CompuServe also maintains a Classified Ads area. Like placing a classified in a newspaper, the cost of putting a classified on CompuServe varies depending on the size of the message and the length of time it is displayed. A 7-day listing costs $1 a line, a 14-day listing costs $1.50 a line, a 56-day listing costs $5.20 a line, and a 182-day listing costs $14.30 a line. (Each line can consist of up to 68 characters.)

Demographics

Here's how CompuServe's demographics break down:

- Membership: More than 2,000,000
- Gender: 80/20 male/female
- Median age: 41.3 years
- Education: 69 percent have a college degree or higher
- Marital status: 72 percent are married
- Average household income: $92,200

Prodigy Services Co.

Designed with the novice user in mind, Prodigy revolutionized the online world when it burst on the scene in 1989. The brainchild of IBM and Sears, Prodigy is part user-friendly videotext service, part Home Shopping Network, reflecting both sides of its unusual lineage.

The first online service to target family computer users, Prodigy also pioneered flat-rate pricing, online advertising, mass-market promotions, classified advertising, and premium-tiered pricing for access to specialized databases. It also boasts the largest percentage of women users—38 percent at last count—of any of the major commercial networks.

Nevertheless, the service has yet to make a profit. In fact, analysts estimate the service has lost over $1,000,000,000 since its inception.

Although CompuServe provides the most extensive information and communications resources of any of the commercial services, Prodigy offers the most feature-rich advertising medium. Not only does Prodigy's colorful, cartoon-like interface make the service easy to master without so much as a glance at a user's manual, but companies can showcase the same kind of display advertising they use to promote products in magazines and newspapers.

Subscribers can use the Prodigy Mall to browse hundreds of online "stores" hawking everything from CDs to flowers, and view real-time drawings and photographs of the products available—something that rival CompuServe has only just begun to offer.

Profile: PC Flowers, which retails flowers through Prodigy, is one of the service's biggest success stories. When PC Flowers first went online in January, 1990, it ranked dead last among the 25,000 FTD florists worldwide. After only 10 months online, it had rocketed to number 2 in terms of wire sales. PC Flowers' strategy: Rather than wait by the phone like other florists, PC Flowers displays its colorful bouquets online and takes customers' orders electronically. PC Flowers then snips a 20-percent commission from every bouquet it sells. Last year, PC Flowers rang up $4 million in sales on Prodigy, taking 115,000 orders from 31,000 Prodigy households.

It's worth noting, however, that Prodigy's in-your-face approach to advertising is controversial. Although advertisers relish the ability to flash commercial messages across the bottom of subscribers' screens, some Prodigy members feel differently—especially now that they're paying by the minute to access Prodigy's bulletin boards and other features.

Nevertheless, Roland Sharette, manager of J. Walter Thompson/OnLine in Detroit, the agency that manages Ford's ads on Prodigy and CompuServe, says that Prodigy has been "very effective" in promoting the automaker's products. Sharette wouldn't release specifics, but a recent *Wall Street Journal* article reported that rival Chrysler, another Prodigy automotive advertiser, has been receiving 48,000 to 60,000 inquiries a year from potential customers through the online service. Those numbers compare favorably with the 35,000 people who request information through Chrysler's toll-free number.

Not only does the Prodigy service enable Ford to run eye-catching *leader ads* across the bottom of subscribers' computer screens, but Prodigy members can "jump" to Ford's online product information center, shown in Figure 12.2, and get the latest on Ford makes and models. What's more, the Prodigy system allows Ford to send targeted e-mail messages to subscribers who have shown interest in the automotive industry.

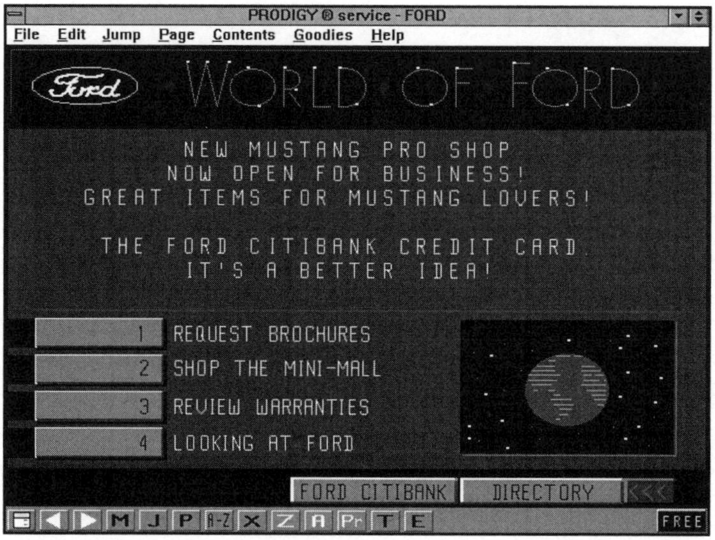

Figure 12.2. Prodigy offers major advertisers such as Ford the capability of setting up online product information centers.

Prodigy has undergone a number of changes over the last year—most of them for the better. The service's decision to scrap its flat-fee pricing plan last year ($14.95 a month for unlimited access to virtually all its offerings), and charge extra for bulletin boards and other features, lost Prodigy some subscribers to rival America Online, but the subscriber base has stabilized and regained its earlier momentum.

To boost its appeal among consumers, Prodigy has rolled out a host of new features and services, including 9,600 bps modem access (which has made the service much zippier to navigate and silenced many critics who complained it was too slow); ESPNET, a joint venture with the television sports network that gives members access to sports news, statistics, photos, bulletin boards, and commentary from ESPN experts; and a Windows front-end that users can use to cut and paste to and from other Windows applications and view real-time news photos with the click of a mouse.

To bolster its business base, Prodigy is engaging in cable tests with Viacom and Comcast and has entered into alliances with large newspaper publishers Times Mirror, Media General, and Cox.

Although Prodigy has come a long way in the last six years, some gaps remain in the service's communications capability. Prodigy only recently added the *live chat* feature common to most other online services for some time now. And to download software on Prodigy, members have to pay extra to tap into the Ziffnet for Prodigy database; it's not available on Prodigy bulletin boards the way it is on other online services.

Business Opportunities

Prodigy charges premium prices for its *display* advertising. A five-screen Standard Advertising Unit (that is, full-screen ads with multiple access points) costs $27,500 a month, a 15-screen buy costs $37,500 a month, and a 30-screen buy costs $54,200 a month.

Prodigy also allows advertisers to send targeted e-mailings to subscribers based on a variety of demographic and interest-group criteria. Creative and production fees cost extra. For targeted mailings, the service charges a cost-per-thousand of $300 to $500 depending on the number of mailings sent. Prodigy charges additional fees for printable coupons, dealer locators, informational databases, advertiser-sponsored bulletin boards, and other promotional services.

Prodigy's business classified advertising rates range from $75 a screen for a two-week display to $200 a screen for a three-month display. Additional screens cost $5 each.

Demographics

Here's how Prodigy's demographics break down:

- Membership: More than 2,000,000 (though some analysts say the number is actually closer to 1,000,000 if only the primary account holders are counted and not the other family members who sign on)
- Gender: 62/38 male/female
- Median age: 41
- Education: 77 percent have attended or graduated college
- Marital status: 66 percent are married
- Median household income: $72,600

America Online

The hippest of the major online services America Online is also the fastest growing—thanks, in part, to its easy-to-use graphical interface. Simply by clicking an icon with a mouse, subscribers can dash off an online message, join in a real-time chat session, drop in on a special-interest discussion group, or download software or clip art from the service's library of more than 70,000 files—all for a monthly fee that's lower than most of its competitors.

America Online bulletin boards range from hardware and software support to wine, aviation, investments, and small business. Its "chat" boards feature electronic "rooms" with names such as *The Flirt's Nook, The Romance Connection,* and *Red Dragon Inn.*

Of all the online services, America Online features the widest assortment of electronic magazines and newspapers, including online editions of *Time, The Atlantic Monthly, The Chicago Tribune,* and *Car and Driver* that offer members the opportunity to read stories, search archives, and swap notes with writers and editors. Subscribers can also access the Internet's Electronic Newsstand, plus a wide variety of Internet newsgroups, mailing lists, and databases.

Though smaller than Prodigy and CompuServe, America Online is coming on strong; it now boasts over 800,000 members, up from 200,000 only 2 years ago. Spurring its rapid growth have been strategic alliances with Tribune Co., Knight Ridder, CNN, *Time Magazine, The New York Times,* Reuters, NBC, *The San Jose Mercury News,* Apple, and Microsoft, and co-marketing agreements with more than 30 companies, including modem manufacturers, magazines, affinity groups, and associations, such as The National Education Association and SeniorNet, a non-profit, international organization for adults 55 and over interested in learning about computers. Pictured below is the *Time Magazine* welcome screen.

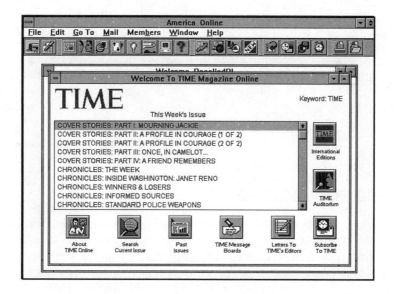

Figure 12.3. America Online features the widest variety of online publications of any of the commercial online services.

Along with America Online's popularity have come some problems, however. Because the service's computer system was designed to accommodate only 6,000 to 8,000 users at any one time, it's often hard to log onto America Online during peak night and weekend periods—and the service has been hard at work expanding the system's capacity.

Primarily a consumer-oriented service, America Online lacks many of the communications capabilities and information resources that make CompuServe attractive to businesses; it also lacks the display ads that make Prodigy a haven for mass-market advertisers.

For example, America Online's software interface lacks many of the off-line, message-handling capabilities afforded by the CompuServe Information Manager, though its unique Download Manager feature saves time and money because users can select a group of files from multiple forums, download them all at once, and log off. And unlike Prodigy, America Online is not a G-rated service; some of the live chat boards feature explicit discussions about gay sex, fetishes, and other adult topics.

Even so, America Online remains a favorite among computing novices and budding entrepreneurs, many of whom like the service's user-friendly interface and low hourly pricing ($3.50 an hour).

Profile: Matthew McDevitt, who recently launched Gutterless Gutters in Pennsauken, New Jersey, says he's tried Prodigy and GEnie but prefers America Online. McDevitt says he's gotten useful tips from AOL members about choosing software and has downloaded files about taxes, partnership agreements, and accounting to help get his business off the ground.

Business Opportunities

As noted previously, America Online does not offer display advertising—at least for now. Its shopping area is also smaller than those of its two larger rivals. As for the cost of establishing a commercial presence on the service, America Online says it does not publicly disclose the details of its arrangements with its information partners. Unlike the other commercial services, however, America Online does not charge a fee for placing classified ads online.

Demographics

Here's how America Online's demographics break down:

- Membership: 900,000
- Gender: 70/30 male/female
- Average age: 39
- Education: Over 50 percent college graduates
- Marital status: N/A
- Average household income: $40,000 to $50,000

GEnie

Launched by General Electric Information Services in 1985, GEnie is now the nation's fourth largest online service, recently overtaken by fast-growing America Online.

In many ways, GEnie resembles a smaller CompuServe. Its roughly 100 bulletin boards, or *roundtables*, feature discussions about everything from romance novels to home business, and users also have access to over 100,000 downloadable software and informational files.

In addition to the standard news, sports, weather, and movie reviews, GEnie provides a variety of technical support forums where subscribers can find answers to questions about IBM, Microsoft, WordPerfect, and other hardware and software products plus gateways to information services such as Dialog and Dow Jones News/Retrieval.

The GEnie Newsstand offers a searchable database of 12 daily newspapers and 900 periodicals. There's also a wide selection of multi-player games plus the chance to participate in public and private conferences with well-known science fiction writers and romance novelists. Figure 12.4 shows GEnie's Science Fiction and Fantasy RoundTable.

Figure 12.4. The nation's fourth-largest commercial service, GEnie resembles a smaller CompuServe, with bulletin boards about topics from science fiction to home-based business.

The trouble with GEnie is that its many treasures are buried beneath a hard-to-use, text-based interface. While the service does provide online help, its bulletin-board menus offer too many choices, and the screen sequence can leave even experienced users lost in cyberspace. Even its DOS-based Aladdin navigational software can be confusing for online novices. The good news is that GEnie just released a Windows version, which should make the service much easier to get around.

Another drawback to GEnie is price. Until recently, GEnie members could pay a flat fee of $4.95 a month for unlimited access to all its services (including e-mail) during off-peak hours; now GEnie has hiked its basic membership fee to $8.95 a month, which includes four hours of access to GEnie services such as e-mail, software downloads, bulletin boards, and real-time chat lines, plus a connect-time charge of $3 an hour for any additional time spent online. Prime-time surcharges of up to $12 an hour also apply.

Nevertheless, GEnie's Home Office/Small Business (HOSB) RoundTable gets favorable reviews from members, though some grumble about GEnie's recent pricing change and its text-based interface that can make the service difficult for novices to navigate. GEnie's home business board, although somewhat smaller than CompuServe's, gets high marks for its helpful members and friendly ambiance.

Profile: "[HOSB] is a very friendly place," says Mary O'Gara, a home-based writer in Albuquerque, New Mexico, who dials the GEnie board for everything from business information to moral support. "It gives me a chance to talk to other women in business about our common problems, to network, to share resources, or just to kick back and complain at the end of the day."

Business Opportunities

Because it is primarily a text-based service, GEnie does not offer display ads. The GEnie Mall charges $3,600 to $15,000 to set up a storefront depending on the type and number of products offered. GEnie classifieds range from 10 cents a line for a seven-day classified to 20 cents a line for a 30-day classified. Each line can be up to 80 characters long.

Demographics

Here's how GEnie's demographics break down:

- Membership: More than 400,000
- Gender: 77/23 male/female
- Age: 64 percent are aged 25 to 44
- Education: 61 percent have college degree or higher
- Marital status: N/A
- Household income: 59.5 percent earn $30,000 to $74,999

Delphi Internet Services

The smallest of the five major commercial online services (roughly 100,000 members), Delphi's main claim to fame is that it's the only one that offers full Internet access. That could change now that America Online has begun offering access to Internet newsgroups, mailing lists, and databases, and CompuServe has announced plans to offer greater Internet access to its subscribers.

At the same time, media mogul Rupert Murdoch's acquisition of the service in 1993 and his publicly announced plans to form alliances between Delphi and News Corp.'s media holdings are expected to give Delphi a boost.

Delphi's other big attraction is price. Delphi members who sign up for the service's 20/20 plan can get 20 hours of online usage for only $20; for another $3 a month, they get full access to the Internet's vast array of discussion groups, databases, software libraries, real-time chatting, and more. There's also a $19 signup fee.

Most other major online services offer only Internet e-mail. Delphi also offers some unique features that its bigger competitors don't, such as a gateway to Latin America through its Delphi/Argentina and Delphi/Miami international gateways, several stock-tip newsletters, and a wealth of trip-planning services, including Commercial Sabre, the professional version of the Easy Sabre service offered by the rest of the online pack. Delphi members can create their own forums for $29.95 plus a $5-a-month maintenance fee where they can meet to discuss matters privately.

Delphi's small size has many disadvantages, however, especially for business users and marketers. Delphi has fewer bulletin boards than CompuServe and Prodigy, its forums tend to be less trafficked, and some of the data files are out of date. Delphi also lacks a graphical interface that would make navigating the system much easier; the Windows software now under development has not yet been released.

In addition, Delphi's rock-bottom pricing is not such a bargain for members who want to log on during the day. Unlike other online services, local telephone access is available only in Boston and Kansas City; members in other locations must call long-distance or pay additional network charges to dial in through Tymnet or Sprintnet gateways.

Nevertheless, Delphi does enjoy its share of fans.

Profile: "I have had accounts with Delphi, CompuServe, America Online, Prodigy, and a couple of local BBSs, and the only one that I use with any consistency is Delphi," says Kurt Remmert, co-owner of Technical Assistant Co., a home-based computer graphics and word processing business in San Antonio, Texas. "While not as big as CompuServe, I don't need to send them my whole paycheck every month."

Pictured in Figure 12.5 is Delphi's Internet SIG, or bulletin board:

```
┌──────────────────────────Terminal - DELPHI.TRM──────────────────▼─┤░│
│ File  Edit  Settings  Phone  Transfers  Help                        │
│                                                                   ▲ │
│            Walt Howe (WALTHOWE), INTERNET SIG Manager               │
│         Andy Eddy (VIDGAMES), Assistant Manager (Library, Mac)      │
│                         > > 0 < <                                   │
│     _Internet Basics, Your Online Access to the Global Electronic Superhighway_ │
│        Order Walt's book, written for Delphi Internet users. Type GUIDES 1. │
│                                                                     │
│           REMINDER: Never give anyone your password online. There is no │
│           legitimate reason to give your password to anyone, even staff. │
│                                                                     │
│    Press RETURN for Internet SIG Menu:                              │
│                                                                     │
│                                                                     │
│    About the Internet     Help                                      │
│    Conference             Exit                                      │
│    Databases (Files)                                                │
│    EMail                  FTP                                       │
│    Forum (Messages)       Gopher                                    │
│    Guides (Books)         IRC-Internet Relay Chat                   │
│    Register/Cancel        Telnet                                    │
│    Who's Here             Utilities (finger, traceroute, ping)      │
│    Workspace              Usenet Newsgroups                         │
│                                                                     │
│    Internet SIG>Enter your selection: W4N~~b                        │
│                                                                   ▼ │
│ ◄                                                                 ► │
└─────────────────────────────────────────────────────────────────────┘
```

Figure 12.5. Delphi is the only one of the five largest commercial online services to offer full access to the Internet.

Business Opportunities

Delphi does not release the cost of setting up an online store on the service or the terms of its online media partnerships. The service does not currently offer classified advertising services for business, though members of Delphi special interest groups can have their own classified ad databases.

Demographics

Delphi has roughly 100,000 members. Other demographic information is not available.

The Future of Commercial Online Services

Despite the soaring popularity of the Internet, the future of the many commercial services appears to be bright as well. Emboldened by the success of CompuServe, Prodigy, and America Online, Microsoft, AT&T, Apple, Hearst, Ziff, Bell Atlantic, and other technology and communications powerhouses are investing heavily in online network development.

At the same time, *The Washington Post, The New York Times*, ESPN, Hachette Fillipache, Scholastic, CMP Publications, Home Shopping Network, QVC, and Viacom are jumping into the online fray to leverage their offerings in other media.

Boosting the fortunes of the commercial networks is the prohibitive cost of wiring the nation's households for interactive television. Even with total cooperation and under the best of prevailing market conditions, it would take at least five years to expand bandwidth and communications for television and build the links that are missing from cable, telephone, and data communications networks, according to Gene DeRose, vice president of Jupiter Communications Co., a New York City-based media research and consulting firm.

In the meantime, both subscribers and businesses are beginning to believe that commerce through the commercial services is the next best thing for now. The commercial services, meanwhile, are rapidly making the transition to multimedia, continuing extensive testing of ISDN and cable-modem delivery in order to speed service and allow for the video, graphics, and sound afforded by greater bandwidth.

Meanwhile, online shopping and other transaction-based services are also beginning to take off on the commercial networks. Once stuck at less than 5 percent of online usage time, services that market retail-oriented applications now report around 10 percent of online time devoted to online banking, shopping, and other commercial applications. DeRose predicts retail and transaction services will grow rapidly over the next few years, especially as online access is combined with TV shopping networks, CD-ROM software publishing, TV infomercials, phone-based product ordering, and credit card processing.

Striking a Balance: Integrating Commercial Networks and the Internet

For most businesses, choosing to do business on the Internet or on the commercial networks is not an either-or decision. Once a business has converted its promotional or informational data into electronic format, there's no reason—and little extra cost—to exploring all online avenues.

Here are several ways to integrate the Internet and the commercial networks in your company's marketing plans:

- **E-mail and networking.** Set up accounts on the Internet and on several large commercial networks so that potential customers on these services can reach you quickly and conveniently. When you have an account on each network, you can participate in online discussion groups and post-press releases and product announcements there.

- **Sales and marketing.**   Set up a storefront on an Internet Gopher server or World Wide Web. Also "rent space" in the CompuServe or Prodigy Malls, if your company can afford it.

- **Customer service.**   Set up an FTP site and a mailing list on the Internet to post FAQ lists and field customer questions. Also set up a technical support forum on a commercial network such as CompuServe or GEnie.

- **Publishing.**   Publish an online edition of your newspaper or magazine on a commercial online service. Post free excerpts of your publication on the Internet as a way of promoting it.

- **Databases.**   Hook up with a commercial network to provide a gateway to your database. Let Internet users access it via telnet or Gopher.

Further Reference: Pricing and Contact Information

America Online
8619 Westwood Center Dr.
Vienna, VA 22182
1-800-827-6364

America Online costs $9.95 a month, which includes 5 hours of connect time; after that, connect time is billed at $3.50 an hour.

CompuServe Information Service
5000 Arlington Centre Blvd.
P.O. Box 20212
Columbus, OH 43220
1-800-848-8199

CompuServe charges $6.30 an hour for 300-bps access, $12.80 an hour for 1,200- and 2,400-bps access, and $22.80 an hour for 9,600-bps access under its pay-as-you-go plan. Even if you don't access CompuServe at all, you're charged a $2.50 monthly membership fee. CompuServe's $8.95-a-month flat-fee plan includes access to basic services such as news reports and travel reservations, the ability to send the equivalent of up to 60 three-page messages a month, and reduced hourly rates on access to specialized bulletin boards ($4.80 to $9.60 an hour).

Delphi Internet Services
1030 Massachusetts Ave.
Cambridge, MA 02138
1-800-695-4005

Under Delphi's 20/20 Advantage Plan, subscribers pay $20 a month (plus a $19 one-time enrollment fee) for 20 hours of usage. Delphi's 10/4 Plan charges a $10 monthly fee for the first 4 hours of evening and weekend use and includes free access to help files, billing information, and other support services; additional connect time costs $4 an hour. Delphi, the only major online service that offers both a gateway to Internet mail plus access to Internet databases and file-transfer capabilities, offers unlimited Internet access for an extra $3 a month.

> General Electric Information Service (GEnie)
> 401 N. Washington St.
> Rockville, MD 20850
> 1-800-638-9636

GEnie's basic membership fee is $8.95 a month, which includes 4 hours of access to GEnie services such as e-mail, software downloads, bulletin boards, and real-time chat lines, plus a connect-time charge of $3 an hour for any additional time spent online. There is also a prime-time surcharge of $9.50 to $12 an hour for access to the service during weekday business hours and a $6 to $8 an hour surcharge for 9,600-bps access.

> Prodigy Services Co.
> 445 Hamilton Ave.
> White Plains, NY 10601
> 1-800-284-5933

Prodigy's Value Plan costs $14.95 a month, which includes unlimited access to the service's "core" features, in addition to two hours of "plus" features such as bulletin boards and the ability to send up to 30 e-mail messages. Additional use of "plus" features costs $3.60 an hour. Prodigy's Alternate Plan costs $7.95 a month, which includes two hours of "core" and "plus" features; there's an extra $3.50-an-hour charge for any additional time spent online. Prodigy also offers volume discounts for heavy users.

THE FUTURE OF INTERNET BUSINESS

By now, you've learned the pros and cons, the pitfalls and the potential of doing business on the Internet. You've also discovered that, although the Internet may not yet be the much-vaunted information highway, the network is far closer to reality than hype—and becoming ever more real by the minute.

Though a relatively small percentage of the world's households and businesses are currently "on the Net," millions of home computer users and thousands of companies, some as tiny as the corner delicatessen, are giving the Internet a try.

What the future holds for companies doing business on the Internet is anybody's guess. But, although no one yet knows whether hordes of shoppers will flock to the Internet cybermalls or whether large numbers of executives and professionals around the world will start doing business on an electronic handshake, plenty of money is betting that the answer will ultimately be a resounding "yes."

In this chapter, we'll look at 10 Internet-business trends worth watching:

- Continued Internet population growth
- Lower network access costs with wider availability of Internet tools
- Easier on-ramps
- An explosion of e-mail
- More sophisticated multimedia technologies
- Tighter security
- More outlets for Flame-Proof advertising
- Persistence of in-your-face advertising
- Geographic specialization
- Internet everywhere

Continued Internet Population Growth

With all the changes swirling around the worldwide network of networks these days, the only certainty about the Internet appears to be growth.

The Internet now has more than 20,000,000 users, and it's estimated to be growing at a rate of 2,000,000 new users a month. If the Internet population continues to expand at its current pace, practically everyone in the world will be "on the Net" by the year 2000 according to recent projections by the Internet Society. Though the Internet's growth will eventually bump up against barriers such as literacy, network access, and computer ownership, observers agree that the Internet still has plenty of room to grow.

Much of this growth is coming from the commercial sector, as opposed to university or government. At current rates, two new Internet accounts are added to the network every four minutes, and one of these accounts is from a commercial site, according to Dataquest, a market research firm in San Jose, California. Subscribers to commercial online services such as Prodigy, CompuServe, and America Online will continue to pour into the Internet, too, accelerating the commercialization trend and drowning out the objections of long-time Internet denizens.

The Internet's continued growth is good news for everybody trying to make money on the Internet—from the access providers who rent the "pipes" to the marketers and publishers who provide the content that Internet users want to read.

Lower Network Access Costs with Wider Availability of Internet Tools

With computers, modems, and Internet access plummeting in price, Internet connections—even the high-powered SLIP and PPP connections needed to run Mosaic—are becoming more widely available.

For less than $100, you can get a high-speed 14.4 Kbps modem; for $60 to $150, you can buy a top-of-the-line communications software package. For as little as $30 a month, you can obtain a SLIP connection from a local Internet access provider; a regular dial-up, or "shell," account starts at less than $10 monthly.

The price of a T1 line—the Internet connection of choice for many large companies—has come down to about $500 a month in some parts of the country. Commercial online services such as CompuServe, America Online, and Delphi offer varying degrees of Internet connectivity as well. (See Appendix A, "Internet On-Ramps," for a list of Internet access providers.)

A host of new and soon-to-be-released software interfaces will open up the Internet to even more users. For example, there are now commercial versions of the Internet's popular Mosaic and Gopher programs that are easier to use and contain more features (see following section). Microsoft is also planning to incorporate TCP/IP support into its next version of Windows.

Easier On-Ramps

With so many new users descending on the Internet, the race is on to introduce graphical interfaces that Internet novices can use to send mail and access data with the click of a mouse.

Showcased in June, 1994, at the Internet World conference in San Jose was Internet in a Box, a soon-to-be-released software package that provides a multimedia Windows interface, a suite of Internet applications such as e-mail, newsgroups, telnet, Gopher, and Mosaic. Internet in a Box requires a SLIP connection or higher and works with both PCs and local-area networks.

New and improved versions of individual Internet software programs are also coming onto the market. WinGopher, developed by Notis Systems of Evanston, Illinois, is a Windows-based Gopher tool with which users can access Internet databases the easy way, without having to type complicated Internet addresses or memorize file locations. WinGopher also supports Archie, Veronica, and WAIS searching plus FTP file transfers and telnet sessions. An image and text viewer are included. WinGopher Complete, which includes Windows-based TCP/IP software and 30 minutes of free connect time from a participating Internet access provider costs $129. The WinGopher graphical interface alone sells for $69.95.

Commercial versions of Mosaic, the popular graphical browser, are also becoming available even as the National Center for Supercomputing Applications (NCSA) at the University of Illinois at Urbana-Champaign continues to upgrade the public domain version of the program, which is available to Internet users at no charge.

Spyglass, Inc. of Savoy, Illinois, announced in mid-1994 an agreement with NCSA to enhance and broadly re-license Mosaic to Internet users. The Windows and Macintosh versions are available now; an X Window version is set for release in July.

An Explosion of E-Mail

Despite the reality that fax machines still outnumber e-mail boxes in offices around the world, e-mail is gathering steam thanks to the Internet. According to Book Marketing Update in Fairfield, Iowa, as much as 75 percent of business-to-business correspondence will take place by fax or e-mail by the year 2000; probably half of all consumer-to-consumer and business-to-consumer correspondence will also be through fax or e-mail, predominantly e-mail, the newsletter predicts.

Even the U.S. Postal Service is hedging its bets. Postmaster General and CEO Marvin Runyon, in his annual report to the Senate Governmental Affairs Committee in May, suggested that "post office lobbies could serve as on-ramps providing access to anyone who wants to be on the electronic highway."

"Maybe we can help certify electronic messages and safeguard their privacy, securing one company's market-sensitive information from the intruding eyes of its competitors," Runyon said.

These days, Internet addresses are fast becoming a fixture on business cards. Sporting an Internet address carries a high-tech cachet; having an Internet address with your company's name on it (for example, yourcompany.com) is considered even classier.

More Sophisticated Multimedia Technologies

Today, the Internet is, for the most part, a silent, text-based expanse of cyberspace with only the quiet clacking of computer keys to break the silence. Audio, video, and other multimedia applications are rarities on the Internet for a host of technological reasons, although there have been innovations such as Internet Talk Radio. (See Chapter 8, "Connecting the World with Internet E-mail.")

That's beginning to change. Soon, Internet videoconferencing will be widely available—at a fraction of the cost of using regular telephone networks. The reason: There's no need to pay a phone carrier $100 a minute to transmit images; once your company is connected to the Internet, there's no extra fee for transmitting video. Besides facilitating "virtual" business meetings, Internet video also potentially enhances the feasibility of telecommuting, telemedicine (remote diagnostics), remote collaboration between workgroups, and distance learning on the network.

Facilitating Internet video transmissions is the Multicast Backbone (MBone), a virtual multimedia network developed by researchers from the University of Southern California Information Services Institute. The service, available through the Internet, provides users with efficient use of bandwidth because a single data packet takes up the same amount of bandwidth whether it is received by one workstation or many. MBone applications such as net video, visual audio tool, and whiteboard can be downloaded from a variety of anonymous FTP locations at no charge. Mbone applications must be run over T1 lines for acceptable video performance, however.

For regular users, Internet videoconferencing still has a long way to go before it's ready for prime time. Right now, it's much slower than the videoconferencing offered by the phone networks—about 15 frames per minute—and the images that appear on conferees' computer screens are rather small (about a quarter of a screen). What's more, concerns have been raised about this use of the network; we share the fears of many experts that traffic jams will become common if too many companies attempt to use the Internet for videoconferencing at the same time.

Nevertheless, some interesting new software programs promise to revolutionize Internet videoconferencing and make it far more widely accessible than it is today.

CU-SeeMe, developed at Cornell University, allows multiple video windows to operate on a single PC or Macintosh screen at the same time with each window able to transmit and receive text as well as audio. Although the black-and-white video is far from perfect—the more windows open, the more bandwidth used and the slower the video—and audio is available only for Mac users, the prospect of live video conferencing is appealing. It's possible to run the program through a modem, but a T1 or faster connection is preferable, its developers say. CU-SeeMe is available for free via anonymous FTP from gated.cornell.edu in the pub/video directory.

A more limited Internet multimedia program is a new public domain program called *Internet VoiceChat* that users can use to conduct through their personal computers live voice conversations over the Internet. The package includes an "answering machine," "call screening," "online help," and other features. The program is available via FTP from several Internet servers, including `b61503.student.cwru.edu`, `www.unb.ca`, and `ftp.demon.co.uk`. For more information, contact author Rich Ahrens at `ahrens26@wharton.upenn.edu`.

Tighter Security

One of the biggest stumbling blocks to Internet commerce is the absence of a secure way of handling credit card, banking, and other financial transactions. But due to a growing demand on the part of businesses, new software programs featuring encryption and digital signatures are now becoming available.

Bank of America, for example, is banking on the Internet to facilitate electronic transactions. The California-based bank, a participant in CommerceNet (see Figure 13.1)— the World Wide Web-based marketplace that's planning to release a "secure" Mosaic in September, 1994— is hoping to use the Internet as a vehicle for payments, wire transfers, and investments. The bank is constructing an electronic kiosk that contains a sample global check as a service the bank plans to offer.

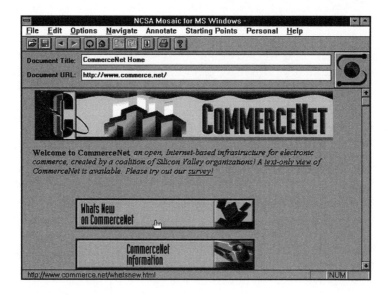

Figure 13.1. CommerceNet.

New versions of encryption software are also coming on-stream. The latest version of PGP, a popular public domain encryption program for e-mail and other files, is now available to Internet users on the Electronic Frontier Foundation server.

According to the Foundation, PGP 2.5 is legal in the United States; previous versions of PGP, with the exception of ViaCrypt's commercial PGP 2.4, arguably violated U.S. patent law. However, PGP still cannot be legally exported from the United States (except to Canada) due to federal export restrictions that categorize cryptographic materials as weapons of war.

PGP and similar material are available from EFF's FTP site in a hidden directory, accessible only to Americans and Canadians. Only the DOS and UNIX versions of PGP 2.5 have been released so far. The UNIX version is in source code form, and so can be readily ported to VMS, NeXT, and many other operating systems. A Macintosh version has yet to be released.

Access to this directory can be obtained by reading and following the instructions in the README.Dist file at

```
ftp.eff.org, /pub/Net_info/Tools/Crypto/
gopher.eff.org, 1/Net_info/Tools/Crypto
gopher://gopher.eff.org/11/Net_info/Tools/Crypto
http://www.eff.org/pub/Net_info/Tools/Crypto/
```

Besides facilitating commercial transactions, encryption is also making possible new forms of Internet business, such as book publishing. A new company called The Internet Bookstore has signed deals with leading print publishers such as Prentice Hall, Oxford University Press, Macmillan, Que, McGraw Hill, Wiley, and Pocket Books to sell text-only electronic versions of popular books for 30 percent of the books' hard-copy price. (Charts, screen shots, photos, and other graphics are not included.) Within 30 seconds of ordering, Internet users can have the entire book, albeit in electronic form, delivered to their computer.

Through The Internet Bookstore, shoppers can search for books via e-mail using a topical wordlist and browse the books' tables of contents, indexes, and other information online. Once they've bought the book, they can use a proprietary software interface to make the type larger, change the page layout, search for topics by keyword, and insert footnotes in research papers. All purchases are charged to a standing credit card number.

What makes The Internet Bookstore possible is a custom hardware encryption technology—in the form of a small decoder that plugs into a personal computer's printer port. Without the decoder, the downloaded book is illegible, thus preventing pirated copies from being made and protecting the publisher's copyright.

In order to "lend" the electronic book to a friend or colleague, the user must also lend the decoder. Each key costs $29.95 and includes a $25 usage credit at the Internet Bookstore, which currently offers approximately 100 titles. Publishers pay a fee to license the technology from The Internet Bookstore but keep all proceeds of the sale.

More Outlets for Flame-Proof Advertising

Probably the biggest controversy on the Internet right now is the issue of commercialization. How can companies market, advertise, and sell their products and services on the Internet without offending the very customers they hope to attract? And how can businesses zero in on their target markets without sending direct mailings and getting flamed?

One advertising model that appears to be catching on is that of passive advertising or sponsorship—posting marketing and advertising information on a World Wide Web server and inviting potential customers to come in and browse for free.

MecklerWeb

One company that has latched onto this concept is Mecklermedia Corp., which offers an advertising platform called *MecklerWeb*. MecklerWeb, expected to be operational by September, 1994, will offer Internet users the chance to access and browse information from sponsoring organizations involved in broad areas of interest such as law, education, technology, medicine, and the arts. Each area, or "domain," will be hosted by a knowledgeable moderator with expertise in that particular area.

Unlike the unwelcome postings splattered throughout the Internet by attorneys Canter & Siegel, the MecklerWeb aims to provide a culturally appropriate advertising forum for companies that want to share information about their products and services.

MecklerWeb provides each sponsor company with 10 to 15 megabytes of space on its server in exchange for a $25,000 annual fee; user access to the site is free. Unlike the more blatant Internet advertising schemes, the audience accesses MecklerWeb voluntarily rather than being bombarded with unwanted, unsolicited e-mail, says Christopher Locke, president of MecklerWeb Corp. in Westport, Connecticut. (To visit MecklerWeb [see Figure 13.2], go to http://www.digital.com/demo.html. The permanent address will be http://www.mecklerweb.com/.)

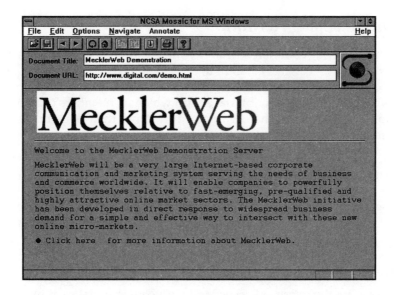

Figure 13.2. Companies such as MecklerWeb are pioneering "politically correct" advertising on the Internet.

MecklerWeb's core technology partners are AlterNet, a large Internet access provider that will provide Internet connectivity; Digital Equipment Corp., which is supplying its Alpha AXP servers and technical support; EIT, which has agreed to contribute its commercial Web server engine, and WAIS, Inc., which will provide the software tools for electronic publishing and information retrieval.

Here's an example of how MecklerWeb is supposed to work:

> Pharmaceutical Information Associates, Ltd., a company that specializes in communicating scientific information to regulatory and health care officials, will host MecklerWeb's Pharmaceutical Information subdomain. On that part of the MecklerWeb server, Internet users will be able to access information about participating drug-companies' products; browse Frequently Asked Questions lists gleaned from relevant newsgroups, e-mail, and other sources; read PIA's monthly electronic newsletter, and access Internet sites of interest to health care professionals. All the information will be provided at no charge to physicians, medical students, pharmacists, nurses, and anyone else with access to the Internet and World Wide Web.

Rather than competing with CommerceNet, an electronic alliance of Silicon Valley companies, MecklerWeb has joined CommerceNet as a member. CommerceNet, in turn, has announced its intention to join MecklerWeb in its business-to-business "domain."

Internet Shopping Network

Another pioneering commercial initiative on the Internet is the Internet Shopping Network, which began market trials in early 1994. Like Home Shopping Network, which displays products on TV that consumers call in to order, Internet Shopping Network offers a Web interface with which its members can browse more than 15,000 software and hardware products from their personal computer or workstation with the click of a mouse.

Like PC Catalog, available on Prodigy and CompuServe, ISN shoppers can search products organized by platform (Mac, DOS, Windows, or UNIX) or by category, such as "children" or "programmers." Orders are processed within 15 minutes of being received and shipped the next business day from one of 12 distribution centers throughout the United States. To avoid the security problems associated with making purchases over the Internet, shoppers must first fax the company a registration card with their credit card number and expiration date; any purchases are charged to that card.

By eliminating the overhead associated with conventional retailing, ISN claims to be able to offer some of the best prices around for the high-tech products it sells. What's more, members of the ISN network get free online access to the entire previous year's contents of *InfoWorld* magazine to help them make better buying decisions. Future services will include more publications, more stores, and electronic downloading of software titles. (To visit ISN, shown in Figure 13.3, connect with your Web browser to URL `http://shop.internet.net`.)

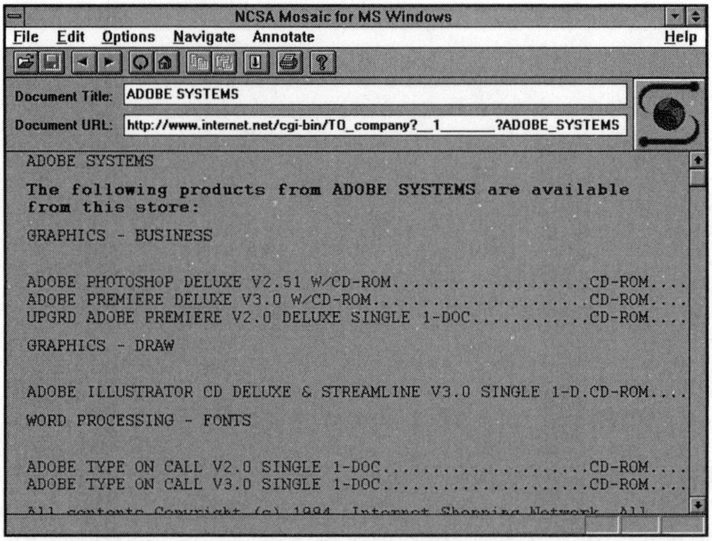

Figure 13.3. Pioneering services like Internet Shopping Network are bringing home shopping to the Internet.

Persistence of In-Your-Face Advertising

At the same time that the Internet's major players are rallying around culturally appropriate advertising platforms such as MecklerWeb, renegade entrepreneurs are trying more blatant sales pitches—with varying degrees of success.

Canter & Siegel, the Arizona immigration law firm that gained Internet-wide notoriety by plastering Usenet newsgroups with "green card" advertisements in the spring of 1994, claims it earned $50,000 on a minimal investment. Now, for $500 a pop, the law firm is helping other companies market their products on the Internet using the same techniques—and has threatened to sue the Internet access provider that kicked it off after the "green card" incident raised a firestorm.

In May, another marketer tried the same thing in Florida. According to *The Miami Herald*, an advertisement for a Miami-based company called U.S. Health, Inc. offering a $29.95 thigh-thinning cream went out over Internet to over 850 electronic mailing lists. The practice, which has become known in Net lingo as "spamming," resulted in nearly 500,000 complaints to the sender and to Shadow Information Services, the Miami company that provided it access to the Internet. U.S. Health's attorney told *The Herald* he knew nothing about the ad and little about the company.

Does this mean advertisers can break the unwritten rules of netiquette and get away with it? Maybe not. Though companies like this may profit in the short-run, blatant advertisers run the risk of turning into Internet pariahs, companies with which no one will do business.

Other companies, meanwhile, are attempting to make money by channeling culturally unacceptable Internet advertising into avenues that are more palatable. The Internet Company, the Cambridge, Massachusetts, consulting firm that operates the Electronic Newsstand, recently announced its intention to set up a new hierarchy of `market.*` newsgroups to accommodate commercial postings in what the company deems to be a culturally acceptable way.

This way, if Internet users don't want to read commercial postings, they don't have to. Likewise, Internet access providers also have the option of not receiving the `market.*` newsgroups at their site. Therefore, the company reasons, the `market.*` postings don't fall into the category of electronic junk mail.

The core newsgroups are `market.announce`, a moderated newsgroup where users can share information about the service with the Internet community, and `market.discuss`, an unmoderated newsgroup dedicated to ongoing discussions about the service. In addition, there are five moderated commercial groups:

> `market.internet.access`, containing marketing information of and about access to the global Internet, including shell accounts, dialup SLIP or PPP services, and dedicated leased-line connections

`market.internet.products`, containing marketing information of and about products available over or in conjunction with the global Internet, including routers or other hardware items, TCP/IP protocol products, applications, and information or publishing products

`market.internet.services`, containing marketing information of and about services available over or in conjunction with the global Internet, including seminars and training services, information retrieval or distribution services, and general Internet-related consulting

`market.internet.publications`, containing marketing information about publications describing or provided over the global Internet

`market.internet.events`, containing marketing information of and about events specific to the global Internet

Other `market.*` newsgroups related to business, computers, consumer products, health, and finance will be added soon after the initial roll-out, the company says. Although placing an advertisement in the `market.internet.*` newsgroups is free, posting a message in the other `market.*` newsgroups will carry charges based on the rate card for the specific newsgroup. The Internet Company has promised that a portion of the revenues generated from this service will be set aside as a "Free Resource Support Fund" to support the free technologies and services on the Internet.

Geographic Specialization

Although the Internet is a worldwide marketplace separated less by geographical boundaries than by interest groups, local Internet access providers are beginning to offer advertising services to hometown businesses seeking to break into the global marketplace.

As an example, CyberGate, an Internet access provider in Deerfield Beach, Florida, recently launched a Gopher site called *The CyberStore on the Shore,* which it hopes will become a bustling marketplace for Florida companies. (To see it, connect with Gopher `gopher.gate.net`.)

Together with a local company called CyberBeach Publishing of Lake Worth, Florida, CyberGate offers a variety of Internet marketing services including a mail reflector "brochure" that is automatically sent to potential customers. Advertisers also get a presence on the Gopher server, a monthly report detailing the number of times their information was accessed and by whom, and a shell account that entitles them to unlimited Internet access. The setup fee is $100, and access charges are $50 a month. Additional services, such as creating World Wide Web documents and setting up an online store, cost extra.

Here's an example of an advertisement posted by CyberBeach Publishing on CyberGate's gopher server:

```
BCyberBeach Publishing, Internet Publishing Services B(1k)                    52%
+----------------------------------------------------------------------+
               CyberBeach Publishing
            Internet Publishing Services

Make your information available on the Internet.  Reach 20
million potential viewers, right at their desks..  Market your
firm or organization globally at affordable prices.
CyberBeach Publishing, in conjunction with CyberGate, provides
Internet publishing services, which will make your firm or
organization a player in the global, electronic highway.  This is
an ideal way for a small firm or organization to enter into the
world of both electronic publishing and the Internet.
Services include:
  * Internet information servers.  Use of the CyberGate
    information servers, which provide 24 hour/7 day a week
    access to your information. Gopher, World Wide Web (WWW),
    WAIS and E-mail servers are available.
+----------------------------------------------------------------------+
```

Internet Is Everywhere

Despite all the hype about interactive TV and its 500 channels, the prohibitive cost of the set-top boxes and fiber optic cable necessary to make that futuristic vision a reality means that the Internet isn't likely to be replaced for at least five or ten years.

We believe that the Internet will never become obsolete; regardless of the networking technology that emerges in the future, the Internet as a "virtual community" of individuals, universities, governments, and businesses will continue to survive and prosper.

"Worldwide, old and new information service organizations are plugging into the Internet and drawing sustenance from its vast and uncharted seas of information and delivering their services to its rising millions of users," writes Vinton Cerf, president of The Internet Society in a recent issue of *Internet Society News.* "Access to its 23,000 networks comprising the Internet is increasingly viewed as a national priority around the world in the research and education sectors, and many governments see the Internet as a microcosm of national and global information infrastructure which is emerging from the rich interplay of ideas, experiments, and collaborations among computer and telecommunications enterprises."

Before You Go...So What Does All This Mean for Your Company?

Although businesses driving onto today's prototype of the information highway aren't guaranteed to strike it rich, companies that stay on the side roads are likely to be left behind. It may be a long time before dispatching an e-mail message over the Internet becomes as commonplace as dialing a phone, but the trend is increasingly clear: The competitive edge will belong to those entrepreneurs prepared to log on, tap in, and reach out to that vast, chaotic and virtually untapped electronic marketplace called *the Internet.*

The Internet is a brave new world in many senses of the phrase, and, although it's likely to prove only the foundation of the coming information superhighway, it's here today and can help you grow your business—regardless of what you sell—if used carefully, thoughtfully, and creatively.

Our advice is to respect the culture of the Internet community, follow the guidelines of the discussion groups you plan to participate in, and offer additional information and value to customers. In short, treat your potential Internet customers as you would friends and you're sure to find the Internet to be an enjoyable and profitable place.

Finally, when you do make the move to connect your firm to the Internet, whether for marketing, sales, or intelligence-gathering, please let us know! We'd love to hear all about the risks you took and rewards you reaped! To contact Rosalind, send electronic mail to `rosalind@harrison.win.net`; to reach Dave, send e-mail to `taylor@netcom.com`.

Above all, remember that the Internet is what we all make of it, so join us in creating an online business community that you would feel comfortable calling home. And, finally, remember our Internet Golden Rule: Advertise unto others as you would like advertised unto you.

INTERNET ON-RAMPS

This appendix lists companies and organizations that provide dial-up access to Internet services for individuals. For more information on different types of Internet access and what to look for in an access provider, see Chapter 2, "Getting Connected: Your Ticket to Ride."

Geographical and Area Code Summary—US and Canadian Providers

Following is a listing of North American Internet provider names arranged by the state or province that the provider services and then by area code. Details and contact information for each provider follow in the next section.

Alabama

205

Nuance Network Service

Alberta

403

Alberta SuperNet Inc.
CCI Networks

Arizona

602

CRL
Data Basix
Evergreen Internet

British Columbia

604

Cyberstore Systems Inc.
DataFlux Systems Limited
Wimsey Information Services

California

213

CRL

310

CERFnet
CRL
Netcom

408

a2i Communications
Netcom
Portal

415

CERFnet
CRL
Institute for Global Communications (IGC)
Netcom
The WELL

510

C—Cnet Communications
CERFnet
CRL
HoloNet
Netcom

619

CERFnet
CTS Network Services
Netcom

707

    CRL

714

    CERFnet
    Digital Express Group (Digex)
    Netcom

818

    CERFnet
    Netcom

909

    Digital Express Group (Digex)

916

    Netcom

Colorado

303

    CNS
    Colorado SuperNet
    Netcom

719

    CNS
    Colorado SuperNet

District of Columbia

202

CAPCON Library Network
Clarknet

Florida

305

CyberGate
Gateway to the World
IDS World Network

407

IDS World Network

Georgia

404

CRL
Netcom

Illinois

312

CICNet
InterAccess Co.
Netcom

708

CICNet
InterAccess Co.
XNet Information Systems

815

InterAccess Co.

Louisiana

504

Neosoft

Manitoba

204

MBnet

Maryland

301

CAPCON Library Network
ClarkNet
Digital Express Group (Digex)

410

CAPCON Library Network
ClarkNet
Digital Express Group (Digex)

Massachusetts

508

The World

617

Delphi
Netcom
North Shore Access
The World

Michigan

313

Msen

810

Msen

Missouri

314

Neosoft

Nevada

702

Evergreen Internet

New Hampshire

603

MV Communications, Inc.

New Jersey

609

Digital Express Group (Digex)
Global Enterprise Services, Inc.

908

Digital Express Group (Digex)

New York

212

Echo
Maestro Information Service
Mindvox
Netcom
Panix
Pipeline

516

Panix

718

Echo
Mindvox

North Carolina

704

Interpath
Northcoast Internet
Internet Access, Inc.

910

Interpath

919

Interpath

Ohio

513

Freelance Systems Programming

614

OARNet

Ontario

416

Internet Online Inc.
UUNorth Incorporated

519

Data Tech Canada
Hookup Communication Corporation

Oregon

503

Agora
Netcom
Teleport

Pennsylvania

412

Telerama

Rhode Island

401

IDS World Network

Quebec

514

Communications Accessibles Montreal, Inc.

Texas

214

Netcom
Texas Metronet

512

Netcom

713

Neosoft

817

Texas Metronet

Utah

801

Evergreen Internet

Virginia

703

CAPCON Library Network
ClarkNet
Digital Express Group (Digex)
Meta Network
Netcom

Washington

206

Eskimo North
Netcom
Olympus
Teleport

Packet Network/Toll-Free Access

CompuServe Packet Network

IDS World Network
The WELL
The World

PSINet

HoloNet

SprintNet

Delphi
Meta Network
Neosoft
Portal

Tollfree/800 Access

CERFnet
CICNet
CNS
CRL
Global Enterprise Services, Inc.
Msen
Neosoft

Tymnet

Delphi
Holonet

Providers in United States and Canada

a2i Communications

E-mail address	info@rahul.net
Dialup number	408-293-9010, log in as guest
Area code(s)	408
Voice phone	408-293-8078
Services provided	Shell, Usenet, e-mail, Internet access, including telnet and FTP

Agora

Area code(s)	503
E-mail address	info@agora.rain.com
Dialup number	503-293-1772
Services provided	Shell, Usenet, FTP, telnet, Gopher, Lynx, IRC, mail, SLIP/PPP coming

Alberta SuperNet Inc.

Area code(s)	403
Voice phone	403-441-3663
E-mail address	info@supernet.ab.ca
Services provided	Shell, e-mail, Usenet, FTP, telnet, Gopher, SLIP/PPP

CAPCON Library Network

Area code(s)	202, 301, 410, 703
Voice phone	202-331-5771
E-mail address	capcon@capcon.net
Services provided	Menu, FTP, Archie, e-mail, FTP, Gopher, telnet, WAIS, Whois, training

CCI Networks

Area code(s)	403
Voice phone	403-450-6787
E-mail address	info@ccinet.ab.ca
Services provided	Shell, e-mail, Usenet, FTP, telnet, Gopher, WAIS, WWW, IRC, Hytelnet, SLIP/PPP

CCnet Communications

Area code(s)	510
Voice phone	510-988-0680
E-mail address	info@ccnet.com
Dialup number	510-988-7140, log in as guest
Services provided	Shell, SLIP/PPP, telnet, e-mail, FTP, Usenet, IRC, WWW

CERFnet

Area code(s)	619,510,415,818,714,310,800
Voice phone	800-876-2373
E-mail address	sales@cerf.net
Services provided	Full range of Internet services

CICNet

Area code(s)	312, 708, 800
Voice phone	800-947-4754 or 313-998-6703
E-mail address	info@cic.net
Services provided	SLIP, FTP, telnet, Gopher, e-mail, Usenet

ClarkNet (Clark Internet Services, Inc.)

Area code(s)	410, 301, 202, 703
Voice phone	800-735-2258, ask for extension 410-730-9764
E-mail address	info@clark.net
Dialup number	301-596-1626, log in as guest, no password
Services provided	Shell/optional menu, FTP, Gopher, telnet, IRC, news, Mosaic, Lynx, MUD, SLIP/PPP/CSLIP, and much more

CNS

Area code(s)	303, 719, 800
Voice phone	800-748-1200
E-mail address	service@cscns.com
Dialup number	719-520-1700, 303-758-2656
Services provided	Shell/menu, e-mail, FTP, telnet, all newsgroups, IRC, 4m, Gopher, WAIS, SLIP, and more

Colorado SuperNet

Area code(s)	303, 719
Voice phone	303-273-3471
E-mail address	info@csn.org or help@csn.org
Services provided	Shell, e-mail, Usenet news, telnet, FTP, SLIP/PPP, and other Internet tools

Communications Accessibles Montreal, Inc.

Area code(s)	514
Voice phone	514-931-0749
E-mail address	info@cam.org
Dialup number	514-596-2255
Services provided	Shell, FTP, telnet, Gopher, WAIS, WWW, IRC, Hytelnet, SLIP/CSLIP/PPP, news

CRL

Area code(s)	213, 310, 404, 415, 510, 602, 707, 800
Voice phone	415-837-5300
E-mail address	support@crl.com
Dialup number	415-705-6060, log in as newuser, no password
Services provided	Shell, e-mail, Usenet, UUCP, FTP, telnet, SLIP/PPP, and more

CTS Network Services (CTSNet)

Area code(s)	619
Voice phone	619-637-3737
E-mail address	support@cts.com
Dialup number	619-637-3660
Services provided	Shell, e-mail, Usenet, FTP, telnet, Gopher, IRC, MUD, SLIP/PPP, and more

CyberGate

Area code(s)	305
Voice phone	305-428-4283
E-mail address	sales@gate.net
Services provided	Shell, e-mail, Usenet, FTP, telnet, Gopher, Lynx, IRC, SLIP/PPP

Cyberstore Systems Inc.

Area code(s)	604
Voice phone	604-526-3373
E-mail address	info@cyberstore.ca
Dialup number	604-526-3676, login as guest
Services provided	E-mail, Usenet, FTP, telnet, Gopher, WAIS, WWW, IRC, SLIP/PPP

DataFlux Systems Limited

Area code(s)	604
Voice phone	604-744-4553
E-mail address	info@dataflux.bc.ca
Services provided	Shell, e-mail, Usenet, FTP, telnet, Gopher, WAIS, WWW, IRC, SLIP/PPP

Data Basix

Area code(s)	602
Voice phone	602-721-1988
E-mail address	info@data.basix.com
Services provided	Shell, Usenet, FTP, telnet

Data Tech Canada

Area code(s)	519
Voice phone	519-473-5694
E-mail address	info@dt-can.com
Dialup number	519-473-7685
Services provided	Shell, e-mail, Usenet, FTP, telnet, Gopher, WAIS, WWW

Delphi

Area code(s)	617, SprintNet, Tymnet
Voice phone	617-491-3393
E-mail address	info@delphi.com
Dialup number	617-492-9600
Services provided	Gopher, FTP, e-mail, Usenet, telnet

Digital Express Group (Digex)

Area code(s)	301, 410, 609, 703, 714, 908, 909
Voice phone	800-969-9090
E-mail address	`info@digex.net`
Dialup number	301-220-0258, 410-605-2700, 609-348-6203, 703-281-7997, 714-261-5201, 908-937-9481, 909-222-2204, log in as `new`
Services provided	Shell, SLIP/PPP, e-mail, newsgroups, telnet, FTP, IRC, Gopher, WAIS, and more

Echo

Area code(s)	212, 718
Voice phone	212-255-3839
E-mail address	`info@echonyc.com`
Dialup number	212-989-3382
Services provided	Conferencing, e-mail, shell, complete Internet access including telnet, FTP, SLIP/PPP

Eskimo North

Area code(s)	206
E-mail address	`nanook@eskimo.com`
Dialup number	206-367-3837
Services provided	Shell, telnet, FTP, IRC, Archie, Gopher, Hytelnet, WWW, Lynx, etc.

Evergreen Internet

Area code(s)	602, 702, 801
Voice phone	602-230-9339
E-mail address	`evergreen@libre.com`
Services provided	Shell, FTP, telnet, SLIP, PPP, others

Freelance Systems Programming

Area code(s)	513
Voice phone	513-254-7246
E-mail address	fsp@dayton.fsp.com
Dialup number	513-258-7745
Services provided	telnet, FTP, FSP, Lynx, WWW, Archie, Gopher, Usenet, e-mail, etc.

Gateway to the World

Area code(s)	305
Voice phone	305-670-2930
E-mail address	m.jansen@gate.com
Dialup number	305-670-2929
Services provided	Dial-up Internet access

Global Enterprise Services, Inc.

Area code(s)	609, 800
Voice phone	800-358-4437
E-mail address	market@jvnc.net
Services provided	Dial-in Internet access

HoloNet

Area code(s)	510, PSINet, Tymnet
Voice phone	510-704-0160
E-mail address	support@holonet.net
Dialup number	510-704-1058
Services provided	Complete Internet access

Hookup Communication Corporation

Area code(s)	519, Canada-wide
Voice phone	800-363-0400
E-mail address	info@hookup.net
Services provided	Shell, e-mail, Usenet, FTP, telnet, Gopher, WAIS, WWW, IRC, Hytelnet, Archie, SLIP/PPP

IDS World Network

Area code(s)	401, 305, 407, CompuServe Network
Voice phone	401-885-6855
E-mail address	info@ids.net
Dialup number	401-884-9002
Services provided	Shell, FTP, Gopher, telnet, Talk, Usenet news, SLIP

Institute for Global Communications (IGC)

Area code(s)	415
Voice phone	415-442-0220
E-mail address	support@igc.apc.org
Dialup number	415-322-0284
Services provided	E-mail, telnet, FTP, Gopher, Archie, Veronica, WAIS, SLIP/PPP

InterAccess Co.

Area code(s)	312, 708, 815
Voice phone	800-967-1580
E-mail address	info@interaccess.com
Dialup number	708-671-0237
Services provided	Shell, FTP, telnet, SLIP, PPP, etc.

Internet Online Inc.

Area code(s)	416
Voice phone	416-363-8676
E-mail address	vid@io.org
Dialup number	416-363-3783, log in as new
Services provided	Shell, e-mail, Usenet, FTP, telnet, Gopher, IRC, Archie, Hytelnet

Interpath

Area code(s)	919, 910, 704
Voice phone	800-849-6305
E-mail address	info@infopath.net
Services provided	Full shell for UNIX, and SLIP and PPP

Maestro Information Service

Area code(s)	212
Voice phone	212-240-9600
E-mail address	info@maestro.com
Dialup number	212-240-9700, log in as newuser
Services provided	Shell, e-mail, Usenet, telnet, FTP, Archie, IRC

MBnet

Area code(s)	204
Voice phone	204-474-9590
E-mail address	info@mbnet.mb.ca
Dialup number	204-275-6132, log in as mbnet with password guest
Services provided	Shell, e-mail, Usenet, FTP, telnet, Gopher, WAIS, WWW, IRC, Archie, Hytelnet, SLIP/PPP

Meta Network

Area code(s)	703, SprintNet
Voice phone	703-243-6622
E-mail address	info@tmn.com
Services provided	Shell, e-mail, FTP, telnet, conferencing

Mindvox

Area code(s)	212, 718
Voice phone	212-989-2418
E-mail address	info@phantom.com
Dialup number	212-989-1550
Services provided	Shell, e-mail, Usenet, FTP, telnet, Gopher, Archie, IRC, conferencing

Msen

Area code(s)	313, 810, 800
Voice phone	313-998-4562
E-mail address	info-request@msen.com
Services provided	Shell, e-mail, telnet, FTP, Usenet, Gopher, IRC, WAIS, SLIP/PPP

MV Communications, Inc.

Area code(s)	603
Voice phone	603-429-2223
E-mail address	info@mv.mv.com
Dialup number	603-424-7428
Services provided	Shell, Usenet, FTP, telnet, Gopher, WAIS, SLIP/PPP

Neosoft

Area code(s)	713, 504, 314, 800, SprintNet
Voice phone	713-684-5969
E-mail address	info@neosoft.com
Services provided	Shell, Usenet, FTP, telnet, Gopher, SLIP/ PPP, etc.

Netcom Online Communications Services

Area code(s)	206, 212, 214, 303, 310, 312, 404, 408, 415, 503, 510, 512, 617, 619, 703, 714, 818, 916
Voice phone	800-501-8649
E-mail address	info@netcom.com
Dialup number	206-547-5992, 212-354-3870, 214-753-0045, 303-758-0101, 310-842-8835, 312-380-0340, 404-303-9765, 408-261-4700, 408-459-9851, 415-328-9940, 415-985-5650, 503-626-6833, 510-274-2900, 510-426-6610, 510-865-9004, 512-206-4950, 617-237-8600, 619-234-0524, 703-255-5951, 714-708-3800, 818-585-3400, 916-965-1371; log in as guest
Services provided	Shell, e-mail, Usenet, FTP, telnet, Gopher, IRC, WAIS, SLIP/PPP

North Shore Access

Area code(s)	617
Voice phone	617-593-3110
E-mail address	info@shore.net
Dialup number	617-593-4557, log in as new
Services provided	Shell, FTP, telnet, Gopher, Archie, SLIP/PPP

Northcoast Internet

Area code(s)	707
Voice phone	707-444-1913
Services provided	Shell, FTP, telnet, Gopher, SLIP/PPP

Nuance Network Services

Area code(s)	205
Voice phone	205-533-4296
E-mail address	info@nuance.com
Services provided	Shell, Usenet, FTP, telnet, Gopher, SLIP/PPP

OARNet

Area code(s)	614
Voice phone	800-627-8101
E-mail address	`info@oar.net`
Services provided	Shell, SLIP/PPP

Olympus

Area code(s)	206
Voice phone	206-385-0464
E-mail address	`ifo@olympus.net`
Services provided	Shell, FTP, telnet, Gopher

Panix Public Access UNIX and Internet

Area code(s)	212, 516
Voice phone	212-787-6160
E-mail address	`info@panix.com`
Dialup number	212-787-3100, 516-626-7863, log in as `newuser`
Services provided	Shell, Usenet, FTP, telnet, Gopher, Archie, WWW, WAIS, SLIP/PPP

Pipeline

Area code(s)	212
Voice phone	212-267-3636
E-mail address	`infobot@pipeline.com`
Dialup number	212-267-6432, log in as `guest`
Services provided	Pipeline for Windows software, e-mail, Usenet, Gopher, telnet, Archie, FTP, WAIS

Portal Communications Company

Area code(s)	408, SprintNet
Voice phone	408-973-9111
E-mail address	info@portal.com
Services provided	Shell, e-mail, Usenet, FTP, telnet, Gopher, IRC, SLIP/PPP

PSI

Area code(s)	North America, Europe and Pacific Basin; send e-mail to numbers-info@psi.com for list
Voice phone	703-709-0300
E-mail address	all-info@psi.com
Services provided	Complete Internet services

Teleport

Area code(s)	503, 206
Voice phone	503-223-4245
E-mail address	info@teleport.com
Dialup number	503-220-1016
Services provided	Shell, e-mail, Usenet, FTP, telnet, Gopher, SLIP/PPP

Telerama

Area code(s)	412
Voice phone	412-481-3505
E-mail address	sysop@telerama.lm.com
Dialup number	412-481-4644
Services provided	Shell, e-mail, telnet, Usenet, FTP, telnet, Gopher, IRC, SLIP/PPP

Texas Metronet

Area code(s)	214, 817
Voice phone	214-705-2900
E-mail address	info@metronet.com
Dialup number	214-705-2901, 817-261-1127; log in as info, with password info
Services provided	Shell, e-mail, Usenet, FTP, telnet, Gopher, IRC, SLIP/PPP

UUNorth Incorporated

Area code(s)	416
Voice phone	416-225-8649
E-mail address	uunorth@north.net
Dialup number	416-221-0200, log in as new
Services provided	E-mail, Usenet, FTP, telnet, Gopher, WAIS, WWW, IRC, Archie, SLIP/PPP

VNet Internet Access, Inc.

Area code(s)	704, public data network
Voice phone	800-377-3282
E-mail address	info@vnet.net
Dialup number	704-347-8839, log in as new
Services provided	Shell, e-mail, Usenet, FTP, telnet, Gopher, IRC, SLIP/PPP, UUCP

The WELL

Area code(s)	415, CompuServe Packet Network
Voice phone	415-332-4335
E-mail address	info@well.sf.ca.us
Dialup number	415-332-6106, log in as newuser
Services provided	Shell, e-mail, Usenet, FTP, telnet, conferencing

Wimsey Information Services

Area code(s)	604
Voice phone	604-936-8649
E-mail address	admin@wimsey.com
Services provided	Shell, e-mail, Usenet, FTP, telnet, Gopher, WAIS, WWW, IRC, Archie, SLIP/PPP

The World

Area code(s)	508, 617, CompuServe Packet Network
Voice phone	617-739-0202
E-mail address	office@world.std.com
Dialup number	617-739-9753, log in as new
Services provided	Shell, e-mail, Usenet, FTP, telnet, Gopher, WAIS, WWW, IRC

XNet Information Systems

Area code(s)	708
Voice phone	708-983-6064
E-mail address	info@xnet.com
Dialup number	708-983-6435, 708-882-1101
Services provided	Shell, e-mail, Usenet, FTP, telnet, Gopher, Archie, IRC, SLIP/PPP, UUCP

Australia

Aarnet

Voice phone	+61 6-249-3385
E-mail address	aarnet@aarnet.edu.au

Connect.com.au P/L

Areas serviced	Major Australian capital cities (2, 3, 6, 7, 8, 9)
Voice phone	1 800 818 262 or +61 3 528 2239
E-mail address	connect@connect.com.au
Services provided	Shell, SLIP/PPP, UUCP

Germany

Contributed Software

Voice phone	+49 30-694-69-07
E-mail address	info@contrib.de
Dialup number	+49 30-694-60-55, log in as guest or gast

Individual Network e.V.

Area serviced	All of Germany
Voice phone	+49 0441 9808556
E-mail address	in-info@individual.net
Dialup number	02238 15071, log in as info
Services provided	UUCP throughout Germany; FTP, SLIP, telnet and other services in some major cities

Inter Networking System (INS)

Voice phone	+49 2305 356505
E-mail address	info@ins.net

Netherlands

Knoware

        E-mail address   `info@knoware.nl`
        Dialup number   030 896775

NetLand

        Voice phone   020 6943664
        E-mail address   `Info@netland.nl`
        Dialup number   020 6940350, log in as `new` or `info`

Simplex

        E-mail address   `simplex@simplex.nl`
        Dialup number   020 6653388, log in as `new` or `info`

New Zealand

Actrix

        Voice phone   (04) 389-6316
        E-mail address   `john@actrix.gen.nz`

Switzerland

SWITCH—Swiss Academic and Research Network

        Voice phone   +41 1 268 1515
        E-mail address   `postmaster@switch.ch`

United Kingdom

Almac

Voice phone	+44 0324-665371
E-mail address	alastair.mcintyre@almac.co.uk

Cix

Voice phone	+44 49 2641 961
E-mail address	cixadmin@cix.compulink.co.uk

Demon Internet Limited

Voice phone	081-349-0063 (London)
	031-552-0344 (Edinburgh)
E-mail address	internet@demon.net
Services provided	SLIP/PPP accounts

The Direct Connection (UK)

Voice phone	+44 (0)81 317 0100
E-mail address	helpdesk@dircon.cu.uk
Dialup number	+44 (0)81 317 2222

HOW TO START YOUR OWN USENET NEWSGROUP

With a bit of help from your local Internet access provider system administration team, starting a mailing list is easy, but if you want to follow the route of DEC, HP, SGI, and other companies and create a Usenet newsgroup (or many newsgroups) that focus on your products and services, it's a bit more tricky to work within the constraints of the Internet culture.

There are two primary avenues for pursuing a newsgroup: either create your own by fiat in the alt.*, biz.*, or market.* hierarchies (we discuss these in various spots within the book) or get involved in the voting and approval process specified by the Usenet community and have your group added as a main-stream addition to the comp.*, sci.*, news.* or one of the other foundation newsgroups.

If you opt for the former strategy, talk with your Internet access provider about the commands needed to create the group, and then work with the Usenet community to publicize it; a succinct announcement to related groups and mailing lists is quite appropriate.

If you want to try to get your newsgroup added to the official Usenet groupings—in order to maximize their distribution—following are the rules of newsgroup formation.

Requirements for Group Creation

These are guidelines that have been generally agreed on across Usenet as appropriate for creating new newsgroups in the "standard" Usenet newsgroup hierarchy. They are not intended as guidelines for setting Usenet policy other than group creations, and they are not intended to apply to "alternate" or local news hierarchies. The part of the namespace affected is comp, news, sci, misc, soc, talk, and rec, which are the most widely-distributed areas of the Usenet hierarchy.

Any group creation request that follows these guidelines to a successful result should be honored, and any request that fails to follow these procedures or to obtain a successful result from doing so should be dropped, except under extraordinary circumstances. The reason these are called guidelines and not absolute rules is that it is not possible to predict in advance what "extraordinary circumstances" are or how they might arise.

It should be pointed out here that, as always, the decision about whether or not to create a newsgroup on a given machine rests with the administrator of that machine. These guidelines are intended merely as an aid in making those decisions.

The Discussion

1. A request for discussion on creation of a new newsgroup should be posted to news.announce.newgroups and also to any other groups or mailing lists at all related to the proposed topic, if desired. The group is moderated, and the Followup-to: header will be set so that the actual discussion takes place only in news.groups. Users on sites that have difficulty posting to moderated groups may mail submissions intended for news.announce.newgroups to newgroups@uunet.uu.net.

   The article should be cross-posted among the newsgroups, including news.announce.newgroups, rather than posted as separate articles. Note that standard behavior for posting software is to not present the articles in any groups when cross-posted to a moderated group; the moderator will handle that for you.

2. The name and charter of the proposed group and whether it will be moderated or unmoderated (and if the former, who the moderator(s) will be) should be determined during the discussion period. If there is no general agreement on these points among the proponents of a new group at the end of 30 days of discussion, the discussion should be taken offline (into `mail` instead of `news.groups`), and the proponents should iron out the details among themselves. Once that is done, a new, more specific proposal may be made, going back to step 1).

3. Group advocates seeking help in choosing a name to suit the proposed charter, or looking for any other guidance in the creation procedure, can send a message to `group-advice@uunet.uu.net`; a few seasoned news administrators are available through this address.

The Vote

The Usenet Volunteer Votetakers (UVV) are a group of neutral, third-party vote-takers who currently handle vote gathering and counting for all newsgroup proposals. Ron Dippold (`rdippold@qualcomm.com`) coordinates this group. Contact him to arrange the handling of the vote. The mechanics of the vote will be handled in accord with the following paragraphs.

1. After the discussion period, if it has been determined that a new group is really desired, a name and charter are agreed on. When it has been determined whether the group will be moderated and if so, who will moderate it, a call for votes may be posted to `news.announce.newgroups` and any other groups or mailing lists that the original request for discussion might have been posted to. There should be minimal delay between the end of the discussion period and the issuing of a call for votes.

   The call for votes should include clear instructions about how to cast a vote. It must be as easy to cast a vote for creation as against it, and vice versa. It is explicitly permitted to set up two separate addresses to mail yes and no votes to (provided that they are on the same machine) to set up an address different than that the article was posted from to mail votes to, or to just accept replies to the call for votes article, as long as it is clearly and explicitly stated in the call for votes article how to cast a vote. If two addresses are used for a vote, the reply addresses must process and accept both yes and no votes, or reject them both.

2. The voting period should last for at least 21 days and no more than 31 days, no matter what the preliminary results of the vote are. The exact date that the voting period will end should be stated in the call for votes.

Only votes that arrive on the vote-taker's machine prior to this date will be counted.

3. A couple of repeats of the call for votes may be posted during the vote, provided that they contain similar clear, unbiased instructions for casting a vote (as the original did) and provided that it is really a repeat of the call for votes on the same proposal (see step 5). Partial vote results should not be included; only a statement of the specific new group proposal, that a vote is in progress on it, and how to cast a vote.

   It is permitted to post a "mass acknowledgment" in which all the names of those from whom votes have been received are posted, as long as no indication is made of which way anybody voted until the voting period is officially over.

4. Only votes mailed to the vote-taker will count. Votes posted to the Net for any reason (including inability to get mail to the vote-taker) and proxy votes (such as having a mailing list maintainer claim a vote for each member of the list) will not be counted.

5. Votes may not be transferred to other, similar proposals. A vote shall count only for the exact proposal that it is a response to. In particular, a vote for or against a newsgroup under one name shall not be counted as a vote for or against a newsgroup with a different name or charter, a different moderated/unmoderated status, or (if moderated) a different moderator or set of moderators.

6. Votes must be explicit; they should be of the form "I vote for the group `foo.bar` as proposed" or "I vote against the group `foo.bar` as proposed." The wording doesn't have to be exact, it just needs to be unambiguous. In particular, statements of the form "I would vote for this group if…" should be considered comments only and not counted as votes.

7. A vote should be run only for a single group proposal. Attempts to create multiple groups should be handled by running multiple parallel votes rather than one vote to create all of the groups.

The Result

1. At the completion of the voting period, the vote taker must post the vote tally and the e-mail addresses—and (if available) names of the voters—received to `news.announce.newgroups` and any other groups or mailing lists to which the original call for votes was posted. The tally should include a statement of which way each voter voted so that the results can be verified.

2. After the vote result is posted, there will be a five-day waiting period, beginning when the voting results actually appear in news.announce.newgroups, during which the Net will have a chance to correct any errors in the voter list or the voting procedure.

3. After the waiting period, and if there were no serious objections that might invalidate the vote and if 100 more valid yes/create votes are received than no/don't create and at least 2/3 of the total number of valid votes received are in favor of creation, a newgroup control message may be sent out. If the 100 vote margin or 2/3 percentage is not met, the group should not be created.

4. The newgroup message will be sent by the news.announce.newgroups moderator at the end of the waiting period of a successful vote. If the new group is moderated, the vote-taker should send a message during the waiting period to David C. Lawrence (tale@uunet.uu.net) with both the moderator's contact address and the group's submission address.

5. A proposal which has failed under step 3 should not be brought up again for discussion until at least 6 months have passed from the close of the vote. This limitation does not apply to proposals which never went to vote.

THE WORLD ACCORDING TO THE INTERNET

Wonder what countries are connected to the Internet? You're not alone. Larry Landweber at the University of Wisconsin has been keeping track of this information and his list of international connectivity is quite impressive.

You can obtain an up-to-date copy of this list by anonymous FTP. Connect via FTP to ftp.cs.wisc.edu, log in as anonymous, and use your e-mail address as the password. Then look in the connectivity_table directory for the file. Also in the same directory is a file in Postscript format that shows a map of the world with countries shaded in to show their level of Internet connectivity (see Figure C.1).

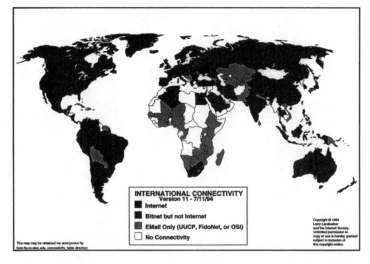

Figure C.1. International Connectivity as of July 11, 1994.

The information in the following list is organized by the ISO international two-letter country abbreviation code. For countries outside of the United States, this two letter abbreviation is usually, but not always, the suffix on the domain name. For example, a host beach in Aruba would be beach.aw as indicated in the following list.

AD	Andorra (Principality of)	AZ	Azerbaijan
AE	United Arab Emirates	BA	Bosnia-Herzegovina
AF	Afghanistan (Islamic Republic of)	BB	Barbados
		BD	Bangladesh (People's Republic of)
AG	Antigua and Barbuda		
AI	Anguilla	BE	Belgium (Kingdom of)
AL	Albania (Republic of)	BF	Burkina Faso (formerly Upper Volta)
AM	Armenia		
AN	Netherlands Antilles	BG	Bulgaria (Republic of)
AO	Angola (People's Republic of)	BH	Bahrain (State of)
		BI	Burundi (Republic of)
AQ	Antarctica	BJ	Benin (People's Republic of)
AR	Argentina (Argentine Republic)		
		BM	Bermuda
AS	American Samoa	BN	Brunei Darussalam
AT	Austria (Republic of)	BO	Bolivia (Republic of)
AU	Australia	BR	Brazil (Federative Republic of)
AW	Aruba		
		BS	Bahamas (Commonwealth of the)

BT	Bhutan (Kingdom of)	FJ	Fiji (Republic of)
BV	Bouvet Island	FK	Falkland Islands (Malvinas)
BW	Botswana (Republic of)	FM	Micronesia (Federated States of)
BY	Belarus		
BZ	Belize	FO	Faroe Islands
CA	Canada	FR	France (French Republic)
CC	Cocos (Keeling) Islands	GA	Gabon (Gabonese Republic)
CF	Central African Republic	GB	United Kingdom (Great Britain and Northern Ireland)
CG	Congo (Republic of the)		
CH	Switzerland (Swiss Confederation)		
		GD	Grenada
CI	Cote d'Ivoire (Republic of)	GE	Georgia (Republic of)
		GF	French Guiana
CK	Cook Islands	GH	Ghana (Republic of)
CL	Chile (Republic of)	GI	Gibraltar
CM	Cameroon (Republic of)	GL	Greenland
CN	China (People's Republic of)	GM	Gambia (Republic of the)
		GN	Guinea (Republic of)
CO	Colombia (Republic of)	GP	Guadeloupe (French Department of)
CR	Costa Rica (Republic of)		
CU	Cuba (Republic of)	GQ	Equatorial Guinea (Republic of)
CV	Cape Verde (Republic of)		
CX	Christmas Island (Indian Ocean)	GR	Greece (Hellenic Republic)
		GT	Guatemala (Republic of)
CY	Cyprus (Republic of)	GU	Guam
CZ	Czech Republic	GW	Guinea-Bissau (Republic of)
DE	Germany (Federal Republic of)	GY	Guyana (Republic of)
		HK	Hong Kong
DJ	Djibouti (Republic of)	HM	Heard and McDonald Islands
DK	Denmark (Kingdom of)		
DM	Dominica (Commonwealth of)	HN	Honduras (Republic of)
		HR	Croatia
DO	Dominican Republic	HT	Haiti (Republic of)
DZ	Algeria (People's Democratic Republic of)	HU	Hungary (Republic of)
		ID	Indonesia (Republic of)
EC	Ecuador (Republic of)	IE	Ireland
EE	Estonia (Republic of)	IL	Israel (State of)
EG	Egypt (Arab Republic of)	IN	India (Republic of)
EH	Western Sahara	IO	British Indian Ocean Territory
ES	Spain (Kingdom of)		
ET	Ethiopia (People's Democratic Republic of)	IQ	Iraq (Republic of)
		IR	Iran (Islamic Republic of)
FI	Finland (Republic of)	IS	Iceland (Republic of)

IT	Italy (Italian Republic)	ML	Mali (Republic of)
JM	Jamaica	MM	Myanmar (Union of)
JO	Jordan (Hashemite Kingdom of)	MN	Mongolia
		MO	Macau (Ao-me'n)
JP	Japan	MP	Northern Mariana Islands (Commonwealth of the)
KE	Kenya (Republic of)		
KG	Kyrgyz Republic	MQ	Martinique (French Department of)
KH	Cambodia		
KI	Kiribati (Republic of)	MR	Mauritania (Islamic Republic of)
KM	Comoros (Islamic Federal Republic of the)		
		MS	Montserrat
KN	Saint Kitts and Nevis	MT	Malta (Republic of)
KP	Korea (Democratic People's Republic of)	MU	Mauritius
		MV	Maldives (Republic of)
KR	Korea (Republic of)	MW	Malawi (Republic of)
KW	Kuwait (State of)	MX	Mexico (United Mexican States)
KY	Cayman Islands		
KZ	Kazakhstan	MY	Malaysia
LA	Lao People's Democratic Republic	MZ	Mozambique (People's Republic of)
LB	Lebanon (Lebanese Republic)	NA	Namibia (Republic of)
		NC	New Caledonia
LC	Saint Lucia	NE	Niger (Republic of the)
LI	Liechtenstein (Principality of)	NF	Norfolk Island
		NG	Nigeria (Federal Republic of)
LK	Sri Lanka (Democratic Socialist Republic of)		
		NI	Nicaragua (Republic of)
LR	Liberia (Republic of)	NL	Netherlands (Kingdom of the)
LS	Lesotho (Kingdom of)		
LT	Lithuania	NO	Norway (Kingdom of)
LU	Luxembourg (Grand Duchy of)	NP	Nepal (Kingdom of)
		NR	Nauru (Republic of)
LV	Latvia (Republic of)	NT	Neutral Zone (between Saudi Arabia and Iraq)
LY	Libyan Arab Jamahiriya		
MA	Morocco (Kingdom of)	NU	Niue
MC	Monaco (Principality of)	NZ	New Zealand
MD	Moldova (Republic of)	OM	Oman (Sultanate of)
MG	Madagascar (Democratic Republic of)	PA	Panama (Republic of)
		PE	Peru (Republic of)
MH	Marshall Islands (Republic of the)	PF	French Polynesia
		PG	Papua New Guinea
MK	Macedonia (Former Yugoslav Republic of)	PH	Philippines (Republic of the)

PK	Pakistan (Islamic Republic of)	SY	Syria (Syrian Arab Republic)
PL	Poland (Republic of)	SZ	Swaziland (Kingdom of)
PM	Saint Pierre and Miquelon (French Department of)	TC	Turks and Caicos Islands
		TD	Chad (Republic of)
		TF	French Southern Territories
PN	Pitcairn	TG	Togo (Togolese Republic)
PR	Puerto Rico	TH	Thailand (Kingdom of)
PT	Portugal (Portuguese Republic)	TJ	Tajikistan
		TK	Tokelau
PW	Palau (Republic of)	TM	Turkmenistan
PY	Paraguay (Republic of)	TN	Tunisia
QA	Qatar (State of)	TO	Tonga (Kingdom of)
RE	Reunion (French Department of)	TP	East Timor
		TR	Turkey (Republic of)
RO	Romania	TT	Trinidad and Tobago (Republic of)
RU	Russian Federation		
RW	Rwanda (Rwandese Republic)	TV	Tuvalu
		TW	Taiwan, Province of China
SA	Saudi Arabia (Kingdom of)	TZ	Tanzania (United Republic of)
SB	Solomon Islands	UA	Ukraine
SC	Seychelles (Republic of)	UG	Uganda (Republic of)
SD	Sudan (Democratic Republic of the)	UM	United States Minor Outlying Islands
SE	Sweden (Kingdom of)	US	United States (United States of America)
SG	Singapore (Republic of)		
SH	Saint Helena	UY	Uruguay (Eastern Republic of)
SI	Slovenia		
SJ	Svalbard and Jan Mayen Islands	UZ	Uzbekistan
		VA	Vatican City State (Holy See)
SK	Slovakia		
SL	Sierra Leone (Republic of)	VC	Saint Vincent and the Grenadines
SM	San Marino (Republic of)	VE	Venezuela (Republic of)
SN	Senegal (Republic of)	VG	Virgin Islands (British)
SO	Somalia (Somali Democratic Republic)	VI	Virgin Islands (U.S.)
		VN	Vietnam (Socialist Republic of)
SR	Suriname (Republic of)		
ST	Sao Tome and Principe (Democratic Republic of)	VU	Vanuatu (Republic of, formerly New Hebrides)
SV	El Salvador (Republic of)	WF	Wallis and Futuna Islands

WS   Samoa (Independent State of)
YE   Yemen (Republic of)
YT   Mayotte
YU   Yugoslavia (Socialist Federal Republic of)
ZA   South Africa (Republic of)
ZM   Zambia (Republic of)
ZR   Zaire (Republic of)
ZW   Zimbabwe (Republic of)

Note: This table was adapted from a list called *International Connectivity*, which is Copyright 1994 Lawrence H. Landweber and the Internet Society.

WORKING WITH THE WORLD WIDE WEB: TIPS AND TOOLS

If you decide to include with your Internet marketing plans support for the thousands of World Wide Web users on the Internet, you'll have to grapple with the issue of transforming your brochures, product descriptions, price lists, pictures, and other information into the hypertext language that Web servers such as Mosaic can read. If you opt for a commercial service to be your Web server, you might find that the operators will perform this format translation for a fee or as part of the setup charge.

You can also produce your own Web-readable hypertext documents in-house using hypertext markup language (HTML). A technician at your firm can either create them directly, write them with the aid of an HTML editor, or convert by hand documents in other formats to HTML. An HTML document can be created with any text editor. If you're accustomed to marking up text in any way (even red-penciling it), HTML should be fairly intuitive.

Fortunately, there are a number of Web tools available on the Internet, including *A beginner's guide to HTML* at URL `http://www.ncsa.uiuc.edu/General/Internet/WWW/HTMLPrimer.html`. An alternate HTML primer is available from Nathan Torkington of New Zealand through the network at the URL `http://www.vuw.ac.nz/who/Nathan.Torkington/ideas/www-html.html`.

Many people, however, prefer an HTML editor because it's graphical and easier to use than writing HTML documents directly in a standard editing environment. Some of the available editors are graphically oriented, offering a "what you see is what you get" metaphor, but others simply assist you in writing HTML by plugging in the desired markup tags from a menu.

The third option is converting documents created in other formats to HTML. A variety of different "filters" that can automatically accomplish this task are available on the Internet for free. The best place to learn about the possibilities is to obtain a copy of the filter list at CERN maintained by Rich Brandwein and Mike Sendall. The URL is `http://info.cern.ch/hypertext/WWW/Tools/Filters.html`.

More Information on the Web and Mosaic

Thanks to the World Wide Web's enormous popularity, a number of Web resources are publicly available on the Internet. The trick is knowing where to find them. Here's where to go to find information on using Web servers and setting up your own server:

The World Wide Web FAQ

An introduction to the World Wide Web project, this FAQ describes the concepts, software, and various access methods. It is aimed at people who know a little about navigating the Internet but want to know more about the Web specifically. The document is posted to `news.answers`, `comp.infosystems.www`, `comp.infosystems.gopher`, `comp.infosystems.wais`, and `alt.hypertext` on the first and fifteenth of every month. The latest version is also available on the Web itself at URL`http://siva.cshl.org/~boutell/www_faq.html`.

World Wide Web Guide

The Guide is intended to be used as a beginner's guide to the World Wide Web in a "hands-on" sort of way and offers answers to many basic questions about the Web. Web statistics, software pointers, information on hypertext and hypermedia, and other topics are covered.

You can find the World Wide Web Guide at URL `http://www.eit.com/web/` `www.guide` or obtain a copy through FTP by connecting to `ftp.eit.com` and looking in the directory `/pub/web.guide`. There you'll find text-only, PostScript, HTML, and FrameMaker 4.0 versions of the Guide.

World Wide Web Discussion Groups

WWW-VM Mailing List

The Web servers can run on a wide variety of systems, but some pose greater difficulties than others. Perhaps the most complex system to set up is VM/CMS, and this list is the best place to find others discussing the problems inherent in this configuration. To subscribe, send e-mail to `listserv@sjuvm.bitnet` or `LISTSERV@sjuvm.stjohns.edu` with the line `SUBSCRIBE WWW-VM firstname lastname` in the body.

comp.infosystems.www newsgroup

This Usenet newsgroup is devoted to discussing technical and other issues related to the World Wide Web, Mosaic, and similar technologies

The Wide World of Webs

With so many Web servers going up these days—some observers estimate their growth at one a day—it's hard to tell what's out there. There are, however, several online resources which provide a great deal of information on new and established servers. Here are three of them:

- The WWW Virtual Library at URL `http://info.cern.ch/hypertext/` `DataSources/bySubject/Overview.html`

- What's New with NCSA Mosaic at URL `http://www.ncsa.uiuc.edu/SDG/` `Software/Mosaic/Docs/whats-new.html`

- The Best of the Web '94 Awards at URL `http://wings.buffalo.edu/` `contest/`. Sponsored by SUNY/Buffalo, these awards are presented in 14 categories: WWW Hall of Fame, Best Overall Site, Best WWW Browser, Best Campus-Wide Information System, Best Educational Site, Best Commercial Site, Best Entertainment Site, Best Professional Site, Best Navigational Aid, Most Important Service Concept, Best Document Design, Best Use of Interaction, Best Use of Multiple Media, Most Technical Merit.

Viewing the Web: World Wide Web Browsers

The best and fastest way to access the Web is to install a browser on your own computer system. Fortunately, browsers are available for many platforms, both in source and executable forms.

Microsoft Windows Browsers

These browsers require that you have SLIP, PPP, or other TCP/IP networking on your PC. SLIP or PPP can be accomplished over phone lines, but only with the active cooperation of your network provider or educational institution. If you only have normal dialup shell access, your best options are to run the Lynx program resident on the UNIX server you dial into or telnet to a public Web browser.

- **Mosaic for Windows.** Developed at the NCSA at the University of Illinois. Available by anonymous FTP from ftp.ncsa.uiuc.edu in the directory PC/Mosaic.

- **Cello.** Developed at Cornell University. Available by anonymous FTP from ftp.law.cornell.edu in the directory /pub/LII/cello.

MS-DOS Browsers

As the Windows browsers do, this browser requires a SLIP, PPP, or other TCP/IP connection or as an alternative, running Lynx or telnetting to a public Web browser.

- **DosLynx.** DosLynx is an excellent text-based browser for use on DOS systems. You can obtain DosLynx by anonymous FTP from ftp2.cc.ukans.edu in the directory pub/WWW/DosLynx.

Macintosh Browsers

As the Windows browsers do, these browsers also require a SLIP, PPP or other TCP/IP connection or, as an alternative, running Lynx or telnetting to a public Web browser.

- **Mosaic for Macintosh.** Developed at NCSA. Available by anonymous FTP from ftp.ncsa.uiuc.edu in the directory Mac/Mosaic.

- **Samba.** Developed at CERN. Available by anonymous FTP from info.cern.ch in the directory /ftp/pub/www/bin as the file mac.

Browsers for Other Platforms

Browsers are also available for other platforms, such as

- **NeXTStep.**   For more information, check `http://www.omnigroup.com/`. You can FTP the package from `ftp.omnigroup.com` in the `/pub/software/` directory.

- **X Window.**   Available by anonymous FTP from `ftp.ncsa.uiuc.edu` in the directory `Mosaic`.

- **VMS.**   Available via anonymous FTP from `ftp.ncsa.uiuc.edu` in the directory `Mosaic`.

- **UNIX.**   Viola for X is available by anonymous FTP from `ora.com` in `/pub/www/viola`; Chimera is available by anonymous FTP from `ftp.cs.unlv.edu` in the directory `/pub/chimera`.

Text-Based Browsers

The following browsers are text-based browsers for UNIX (and in some cases also VMS) systems. Many Internet access sites have these programs already installed on their server.

- **Line Mode Browser.**   This program gives Web readership to anyone with a dumb terminal. Available by anonymous FTP from `info.cern.ch` in the directory `/pub/www/src`.

- **Lynx Full Screen Browser.**   This is a hypertext browser for VT100 terminals using full screen, arrow keys, highlighting, and so on. Available by anonymous FTP from `ftp2.cc.ukans.edu`.

- **Tom Fine's perlWWW.**   A TTY-based browser written in perl. Available by anonymous FTP from `archive.cis.ohio-state.edu` in the directory `pub/w3browser` as the file `w3browser-0.1.shar`.

- **Dudu Rashty's Full Screen Client.**   Based on VMS's SMG screen management routines. Available by anonymous FTP from `vms.huji.ac.il` in the directory `www/www_client`.

- **Emacs w3-mode.**   Web browse mode for emacs. Uses multiple fonts when used with Lemacs or Epoch. See the documentation. Available by anonymous FTP from `moose.cs.indiana.edu` in the directory `pub/elisp/w3` as the files `w3.tar.Z` and `extras.tar.Z`.

Creating Web Documents (HTML Editors)

HTML editors make creating Web documents a good deal easier. Here are editors for some of the more popular platforms:

- **EMACS.**   Within the popular EMACS editor are a couple of macro packages to ease HTML creation. Via FTP connect to `www.reed.edu` and look in `~nelson/tools/` or FTP to `ftp.ncsa.uiuc.edu` and look for `/Web/elisp/html-mode.el`.

- **Microsoft Windows.**   HTML Assistant can be obtained via anonymous FTP from `ftp.cs.dal.ca` in the directory `/htmlasst/`.

- **X Window.**   TkWWW, also a Web browser, supports WYSIWYG HTML editing. Because it's a browser, you can try links immediately after creating them.

- **Macintosh.**   BBEdit HTML extensions allow the BBEdit and BBEdit Lite text editors for the Macintosh to edit HTML documents. Available from `http://www.uji.es/bbedit-html-extensions.html`.

- **Other HTML Tools.**   NCSA's List of Filters and Editors, for which the URL is `http://www.ncsa.uiuc.edu/SDG/Software/Mosaic/Docs/faq-software.html#editors>`, mentions several editors, including two for Microsoft Windows.

THE FULL SCOOP ON GOPHER

The World Wide Web isn't the only way to use the Internet to distribute information to your customers or clients. E-mail is an excellent alternative, as we discuss extensively in Chapters 6, 7, and 8, and the Gopher service, invented at the University of Minnesota, is perhaps the best way to distribute textual information.

This appendix takes a closer look at Gopher, including listing various references and resources available on the Net for setting up servers, organizing information, and obtaining client programs that can help you see what's available on the network.

Much of this information comes from the excellent *Common Questions and Answers about the Internet Gopher*, a document posted to the Usenet groups comp.infosystems.gopher, comp.answers, and news.answers every two weeks. You can also obtain this document through anonymous FTP by connecting to either rtfm.mit.edu and looking in the directory /pub/usenet/news.answers or connecting to ftp.uu.net and searching /usenet/news.answers. Finally, you can obtain a copy of the FAQ through electronic mail by sending a message to mail-server@rtfm.mit.edu with the subject of send usenet/news.answers/gopher-faq.

Gopher Client Software

The best place to look for a Gopher client program is at the University of Minnesota. Connect with anonymous FTP to the system `boombox.micro.umn.edu` and then look in the directory `/pub/gopher`. There is a wide variety of different hardware platforms that have client programs written; all of the following are available at Boombox with FTP:

UNIX curses and Emacs	Unix/gopher+2.0.tar.Z
X Window (Athena)	Unix/xgopher.1.3.tar.Z
X Window (Tk)	Unix/moog-0.2.tar.Z
X Window (Xview)	Unix/xvgopher
Macintosh Hypercard	Macintosh-TurboGopher/old-versions
Macintosh	Macintosh-TurboGopher/
DOS w/Clarkson Driver	PC_client/
NeXTstep	NeXT/
VM/CMS	Rice_CMS/ or VieGOPHER/
VMS	vms/
OS/2 2.0	os2/
MVS/XA	mvs/

There are more if those don't fit the bill:

The Gopher Book, for Microsoft Windows with WinSock at `sunsite.unc.edu:/pub/micro/pc-stuff/ms-windows/winsock/apps/gophbook.zip`

MacGopher for the Macintosh, at `ftp.cc.utah.edu:/pub/gopher/Macintosh` *

GopherApp, also for the Macintosh at `ftp.bio.indiana.edu:/util/gopher/gopherapp` *

A port of the UNIX curses client for DOS with PC/TCP at `oac.hsc.uth.tmc.edu:/public/dos/misc/dosgopher.exe`

A port of the UNIX curses client for PC-NFS at `bcm.tmc.edu:/nfs/gopher.exe`

A VMS DECwindows client for use with Wollongong or UCX at `job.acs.ohio-state.edu:XGOPHER_CLIENT.SHARE`

Publicly Available Gopher Logins

If for some reason a Gopher client isn't available to you, you can telnet to one of the public Gopher clients:

Hostname	Login	Region
consultant.micro.umn.edu	gopher	North America
ux1.cso.uiuc.edu	gopher	North America
panda.uiowa.edu	panda	North America
gopher.msu.edu	gopher	North America
gopher.ebone.net	gopher	Europe
gopher.sunet.se	gopher	Sweden
info.anu.edu.au	info	Australia
tolten.puc.cl	gopher	South America
ecnet.ec	gopher	Ecuador
gan.ncc.go.jp	gopher	Japan

Gopher Server Software

The best way to find the appropriate Gopher server for your system is to use anonymous FTP to connect to the site boombox.micro.umn.edu and look in the directory pub/gopher. Here's a rundown of what's available there:

UNIX	Unix/gopher+2.0.tar.Z
VMS	VMS/
Macintosh	Mac_server/
VM/CMS	Rice_CMS/ or Vienna_CMS/
MVS	mvs/
DOS PC	PC_server/
OS/2	os2

Discussion Lists

gopher

You can contact the developers of the Gopher protocol and many of the client and server software programs by sending mail to this list: gopher@boombox.micro.umn.edu. You can't join the list currently without an invitation.

comp.infosystems.gopher

A Usenet newsgroup that focuses on the many facets and aspects of Gopher servers, clients, and information.

gopher-news

The best place to learn general Gopher news, including information about new clients, servers, and media coverage of the programs and software. To sign up for the list, send a message to gopher-news-request@boombox.micro.umn.edu requesting to be added.

VMSgopher

A list discussing topics of interest to VMS users and developers. Send e-mail to listserv@trln.lib.unc.edu with the message subscribe VMSgopher-L *your full name*.

MVSGOPHER

A mailing list for MVS Gopher developers and users is also available. To subscribe to the list, send mail to listserver@lists.acs.ohio-state.edu, containing the message SUBSCRIBE MVSGOPHER *your full name*.

Hooking Your Gopher Server into Gopherspace

The way to hook your Gopher to the overall Gopher space is to get it all set up and then send an e-mail note to the Gopher administration team. If you're in Europe, send mail to gopher@ebone.net. If you're anywhere other than Europe, send e-mail to gopher@boombox.micro.umn.edu with the following information:

Server's name (as it will appear on the menu)
Hostname
Port number
Administrative contact
Selector string (optional)

Symbols

:-) (smileys) e-mail, 154
<g> (grin) e-mail, 154
> (arrow) Usenet
   postings, 142
>> (double arrow) Usenet
   postings, 142
@ (at sign) e-mail
   addresses, 6
3Com Products mailing
   list, 172

A

*A Beginner's Guide to
   HTML*, 378
a2i Communications, 337,
   347
Aarnet, 361
Acceptable Use Policies
   (AUPs), 52
   access providers, 117
   NSFnet, 117
access providers, 50
   AT & T, 212
   AUPs (Acceptable Use
      Policies), 117
   CIX, 47
   connection speed,
      51-52
   costs, 46, 61
   dialup accounts, 54-57

leased-line direct
   connections, 60
listing of, 336-364
local phone access, 53
MCI, 212
network reliability,
   50-51
network
   restrictions, 52
PPP connections, 58
security, 52
services, 53-54
SLIP/IP
   connections, 58
Sprint, 212
technical support,
   53-54
see also commercial
   online services
accessing commercial
online services,
194-195
account names (e-mail
addresses), 5
accounts, *see* connections
Actrix, 363
addresses (e-mail), 220
   @ (at sign), 6
   account names, 5

cc:Mail, 213
computer names, 5
domains, 5-6, 220
finding, 189-190, 221
incompatibility of
  addressing systems,
  224-225
Internet, 213
*Internetwork Mail
  Guide*, 221
mailinglists, 125
Microsoft Mail, 213
SRI International, 213
X.400 messaging
  system, 213
ADMDs (Administration
  Management
  Domains), 213
advertising, 145-146,
  331-332
  commercial online
    services, 300, 303,
    306-308
  consumer opinions,
    122
  costs, 118
  discussion groups,
    156-158
    flame wars,
      140-144
    jobs, 161-163
    postings, 331
    spamming, 142,
      331
  e-mail signatures,
    131-132
  expert advice, 122-123
  finger service (UNIX),
    131-133
  Global Network
    Navigator, 95
  Internet Shopping
    Network, 330

jobs, 123
mail reflector
  brochures
  (Cybergate), 332
strategies
  in-your-face
    marketing,
    143-144
  passive
    advertising, 124
  press releases, 124
  sponsorships, 124
URLs (uniform
  resource locators),
  91
World Wide Web, 90,
  271
  MecklerWeb,
    328-329
  Mosaic browser,
    115, 136-142
advertising agencies, 90
  Bernard Hodes
    Advertising, 123
  Bonney & Co., 115
Agora, 344, 347
airlines
  Lufthansa (German
    airline), 281-282
  see also travel services
Aladdin navigational
  software (GEnie), 314
Alain Pinel Realtors,
  88-89, 212
Alberta SuperNet Inc.,
  336, 347
Aldea Corp. Internet
  directories, 104
AlliedSignal Inc., 211
Almac, 364
alt (alternative) Usenet
  newsgroups, 21

alt.security Usenet
  newsgroup, 81
Ambient Monitoring
  Technology
  Information Center
  database, 203
America Online, 299,
  310, 319
  advertising, 312
  BBBes (Bulletin Board
    Systems), 311
  chat boards, 311-312
  costs, 312, 319
  demographics, 313
  e-mail, 4
  logon capacity, 312
  Microsoft Small
    Business Center, 261
  online publications,
    311
  see also commercial
    online services
Americans with
  Disabilities Act
  database, 203
announcements to
  dicussion groups, 159
  see also press releases
anonymous FTP, 26
Apollo Advertising, 90
AppleLink
  costs, 48
  e-mail, 4
Archie, 30-33
archives (FTP archives),
  searching, 30-33
ARPAnet, 47
articles
  discussion groups
    libel, 267
    posting, 151
    reading, 151
    writing, 152-154

magazine articles
about virtual
corporations, 269
The Electronic
Newstand, 280
ASCII (American
Standard for Computer
Information
Interchange), 27
ASCII mode (UNIX
FTP), 27
ASET software (network
security), 74
AT&T, 212
catalog/inventory
posting service, 95
EasyLink e-mail, 4,
213
Internet directories,
104
*The Atlanta Journal and
Constitution*, 100
*The Auction Directory &
News*, 282
audio-conferencing, 254
AUPs (Acceptable Use
Policies), 52
access providers, 117
NSFnet, 117
Australian culture
newsgroups, 170
auto manufacturers, 212
automated credit card
processing service, 265
automated mail
servers, 8
The Avid Explorer, 283

B

Background Notes
database, 205
banking, 326

Basic Guide to Exporting,
200
BBBs (Bulletin Board
Systems)
Clean Air Act
Amendments BBS,
204
commercial online
services, 302-304
America Online,
311
Delphi, 316
GEnie, 313
networking, 302
customer support, 233
Food and Drug
Administration BBS,
204
Patent and
Trademark Office
BBSes, 206
BBEdit HTML editors,
382
Berkeley Mail, *see* Mail
Bernard Hodes
Advertising, 123
The Best of the Web '94
Awards, 379
beverage vendors
Murchies Tea and
Coffee, 275
Watson's Barrels and
Wine Making
Supplies, 275
billing customers online,
96
binary files, sending via
e-mail, 223
binary mode (UNIX
FTP), 27
BITNET mailing lists,
finding, 149
biz (business) Usenet

newsgroups, 21
Bonney & Co.
advertising agency, 115
book sellers/publishers
Book Stacks
Unlimited, 25-26, 93
Computer Literacy,
92-93
encryption, 327-328
Future Fantasy
bookstore, 93
Infinity Link Network
Services, 94
The Internet
Bookstore, 327-328
JF Lehmanns
Fachbuchhandlung,
94
Macmillian Computer
Publishing, 145
Moe's Books, 93
The Online Bookstore,
93
O'Reilly & Associates,
95
Roswell Electronic
Computer
Bookstore, 94
Softpro Books, 94, 285
Book Stacks Unlimited,
25-26, 93
books
on security issues, 81
virtual corporations,
269
bps (bits per second), 51
break-ins (Internet),
64-66
reporting, 78
spotting potential
intruders, 259
Brigham and Women's
Hospital, 256-257

brochures
    mail-reflector bro-
        chures (Cybergate),
        332
    placing on the
        Internet, 9
Brock, Jack L., 65
browsers (World Wide
    Web)
    Cell, 380
    Chimera, 381
    DosLynx, 380
    Dudu Rashty's Full
        Screen Client, 381
    Emacs w3-mode, 381
    Line Mode Browser,
        381
    Lynx Full Screen
        Browser, 381
    Mosaic, 287-293, 380
    NeXTStep, 381
    Samba, 380
    Tom Fine's
        perlWWW, 381
    UNIX Viola for X, 381
    VMS, 381
    X Window, 381
Buckeye Pipeline Co.,
    211
Bureau of Labor
    Statistics, 191
Business Resources on the
    Net, 180

C

C-Cnet Communica-
    tions, 337
Canadian culture
    newsgroups, 170
canceling subscriptions
    to Listservs, 10
Canter & Siegel law
    firm, 120, 331

CAPCON Library
    Network, 339-340, 345,
    347
Case, Steve, 114
catalogs, 84
    Enterprise Integration
        Technology catalog
        posting service, 95
    PC Catalog, 330
    posting, 95
CB Simulator chat area
    (CompuServe), 305
cc:Mail
    addressing messages,
        213
    encryption, 76
CCI Networks, 336, 348
CCnet Communications,
    348
cd (change directory)
    command (UNIX FTP),
    27
CD vendors
    Compact Disc Con-
        nection, 93
    The Expert Center for
        Taxonomic
        Identification, 94
    Infinity Link Network
        Services, 94
    JF Lehmanns
        Fachbuchhandlung,
        94
Celestin Company,
    132-133
Cell browser (World
    Wide Web), 380
Census Bureau, 191-194
    Census Information
        database, 198
    Census of Population
        and Housing
        database, 198

Ceram Corporation, 93,
    114
CERAM Email
    Marketplace, 94
CERFnet, 85, 337-338,
    346, 348
CERT (Computer
    Emergency Response
    Team), 64, 79-80
    reporting network
        break-ins, 78
    security breaches,
        66-67
Chameleon
    (Netmanage), 58
chatting online
    America Online,
        311-312
    CompuServe, 305
    Internet VoiceChat,
        326
    Prodigy, 309
Chevrolet, 212
Chimera browser
    (World Wide Web), 381
Chinook College
    Funding Services, 274
Chrysler, 212
CICNet, 339-340, 346,
    348
CIM (CompuServe
    Information Manager),
    306
CIX (Commercial
    Internet Exchange), 47,
    85, 364
ClarkNet (Clark Internet
    Services, Inc.), 339-340,
    345, 349
    SLIP/PPP
        connections, 58
classified ads, 303
    America Online, 312
    CompuServe, 307

Delphi, 317
GEnie, 315
Prodigy, 310
Clean Air Act
  Amendments BBS, 204
Clean Water Act
  database, 204
Clearinghouse for
  Inventories/Emission
  Factors (CHIEF)
  database, 204
client software
  e-mail, 216
    Elm, 216-218
    Eudora, 217, 227
    Mail, 216-217
    MailTool, 217
    Mush, 217
    Netcom, 219
    Pine, 216-218
    Pipeline, 217, 219
    PSI, 219
    WinNET, 217, 219,
      223
    XMH, 217
    ZMail, 217
  Gopher, 384
clothing vendors
  Gymboree, 272
  Joe Boxer
    Corporation, 236
CNS, 338, 346, 349
Code of Federal
  Regulations databases,
  206
colleges, *see* universities
Colorado SuperNet, 338,
  349
com (commercial sites)
  domain, 6
commands (UNIX
  FTP), 27
Commerce Business Daily,
  200

CommerceNet, 265, 326
Commercial Internet
  Exchange, *see* CIX
commercial online
  services, 299-300,
  317-318
  accessing
    telnet, 22
    through The
      World, 194-195
  advertising, 300, 303,
    306-308
  America Online,
    310-313
  CompuServe, 304-307,
    319
  costs, 48, 300-301
  credit card
    transactions, 265
  culture, 301
  Delphi, 315-317, 319
  demographics, 301,
    304
    America Online,
      313, 319
    CompuServe, 305,
      307
    Delphi, 317
    GEnie, 315
    Prodigy, 310
  dialup accounts, 55
  discussion groups,
    302
  e-mail, 4, 210
    costs, 4, 310
    sending, 4
    targeting to
      potential
      customers, 303
  GEnie, 313-315, 320
  information services,
    302, 304
  infrastructure, 301

Internet access, 323
  magazines, 303
  marketing, 112
  newspapers, 303
  population growth,
    322
  Prodigy, 307-310, 320
  security issues, 72-73
  sponsorship
    advertising, 303
  walls, 302
Commercial Sabre
  (Delphi), 316
CommerNet (World
  Wide Web), 137
*Common Questions and
  Answers about the
  Internet Gopher*, 383
communications, 84-89
  e-mail, 210-212
  foreign language
    communications,
    104
Communications
  Accessibles Montreal,
  Inc., 344, 349
comp (computers)
  Usenet newsgroups, 21
comp.infosystems.gopher
  Usenet newsgroup, 386
comp.infosystems.www
  newsgroup, 379
comp.risks Usenet
  newsgroup, 81
comp.security.announce
  Usenet newsgroup, 80
comp.security.misc
  Usenet newsgroup, 80
comp.virus Usenet
  newsgroup, 81
Compact Disc
  Connection, 93
The Company
  Corporation, 92, 282

company mailboxes, 273-276
compressed files, uncompressing, 150
CompuServe, 299-300, 304, 319
    advertising
        classifieds, 307
        Electronic Mall, 306-307
    CB Simulator chat area, 305
    communications links, 304
    CompuServe Information Manager (CIM), 305-306
    costs, 305-306, 319
    databases, 304
    demographics, 305, 307
    e-mail, 4
    Executive News Service, 305
    forums, 305
        Entrepreneurs Forum, 261
        Legal Forum, 268
        Working From Home Forum, 261
    see also commercial online services
CompuServe Information Manager (CIM), 306
CompuServe Packet Network, 346
Computer Database Plus (Ziff-Davis), 302
Computer Emergency Response Team, see CERT

Computer Fraud and Abuse Act of 1986 (18 U.S.C. Section 1030), 269
computer hardware/ software vendors
    Ceram Inc., 93-94
    customer support, 96-99, 232
    Digital Equipment Corp. (DEC), 240-241
    Front Porch Computers, 305
    Hewlett Packard HP SupportLine, 245-249
    InterCon Systems, 235
    The Programmer's Shop, 94
    Silicon Graphics, 237-239
    Sun Microsystems, 234, 243-245
Computer Law database, 206
Computer Literacy, 92-93
computer names (e-mail addresses), 5
Computer Witchcraft, 104
concert ticket vendors (Planet Earth Management), 94
conferences
    announcing in discussion groups, 159
    online, 254, 325
Connect.com.au P/L, 362

connecting to remote computers, see telnet
connections
    access providers, 50-54
        CIX, 47
        costs, 46
        listing of, 336-364
        network reliability, 50-51
    commercial online services, 323
    costs, 61, 323
    determining needs, 48-50
    dialup accounts, 46, 54-57
    e-mail, 225-227
    Gopher servers to Gopherspace, 387
    international connections, 371-376
    leased-line direct connections, 46, 60-61
    PPP (Point-to-Point Protocol) connections, 46, 57-59
        costs, 58
        client software, 58
    security issues, 71
        commercial online services, 72-73
        firewalls, 71, 75
        university connections, 72
    SLIP (Serial Line Interface Protocol) connections, 46, 57-59
        client software, 58
        costs, 58, 323

consulting firms
(Internet)
CyberGate, 332-333
INFOMARK, 92
Information
Researchers, 273-276
The Internet
Company, 331
The Internet Group,
105
contracts (e-mail con-
tracts), 263
digital signatures, 263
legal tips, 268-269
Uniform Commercial
Code, 263
Contributed Software,
362
converting documents to
HTML, 378
COPS software (network
security), 74
copyrights, 266
Copyright
Information
database, 206
government
documents, 192
Cornell Law School
Legal Information
Institute, 187, 206
country codes (e-mail
domain names), 6,
371-376
Country Fare restaurant,
163, 282
*Country Reports on
Economic Policy and
Trade Practices*, 200
Country Studies and
Area Handbooks
database, 205
crackers, 65-67

crafts vendors
(McCrerey Farm), 94
credit card transactions
automated credit card
processing service,
265
commercial online
services, 265
digital signatures, 264
legal tips, 268-269
Mosaic (World Wide
Web browser), 290
security issues, 67-70
credit reporting services
(Infotech Information
Technologies), 91
CRL, 336-339, 346, 350
CTS Network Services
(CTSNet), 55, 337, 350
CU-SeeMe, 325
The Cuckoo's Egg, 259
culture
commercial online
services, 301
see also netiquette
currency, *see* credit card
transactions; digital
currency
customer profile
services, 239
customer support, 96,
231-232
BBBs, 233
by fax, 233
by phone, 232
by postal mail, 233
computer hardware/
software vendors,
96-99
customer profile
services, 239
discussion groups,
160

integrating on
commercial services
and Internet, 319
Internet, 233, 251
costs, 234, 249-250
databases, 243-245
e-mail, 235-236
FAQs, 240-241
FTP sites, 241-243
newsgroups,
237-239
online ordering
services, 242-243
Mosaic (World Wide
Web browser),
245-249
public relations,
234-235
"virtual" focus
groups, 233
World Wide Web, 97
CyberBeach Publishing,
332-333
CyberGate, 104, 332, 339,
350
cybermalls, 271-272
Virtual Mall, 275
World Wide Web,
271, 282-286, 296
costs for setting up
shops, 285
home pages, 283
renting space, 295
see also storefronts;
stores
CyberSpace
Development, 276
The CyberStore on the
Shore, 332
CyberStore Systems Inc.,
336, 350

D

Daniels, Frank, 102
Data Basix, 336, 351
data encryption
   book publishing,
      327-328
   e-mail, 75, 259, 327
      digital signatures,
         263-265
      encrypting hard-
         ware suppliers, 76
      PEM (Privacy-
         Enhanced Mail),
         77
      PGP (pretty good
         encryption), 77
      private key
         encryption, 76
      public key
         encryption, 76
Data Tech Canada, 343,
   351
databases
   commercial online
      services, 302, 304
   customer support,
      243-245
   demographics
      databases
      Census Informa-
         tion database, 198
      Census of
         Population and
         Housing
         database, 198
   financial databases
      *Basic Guide to
         Exporting*, 200
      *Business Resources
         on the Net*, 180
      *Commerce Business
         Daily*, 200

Country Reports
   on Economic
   Policy and Trade
   Practices, 200
Disclosure, 179
EconData, 200
Economic Bulletin
   Board, 200
EDGAR, 178-179,
   181-184, 200
Empowerment
   Zones and
   Enterprise
   Communities, 200
Financial
   Economics
   Network (FEN),
   201
General Agreement
   on Tariffs and
   Trade (GATT),
   201
Gross State
   Product Tables,
   201
Industry Profiles,
   201
International
   Business
   Practices, 201
Labor News, 201
LabStat, 202
Microsoft Corp.,
   195
MIT Experimental
   Stock Market
   database, 202
NAFTA (North
   American Free
   Trade
   Agreement), 202

National Export
   Strategy database,
   202
Occupational
   Outlook Hand-
   book database,
   202
Overseas Business
   Reports database,
   202
QuoteCom data-
   base, 202
Regional Economic
   Information
   System (REIS),
   203
State Small
   Business Profiles
   database, 203
U.S. Industrial
   Outlook database,
   203
Uniform
   Commercial Code
   database, 203
general information
   databases
   FedWorldNational
      Technical
      Information
      Service, 197
   Library of Con-
      gress, 197
   National Trade
      Data Bank, 197
   SunSITE Archives,
      197, 243-245
   U.S. Government
      Gophers, 198
   U.S. Government
      Publications
      Index, 198
   zip codes database,
      198

government
databases
Ambient
Monitoring
Technology
Information
Center database,
203
Americans with
Disabilities Act
database, 203
Bureau of Labor
Statistics, 191
Census Bureau,
191-194
Clean Air Act
Amendments
BBS, 204
Clean Water Act
database, 204
Clearinghouse for
Inventories/
Emission Factors
(CHIEF) database,
204
Economic Bulletin
Board, 185-187
Environmental
Protection
Agency database,
204
Federal Com-
munications
Commission, 191
Federal Deposit
Insurance Corp,
191
Food and Drug
Administration
BBS, 204
Food Labeling
Information
database, 204

*Government Sources
of Business and
Economic Informa-
tion on the
Internet*, 180
Health Care
Reform
Information
database, 204
*Internet Sources of
Government
Information*, 180
National Air Toxics
Information
Clearinghouse,
204
Occupational
Safety and Health
Administration
database, 205
Patent Office, 191
State Department
Travel Adviso-
ries, 179, 205
state goverment
databases, 191
TOXNET database,
205
integrating on
commercial services
and Internet, 319
international trade
databases
Background Notes
database, 205
Country Studies
and Area Hand-
books database,
205
International
Organizations
database, 205

World Bank Public
Information
Service database,
206
legal databases
Code of Federal
Regulations
databases, 206
Computer Law
database, 206
Copyright
Information
database, 206
Cornell Law School
Legal Information
Institute, 187, 206
Internet Patent
News Service, 206
Patent and
Trademark Office
BBSes, 206
Patent Office
Reform Panel
Final Report
database, 207
Supreme Court
Decisions
database, 207
Venable, Baetjer,
Howard &
Civiletti, 207
market research
databases
Public Opinion
Item Index
database, 198
U.S. Department of
Agriculture
Economics and
Statistics gopher,
199

searching
  telnet, 23-26
  WAIS, 187-189
technology databases
  Information
    Infrastructure
    Task Force
    Gopher, 199
  Merit Network
    Information
    Center, 199
  National
    Information
    Infrastructure
    Agenda, 199
DataFlux Systems
  Limited, 336, 351
datagrams (Internet
  Protocol), 214
decoding e-mail binary
  files, 223
Delphi, 299, 319, 341,
  346, 351
  advertising, 317
  BBBs (Bulletin Board
    Systems), 316
  costs, 316, 320
  demographics, 317
  forums, 316
  Internet access, 315
  Latin America
    gateways, 316
  navigating, 316
  travel services
    (Commercial Sabre),
    316
  see also commercial
    online services
demographics
  commercial online
    services, 301, 304
    America Online,
      313

CompuServe, 305,
  307
Delphi, 317
GEnie, 315
Prodigy, 310
databases
  Census Informa-
    tion database, 198
  Census of
    Population and
    Housing
    database, 198
Internet, 113-116
The Detroit Free Press, 100
dialup accounts, 46
  access providers,
    54-57
  commercial online
    services, 55
  Freenets, 56
  government, 55-56
  modems, 57
  nonprofit
    organizations, 55-56
  terminal emulation
    software, 57
  universities, 55-56
dialup network
  extensions, see PPP;
  SLIP
digest format mailing
  lists, 12
digital currency, 265-267
Digital Equipment Corp.
  (DEC), 97, 240-241
Digital Express Group
  (Digex), 338-342, 345,
  352
digital signatures
  (e-mail), 76-77, 262-263
  credit card
    transactions, 264
  encryption, 263-265

dir (directory) command
  (UNIX FTP), 27
The Direct Connection
  (UK), 364
direct marketing, 86,
  124-125
  discussion groups,
    118-119
  e-mail (direct mail),
    125-126
  international markets,
    118
  Listservs, 13-14
  mail reflector bro-
    chures (Cybergate),
    332
  see also marketing
directories
  e-mail addresses, 221
  Internet directories,
    104
  legal directories, 187
directory assistance
  tools, 221
Disclosure financial
  database, 179, 302
discussion groups,
  147-148
  advertising, 156-158
    flame wars,
      140-144
    spam attacks, 142
  commercial online
    services, 302
  creating, 163-166
  customer support, 160
  employee
    recruitment, 161-163
  expert advice, 159-160
  finding, 149-150
  Gopher, 386

marketing, 115
  direct marketing,
    118-119
  press releases, 121,
    124
monitoring industry
  trends, 158-160
netiquette, 148, 152
  Emily Postnews,
    154-155
  shouting, 152
  smileys, 154
World Wide Web, 379
see also mailing lists;
  newsgroups
display ads (Mosaic),
  136-142
The Document Center,
  91, 282, 286
doll vendors (McCrerey
  Farm), 94
domain names, 220
  e-mail addresses, 5-6,
    371-376
  trademarks, 267
DosLynx browser
  (World Wide Web), 380
Dow Jones News/
  Retrieval database, 302
Dudu Rashty's Full
  Screen Client browser
  (World Wide Web), 381

E

e-mail, 4, 209-212
  addresses, 220
    @ (at sign), 6
    account names, 5
    cc:Mail, 213
    computer names, 5
    domains, 5-6, 220,
      371-376

finding, 221
incompatibility of
  addressing
  systems, 224-225
Internet, 213
Internetwork Mail
  Guide, 221
Microsoft Mail, 213
SRI International,
  213
X.400 messaging
  system, 213
automated mail
  servers, 8
client programs, 216
  Elm, 216-218
  Eudora, 217, 227
  Mail, 216-217
  MailTool, 217
  Mush, 217
  Netcom, 219
  Pine, 216-218
  Pipeline, 217, 219
  PSI, 219
  WinNET, 217, 219,
    223
  XMH, 217
  ZMail, 217
commercial online
  services, 4, 210
  costs, 4, 301
  targeting to
    potential
    customers, 303
company mailboxes,
  273-276
composing messages,
  216
connections, 225-227
contracts, 263
  legal tips, 268-269
  Uniform
    Commercial
    Code, 263

costs, 212
customer support,
  235-236
digital signatures,
  76-77, 262-265
encryption, 75, 259,
  327
  encrypting
    hardware
    suppliers, 76
  PEM (Privacy-
    Enhanced Mail),
    77
  PGP (pretty good
    encryption), 71,
    77
  private key
    encryption, 76
  public key
    encryption, 76
finding addresses,
  189-190
flame wars, 112, 266
foreign languages,
  213
GUIs (graphical user
  interfaces), 227
headers, 215-216
integrating on
  commercial services
  and Internet, 318
interoperability, 228
letters to the editor
  (newspapers),
  235-236
mail reflectors, 241
mailing lists
  Listserv, 9-12
  majordomo, 14
marketing, 115
  direct mail, 125-126
  e-mail mailing lists,
    125

junk mail, 119-123
mass mailings, 121
multimedia, 228-229
netiquette, 152
security issues, 222
sending, 4
server programs, 216
shouting, 152
signatures, 154
advertising,
131-132
smileys, 154
transmission, 215
binary files, 223
MIME (Multipur-
pose Internet Mail
Extensions), 223
SMTP (Simple Mail
Transfer
Protocol), 215
U.S. Postal Service,
324
EasyLink, *see* AT&T,
EasyLink e-mail
Echo, 342, 352
EconData, 200
Economic Bulletin Board
(U.S. Commerce
Department), 185-187,
200
EDGAR financial
database, 178-184, 200
edu (educational sites)
domain, 6
electrical engineering
mailing lists, 168
electronic books, 327-328
Book Stacks
Unlimited, 25-26, 93
Computer Literacy,
92-93
encryption, 327-328

Future Fantasy
bookstore, 93
Infinity Link Network
Services, 94
The Internet
Bookstore, 327-328
JF Lehmanns
Fachbuch-
handlung, 94
Macmillian Computer
Publishing, 145
Moe's Books, 93
The Online
Bookstore, 93
O'Reilly &
Associates, 95
Roswell Electronic
Computer
Bookstore, 94
Softpro Books, 94, 285
Electronic
Communications
Privacy Act of 1986 (18
U.S.C. Section 2701),
269
electronic mail, *see*
e-mail
Electronic Mall
(CompuServe), 306
The Electronic
Newsstand, 278-282
electronic signatures, *see*
digital signatures
Elm e-mail client
program, 76, 216-218
EMACS editor (HTML),
382
Emacs w3-mode
browser (World Wide
Web), 381
Emily Postnews, 154-155
emoticons, 154

employees
recruiting, 123,
161-163
virtual workers, 255,
261-263
Empowerment Zones
and Enterprise
Communities database,
200
encryption
book publishing,
327-328
e-mail, 75, 259, 327
digital signatures,
263-265
encrypting
hardware
suppliers, 76
PEM (Privacy-
Enhanced Mail),
77
PGP (pretty good
encryption), 77
private key
encryption, 76
public key
encryption, 76
Enews, 278-282
engineering discussion
groups, 168
Enterprise Integration
Technology catalog
posting service, 95
entrepreneur
newsgroups, 168
Entrepreneurs Forum
(CompuServe), 261
Environmental
Protection Agency
database, 204
Eskimo North, 345, 352
ESPNET (Prodigy), 309

etiquette, *see* netiquette
Eudora e-mail client
    program, 217, 227
Evergreen
    Communciations, 58,
    336, 341, 345, 352
eWord (e-mail), 4
Executive News Service
    (CompuServe), 305
expert advice
    discussion groups,
    159-160
    marketing products/
    services online,
    122-123
The Expert Center for
    Taxonomic
    Identification, 94

F

FAQs (Frequently Asked
    Questions), 149
    customer support,
    240-241
    Gopher, 383
    The World Wide Web
    FAQ, 378
fax service customer
    support, 233
Federal Communica-
    tions Commission, 191
Federal Deposit
    Insurance Corp, 191
FedWorldNational
    Technical Information
    Service, 197
FEN (Financial Econom-
    ics Network), 195, 201
Fetch, 27-29
file transfer protocol, *see*
    FTP

files
    transferring with
    UNIX FTP, 27-28
    uncompressing, 150
filters
    HTML, 378, 382
    Internet information,
    105
financial databases
    *Basic Guide to
    Exporting*, 200
    *Business Resources on
    the Net*, 180
    *Commerce Business
    Daily*, 200
    Country Reports on
    Economic Policy and
    Trade Practices, 200
    Disclosure financial
    database, 179
    EconData, 200
    Economic Bulletin
    Board, 185-187, 200
    EDGAR, 178-184, 200
    Empowerment Zones
    and Enterprise
    Communities, 200
    Financial Economics
    Network (FEN), 195,
    201
    General Agreement
    on Tariffs and Trade
    (GATT), 201
    Gross State Product
    Tables, 201
    Industry Profiles, 201
    International Business
    Practices, 201
    Labor News, 201
    LabStat, 202
    Microsoft Corp., 195

MIT Experimental
    Stock Market
    database, 202
    NAFTA (North
    American Free
    Trade Agreement),
    202
    National Export
    Strategy database,
    202
    Occupational Outlook
    Handbook database,
    202
    Overseas Business
    Reports database,
    202
    QuoteCom database,
    202
    Regional Economic
    Information System
    (REIS), 203
    State Small Business
    Profiles database,
    203
    U.S. Industrial
    Outlook database,
    203
    Uniform Commercial
    Code database, 203
Financial Economics
    Network (FEN), 195,
    201
finding
    databases (WAIS),
    187-189
    discussion groups,
    149-150
    e-mail addresses,
    189-190, 221
    mailing lists, 149
    newsgroups, 150
finger service
    (UNIX), 221
    advertising, 131-133

firewalls, 71, 258-259
  building, 75
  Itelnet software-only
    firewall gateway, 75
flame wars, 112
  advertisers, 140-144
  libel, 266
florists
  Grant's Florist and
    Greenhouse, 94, 285
  PC Flowers, 308
focus groups, 233
food and beverage
  vendors
  Murchies Tea and
    Coffee, 275
  Myers' Gourmet
    Popcorn, 274
  River View Herbs,
    275-276
  Rogers Chocolates,
    275
  Watson's Barrels and
    Wine Making
    Supplies, 275
  see also restaurants
Food and Drug
  Administration BBS,
  204
Food Labeling
  Information database,
  204
Ford, 212
foreign countries
  e-mail addresses, 6,
    371-376
  foreign language
    communications,
    104, 213
forums
  CompuServe, 305
    Entrepreneurs
    Forum, 261

Legal Forum, 268
  Working From
    Home Forum, 261
Delphi, 316
GEnie, 313
see also discussion
  groups
Freelance Systems
  Programming, 343, 353
Freenet dialup accounts,
  56
Front Porch Computers,
  132, 305
FTP (file transfer
  protocol), 26
  anonymous FTP, 26
  Archie, 30-33
  customer support,
    241-243
  graphical interfaces,
    27-28
  uncompressing files,
    150
  UNIX FTP, 27-28
Future Fantasy
  bookstore, 93

G

game vendors
  (Harmony Games),
  276-278
Gary, Dain, 67
Gateway to the World,
  104, 339, 353
GATT (General
  Agreement on Tariffs
  and Trade) database,
  201
Gazeta Wyborcza (Polish
  newspaper), 291

general information
  databases
  FedWorldNational
    Technical
    Information Service,
    197
  Library of Congress,
    197
  National Trade Data
    Bank, 197
  SunSITE Archives,
    197
  U.S. Government
    Gophers, 198
  U.S. Government
    Publications Index,
    198
  zip codes database,
    198
GEnie, 299, 313, 320
  advertising
    classifieds, 315
    GEnie Mall, 315
  Aladdin software, 314
  costs, 48, 314, 320
  demographics, 315
  e-mail, 4
  forums, 313
  online publications,
    313
  roundtables, 313
  see also commercial
    online services
geographic
  specialization, 332-333
gift vendors (McCrerey
  Farm), 94
The Global Basins
  Research Network, 257
Global Enterprise
  Services, Inc., 342, 346,
  353

Global Network
Navigator, 95
Gopher, 33, 383
  client software, 384
  *Common Questions and
  Answers about the
  Internet Gopher*, 383
  discussion groups,
  386
  gateways, 34
  Gopherspace, 33-34
    connecting Gopher
    server to
    Gopherspace, 387
    searching with
    Veronica, 37-39,
    184
  GUIs (graphical user
  interfaces), 323
  menus, 34-35
  selling products
  online, 35-37
  server software, 385
  shopping online,
  35-41
  storefronts, 276-278
  telnet sites, 384-385
  TurboGopher, 33-36
  U.S. Government
  Gophers, 198
  Winsock Gopher,
  33-34, 323
gov (government sites)
  domain, 6
government
  databases
    Ambient
      Monitoring
      Technology
      Information
      Center database,
      203

Americans with
  Disabilities Act
  database, 203
Bureau of Labor
  Statistics, 191
Census Bureau,
  191-194
Clean Air Act
  Amendments
  BBS, 204
Clean Water Act
  database, 204
Clearinghouse for
  Inventories/
  Emission Factors
  (CHIEF) database,
  204
Economic Bulletin
  Board, 185-187
Environmental
  Protection
  Agency database,
  204
Federal
  Communications
  Commission, 191
Federal Deposit
  Insurance Corp,
  191
Food and Drug
  Administration
  BBS, 204
Food Labeling
  Information
  database, 204
*Government Sources
  of Business and
  Economic Informa-
  tion on the
  Internet*, 180
Health Care
  Reform
  Information
  database, 204

Internet Sources of
  Government
  Information, 180
National Air Toxics
  Information
  Clearinghouse,
  204
Occupational
  Safety and Health
  Administration
  database, 205
Patent Office, 191
State Department
  Travel
  Advisories, 179
state goverment
  databases, 191
TOXNET database,
  205
dialup accounts, 55-56
documents
  copyrights, 192
  Government
    Printing Office
    Electronic
    Information
    Access
    Improvement
    Act, 191
  regulation, 145, 212
*Government Sources of
  Business and Economic
  Information on the
  Internet*, 180
Grant's Florist and
  Greenhouse, 94, 285
graphical interfaces, 3
Gross State Product
  Tables database, 201
GUIs (graphical user
  interfaces), 3, 227
  e-mail, 227
  FTP, 27-28

Gopher
  TurboGopher, 33-36
  WinGopher, 33-34, 323
  Internet, 323
  World Wide Web, 41-43
Gymboree, 272

H

Hahnemann University medical school, 211
hardware and software vendors
  Ceram Inc., 93-94
  customer support, 96-99, 232
  Digital Equipment Corp. (DEC), 240-241
  Front Porch Computers, 305
  Hewlett Packard HP SupportLine, 245-249
  InterCon Systems, 235
  The Programmer's Shop, 94
  Silicon Graphics, 237-239
  Sun Microsystems, 234, 243-245
Harmony Games, 276-278
headers (e-mail), 215-216
Health Care Reform Information database, 204
Hewlett Packard HP SupportLine, 245-249

High Performance Computing and Communications: Toward a National Information Infrastructure, 199
HoloNet, 337, 346, 353
Home Office/Small Business RoundTable (GEnie), 314
home pages (World Wide Web), 40, 283
Honda, 212
Hookup Communication Corporation, 343, 353
HOTT (Hot Off The Tree) newsletter, 103
HTML (hypertext markup language)
  creating Web-readable documents, 377-378
  filters, 382, 378
  HTML editors, 378, 382
  Mosaic (World Wide Web browser), 293
HTML Assistant (Microsoft Windows) HTML editor, 382
hypermedia (World Wide Web), 287
hypertext (World Wide Web), 287

I

IBM 9370 Computers mailing list, 172
IDS World Network, 339, 344-346, 354

IETF (Internet Engineering Task Force), 228
in-your-face marketing, 143-144
incorporation services (The Company Corporation), 92
Indian culture newsgroup, 170
Individual Network e.V., 362
Industry Profiles database, 201
industry trends, monitoring through discussion groups, 158-160
Infinity Link Network Services, 94
INFOMARK, 92
Information Infrastructure Task Force Gopher, 199
Information Researchers, 273
information services, 86
  auctions (The Auction Directory & News), 282
  commercial online services, 302-304
  credit reporting services (Infotech Information Technologies), 91
  document delivery (The Document Center), 91
  international trade (International Trade Network), 92

Internet information
filters, 104-105
online merchants
(Global Network
Navigator), 95
see also consulting
firms (Internet)
Infotech Information
Technologies, 91
Institute for Global
Communications
(IGC), 337, 354
Intel Computer Systems
mailing list, 173
Inter Networking
System (INS), 362
InterAccess Co., 55,
339-340, 354
InterCon Systems, 235
International Business
Practices database, 201
international
connections, 371-376
international markets
Economic Bulletin
Board, 185-18
databases, 202,
205-206
mailing lists, 170-172
marketing, 118
newsgroups, 170-172
trade (International
Trade Network), 92
Internet
demographics,
113-116
directories, 104
Internet Access, Inc., 343
The Internet Bookstore,
327-328
The Internet Company,
331
Internet Direct, 55

Internet Distribution
Services, 282-283
Internet Engineering
Task Force (IETF), 64,
228
The Internet Group, 105
Internet in a Box, 323
Internet Mall, 86, 93-94
Internet Online Inc., 343,
354
Internet Patent News
Service, 206
Internet Protocol (IP),
214
Internet Shopping
Network, 9, 139-140,
330
The Internet Society, 114
*Internet Sources of
Government Information*,
177-178, 180
Internet VoiceChat, 326
Internet: Mailing Lists,
149
Internetwork Mail Guide,
221
internetworks (Internet),
114
interoperability (e-mail),
228
Interpath, 343, 355
inventories, posting, 95
Itelnet software-only
firewall gateway, 75

J-K

Japanese culture mailing
list, 171
JF Lehmanns
Fachbuchhandlung, 94
job listings, 123, 161-163

Joe Boxer Corporation,
236
Johnson, Bill, 101
joining
mailing lists, 150-151
newsgroups, 150
journalism discussion
groups, 168-169
junk mail, 119-123

KinderCare, 272
Knight-Ridder, Inc, 101
Knoware, 363
KnowledgeNet, 260-261
Korean culture
newsgroup, 171

L

Labor News database,
201
LabStat database, 202
LANs (Local Area
Networks) (e-mail),
224-225
law firms, 90
Canter & Siegel, 120,
331
Venable, Baetjer,
Howard & Civiletti,
90, 207
*The Law of Electronic
Commerce*, 263
leader ads (Prodigy), 308
Learned Information,
Ltd., 290
leased-line direct
connections, 46, 60
access providers, 60,
336-364
software
requirements, 60
T1 lines, 60
T3 lines, 60

legal databases
  Code of Federal
    Regulations
    databases, 206
  Computer Law
    database, 206
  Copyright
    Information
    database, 206
  Cornell Law School
    Legal Information
    Institute, 187, 206
  Internet Patent News
    Service, 206
  Patent and
    Trademark Office
    BBSes, 206
  Patent Office Reform
    Panel Final Report
    database, 207
  Supreme Court
    Decisions database,
    207
  Venable, Baetjer,
    Howard & Civiletti
    WWW server, 207
legal directories (West
  Publishing Company
  legal directory), 187
Legal Forum
  (CompuServe), 268
legal issues
  Computer Fraud and
    Abuse Act of 1986
    (18 U.S.C. Section
    1030), 269
  copyrights, 266
  e-mail contracts, 263
  Electronic
    Communications
    Privacy Act of 1986
    (18 U.S.C. Section
    2701), 269

libel
  articles (published
    on the Internet),
    267
  flame wars
    (e-mail), 266
  newsgroup
    postings, 267
  newsgroups, 168
  trademarks, 267
  transactions
    (monetary), 268-269
  wire fraud statute
    (18 U.S.C. Section
    1343), 268
LensDirect, 272
Lewis, David, 103
libel
  articles (published on
    the Internet), 267
  flame wars (e-mail),
    266
  newsgroup postings,
    267
library card catalogs, 194
  Library of Congress,
    194, 197
  The New York Public
    Library, 194
  searching with telnet,
    23-26
  universities, 194
The Library of Congress,
  194, 197
Line Mode Browser
  (World Wide Web), 381
List of Lists, 149
Listserv software
  mailing lists, 10-12, 166
  canceling
    subscriptions, 10, 15
  dissemating
    information, 13-14

  obtaining a copy of
    lists, 10
  subscribers, 12
  subscribing, 10, 14-19,
    150
Local Area Networks
  (LANs) (e-mail),
  224-225
Lockheed, 87-88, 212
Lufthansa (German
  airline), 281-282
Lynx Full Screen
  Browser (World Wide
  Web), 381
Lynx interface (World
  Wide Web), 41

M

Mac Fetch, 27, 29
Macintoshes
  e-mail client
    programs, 217
  newsgroups, 173
Macmillian Computer
  Publishing, 145
Maestro Information
  Service, 342, 355
magazines
  articles about virtual
    corporations, 269
  commercial online
    services, 303
  e-mail letters to the
    editor, 235-236
  The Electronic
    Newsstand, 278-282
  *Mother Jones
    Magazine*, 291
Magma, 119
Mail e-mail client
  program, 216-217

mail order businesses, 273-276
mail reflectors (e-mail), 241
  brochures (Cybergate), 332
mail, *see* e-mail
mail servers, 8
mailboxes, *see* company mailboxes
mailing lists, 9
  advertising, 156-158
  announcements, 159
  articles
    posting, 151
    reading, 151
    writing, 152-154
  BITNET, 149
  creating, 163-166
  customer support, 160
  digest format, 12
  e-mail addresses, 125
  employee recruitment, 161-163
  expert advice, 159-160
  FEN (Financial Economics Network), 195
  finding, 149
  marketing, 12-14, 115
    direct marketing, 118-119
    press releases, 121, 126
  moderated mailing lists, 12
  netiquette, 152
  obtaining a copy of lists, 10
  software
    LISTSERV, 10-12, 166
    majordomo, 14-15, 151, 166

  subscriptions, 14-19, 150-151
    canceling subscriptions, 15
  topics
    3Com Products, 172
    engineering, 168
    IBM 9370 Computers, 172
    Intel Computer Systems, 173
    Japanese culture, 171
    journalism, 169
    medicine, 169
    Mexican culture, 171
    monitoring industry trends, 158-160
    museum professionals, 169
    NeXT Computers, 173
    oil and gas exploration, 169
    OS/2 mailing list, 173
    Russian culture, 172
    VALERT-L mailing list, 80
    veterinary medicine, 170
    Vietnamese culture, 172
    VIRUS-L mailing list, 80
    WWW-VM Mailing List, 379
  unmoderated mailing lists, 12

MailTool e-mail client program, 217
majordomo (mailing list software), 14-15, 151, 166
Malaysian culture newsgroup, 171
malls
  Electronic Mall (CompuServe), 306
  GEnie Mall, 315
  Prodigy Mall, 308
  see also cybermalls
manners, *see* netiquette
MAPI (Messaging Application Programming Interface), 228-229
Marion Merrell Dow Inc., 211
market research, 176-177
  Public Opinion Item Index database, 198
  U.S. Department of Agriculture Economics and Statistics gopher, 199
market.announce Usenet newsgroup, 331
market.internet.access Usenet newsgroup, 331
market.internet.events Usenet newsgroup, 332
market.internet.products Usenet newsgroup, 332
market.internet.publications Usenet newsgroup, 332
market.internet.services Usenet newsgroup, 332
marketing, 145-146
  commercial online services, 112
  consumer opinions, 122

direct marketing, 86, 124-125
- discussion groups, 118-119
- international markets, 118
- LISTSERVs, 13-14
- mail reflector brochures (Cybergate), 332

discussion groups, 21, 115, 156-158
- flame wars, 140
- press releases, 121, 126-130
- spam attacks, 142

e-mail, 115
- direct mail, 125-126
- e-mail mailing lists, 125
- junk mail, 119-123
- mass mailings, 121

expert advice, 122-123

Gopher sites (marketplaces), 35-37

integrating on commercial services and Internet, 319

posting press releases, 112

strategies
- developing, 92
- in-your-face marketing, 143-144
- passive advertising, 124
- press releases, 124
- relationship marketing, 133-135

sponsorships, 124
see also international markets

marketplaces (Gopher), 35-37

mass mailings, 121

MBnet, 340, 355

MBone (The Multicast Backbone), 325

McCrerey Farm, 94

MCI Communications Corp., 4, 212-213

mechical engineering mailing list, 168

MecklerWeb, 136-137, 328-329

media mailing lists, 169

medicine
- mailing lists, 169
- research and development, 256-257

menus (Gopher), navigating, 34-35

merchants, *see* online merchants

Merit Network Information Center, 199

Messaging Application Programming Interface (MAPI), 228-229

Meta Network, 345-346, 355

Mexican culture mailing lists, 171

Microsoft Corp. financial database, 195

Microsoft Mail, 213

Microsoft Small Business Center (America Online), 261

mil (military sites) domain, 6

MILNET, 5-6

MIME (Multipurpose Internet Mail Extensions) protocol, 223

Mindvox, 342, 356

misc (miscellaneous) Usenet newsgroups, 21

MIT Experimental Stock Market database, 202

modems (dialup accounts), 57

moderated mailing lists, 12

moderated Usenet newsgroups, 16

Moe's Books, 93

Monterey Bay Aquarium Research Institute, 257-258

Morning Star Technologies, Inc. encryption hardware, 77

Morris, Robert T., 65

Mosaic (World Wide Web browser), 41-43, 158-159, 287-290
- accessibility, 294
- advertising, 115, 136-142, 271
- commercial versions, 324
- CommerNet, 137
- credit card transactions, 290
- customer support, 245-249
- HTML (hypertext markup language), 293

The Internet Shopping Network, 139-140
Macintosh version, 380
MecklerWeb, 136-137
publishing, 290-298
searching capabilities, 294
security, 138, 294, 297
speed, 294
Windows version, 380
Mother Jones Magazine, 291
Motorola, 258
Msen, 341, 346, 356
The Multicast Backbone (MBone), 325
multimedia, 325
e-mail, 223, 228-229
newsgroups, 173
video-conferencing CU-SeeMe, 325
The Multicast Backbone (MBone), 325
Multipurpose Internet Mail Extensions (MIME) protocol, 223
Murchies Tea and Coffee, 275
Murdoch, Rupert, 316
museum professionals mailing lists, 169
Mush e-mail client program, 217
MV Communications, Inc., 342, 356
Myers' Gourmet Popcorn, 274

N

NAFTA (North American Free Trade Agreement) database, 202
National Air Toxics Information Clearinghouse database, 204
National Export Strategy database, 202
National Information Infrastructure Agenda, 199
National Real Estate Services, 92, 283
National Science Foundation network, *see* NSFnet
National Trade Data Bank, 197
navigational tools, 2-3
Archie, 30-33
Gopher, 33-37
Veronica, 37-39
WAIS (Wide Area Information Server), 187-189
whois, 190-191, 195
World Wide Web, 39-43, 158-159
needs assessment for Internet connections, 48-50
Neosoft, 340-341, 345-346, 356
net (network sites) domain, 6
Netcom, 4, 337-339, 341-345
e-mail client program, 219
leased-line direct connections, 60
SLIP connections, 58
Netcom On-Line Communications Services, 357
netfind, 221
netiquette, 148, 152
Emily Postnews, 154-155
shouting, 152
smileys, 154
NetLand, 363
NetPages (Aldea Corp.), 104
NetPro Computing, 135
networking
commercial online services, 302
integrating on commercial services and Internet, 318
The New York Public Library, 194
The New York Times, 100
newreaders (Usenet newsgroups), 17
The News & Observer (Raleigh, NC), 101-102, 290
news (Usenet) Usenet newsgroup, 21
newsgroups, 16, 21-22
advertising, 156-158, 331
announcements, 159
articles
posting, 152
reading, 152
writing, 152-154
creating a newsgroup, 163, 365-369

customer support,
160, 237-239
employee recruit-
ment, 161-163
expert advice, 159-160
finding, 150
joining, 150
libel, 267
marketing, 21, 115
    direct marketing,
    118-119
    press releases, 121
moderated
newsgroups, 16
monitoring industry
trends, 158-160
multimedia, 173
netiquette, 152
newsreaders, 17
    rn newsreader, 17
    tin newsreader, 17,
    19-20
    trn newsreaders, 17
obtaining a list of
newsgroups, 17-19
topics
    Australian culture,
    170
    Canadian culture,
    170
    computers, 80-81,
    379, 386
    entrepreneurs, 168
    India culture, 170
    jornalism, 168
    Korean culture, 171
    legal issues, 168
    Macintoshes, 173
    Malaysian culture,
    171
    marketing, 331-332
unmoderated
newsgroups, 16

Usenet Volunteer
Votetakers (UVV),
367
newsletters, 103, 165
    The Electronic
    Newstand, 278-282
    HOTT (Hot Off The
    Tree) newsletter, 103
newspapers, 100-103,
165
    The Atlanta Journal and
    Constitution, 100
    commercial online
    services, 303
    e-mail letters to the
    editor, 235-236
    The Electronic
    Newstand, 278-282
    Gazeta Wyborcza
    (Polish newspaper),
    291
    The New York Times,
    100
    The News & Observer
    (Raleigh, NC),
    101-102, 290
    The Palo Alto Weekly,
    282, 290
    The San Jose Mercury
    News, 100-101
    The Seattle Times
    seatimes.ptech
    newsgroup, 164
newsreaders, 17
    rn newsreader, 17
    tin newsreader, 17,
    19-20
    trn newsreaders, 17
NeXT Computers
mailing list, 173
NeXTStep browser
(World Wide Web), 381

nonprofit organizations
(dialup accounts),
55-56
North American Free
Trade Agreement
(NAFTA) database, 202
North Shore Access, 341,
357
Northcoast Internet, 343,
357
NSFnet (National
Science Foundation
network), 47
    Acceptable Use
    Policies (AUPs), 117
Nuance Network
Services, 336, 357

O

OARNet, 343, 358
Occupational Outlook
Handbook database,
202
Occupational Safety and
Health Administration
database, 205
oceanography research
and development
(Monterey Bay
Aquarium Research
Institute), 257-258
oil and gas exploration
mailing lists, 169
    research and
    development (The
    Global Basins
    Research Network),
    257
Olympus, 345, 358
online accounts, see
dialup accounts

The Online Bookstore, 93
online merchants, finding with Global Network Navigator, 95
online ordering services, 242-243
O'Reilly & Associates, 95, 145
org (organization sites) domain, 6
OS/2 mailing list, 173
Overseas Business Reports database, 202
overseas markets
  Economic Bulletin Board, 185-187
  mailing lists, 170-172
  marketing, 118
  newsgroups, 170-172
  Overseas Business Reports database, 202

P

The Palo Alto Weekly, 101, 282, 290
Panix (Public Access UNIX and Internet), 342, 358
passwords (security issues), 73-74
Patent and Trademark Office BBSes, 191, 206
Patent Office Reform Panel Final Report database, 207
PC Catalog, 330
PC Flowers, 308
PEM (Privacy-Enhanced Mail), 77

Performance Systems International (PSI), 85, 104, 124
  leased-line direct connections, 60
  security, 72
PGP (pretty good encryption) program, 71, 77, 327
phone-in service customer support, 232
Pine e-mail client program, 216-218
Pipeline, 104, 342, 358
Pipeline e-mail client program, 217-219
Planet Earth Management, 94
Point-to-Point Protocol, *see* PPP
population growth
  commercial online services, 322
  Internet, 114, 322
Portal Communications Company, 337, 346, 359
The Posse, 66
postal service for customer support, 233
postings (discussion groups)
  advertisements, 331
  articles, 151-152
  catalogs, 95
  libel, 267
  press releases, 112, 124, 126-130
PPP (Point to Point Protocol) connections, 46, 57-59
  access providers, 58, 336-364
  client software, 58
  costs, 58

Predicasts database, 302
press releases, 121
  discussion groups, posting, 13-14, 112, 124, 126-130
  see also announcements
price lists, placing on the Internet, 9
Privacy-Enhanced Mail (PEM), 77
private key encryption (e-mail), 76
Procomm Plus terminal emulation software, 57
Prodigy, 299-300, 307, 320
  advertising, 307, 310
    classified ads, 310
    leader ads, 308
    Prodigy Mall, 308
    targeted e-mail ads, 308
  chatting services, 309
  costs, 309, 320
  demographics, 310
  ESPNET, 309
  navigating, 309
  see also commercial online services
product development, 99-100
  market research, 176-177
  medicine, 256-257
  Motorola, 258
  security issues, 258-259
  Sun Microsystems, 259-260
  see also research and development

product display ads
(Mosaic), 136-142
The Programmer's Shop,
94
PSI, 359
e-mail client program,
219
PSINet, 346
Public Access Network
Corp., 66
public key encryption
(e-mail), 76
Public Opinion Item
Index database, 198
public relations
(customer support),
234-235
publishing, 100
databases, 243-245
electronic books,
327-328
integrating on com-
mercial services and
Internet, 319
magazines
commercial online
services, 303
e-mail letters to the
editor, 235-236
The Electronic
Newsstand,
278-282
Mosaic (World Wide
Web browser),
290-298
newsletters, 103, 165
The Electronic
Newsstand,
278-282
newspapers, 100-103,
165, 290
commercial online
services, 303

e-mail letters to the
editor, 235-236
The Electronic
Newsstand,
278-282
World Wide Web,
39-43

Q

Qualcomm, Inc., 227
QuoteCom database, 202

R

Racal-Guardata, Inc.
encryption hardware,
76
RAS (Remote Access
System) encryption, 76
readers, *see* newsreaders
reading
mailing list articles,
151
newsgroup articles,
152
real estate, 88-89
Alain Pinel Realtors,
212
National Real Estate
Services, 92, 283
RealtyNet, 92-93
TKO Real Estate
Advisory Group,
165
RealtyNet, 92-93
rec (recreation) Usenet
newsgroups, 21
recruiting employees,
123, 161-163
Regional Economic
Information System
(REIS) database, 203

relationship marketing,
133-135
replying
mailing list articles, 152
newsgroup articles,
152
research and
development, 99-100
market research,
176-177
medicine, 256-257
Motorola, 258
oceanography
(Monterey Bay
Aquarium Research
Institute), 257-258
oil (The Global Basins
Research Network),
257
security issues,
258-259
Sun Microsystems,
259-260
restaurants (Country
Fare), 163, 282
see also food and
beverages
River View Herbs,
275-276
rn newsreaders, 17
Rogers Chocolates, 275
Roswell Electronic
Computer Bookstore,
94
roundtables (GEnie), 313
routers
dividing network into
subnets, 75
programming to deny
requests, 75
Ruf Corp., 211
Runyon, Marvin, 324
Russian culture mailing
list, 172

S

S&P Online database, 302
sales
    billing customers, 96
    catalogs, 84
    direct marketing, 86
    discussion groups, 156-158
    integrating on com-
        mercial services and
        Internet, 319
    online ordering
        services, 242-243
    real estate, 88-89
    visibility, 96
Samba browser (World
    Wide Web), 380
*The San Jose Mercury
    News*, 100-101
sci (science) Usenet
    newsgroups, 21
searching
    databases
        telnet, 23-26
        WAIS, 187-189
    discussion groups,
        149-150
    e-mail addresses,
        189-190
    The Electronic
        Newstand, 280
    FTP archives, 30-33
    Gopherspace, 37-39
        Veronica, 184
    World Wide Web, 42,
        294
The Seattle Times'
    seatimes.ptech
    newsgroup, 164
Securemax network
    security software, 74

Securities & Exchange
    Commission EDGAR
    database, 178-179
security issues, 63-64,
    77-78, 81
    books, 81
    break-ins, 64-66
        reporting, 78
        spotting potential
            intruders, 259
    CERT (Computer
        Emergency Re-
        sponse Team), 64
    connections, 71
        access providers,
            52
        commercial online
            services, 72
        universities, 72
    crackers, 65, 67
    credit card
        transactions, 67-70
    e-mail, 222
        digital signatures,
            76
        encryption, 71,
            75-77
    firewalls, 71, 75,
        258-259
    Internet Engineering
        Task Force (IETF), 64
    passwords, 73-74
    viruses, 80
    worms, 65
sending e-mail, 4
Serial Line Interface
    Protocol, *see* SLIP
server software
    e-mail, 216
    Gopher, 385
servers
    leased-line direct
        connections, 60

    mail servers, 8
    World Wide Web,
        295-296, 379
SGML (standardized
    graphic markup
    language), 293
shopping online
    Gopher, 35-41
    telnet, 25-26
    see also cybermalls;
        malls
shouting (e-mail), 152
signatures (e-mail), 154
    advertising, 131-132
    see also digital
        signatures
Silicon Graphics, 98, 134,
    237-239
Simplex, 363
SLIP (Serial Line Inter-
    face Protocol)
    connections, 46, 57-59
    access providers, 58,
        336-364
    client software, 58
    costs, 58, 323
small businesses, 89
    incorporation services
        (The Company
        Corporation), 92
    KnowledgeNet,
        260-261
    relationship
        marketing, 134-135
    virtual corporations,
        260
smileys, 154
SMTP (Simple Mail
    Transfer Protocol), 215
SNPP (Simple Network
    Paging Protocol), 229
soc (social topics) Usenet
    newsgroups, 21

SoftLock Services, 265-266
Softpro Books, 94, 285
software
  client software
    e-mail, 216-219
    Gopher, 384
    firewalls (Itelnet software-only firewall gateway), 75
  Internet in a Box, 323
  mailing lists, 166
  network security software, 74
  server software
    e-mail, 216
    Gopher, 385
  TCP/IP software, 60
  terminal emulation software, 57
  video-conferencing software, 325
  see also hardware and software vendors
software requirements
  dialup accounts, 57
  leased-line direct connections, 60
  PPP connections, 58
  SLIP connections, 58
soliciting customers by e-mail, 119-123
spamming, 142, 331
sponsorships (commercial online services), 124, 303
Sprint Corp., 211-212
SprintNet, 346
Spyglass, Inc., 324
SRI International, 212
standardized graphic markup language (SGML), 293

Stanford Netnews Filtering Service, 105
State Department Travel Advisories, 179, 205
state goverment databases, 191
State Small Business Profiles database, 203
stock market
  QuoteCom database, 202
  see also financial databases
store-and-forward network, 215
storefronts, 272, 276-278
  see also cybermalls; malls
stores, 272, 278-282
  The CyberStore on the Shore, 332
  see also cybermalls; malls
subscribing
  mailing lists, 10-19, 150-151
  newsgroups, 150
Sun Microsystems
  customer support, 99
  SunSITE, 197, 243-245
  SunSolve, 99, 234
  research and development, 259-260
Supreme Court Decisions database, 207
SWITCH—Swiss Academic and Research Network, 363
System 7 encryption, 76

T

T1 lines, 60
T3 lines, 60
talk (debated topics) Usenet newsgroups, 21
TAMU toolkit (network security), 74
targeting e-mail to potential customers, 303
TCP (Transmission Control Protocol), 214
TCP/IP (Transmission Control Protocol/Internet Protocol), 57, 60, 214
technical suport, 232
  access providers, 53-54
  BBSes, 233
  by fax, 233
  by phone, 232
  by postal mail, 233
  customer profile services, 239
  discussion groups, 160
  Internet, 233, 251
    costs, 234, 249-250
    databases, 243-245
    e-mail, 235-236
    FAQs, 240-241
    FTP sites, 241-243
    newsgroups, 237-239
    online ordering services, 242-243
  Mosaic (World Wide Web browser), 245-249
  public relations, 234-235
  "virtual" focus groups, 233

The Technology Board
  of Trade, 282
technology databases,
  199
telephone service
  customer support, 232
telephone network, *see*
  telnet
Teleport, 344-345, 359
Telerama, 344, 359
telnet, 22, 185-187
  Archie sites, 31-32
  commercial services,
    22
  Gopher, 384-385
  searching databases,
    23-26
  shopping online,
    25-26
Templeton, Brad, 154
terminal emulation
  software for dialup
  accounts, 57
Texas Metronet, 344-345,
  360
ticket sales
  airline tickets
    (Lufthansa German
    airline), 281-282
  concert tickets (Planet
    Earth Management),
    94
tin newsreader, 17, 19-20
TKO Real Estate
  Advisory Group, 165
TkWWW (X Window)
  HTML editor, 382
Tom Fine's perlWWW
  browser (World Wide
  Web), 381

tools
  directory assistance
    tools
    finger system, 221
    netfind, 221
    whois, 221
  navigational tools
    Archie, 30-33
    Gopher, 33-37
    Mosaic (World
      Wide Web
      browser), 158-159
    Veronica, 37-39
    WAIS (Wide Area
      Information
      Server), 187-189
    whois, 190-191, 195
    World Wide Web,
      39-43
TOXNET database, 205
Toyota, 212
trade (international
  trade)
  databases, 205-206
  International Trade
    Network, 92
trademarks, 267
transactions
  banking, 326
  credit card
    transactions
    automated credit
      card processing
      service, 265
    commercial online
      services, 265
    digital signatures,
      264
    Mosaic (World
      Wide Web
      browser), 290
  e-mail contracts, 263

legal issues, 268-269
  Computer Fraud
    and Abuse Act of
    1986 (18 U.S.C.
    Section 1030), 269
  Electronic
    Communications
    Privacy Act of
    1986 (18 U.S.C.
    Section 2701), 269
  wire fraud statute
    (18 U.S.C. Section
    1343), 268
transferring files with
  UNIX FTP, 27-28
Transmission Control
  Protocol (TCP), 214
Transmission Control
  Protocol/ Internet
  Protocol (TCP/IP), 57,
  60, 214
travel services
  The Avid Explorer,
    283
  Commercial Sabre
    (Delphi), 316
  State Department
    Travel Advisories,
    179
  see also airlines
trends, monitoring
  through discussion
  groups, 158-160
Tripwire auditing
  package (network
  security), 74
TurboGopher, 33-34
Tymnet, 346

U

U.S. Commerce
Department Economic
Bulletin Board, 185-187
U.S. Department of
Agriculture Economics
and Statistics gopher,
199
U.S. Government
Gophers, 198
U.S. Government
Publications Index, 198
U.S. Industrial Outlook
database, 203
U.S. Postal Service
e-mail, 324
uncompressing files, 150
Uniform Commercial
Code
database, 203
e-mail contracts, 263
universities
connections
security issues, 72
dialup accounts,
55-56
library card catalogs,
194
UNIX
e-mail client
programs, 216
finger service
(advertising),
131-133
World Wide Web
browsers, 381
UNIX FTP
ASCII mode, 27
binary mode, 27
transferring files,
27-28

UNIX Viola for X
browser (World Wide
Web), 381
unmoderated mailing
lists, 12
unmoderated Usenet
newsgroups, 16
Unocal, 100
unsolicited e-mail,
119-123
URLs (uniform resource
locators), 91
World Wide Web
sites, 288-290
Usenet newsgroups, 16,
21-22
advertising, 156-158
alt (alternative)
newsgroups, 21
announcements, 159
biz (business)
newsgroups, 21
comp (computers)
newsgroups, 21
creating a newsgroup,
163, 365-369
customer support,
160, 237-239
employee recruit-
ment, 161-163
expert advice, 159-160
finding, 150
joining, 150
marketing, 21, 115,
331-332
direct marketing,
118-119
press releases, 121
misc (miscellaneous)
newsgroups, 21
moderated
newsgroups, 16

monitoring industry
trends, 158-160
multimedia, 173
netiquette, 152-154
news (Usenet)
newgroup, 21
newsreaders, 17
rn newsreaders, 17
tin newsreader, 17,
19-20
trn newsreaders, 17
obtaining a list of
newsgroups, 17-19
rec (recreation)
newsgroups, 21
sci (science)
newsgroups, 21
soc (social topics)
newsgroup, 21
talk (debated topics)
newsgroups, 21
unmoderated
newsgroups, 16
Usenet Volunteer
Votetakers (UVV),
367
writing articles,
152-154
uudecode tool, 223
uuencode tool, 223
UUNet Technologies,
Inc., 85
encryption hardware,
77
leased-line direct
connections, 60
UUNorth Incorporated,
343, 360
UUTool, 223

V

VALERT-L mailing list, 80

Venable, Baetjer, Howard & Civiletti WWW server, 90, 207

Veronica, 37-39
  gopherspace searches, 184
    keyword searches, 37-38
    search results, 38-39
  sites, 38

VersaTerm terminal emulation software, 57

veterinary medicine mailing lists, 170

video-conferencing, 254, 325
  CU-SeeMe, 325
  The Multicast Backbone (MBone), 325

Vietnamese culture mailing list, 172

virtual corporations, 254
  books, 269
  credit card transactions, 263-269
  e-mail contracts, 262-269
  KnowledgeNet, 260-261
  legal issues
    copyrights, 266-267
    trademarks, 266-267
  magazine articles, 269
  research and development, 256-259
  small businesses, 260
  virtual workers, 255, 261-263

"virtual" focus groups, 233

Virtual Mall, 275

viruses, 80

VMS browser (World Wide Web), 381

VNet Internet Access, Inc., 360

W

WAIS (Wide Area Information Server), 187-189

walls (commercial online services), 302

want ads, 123
  discussion groups, 161-163
  see also advertising

Watson's Barrels and Wine Making Supplies, 275

Web, see World Wide Web

The WELL, 337, 346, 360

West Publishing Company legal directory, 187

What's New with NCSA Mosaic, 379

whois, 190-191, 195, 221

Wimsey Information Services, 336, 361

Windows
  e-mail client programs, 217
  FTP, 27-29
  Gopher, 33-34, 323

WinGopher, 323

Wingra Technology, 98

WinNET e-mail client program, 217, 219, 223

Winsock Gopher, 33-34

wire fraud statute (18 U.S.C. Section 1343), 268

Working From Home Forum (CompuServe), 261

The World, 194-195, 341, 346, 361

World Bank Public Information Service database, 206

World Wide Web, 39
  advertising, 90, 271
  browsers, 380-381
  customer support services, 97
  cybermalls, 271, 282-286, 296
    costs for setting up shops, 285
    home pages, 283
    renting space, 295
  discussion groups, 379
  FAQs, 378
  home pages, 40
  HTLM (hypertext markup language), 377
  hypermedia, 287
  hypertext, 287
  Lynx interface, 41
  Mosaic browser, 41-43, 158-159, 287-290, 296-298
    accessibility, 294
    advertising, 115, 136-142
    commercial versions, 324
    CommerNet, 137
    customer support, 245-249

credit card
   transactions, 290
HTML (hypertext
   markup
   language), 293
The Internet
   Shopping
   Network, 139-140
MecklerWeb,
   136-137
publishing, 290-298
searching
   capabilities, 294
security, 138, 294,
   297
speed, 294
searching, 42
servers, 295-296, 379
sites, 288-290
World Wide Web Guide,
378
worms, 65
writing
   mailing list articles,
   152-154
   newsgroup articles,
   152-154
WWW, *see* World Wide
Web
WWW Virtual Library,
379
WWW-VM Mailing List,
379

X-Y-Z

X Window browser
   (World Wide Web), 381
X.400 messaging system,
   213
XMH e-mail client
   program, 217
XNet Information
   Systems, 340, 361

Ziff-Davis Computer
   Database Plus, 302
zip codes database, 198
ZMail e-mail client
   program, 217

Add to Your Sams Library Today with the Best Books for Programming, Operating Systems, and New Technologies

The easiest way to order is to pick up the phone and call

1-800-428-5331

between 9:00 a.m. and 5:00 p.m. EST.

For faster service please have your credit card available.

ISBN	Quantity	Description of Item	Unit Cost	Total Cost
0-672-30464-3		Teach Yourself UNIX in a Week	$28.00	
0-672-30520-8		Your Internet Consultant: The FAQs of Life Online	$25.00	
0-672-30519-4		Teach Yourself the Internet: Around the World in 21 Days	$25.00	
0-672-30466-X		The Internet Unleashed (book/disk)	$44.95	
0-672-30485-6		Navigating the Internet, Deluxe Edition (book/disk)	$29.95	
0-672-30457-0		Learning UNIX (book/disk)	$39.95	
0-672-30382-5		Understanding Local Area Networks	$26.95	
0-672-30209-8		NetWare Unleashed (book/disk)	$45.00	
0-672-30173-3		Enterprise-Wide Networking	$39.95	
0-672-30501-1		Understanding Data Communications	$29.99	
0-672-30119-9		International Telecommunications	$39.95	

❏ 3 ½" Disk

❏ 5 ¼" Disk

Shipping and Handling: See information below.		
TOTAL		

Shipping and Handling: $4.00 for the first book, and $1.75 for each additional book. Floppy disk: add $1.75 for shipping and handling. If you need to have it NOW, we can ship product to you in 24 hours for an additional charge of approximately $18.00, and you will receive your item overnight or in two days. Overseas shipping and handling adds $2.00 per book and $8.00 for up to three disks. Prices subject to change. Call for availability and pricing information on latest editions.

201 W. 103rd Street, Indianapolis, Indiana 46290

1-800-428-5331 — Orders   1-800-835-3202 — FAX   1-800-858-7674 — Customer Service

Book ISBN 0-672-30530-5